VOICES FROM THE FRONT

PETER HART

VOICES

FROM THE

FRONT

AN ORAL HISTORY OF THE GREAT WAR

PROFILE BOOKS

First published in Great Britain in 2015 by
PROFILE BOOKS LTD
3 Holford Yard
Bevin Way
London WC1X 9HD
www.profilebooks.com

1 3 5 7 9 10 8 6 4 2

Typeset in Stone Serif by MacGuru Ltd
info@macguru.org.uk
Printed and bound in Great Britain by
Clays, St Ives plc

A CIP catalogue record for this book is available from the British Library.

ISBN 978 1 78125 474 5
eISBN 978 1 78283 172 3

Dedicated to the men that didn't come home,
Men a long time dead,
Dead long before their time.

Peter Hart, 8 August 2015

CONTENTS

PREFACE

THIS IS AN ORAL HISTORY of the British military involvement in the Great War based on the 183 interviews with veterans that I carried out for the Imperial War Museum Sound Archive in the 1980s and early 1990s. The length varied from some thirty minutes to a stupendous twenty-two hours; they were always fascinating, but since the passing of the last few veterans they are now a unique source of authentic voices from the front line. They have never been 'forgotten'; the recordings were deliberately created by IWM staff as part of their ongoing mission to expand our historical record. Previous authors have done little more than skim lightly over the surface of these treasures.

During the Great War people lost control of their lives as events overwhelmed them. Illustrious statesmen and politicians, industrialists and trades unionists, generals and admirals were all rendered impotent by forces that seemed to dwarf the efforts of mere individuals. Armies marched in millions and mankind apparently reduced to the level of a 'resource' to be enumerated in the same manner as ships, guns, munitions, grain, horses, oil and steel. It was a war of 'big battalions'. The war exerted a catalytic effect on the history of the twentieth century. Empires fell, others were crippled and new contenders arose to redefine entirely the balance of power in the post-war years. Strong economies were dragged down by the debts incurred in the fighting. The established political orthodoxies were challenged by communism and the spectre of fascism lurked menacingly in the wings. Even now, an understanding of the war is crucial to a grasp of the internecine conflicts that rage across the Middle East and the Balkans. It changed the map of the world, but it also radically affected the lives of all those caught up in the maelstrom. In this book I have tried to bring individuals back to centre-stage; their voices loud and clear for all those who care to listen.

What a breadth of experience our veterans amassed between them in the Great War. For this was a global conflict that raged across most of western and central Europe, enfolded most of the Middle East and spread deep into Africa while also probing deep into the extremities of the Far East and Americas. And what destruction and mayhem these veterans witnessed. The Great War posed the most intractable set of military problems hitherto encountered in modern warfare. Artillery ruled the battlefield along with trenches, barbed wire and machine guns. The much abused generals were no 'donkeys', but even without mistakes, beating the main German Army in the field was always going to cost the lives of hundreds of thousands of men.

Every positive step forward was immediately countered by new defensive tactics, as trench warfare mutated constantly to create hitherto unforeseen problems, traps and pitfalls. The conditions in the trenches have become bywords for suffering: mud and blood; death and destruction; courage and sacrifice; hopelessness and despair. Archaic terms, techniques and weapons from the half-forgotten era of siege warfare made a return to prominence as mining expanded from small beginnings to huge underground operations that had the power to blow up whole ridges in the blink of an eye. The first tanks rumbled their way across battlefields, slow-moving and unreliable, but a potent sign of the future nonetheless. Poison gas made its terrifying entrance – even the very air that they breathed was turned against the troops.

At sea, huge fleets faced each other across the North Sea and in the Mediterranean. The hopes and fears of entire nations were bound up in the technological marvels of the dreadnoughts that defined the arms race of the day. When they clashed in battle, thousands of men lost their lives in minutes, but somehow nothing ever seemed to change. Smaller cruisers roamed across the globe from the Atlantic to the Pacific, spreading across the Indian Ocean, the Black Sea, the Baltic, the China Seas, even right up to the Arctic and the Antarctic Oceans. Under the waves, submarines menaced the sea lanes, sinking troopships, merchant-men, liners and even hospital ships. Disguised armed vessels – known as 'Q' ships – sought to take murderous advantage of any submarine commander gentlemanly enough to allow a ship's crew and passengers the opportunity to escape. Controversy raged, but in truth both sides stretched the long-standing rules of war until they snapped.

Above them, an air war raged. Just over a decade after the first air-craft had flown, it was evident that warfare had gained a deadly new dimension. The development of wireless-carrying army cooperation air-craft meant that the war reached deep behind the front-line trenches, as targets could be first pinpointed and then destroyed by shell fire directed by observers perched high in the sky. The bombing of cities soon blurred the traditional acceptance that civilians were non-combatants. This was an escalation of warfare – everyone would be caught up in the new Armageddon.

Oral history is a strange business. It can be the cold and unemo-tional process of sitting in a museum environment listening to disem-bodied voices recorded long ago by complete strangers. Or it can be like stepping into your own past. Throughout, my aim was to make this book deeply personal, to reflect the stories told personally to me, not gleaned remotely at second-hand.[1] For me, this book is real life. As I sit down to listen to the recordings I made in my late twenties and thir-ties (some thirty years past) my mind is transported back to the myriad front doors, halls, kitchens and living rooms of the elderly veterans I interviewed. These were men who had actually experienced the horrors and witnessed the cataclysmic events of the Great War that I had only ever read about. Some rich, some poor, some hale and hearty, some sadly on their last legs. Many were warm and welcoming, but others were nervous or withdrawn – at least at first. A number were chronically lonely, an indictment of a society that no longer places much value on experience. A kaleidoscope of tea and coffee made in every imaginable manner, fancy napkins and best china, broken cups and filthy mugs, plain biscuits and fancy cakes – all part of the process of getting to know one another. Sitting opposite each other on chairs that chronicled the passing fads of a century of furniture design, some of which you can clearly hear creaking on the tapes! Rooms heated to a furnace-like intensity; others bitterly – worryingly – cold. Once we started recording, then I sat opposite them, watched their faces, their body language, as they told their story. Most would soon lose track of time and place, immersing themselves in their past and carrying you along with them on their journey through a lifetime.

Yet while oral historians may develop warm personal feelings and a deep admiration for their informants, once an interview is recorded, just as with any other historical source it becomes evidence to be assessed on its merits. A robust defence of oral history must start with a recognition that it is invaluable in correcting misconceptions garnered through the uncritical study of more traditional forms of historical evidence, such as, ironically, the unit war diaries, which were subsequently enshrined in the pages of regimental histories. At times, however, the prime function of these was to help absolve senior officers from any possible criticism of their performance in battle! This explains the unbelievable number of times that a 'retirement' is ordered to 'conform' with the 'retreat' of the unit next in line. Even ordinary personal diaries can be highly inaccurate, filtered through the transient and contradictory emotions of the writer, who often incorrectly gives the impression of being at the centre of events. Finally, the tone and content of letters depend to a large degree on the person destined to read them. Soldiers frequently minimise the risks they face in letters to their mothers, while exaggerating to male contemporaries and making frankly nonsensical boasts to their girlfriends. Very rarely do men refer to the mundane horrors of war in any great detail – the lice, the stench, and above all the deep personal humiliations inflicted upon them by diseases like dysentery. Such things, if mentioned at all, are concealed, rather than revealed, by coy euphemisms.

So what is oral history good for? Well if you want to know what life was really like for the men fighting the Great War, then reading this book a hundred years later is surely the closest you can get. Oral history brings the past into sharp focus – revealing and explaining all the nitty-gritty fundamentals that define the spirit of the age, the little wrinkles that allow you to feel what people were going through. Some

elements are strangely familiar; other once commonplace habits or attitudes now seem alien. Oral history can also simplify a convoluted situation. An amusing anecdote can cut through the complexities to reveal
what was really happening in a way that a dry narrative often cannot.
But above all it is the emotions heightened by war that are revealed in
interviews. Given time to consider, men and women open up as to what
they were really thinking, untrammelled by pressure to conform to a set
perspective. It is very apparent from oral history interviews that once
men became aware of the horrors of war, then few of them had much
enthusiasm for fighting and many were just plain terrified. This makes
their courage in 'going over the top' all the more remarkable, even if it
rather undercuts the official sanctioned view that the lads were 'dying
to have another bash at the Hun'. Terrible tragedies are often exposed in
heart-rending memories of much loved relatives or comrades that were
killed, mangled or mentally shattered by war.

Oral history gives us much needed variety. All human nature is here
and indeed, I encountered 'all sorts' as I carried out the interviews. Quiet
bespectacled types, rough diamonds, stolid Bible-readers, intellectuals,
eccentrics, even a few who still 'liked a drink'. Brave men who could
take all their enemies could throw at them and ask for more; nervous
types who had to dig deep. Many got through without a scratch, but
some were dreadfully wounded, their lives ruined or changed forever.
Few had ever written anything down or preserved their contemporary
letters, so without these oral history interviews their experiences would
have been lost.

Yet it is undeniable that there *are* problems with the unthinking
usage of oral history, normally by people who think of it as 'testimony'.
In particular, veterans of junior rank are inherently unlikely to understand the military strategy and tactics of the day. As such they are *not*
authorities on what the generals were thinking, or of what should have
been done. It is also true that some men, lacking confidence in their
own recall of events, begin to draw on the views peddled in post-war
books or popular television programmes. These false memories can
become their reality. There were also a very few sad fantasists who
had been lying about their exploits for years and could no longer distinguish truth from fiction. Such cases can generally be exposed by a

combination of competent interviewing and diligent historical analysis: to put it bluntly, it is usually evident when veterans are unreliable informants. Yet one very real problem with oral history does remain: people in battle are under severe stress and often in a state of physical shock, with all the mental confusion and dislocation from events that this entails. The result is that their recollections of actual fighting are often vague, sometimes dreamlike, or they may even have had a blackout and be reliant on what they have been subsequently told of the incident. Witness statements can often differ radically just minutes after the event – never mind after a gap of several decades. Thus oral history 'action' stories always need to be carefully checked for internal inconsistencies and alongside other sources of evidence. In many ways interviews are best used to give a sense of what it was like to be in an attack, rather than the fine details of what actually happened.

In the final analysis, oral history is *not* testimony – a word that provides a wholly unnecessary smokescreen of reverence combined with the sulphurous whiff of legal depositions. On the contrary, as a source of evidence, interviews are by no means perfect and the veterans are not saints. When using oral history you have to be sceptical. But this is surely one of the ground rules of any historical research: if something is frankly unbelievable, then don't believe it without a great deal of solid confirmation – whatever the source. In the end, historical evidence is made up of many constituent parts. Oral history is just one part of the big picture, but it does have an important role in that it humanises the record and provides a grounding with its strong roots in real life. Rely solely on contemporary documents and you will eventually end up with a sanitised romantic view of war that significantly underplays the horror and moral ambivalence that defined the experience for the majority.

All the voices preserved in the IWM recordings have now fallen silent. With the deaths of Harry Patch and Henry Allingham in 2009, the last of the known Great War veterans living in Britain, we collectively marked the passing of a wonderful generation. The men I interviewed had survived the war and the economic hardships of the 1920s and 1930s; they had experienced for the most part all the mixed joys and challenges of marriage, parenthood and family life. Some served again in the Second World War; others endured the whistling bombs of the Blitz. Most grew old and infirm together, reliving their comradeship through the Royal British Legion or their much-treasured regimental associations; then gradually, almost imperceptibly, they faded away. Most were grateful that they had had the chance to enjoy a full life; a chance that had been snatched away from many of their mates who died when they were all so very young. Many felt a residual guilt that they had survived when so many of their friends had not. Sacrifice is a cliché, but the dead of the Great War truly did forfeit their tomorrows: not just a few hours, weeks, or at most months, as it may have seemed in the midst of that mass slaughter, but they lost sixty, seventy, or even eighty years of potential life and happiness. It is to reflect the veterans' heartfelt awareness of their deep indebtedness to their friends that died that this book is dedicated: to all those who did not survive; men a long time dead; men dead long before their time.

1

ALL OVER BY CHRISTMAS!

THE GENESIS OF THE GREAT WAR was not a simple matter, but it can be stated in simple terms. Europe was beset by political and economic rivalries that reflected both the bloody history of the continent and the conflicting ambitions of its constituent nation states. That these nation states cared little for the common weal, but only for their own ambitions, is undeniable. There were many possible causes, many underlying threats to the peace of Europe in 1914: the explosive powder keg of the Balkans, the wide-ranging rise of separatist nationalist ambitions, the colonial stresses between the great empires, German insecurities at being surrounded by enemies, French determination to regain her lost provinces from Germany, the economic determinism that set the leading capitalist economies in a vicious winner-takes-all competition – or even the increasing willingness to contemplate violence that seemed to permeate everything from domestic politics to art and literature. All this is true. Any one of these factors, alone or in concert, may have had the power to trigger war. But the fact is that in the end they were not the *prime* cause of war.

What caused the war in August 1914 was the underlying threat emanating from the German Empire, a militaristic power that was actively seeking to establish the domination of Europe. Behind the blustering persona of Kaiser Wilhelm II lay a very real threat to the status quo in Europe. Modern Germany had been forged on the anvil of war, first by victory over Austria in 1866 and then by the stunning defeat of France in 1870–71. By 1914, the German Army, based on an efficient conscription system, was the most powerful in the world. It had a long-standing general staff which had mastered – at least to their own satisfaction – the study of the art of war. The infantry, cavalry and artillery were all equipped on a de luxe scale, and their regular drill and constant training-ground exercises had burnished their collective military skills to a fearsome degree. Germany's economy was booming, penetrating markets across the globe and offering competition where Britain and others would rather have preserved a privileged monopoly. Then in 1898 came the final piece in the jigsaw: successive Naval Laws began a programme of warship construction that presented a serious challenge to the pre-eminence of the Royal Navy.

The rise of Germany had not gone unnoticed in London. The defeat of Napoleonic France at Waterloo in 1815 had left a Europe free from domination of any one power. The Great Powers were in balance – not harmony – but at least a rough equilibrium that prevented any country attaining supremacy. For most of the nineteenth century the Royal Navy had ruled the waves and, with her huge colonial empire covering significant sections of the globe, Great Britain was *apparently* the strongest power in the world, even though chronic unwillingness to invest in the sinews of Imperial governance left her with a laughably weak army. The rise of Germany changed everything. It was axiomatic to any British statesman worth his salt that no one state could be allowed to secure the hegemony of Europe, so the threatened permanent defeat of France by Germany could not be countenanced.

The signs of this underlying change in British attitudes were soon evident. A colonial rapprochement of the *entente cordiale* was reached with France in 1904. This smoothed away many of the historical conflicts by allowing both countries clearly defined untrammelled spheres of influence in Africa and the Middle East. A far more serious signal that the ground was shifting occurred with the signing of the Anglo-Russian

Convention in 1907. Britain and Russia had been playing the 'Great Game' for most of the previous century, competing for power and influence across a great swathe of central Asia from Persia to Tibet. Now the threat of Germany far closer to home meant that these rivalries were buried by an agreement that managed to define borders and areas of 'interest' to their mutual satisfaction.

With both her main former rivals safely 'within the tent' of a loose Triple Entente, the British began to explore what war with Germany might mean. Step by step military arrangements were negotiated, which drew Britain ever closer to the French. It was a marriage of convenience as the two countries had interlocking strengths and weaknesses. The German Navy was such a threat that the Royal Navy had to gather all its forces together to face the German High Seas Fleet across the North Sea. In consequence, arrangements were drawn up whereby the British would undertake to protect the French Atlantic coastline, while the French Navy would concentrate its forces to secure Anglo-French interests in the Mediterranean area. Secret staff talks were also underway to commit the British Army to supplying an expeditionary force to fight alongside the French on the mainland. From the French perspective the actual numbers contributed were of little matter compared to the symbolism of the British Expeditionary Force (BEF) fighting at their side, giving a clear indication of positive intent that, in due time, the whole strength of the British Empire would be thrown into the fight.

The Boer War of 1899–1902 had drawn attention to the manifold imperfections of the British Army. The most obvious fault was its inadequate size. Over the course of four years, some 450,000 men had been deployed to South Africa, but even a mobilisation on this scale would have been of little relevance in a full-scale continental war. That would be a war of heavyweights. Yet this fault would never be resolved in peacetime, for British governments lacked the political resolve to embark either on the serious increases in taxation, or on the introduction of conscription, which would be required to compete on an equal military footing with Germany. Any reforms to improve the army would have to be made from within existing parameters. It was certainly unhelpful that the army was not highly regarded in polite society throughout the Victorian and Edwardian eras. Although there was a superficial sentimentality over the 'thin red line', this masked an indifference to the fate of the men that actually had to police the Empire.

It is therefore no surprise that conditions of service in the British Army were at times dire. Barrack accommodation was often run down and lacking in basic amenities, the food was barely adequate and the pay dreadful. But in this the army was not unique, for Edwardian Britain was a relatively harsh social environment, and the army still offered a way out for youths dogged by unfortunate personal circumstances or trapped in mundane jobs. Young William Holbrook from the Hornchurch area was one such recruit to the colours. His family had fragmented after the death of their father and Holbrook had subsequently endured, for a period, the tender mercies of parish relief. After working as a greengrocer, a farm labourer and a household servant, by the autumn of 1908, aged 15, he was ready for something different. From Holbrook's experience of the recruitment process there would still appear to have been a relaxed attitude to legal requirements.

This gardener he'd been in the army and he used to tell me all the tales about India and all these rajahs he made out he'd seen. I thought, 'This is the job for me!' So one morning, instead of going to work, I went up the post office where I saw, 'Recruits wanted in the army: 30 Southchurch Street, East Ham.' I found the place and knocked – a woman came to the door and she said, 'Yes?' I said, 'I want to join the army, please.' She said, 'How old are you?' I said, '15!' She said, 'You can't join the army at 15; you've got to be 18. Come in I'll make you a cup of tea – you stop here till my husband comes home and you talk to him.' About an hour later he came in, a smart looking man with an army uniform, khaki cap. He looked and said, 'What have we got here?' 'He wants to join the army.' 'You can't join the army. When you're 18 I'll put you in the finest regiment in the British Army, but not before.' I suppose I looked miserable because he said, 'Stand up against that door.' So I stood against the door and it was marked off in inches. He said, 'You're a tall boy, you know.' I was about 5 feet 8 inches. He said, 'Can you tell a white lie? Can you say you're 17?' I said, 'Yes!' He said, 'Right, tomorrow morning you come with me.' Next morning he took me up to Stratford to the doctor. When it was my turn to go in he said, 'Strip'.

I took everything off, I'd never done it in front of anybody so I was a bit nervous at first! He said, 'Hop on your left foot and right foot alternately.' Well that done me. I'd never heard the word alternately, what that meant. So I started hopping, 'The other left foot you bloody fool!' I thought, 'I've come to the right place!' Never been spoken to like that before! Anyway I passed.[1]

William Holbrook

He would hear plenty more language in a similar vein before he was a civilian again.

The British Army may have been small, but the regular soldiers were extremely well trained. The standard of drill was first rate, as recruits underwent the classic parade-ground regime that sought to break them down as individuals before building them back up into the standard mould of a trained soldier. There was a particular concentration on musketry, with both accuracy and speed prized highly. It was expected that the trained regular would be able to achieve some fifteen aimed rounds per minute. Whether infantryman, sapper, cavalry, gunner or medic, they were all inculcated with the principle that they were fortunate above measure to be a member of the best unit in the whole British Army. It may seem trite, but it had the enormous advantage in that it worked.

One of the first things that happened was Captain Lock explained our cap badge to us. He said, 'This is your cap badge. There is a Latin motto at the foot, "*In Arduis Fidelis*" – faithful in difficulties – that's the translation from the Latin. That's the *esprit de corps*.' In other words you were there to look after other people and be faithful to them. That used to drum itself into me on the battlefield, I used to say to myself, 'Boy, no matter how afraid you are, you have got to live up to your cap badge'. And it helped.[2]

Stretcher Bearer William Collins, Base Depot, Royal Army Medical Corps, McGrigor Barracks, Aldershot

In the contest of a continental war, this elite force of just 250,000 men was nigh-on irrelevant. In a logical world it might have been best used to provide a reservoir of the officers, NCO instructors and trained soldiers from which a mighty new volunteer army might be created, yet to achieve this, Britain would have had to renege on her commitments to the French. The BEF was therefore duly dispatched to war on the Western Front, with the inevitable result that the training of the greater armies that were later needed would be left to older soldiers returning to the colours.

An important additional layer was, however, added to the British Army before 1914. This was the Territorial Force created from the Haldane reforms of 1908 which had swept away the previous ramshackle system of 'Volunteer' units. It allowed each of the county regiments to create additional Territorial battalions that would recruit 'part-time' soldiers locally, aged between 17 and 38, who would be liable to call-up for Home Service on the outbreak of any war. The 'Terriers' would undergo basic training at least one night a week at local drill halls and would mobilise once a year for a two-week summer camp. Their perceived role was to replace the regular units when the BEF deployed overseas. Their officers would be a mixture of old regulars and socially acceptable young men who had usually been given their introduction to military life with the Officers' Training Corps (OTC) run by most public schools. One such was Cyril Dennys, the son of an Indian Army officer who was a member of the OTC at Malvern School.

> The war they were preparing for was something like the Boer War: great emphasis on musketry; no emphasis on artillery at all; the machine gun simply wasn't visible at all. One would be manoeuvred in columns of companies and then broken up into lines of skirmishers which would be very much what they would have done in the Boer War.[3]
>
> Cyril Dennys, OTC, Malvern School

In fairness, it should be recognised that the Boer War was the most recent conflict experienced by the British Army.

THE STORY OF THE STUMBLING RACE TO WAR in 1914 is a tragedy from start to finish. The assassination of Archduke Franz Ferdinand in Sarajevo on 28 June 1914, by a Serbian nationalist Gavrilo Princip, was the trigger. The exact sequence of events and motivations will forever be debated, but in the diplomatic crisis that followed it is clear that, rather than working for a negotiated peace settlement, Germany was offering unconditional support to her ally the Austro-Hungarian Empire and actively encouraging them to threaten Serbia. This culminated in the Austrian declaration of war on Serbia on 28 July. As the rash of mobilisations and counter-mobilisations began, the process became irreversible.

The Germans were ready for war. Their strategy was based on the Schlieffen Plan, which sought to hold the slowly mobilising Russians in the east while seeking a quick decision on the Western Front. It envisaged a strong force bludgeoning through Belgium and northern France before moving south, pushing strongly towards Paris before finally encircling the French Army. For Britain, it would be the invasion of Belgium by Germany that at a stroke clarified the tangle of issues and doubts. It indicated without any ambiguity the true nature of the German state and her ambitions, at any price, for hegemony over Europe. Yet there was still a considerable degree of anti-war sentiment in Britain, as was witnessed by 16-year-old schoolboy Harold Bing.

> When I heard that a big anti-war demonstration was to be held in Trafalgar Square on Sunday, 2nd August 1914, and that Keir Hardie[4] was to be one of the speakers, I walked up from my home to Trafalgar Square – about 11 miles – took part in that demonstration, listened to Keir Hardie and of course walked home again afterwards, which perhaps showed a certain amount of boyish enthusiasm for the anti-war cause. It was quite a thrilling meeting with about ten thousand people there and certainly very definitely anti-war. But at the very same time while we were demonstrating in Trafalgar Square, the Cabinet was sitting at Downing Street deciding on the ultimatum which brought the country into the war two days later on 4th August.[5]
>
> Harold Bing

With the Germans massed on the Belgian frontier on 2 August, the British Cabinet could hesitate no longer; the Germans were going too far. News of the German declaration of war on Belgium drew a final ultimatum and Britain joined the war at midnight on 4 August.

As the last hours of peace trickled away, the popular reaction was generally enthusiastic. Jobbing actor Jim Davies was caught up in the thronging crowds in London on that fateful day. There was a real holiday atmosphere.

> We expected war to be declared, so I rushed down by 11 o'clock down to Big Ben. The crowds were there and as Big Ben struck 11 everybody cheered! We sang, 'Rule Britannia' and 'Britons never shall be slaves' and then someone said, 'Let's march back to Buckingham Palace.' We all marched back, right down Whitehall, down the Mall. It was very late then, getting on for midnight, and we were shouting for the King and singing songs. I'd met a couple of medical students and we climbed up by the big gates. The King came out and the Queen, we all cheered and sang some more. We said we'd join the army the next day: full of enthusiasm – not drink – just enthusiasm. Next day, I thought, 'Christ, I'm going to join the army, I've got to give two weeks' notice in!' I was young and stupid I suppose, full of patriotism and the *Boys Own Paper* on which my boyhood was based.[6]
>
> Jim Davies

The influence of jingoistic comics and books was marked on men who were too young to have any real experience of life. The horrors of the Boer War had been filtered through a prism of heroism and sacrifice which gave the impression that 'bad things' could only happen to someone else. Every individual thought of himself as the inviolable hero in their very own adventure story: nothing could happen to them.

> I thought it would be like I had read about in the Boer War. I'd read about the Siege of Mafeking, about Baden Powell and how he held out at Ladysmith. Everything was a victory as far as we were concerned. I remember a drawing of Spion Kop and there was a chap lying there with his leg off, in a pool of blood with his hat on one side. I thought, 'How terrible – the chap's lost his leg.' Never did I realise that I would lose my own leg![7]
>
> Jim Davies

From end to end the country was buzzing with excitement as everyone realised that nigh on one hundred years after Waterloo, they would once again be at war with a western European power.

It was a lovely morning. I can remember it; I see it as plain as now. I was going to work for 7 o'clock. As I got to the end of Richmond Road, there was a newsagent's shop and outside was a big placard, 'War Declared on Germany'. Mobilisation had taken place. In the evening I went to Bellevue Barracks. There were crowds round there, everybody was excited. Anytime they saw a soldier he was right at the top of the tree – cheering and all that. The people welcomed it: a challenge had been thrown down over Belgium and they were eager to take that challenge. Everybody was stood in groups talking, 'We've got to beat the Germans!' Quite a number were already setting off to enlist that day as it broke out. Very patriotic songs singing – 'Rule Britannia', 'Land of Hope and Glory'. All the favourites. I stayed there till late at night – half past ten – I should have been back by nine![8]

Horace Calvert

The minority who continued to hold on to their anti-war views found themselves overwhelmed in the popular rush to war.

The Regular Army was mobilised on 5 August. The regiments called in their reservists – older men who had already served their time with the colours, left the army and started to build a new life. By this time often married, drifting into middle-age with a sedentary civilian life-style, they suddenly found themselves pitched back into the army, some struggling to reach the required fitness levels. It would be these men that formed a significant element within the BEF dispatched to France.

The advent of war meant that the Territorials also found themselves called up for war service. One young Territorial officer was Lieutenant Eric Wolton whose time in the OTC qualified him to command a platoon in the 1/5th Suffolk Regiment. He and the volunteers of Lavenham had trained together and would now go to war together. It was a strangely happy time.

About 2 o'clock in the morning of August 5th the post office man came along. My brother had made arrangements, showed him in which bedroom he slept. He made a noise outside and then delivered the telegram. I at once had to go down and wake up the sergeant major in Lavenham and he sent people out to the villages round about to tell them they must come in. The local haberdashery opened straight away so that people could get their kits all completed. The whole village was woken up. One felt one was taking part in history; the excitement – it was like a holiday – everybody was moving about. We paraded in the market place at about half past nine – full marching order. My brother had to go off early to Bury St Edmunds, so I was in charge of the detachment. We paraded on the Market Hill, crowds all round us. The Salvation Army band had all turned up so we marched to the station with the band. My father and mother said goodbye to us all there. My three brothers and my cousin were all of us in the Territorials before the war. We went to Bury St Edmunds, marched up to the old barracks. As every detachment was coming in we'd greet them, laugh at them and say, 'You're late! Are you afraid of war?' A wonderful spirit. Whether it was sensible or not I don't know but the whole spirit was ecstasy – Rupert Brooke has got it absolutely right in his poems.[9]

Lieutenant Eric Wolton, 1/5th Suffolk Regiment

With this kind of atmosphere it was hardly surprising that many of the Territorials were more than keen to waive the right that they should only be employed on Home Service and not sent overseas to war. The dominant mood was of pride in themselves, their friends and their Territorial status, though many were unknowingly signing their lives away. These Territorials represented at least a small investment for the future, but most were not ready to be sent into action until 1915. In the summer of 1914, the regulars of the pitiably small BEF would have to face the might of the German Army, participating in the battles on the Western Front that would decide the future of the world.

2

1914: THE DEATH OF AN ARMY

WHILE THE MEN OF BRITAIN rushed to the colours, or warily pondered their options, the Regular Army was mobilised on 5 August 1914 in accordance with the detailed plans that had been prepared by staff officers and lodged at the headquarters of every constituent unit. The bulk of the BEF was going to France to take up its allotted position on the left flank of the French Army, to participate in what would become known as the Battle of the Frontiers. Four infantry divisions were dispatched straight away, arriving in France on 17 August, while two divisions were held back in case of a German attack on the British mainland. The division was the basic fighting unit for most of the war. It was a partially self-sufficient formation and the original regular divisions were composed of four infantry brigades each with four battalions of 1,000 men, while their artillery was composed of nine six-gun batteries of 18-pounder guns, three six-gun batteries each of six 4.5-inch howitzers and one four-gun battery of the 60-pounders. Each division also had engineer, medical and logistical support units with an attached cavalry squadron. Two or more divisions formed an army corps.

The BEF was under the command of Field Marshal Sir John French.

Although a brilliant cavalry commander who had shone in the Boer War, there were doubts as to whether his relatively shallow experience in senior staff roles, coupled with his overall irascibility, might mean his promotion to command the BEF was a step too far. The I Corps was commanded by Lieutenant General Sir Douglas Haig, while the II Corps would be led by Lieutenant General Sir Horace Smith-Dorrien.

ALL THE DETAILED ADVANCE PLANNING paid its dividends as with few hitches the BEF mobilisation proceeded. The telegrams held in readiness were duly dispatched, the warning posters displayed and notices published in the newspapers. Every reservist already had his personal instructions, documentation and a railway warrant to get to their regimental depot.

> The reservists were called up. We in the battalion had to hand in all our spare kit, our second suits of khaki, puttees and our ceremonial uniform. We just had our service dress, our greatcoat, small kit, a couple of pairs of socks, mess tins and that kind of necessary thing. Anything else was handed into stores for what might be required later on. And we had our first lot of reservists. They came to us about three days after war was declared.[1]
>
> Sergeant Thomas Painting, 1st King's Royal Rifle Corps

It all worked with remarkable smoothness. Then the railways transported the troops in some 1,800 special trains to Southampton where the troopships were waiting.

> We entrained down to Southampton, marched out of the train into the docks and boarded a vessel. We were issued with our first aid kit that we placed inside our tunics in a little pocket. A bandage, a safety pin and a tube of iodine to put on a wound, bandage it up and pin it. We were issued with our pay books and a leaflet from Kitchener – reminding us we were British soldiers and ambassadors representing our country. In part it read very much like a parson's advice to a party of parishioners going off on a weekend binge to Paris. I'm referring to his advice on the temptations of wine and women. The ordinary fighting soldier had neither the means nor facilities to indulge in such

fantasies – not where he was going! Kitchener who was Sirdar of Egypt and used to that kind of thing – we were going out to fight![2]

Private Basil Farrer, Royal Army Medical Corps

On arrival in France many of the soldiers were given an uncompromising warning as to their future conduct.

> We were formed on parade and the Riot Act was read out to it. The Riot Act was that part of King's Regulations appertaining to the crimes and punishment of troops whilst on active service. No doubt this was an order to every regiment – the CO had to read it out to the troops. The list he read out of the different crimes was pretty lengthy, quite a list of things, but the penalty for every one of them was death. So we were warned and there was no question of ignorance if we were caught.[3]

Private Basil Farrer, Royal Army Medical Corps

From the ports the BEF was once again entrained to move to the concentration area around Mauberge, where it would slot neatly into its designated position to the left of the mighty French Army. Meanwhile, great events beyond any individual's comprehension were unfolding apace all around them.

WHILE THE FRENCH ARMIES launched massive disastrous offensives into Alsace-Lorraine and the Ardennes, the BEF and the neighbouring French Fifth Army found themselves in the path of an enormous onrushing juggernaut. The Royal Flying Corps (RFC) flew several reconnaissance missions, but it is unfortunate that many of the reports they made were not taken seriously.

> I started out that morning from Mauberge and we were told to go to a given area – east – and we were told we should see advancing German troops. As soon as we got over our area instead of seeing a few odd German troops I saw the whole area covered with hordes of field grey uniforms – advancing infantry, cavalry, transport and guns. In fact it looked as though the place was alive with the Germans. My pilot and I were completely astounded because it was not a little more than we'd been looking for – it was infinitely more. I was completely

horrified. We came roaring back and we landed, whereupon I was put into a motor car by my squadron commander and taken off to GHQ which was in a chateau some miles away. As we arrived we were ushered in and we went into a room with a lot of elderly gentlemen covered in gold lace and all the rest of it. All these senior generals, it was Sir John French's own personal conference that was going on. Somebody announced us and he said, 'Well, here's a boy from the Flying Corps, come here and sit down.' I was put to sit next to him rather terrified. Then he said, 'Now, where have you been, have you been flying, what have you been doing?' He called up to some man, 'Come here and just look at this.' I showed him a map all marked out. He said, 'Have you been over that area?' and I said, 'Yes, Sir'. I explained what I had seen and they were enormously interested. Then they began reading the figures that I had estimated, whereupon I feel that their interest faded – they seemed to look at each other and shrug their shoulders. I again tried and he looked at me and said, 'Yes, this is very interesting, but our information proves that I don't think you could have seen as much as you think. I quite understand that you may imagine that you have, but it's not the case.'[4]

Lieutenant Euan Rabagliati, 5 Squadron, RFC

The German First and Second Armies smashed through the Belgian frontier forts and were sweeping round the left of the French Army. Here, on 23 August 1914, they encountered the BEF at the Battle of Mons.

The British took up defensive position with the II Corps line stretching from the town of Mons along the Mons-Condé Canal. In the Battle of Mons, superior German skills in using concentrations of artillery and machine guns forced the British to retire in a matter of hours. Nevertheless, several British battalions gave a good account of themselves, demonstrating that British musketry was capable of delivering a bloody nose to unwary attacking German formations. Young Private William Holbrook of the 4th Royal Fusiliers found himself in a very tight spot by the canal bridge at Nimy.

We were on the bank of the river – a bit of cover, nothing much, no trenches. The ground was rather rough and hilly, quite a few rises in the ground. The machine guns were on the bridge on my left. Most of the fighting started early on the 23rd, shrapnel shells, machine-gun

14

fire and rifle fire across the canal. They were getting close to the canal bank, very near, waves coming over. Our fellows were very rapid, the fire from the bank was more like machine-gun fire, different altogether from the German fire, our fire was terrific. Every man was firing what he'd been taught to fire, fifteen rounds per minute. They were being reinforced, they didn't fall back from the canal bank, they were doing their best to get across, there were so many of them. We had a few casualties where I was, they had the worst part on the bridge, quite a number got killed and wounded. Lieutenant Dease[5] in charge of the machine-gun party, he wasn't with them at first, but when things got very close he was wounded about three times, but he still went to the gun. Godley was firing it. Dease died there, leaving Godley[6] in charge of the gun. There were some village kids up there, quite near the canal bank and I remember Godley shouting at them, 'Get out of the way! Get away!' These kids were within about 50 yards – during the attack. When they started crossing the bridge, Godley had sense enough to take the breech block out of the gun and pitched the gun over into the water, so they couldn't use it on us as we retreated. He got captured there.[7]

Private William Holbrook, 4th Royal Fusiliers

The British retirement conformed to the retreat of the neighbouring French Fifth Army. But in the titanic clashes between the huge French and German armies, the BEF was still a relatively minor player. This was a war between nations at arms.

The BEF fell back from Mons in reasonable order, but were soon being hard-pressed by the German First Army, and as a result the I and II Corps found themselves physically separated as they marched back on either side of the Forest of Mormal. By this time some of the troops, particularly the reservists softened by civilian life, were beginning to show signs of fatigue. As a result, rightly or wrongly, Smith-Dorrien on his own initiative decided that the II Corps must stand and fight. The battlefield selected ran along a 10-mile front from the town of Le Cateau. There was little time to dig in.

We lined up on this road and were told to get ourselves some head cover. We hardly got our head cover before the ridge, about three-quarters of a mile away, was literally swarming with Germans in their field grey uniforms and they advanced and we would receive the order for rapid fire. It was probably three-quarters of a mile away, an extreme range for a rifle but we rapid fired at fifteen rounds a minute at these advancing Germans and they broke up into smaller groups of six or eight, advancing through the cornfield where the corn was in stooks; as we rapid fired they took cover behind the stooks. Well, we received orders to fire into these stooks, which we did and after probably an hour or so they retired back over the ridge and we advanced to the position where they had been taking cover. Behind these stooks we found quite a lot of dead and wounded Germans.[8]

Private Henry Dally, 2nd Royal Inniskilling Fusiliers

The Germans were soon feeling round the exposed flanks of the II Corps and the meagre reserves had to be deployed for action.

The Hun came along, in his hordes. I was with my platoon officer, a gentleman by the name of Campbell, and a young sergeant called Johnny Fair,[9] who got killed. We were just lined up in a cornfield. I shall never see a picture like this in my life again – these Germans literally came in their hordes and were just shot down. But they still kept coming. There were sufficient of them to shove us out of the field eventually. Then, the realisation of what war meant: when you see my Company Sergeant Major Sim, wounded in the mouth, going back dripping blood.[10]

Private Charles Ditcham, 2nd Argyll and Sutherland Highlanders

The battle was fierce at times and British casualties were high at 7,812. German losses have been estimated at around 2,000 casualties.

As the Great Retreat continued, the men were becoming increasingly exhausted and the logistical arrangements that supported them were disintegrating.

Your rations was dished up as you passed by from ration carts. You got bully beef in 7-pound tins; we used to open our tins and get on with it. We ate on the march. You had to cut it open, dish it out as fair as you could, you couldn't expect a man to carry a 7-pound tin, particularly in hot weather – it was jolly hard work. Well, that was the ration: bully beef, biscuits and water, no time for anything else.[11]

Sergeant Thomas Painting, 1st King's Royal Rifle Corps

The reservists suffered most: their fitness was suspect and they had not had a chance to 'wear in' their ammunition boots, so their feet were soon badly chafed and blistered. Worse still, once they took their boots off, they often could not get them back on as their feet had swollen up.

> We picked up men as we went along. The original stragglers were members of the regiments that were down on some business and got caught in the retreat – they were all right. But a lot of men fell out of the retreat and they had to be picked up. We had to carry their rifles! Some were in a bad way, reservists, some of them were 40 years of age. I saw a couple; their feet were so bad they were bleeding. They took their puttees off, threw their boots away and tied their puttees round their feet and marched back in their puttees. When we got to St Quentin, we halted. They were in a bad way; some of them were sitting at the side of the road crying. There was a toy shop and Bridges[12] went in the shop and got this drum out of the shop window – whether he paid for it or not I don't know! He came out, 'Come on, we're all right now!' He got this drum going, got them together and they marched behind the drum. One helped another; the more fit stragglers helped the elderly ones. Some were left behind – you couldn't get them all back.[13]
>
> Private William Holbrook, 4th Royal Fusiliers

Those that could not rally were captured. Back and back they went, in a retreat that would continue for the best part of two weeks.

Then, after the BEF had fallen back across the River Marne, suddenly everything changed. The French Commander in Chief, Joseph Joffre, launched a concerted counter-attack on the German right flank as they swept past east of Paris during the Battle of the Marne. The BEF found itself advancing, albeit slowly, alongside the French Fifth Army, into a yawning gap between the two German armies. On 9 September the Germans, fearing disaster, reluctantly began to fall back.

There was much optimism in the Allied camp that they were embarked on an advance to victory, that Germany was beaten and that the war was as good as won. Sergeant Thomas Painting exulted in a promising minor action at Hautevesnes that seemed to promise a great deal.

We formed up and made the attack on the Germans, a Jäger Battalion, a rifle battalion same as we were. They were in a sunken road which was good cover. We'd got to go 1,500 yards over a cornfield which had been cut and cleared. It was just stubble, no cover at all. We advanced by covering fire. One section would advance under the covering fire of another section, leapfrogging each other as the others were firing to keep Jerry's heads down. When we got to within 200 yards of them my company was going in with the bayonet, on the flank of them. Jerry put white flags up, surrendered. After we roped them up and disarmed them we said, 'Well, why did you surrender?' They said, 'Well, your fire was so accurate we couldn't put our heads up to shoot at you.'[14]

Sergeant Thomas Painting, 1st King's Royal Rifle Corps

After falling back just 40 miles, German forces took up positions on the commanding heights of the Chemin des Dames Ridge overlooking the River Aisne. Here the Germans dug in and prepared a warm welcome for their pursuers.

We went off to cross the Aisne next morning. And my God it was a cross! It was very, very high. What the engineers had to do was throw a bridge from one side to the other – a distance of 10 to 15 feet. We had to cross these planks – it was half dark when I got across. No railing, just bare planks. They kept moving as you walked: no supports, no rope to hold on by. As you put one foot down, the weight of your body, as you lifted your foot, the plank sprang up and met your other foot before you could get it down. It was a hell of a job. One or two shells coming over. You could hear the roaring water of the river rushing by 20 or 30 feet below. We lost a few men drowned, fell over. Eight or nine hundred men across a plank, marvellous it was really.[15]

Private William Holbrook, 4th Royal Fusiliers

When they got to the other side the BEF found themselves facing the German entrenched positions snaking along the top of the ridge and supported by plentiful artillery that could rain down shells on the attacking British infantry. But German counter-attacks were also shot to pieces. By nightfall on 14 September there was a clear stalemate, and the British were digging their own trenches.

They were roughly dug. Still, they weren't like a permanent fixture. We had an entrenching tool which you scraped out, when you was lying there, and put a bit of head cover up so just your body could go in. And gradually that was connected up and made a trench. It was head cover you could get down underneath it, but nothing elaborate. But it was nothing elaborate like it was afterwards.[16]

Sergeant Thomas Painting, 1st King's Royal Rifle Corps

Lance Corporal Joe Armstrong remembered a macabre incident that in a way seemed almost funny, but which at the same time demonstrated all too brutally why the gap between the British and German trenches would soon became known as No Man's Land.

The trench would be about 4 feet deep, that's all, with sandbags on the front. In between us and the German trenches there were some potatoes growing. One chap said, 'I'm going to have some of those potatoes if they blow my blinking head off!' He got out of the trench, he got the potatoes but a shell took his head clean off his shoulders. That happened, it sounds a bit fantastic but it's true.[17]

Lance Corporal Joe Armstrong, 1st Loyal North Lancashire Regiment

Gradually they worked at strengthening the trenches, digging deeper and improving the parapet in front of the trench. No one imagined it would be more than a temporary expedient; most expected the offensive to resume at the first available opportunity.

With the two sides entrenched above the Aisne, the 'Race to the Sea' began, as both the French and Germans forces strove to find and exploit an open flank to the north. As they smashed into each other, so rough trench lines would be dug and they would try again. They were not racing to the sea; far from it: they were racing to turn their opponent's flank *before* it reached the sea. Meanwhile, the BEF remained in their trenches on the Aisne until Sir John French requested that they be moved to the left of the French line. Here they would be nearer the Channel ports, thereby shortening stretched lines of communication. On 1 October the BEF were duly dispatched in stages to northern France and Flanders, where many would lose their lives at the obscure Belgian city of Ypres.

YPRES MARKED THE FINAL STAGE of the race to the sea as both sides made one last desperate attempt to outflank each other. For the Germans the prize was obvious. If they could only break through then they would surely be able to overrun the Channel ports. But the British and French also had the vision of breaking through to the strategic-ally crucial Roulers rail hub and the port of Ostend. Ypres itself was irrelevant, but it guarded the gateway to key objectives for both sides. The newly formed British IV Corps under the command of Lieutenant General Sir Henry Rawlinson arrived on 14 October, and were joined on 19 October by Haig's I Corps. They were intent on attacking towards Menin, but instead found themselves squarely in the path of a one last German offensive using formations of half-trained troops. The fighting that followed would be horrendous.

The German assault fell on Haig's I Corps, which was situated directly in front of Ypres on either side of the Menin Road. The Germans pressed hard and at times seemed to be on the point of breaking clean through. Lance Corporal Joe Armstrong was with the Loyal North Lan-cashires in the Langemarck sector. He remembered one tragic incident.

> We were told to fix our bayonets. I was behind a hedge with a chap by me, ready to move off with the rest. This shell came through and practically took his leg off; it was hanging on by a few bits of skin. I got hold of him, got him a little bit safer. He emptied his water, used his bandage. He emptied my water bottle! I used my bandage. I didn't know about a tourniquet. I got him on my shoulder and put him underneath a tree. He was a Cockney, he said, 'Cor blimey mate, you aren't half a toff.' What could I do? Do you know what he did? He just got hold of the rest of the leg and threw it! I had to leave him, no doubt he'd die, without some stretcher bearers to do the job properly with a tourniquet. It might have congealed enough to save his life, I wouldn't know.[18]
>
> Lance Corporal Joe Armstrong, 1st Loyal North Lancashire Regiment

He then found himself in a trench captured from the Germans in a brief counter-attack.

> Their sandbags are this way – facing us. It was a bit too laborious to get the sandbags and put them on the other side. It was far easier to

put German dead bodies there – which I did along with others. You had your rifle and your elbow on a dead German. I was given the job of taking a party to bury some of our dead, which we did in a farmyard. There was about four to six in this party but the first thing they seemed to think about was taking the blinking wristwatches and the money out of their pockets. I swung me rifle and I said, 'The first man that takes anything I'll split his blasted head open!'[19]

Lance Corporal Joe Armstrong, 1st Loyal North Lancashire Regiment

Although the First Battle of Ypres is often portrayed as an infantry battle, as shells rained down the artillery on both sides made their presence felt in no uncertain terms.

Jerry hit my platoon four times in one morning with heavy shells. The first one hit the trench, blew it in. Well, we dug them out and built up the trench. One of my lads he was lying back there, I couldn't see a wound on him, but he couldn't move. I think the explosion had blown him against the wall of the trench and had dislocated his spine because he had no feeling downwards. Anyway, we couldn't do anything for him. The last shell found me 'at home': it blew the platoon's ammunition sky high, smashed my rifle in front of me, buried me in the trench – and didn't hurt me! They came and dug me out.[20]

Sergeant Thomas Painting, 1st King's Royal Rifle Corps

The fighting reached fever pitch on 31 October as the German attacks bore down on the 1st Division holding the line at the village of Ghelu-velt. The Germans swiftly overran Lance Corporal Joe Armstrong and the men of the Loyal North Lancashires.

Nothing happened till first light. About 2 or 300 yards away I saw bodies moving between bushes. I took a few snapshots at them. Quite frankly, looking back now, I hope I didn't hit anybody. Later on we heard such a hullabaloo on our left. We didn't know what had happened until about 11 o'clock. They'd broken through, swept right through, captured our artillery, captured the headquarters and they just swept us all in. The officer in charge, when he saw them coming across this way, he tried to do a bunk that way, but he only ran into them – he scuttled back as quick as he could. What could you do?

There was no point at all – resistance would have been suicide. I was in a trench with the others. Same as the others I scrambled out – I nearly got blinking bayoneted for having my rifle in my hand until I threw it down – you don't get any instructions as regards what to do in the event of being captured, you know. They marched us a bit further along, put us in fives. I had a pipe in my mouth and when the officer came to me, I was flank man, he saw this pipe, grabbed hold of it and tried to tug it out. I thought, 'Good crikey, this is my pipe!' And I stuck to it. A Corporal Taylor behind me shouted, 'Let go of that bloody pipe, you fool!' It's a good job I did because almost at the split second I let it go, his revolver was round my temples. It must have been a near thing.[21]

Lance Corporal Joe Armstrong, 1st Loyal North Lancashire Regiment

The Germans seemed poised to sweep forwards, breaking through to Ypres. But at a crucial moment a small but desperate counter-attack on the Gheluvelt Chateau by the 2nd Worcesters seemed to tip the balance. Lance Corporal William Finch was there at the sharp end.

When the charge went, the bugle went, we had to go for them, that's all. You know how excited a crowd would be at a football match when they score a goal, tremendous uproar, that's just how the charge started. Shouting of course, make as much noise as you can. During the charge I couldn't tell you whatever happened. We all go into the Germans, charge into Germans – they were very close. I had control of myself all of the way, but what happened I could never say.[22]

Lance Corporal William Finch, 2nd Worcestershire Regiment

As they reached the Gheluvelt area, Finch suddenly ran out of luck.

Jerry opened fire straight across the Menin Road at me, which was the other side of the hedge, with a machine gun. That's when I got hit in the leg. As I dropped down, I called out for help. I had to lay on me back. As I got up, Jerry hit me in the back, and the metal ration tin saved me from having my backbone broken. Anyway, I was calling out for help and a fellow gets over to me, laying there by myself, gets me kit off, cuts me trousers off and tied just above me knee, then a second tie in the thick of me thigh. I saw the blood come down his shoulder, he'd been hit and I said to him, 'For God's sake, leave me!

22

I shall be all right.' But he finished the tying of the second tie on the thigh. He said, 'Well, Corporal Finch, I shall get you back again.'[23]

Lance Corporal William Finch, 2nd Worcestershire Regiment

Finch was helpless lying out on the battlefield.

With the rain I got this German oil sheet and kept myself covered. All of a sudden in the daylight of the morning, this sheet was thrown off me and it was a German officer stood by me with his revolver at my head. I shouted, 'Have mercy on me.' He searched me and I said, 'Well, I can't do you any harm now!' As he was going through he pulled out my wallet – two kiddies' pictures. I was asking him for a drink of water and he wouldn't. Then he threatened me again as he walked away.[24]

Lance Corporal William Finch, 2nd Worcestershire Regiment

Alone again, Finch tried to drag himself to a ditch.

It was only a few yards, but it seemed a hell of a way to drag myself, but anyway with the aid of me gun under the bad leg, my hands and elbows, I pulled myself into this ditch – where I lay for three and a half days without being found. The rain, I'd got a handkerchief in my pocket, and I put it into the sheet above me, into the puddle of water and kept squeezing it into me mouth and spitting it out. I'm still laying in the ditch with the water going under me. As I lay there for the third day, I said, 'I hope, please God, I'll be found today.' Which I was – the German oil sheet was flung open and there was two bayonets towards my head. I shouted quick to the fellows with the bayonets, 'Have mercy, I'm English!' They said, 'What brings you here? What regiment are you?' I told them, 'The Worcesters'. They were two Coldstream Guardsmen. They went away and brought back a stretcher, put me onto it and carried me into their lines.[25]

Lance Corporal William Finch, 2nd Worcestershire Regiment

Finch had six bullets in his leg for the rest of his life. He was a very lucky man to have survived such an ordeal.

On 2 November, Sergeant Thomas Painting had moved forward to take up positions by the Menin Road. He and his men found a smattering of shallow unconnected trenches with no protective barbed wire in front of them. As a professional soldier Painting tried his best.

> I made the lads improve the trenches. And then we had a couple of hours lie-down, stood to next morning at dawn and fired away at Jerry. We suffered heavy shelling. It finished up with four of us left to use a rifle, half of us had gone. Jerry must have broken the line somewhere to the left of the Guards and to the right of us – they came round behind. He took our Support Company before he took us in the line. I was busy firing away at Jerry in front. You've got nothing to command, everybody for themselves – Jerry out 150 yards in front. I saw the platoon on my left going forward. I thought 'Well, that's funny. They're moving without telling me.' However, they'd been scooped up. Three Jerries walked round the trench just behind me. One had me covered with a rifle, another with a revolver, another with a bayonet. Well, I'd just emptied my rifle and was in the act of putting another five in. The breech was open. I couldn't shoot because I hadn't got anything in there. I'd got a very bad position to get a grip on my rifle with the butt being back. Jerry gave me the chance to put my rifle down. He could have shot me in the back or he could have bayoneted me. But he gave me a chance to put my rifle down – I had to put it down. That was the last thought in my life! I thought I might be killed or wounded, but I never thought of being taken prisoner. And it broke my heart. I thought I was a better man than Jerry, you know, man for man. But there you are, you couldn't do anything about it.[26]
>
> Sergeant Thomas Painting, 1st King's Royal Rifle Corps

Painting and the survivors were escorted back from the line by their captors until they reached a small hollow.

> Our artillery opened fire and they were dead on the mark. It hadn't got a lot of noise, but it's got a nasty sweep, our shrapnel. The bullets burst and a German officer said 'Ah, Englander – the English artillery no good'. He'd hardly said that before he was killed – it was too good for him![27]
>
> Sergeant Thomas Painting, 1st King's Royal Rifle Corps

Painting also had the chance to see the execution that the British had

24

inflicted on the Germans in their advance, as corpses were strewn across the battlefield.

> Going through the German lines as a soldier, I was pleased to see the number of dead the price they'd had to pay for their success. But as a human being I thought, 'Look at that. Look at the trouble that's going home to wives, mothers and sweethearts.'[28]
>
> Sergeant Thomas Painting, 1st King's Royal Rifle Corps

The Germans pressed on, occasionally thrown back by counter-attacks, but still creeping forward towards Ypres, moving remorselessly from ridge to ridge, wood to wood and village to village. On 11 November another desperate German lunge hit the 4th Royal Fusiliers.

> Next morning they drove us back about 100 yards towards the Menin Road. It was Prussian Guard attack, big bloody fellows, thousands of them. You couldn't see them in the half dark. Not only that, they were among trees and bushes, no clear field of fire at all. You couldn't see them until they were quite near you, you heard the noise. You were more or less firing, not knowing what you were firing at. They drove us out of our trenches, killed Colonel McMahon.[29] I was about 20 to 30 yards along the line. A fellow named Corporal Chaney said, 'The Colonel's been killed.' 'Been killed. No! Just along here?' He said, 'Yes!' God, it frightened the life out of me. I looked upon him more as a father than anything else. Chaney gave me his pocket book and revolver, so I knew he was dead. I didn't know what to do with myself for days, neither did the men that was left. When he got killed it was as if somebody had obliterated the whole battalion, they thought so much of him. No other officer made them feel like that. We got driven back, you see how far they got, they got down to our dressing station and killed our doctor, Major Macgregor, killed him looking after the wounded. We fell back. When the morning came on my birthday [12th November] we had no officers left and thirty-four men out of 900.[30]
>
> Private William Holbrook, 4th Royal Fusiliers

The British were reaching the end of their tether. Many of them had been in almost unremitting action for the best part of three months. Units were beginning to fall apart and desperate defensive measures were required by Haig and his commanders to keep the line intact. Battalions, companies and even platoons were shuffled about the battlefield to fill the gaps. In the course of the First Battle of Ypres the BEF suffered over 54,000 casualties, bringing the total losses since the campaign to nearly 90,000. The regulars who had marched to war in August 1914 were no more; the Germans, too, were close to exhaustion. Their losses in the Ypres battles numbered some 80,000 and many of the advancing new German formations who had been thrust unprepared into battle were filled with inexperienced reservists or wartime volunteers who had barely completed their training. At times their tactics degenerated into the kind of mass attacks that just exacerbated the slaughter amidst their ranks. In the end they simply ran out of steam and the battle ended on 22 November. The Germans had almost broken through, but together the British and French still held a shallow salient in front of Ypres.

The final stalemate at Ypres introduced a new phase of the war. There were no more open flanks for anyone on either side to exploit. The only way forward was by frontal attacks on prepared defensive positions. No one had any relevant experience and they were all learning together on the most bloody of battlefields. In one of the early actions Lieutenant Philip Neame, a sapper officer of the 15th Field Company, distinguished himself during a frenetic night attack on 18–19 December in the Neuve-Chapelle sector.

I got up to the front and started throwing bombs back at the Germans, and that's how the whole affair started. There were crowds of our infantry all crowded up into the remaining bit of trench we'd captured and the Germans were throwing their bombs at us from two different directions. So I had rather a business – being the only person there who knew how to light our bombs. I quickly shouted for all our available bombs to be sent up to me and told two or three of the infantry – the West Yorks – to stay by me in a bit of trench alongside me in case the Germans tried to rush us. I then started lighting and throwing bombs in the two different directions from which the Germans were throwing bombs at us. I very quickly stopped the Germans bombing from a trench away on the right which didn't run into ours – it was some branch trench – and any further trouble from that stopped. Then I had a good deal of bombing coming from straight in front of me from Germans throwing from about 20 or 30 yards away. So I quickly threw several bombs as quick as I could and with as good aim as I could. To do this I had to stand up on the fire step and expose myself so that I could see where I was throwing with some accuracy. Every time I stood up a German machine gun fired at me, but luckily he was a bit slow and I always managed to pop down again having thrown my bomb before the stream of machine-gun bullets came over more or less where I'd been standing. Anyway, after I'd thrown one or two bombs I heard what sounded like shouts and screams from the Germans in the trench. Then I got a message to say that all the British troops had got back and we were to come back. I gave a quick two or three bombs as a final goodbye to the Germans – really to keep them quiet.[31]

Lieutenant Philip Neame, 15th Field Company, Royal Engineers

Neame retired under heavy fire, assisting some of the wounded as he went. His various courageous actions had not gone unnoticed, however, and he was awarded the Victoria Cross. Philip Neame would go on to serve throughout the war and subsequently rose to the rank of lieutenant general.

Trench warfare, with all its attendant horrors, was the future. There was little honour and glory of the 'old style' to be had fighting in ditches, and a heartless new brutality would hold sway for years to come. But there was a last flicker of humanity at the end of December, when Christmas seemed, just for a moment, to break the ice and thaw relations between the entrenched enemies.

It came 11 o'clock. We'd been standing up on the firing parapet and nobody was shooting. So one or two fellows jumped out on top; another two stopped in the trench with their rifles ready. But they didn't need. As these two fellows got up others followed and there were scores of us on top at the finish. It was grand, you could stretch your legs and run about on the hard surface. We tied an empty sandbag up with its string and kicked it about on top – just to keep warm of course. And Jerry – he was sliding on an ice pond just behind the line – we could tell the way he started off, went so gently across to the other end and then another followed. We did not intermingle. Part way through we were all playing football, all on top. Some

Germans came to their wire with a newspaper, they were waving it.
A corporal in our company went for it, went right to the wire and
the Germans shook hands with him, wished him 'Merry Christmas'
and gave him the paper. Of course we couldn't read a word of it so
it had to go to an officer. There was fellows walking about on top of
our trench at 5 o'clock of teatime. Not a shot had been fired and the
Armistice finished at 1 o'clock. It was so pleasant to get out of that
trench from between them two walls of clay and walk and run about
– it was heaven.[32]

Private George Ashurst, 2nd Lancashire Fusiliers

Ashurst was a recent arrival, one of the drafts of newly trained recruits
who would restock the old regular battalions with new blood. Not far
away was Private Henry Williamson, serving with one of the first Territorial units to reach the front line, bolstering the regulars just when
they needed it most.

A German voice began to sing 'Heilige Nacht' and after that
somebody said, 'Come over Tommy, come over'. We still thought
it was a trap, but some of us went over at once and came to this
barbed wire fence between us which was five strands of wire hung
with empty bully beef tins to make a rattle. Very soon we were
exchanging gifts. The whole of No Man's Land as far as we could see
was grey and khaki, there was smoking and talking, shaking hands,
exchanging names and addresses for after the war to write to one
another. The Germans started burying their dead which had frozen
hard, and we picked up ours and we buried them. Little crosses of
ration box wood were nailed together, quite small ones, and marked
in indelible pencil. They were putting in the Germans, 'Für Vaterland
und Freiheit', 'For Fatherland and Freedom'. I said to a German,
'Excuse me, but how can you be fighting for freedom? You started the
war, and we are fighting for freedom!' He said, 'Excuse me English
comrade, but we are fighting for freedom for our country. I have also
put, "Here rests an unknown hero known to God", oh yes, God is on
our side!' But I said, 'He is on our side!' And that was a tremendous
shock, I began to think that these chaps were like ourselves, whom we
liked and who felt about the war as we did. They said, 'It will be over
soon because we shall win the war in Russia' and we said, 'No, the

Russian steamroller is going to win the war in Russia'. 'Well, English comrade, do not let us quarrel on Christmas Day.'[33]

Private Henry Williamson, 1/5th London Regiment (London Rifle Brigade)

Of course it couldn't last. The men weren't really 'peace campaigners' desperate for an end to war; they were more motivated by curiosity, a desire to stretch their legs. But behind them were others, less caught up in the moment, who needed to reassert their national priorities and get everyone shooting at each other as soon as possible.

We got orders come down the trench by word of mouth, 'Get back in your trenches – every man'. 'Everybody back in your trenches.' And shouting. Of course some of us took no damn notice. The generals behind must have seen it, got a bit suspicious and they gave orders for a battery of guns to fire, a machine gun to open out and officers to fire their revolvers at the Jerries. Of course that started the war again.[34]

Private George Ashurst, 2nd Lancashire Fusiliers

The war would continue for nearly four long years before the guns fell silent again.

3

READY FOR WAR?

LORD KITCHENER WAS APPOINTED as Secretary of State for War on 5 August 1914. The appointment of the greatest British soldier of the age was undoubtedly popular across the country. Yet Kitchener's assessment of the situation was stark and uncompromising: he had the sense to realise that it would be a long painful business to defeat Imperial Germany, with its huge army, strong navy and vibrant economy. Hundreds of thousands, indeed millions, of men would be needed to serve over the next few years, and it was his opinion that the Territorial Force could not be relied on to provide the infrastructure for massed armies. He instead sought to raise 500,000 men in a series of separate 100,000s, which would be numbered sequentially from K1 to K5 and form a whole new structure of 'Service Battalions' linked to the existing regiments. One recruiting campaign that has since loomed large in the popular imagination was an iconic poster designed by Alfred Leete picturing Kitchener's own stern mustachioed head and a pointing arm with the uncompromising caption: 'Your country needs you'. Yet for the first couple of months there was little need to point – men were flocking to the colours in unprecedented numbers.

Soon recruiting offices were everywhere, and the rapidly growing army was billeted in drill halls, requisitioned factories, church halls, schools or tented camps. Everywhere there was the hustle and bustle of men undergoing their basic training. Horace Calvert was only 15 and working at a small general engineering shop in Bradford. Opposite was an ice-skating rink which had been taken over by the army. Fascinated, Calvert mingled with the new recruits and by September 1914 he felt he could wait no longer.

> I thought it might be more exciting. I looked on it as a big adventure, having read all those adventure stories in the local library. Instead of going to work, I left my working clothes in the scullery head, went out in my better clothing. I walked into the barracks and lined up. The doctor tested you here and there, your particulars were taken, you were sworn in and it all took place inside an hour. You received your King's shilling and I was given a number: 3274. I just said, 'I'm 18', and that was it.[1]
>
> Horace Calvert

The actual legal age of enlistment was 19. However, whatever the age of the potential recruit, he was liable to be accepted if he fitted the bill through his size, general appearance, fitness and intelligence. Harold Hayward was only 17, but found a cooperative recruiting sergeant.

> I went down to Colston Hall with the hope of enlisting in the newly formed battalion by the City, called 'Bristol's Own'; official title, 12th Battalion, The Gloucestershire Regiment. I went to the table and the recruiting sergeant was there. I knew that the age of enlistment was 19 so that it was no good me telling the truth – I would say I was 19 instead of 17½. But I wasn't asked how old was I – I was asked, 'When were you born?' I gave the answer I'd given throughout my life – 12th February, 1897! The Recruiting Sergeant said, 'Well, I don't know whether we can take you at that age.' He must have seen my sad looks and he said, 'But if you go outside the Colston Hall, run round the building three times – you'll be three years older when you come back.' That was a good enough hint for me! When I came back he said, 'How old are you?' and I said, '20!' So that got me into the battalion.[2]
>
> Harold Hayward

Newspapers and weekly war-illustrated magazines hammered home their message in a relentless fashion. More and more posters appeared, appealing to simple patriotism, or intent on shaming those 'hanging back'. George Cole was working as a trapper and pony driver at Seaham Colliery when all this insidious pressure finally got too much for him by January 1915.

> I was 18 in November and then in the New Year I saw this one joining up, that one joining up, another one joining up – so off I went and joined up on the 28th January. One of the things was seeing a poster, I can see it now: there was a fellow lying wounded and another one standing up there with his bandage on his head and the words were, 'Will they never come?' So I joined up. The man at the Seaham Drill Hall was Joe Newby and he only lived about five or six doors from where I was. He looked at me when I went in and he says, 'Well, I know your name; I know where you live.' He put that down! He says, 'Are you 19?' I said, 'Yes!' He says, 'Well, I know you're telling a lie, but suit yourself!' He knew I wasn't 19 but he put it down and I joined up. He was killed in the war and his name is the last one in the War Memorial[3] in the park up there.[4]
>
> George Cole

Even if they did not join up straight away, young men found that the dramatic news pouring in from the front, combined with the all-pervasive influence of their peer group, was a potent combination. This was particularly the case in what became known as the 'Pals' Battalions which were locally raised within narrow communities. The friendships they had made at school, on the factory shop floor, down the pit, or even on the football field exerted a pull that most found difficult to resist. James Snailham endured a fairly dull weekday life working at the Chorley rubber works and he only truly came to life at the weekends – when Saturday came! Although only 16 he had already become a regular player for his local football team and had even had a trial for Preston North End who were at the time riding high in the Second Division in the 1914–15 season.

> As far as I was concerned the only object I had in life was football. I played in the Chorley and Preston Leagues in my village team –

Witley Woods. One Saturday, coming off after the match I could hear chaps older than me talking, that they were going enlisting in the morning. As we were changing after the match they said, 'Jimmy, we're going and enlisting, are you coming with us?' They were older than me but I had a permanent position in the football team! I said, 'Eeeeh, I don't know, I think I will!' I wanted to be with the lads I played football with. Well I was only 16. So away we go from our village 3 miles to Chorley. Eventually it came to be my turn, last man of the lot. Doctor Rigby said, 'My lad what the devil are you doing here?' He could see I was only young. Well I says, 'Sir, they're joining and I play with them every Saturday and I wanted to go with them.' He said, 'Go home and come back after dinner and I'll pass you.' Away I went and I ran damn near. I wanted to be with the lads you see – they were going and I was going! I came back and he passed me 'A1' straight away. And that was how I came to join the 'Chorley Pals', one company of the 'Accrington Pals'. The whole eleven of us went.[5]

James Snailham

The actions of that doctor would change the enthusiastic young foot-baller's life forever.

Amidst all the war fever, popular sentiments stirred up against the Germans were so powerful that at times there were unfortunate instances of attacks on expatriate German civilians who had settled peacefully in Britain. Such incidents could be triggered by some event, or just plain xenophobic hatred and a corrosive jealousy of foreigners prospering in their community. Ernie Rhodes was an apprentice weaver at the Eccles Cotton Mill when he was caught up in one such attack.

A gang of young fellows came with bricks, half-bricks, throwing them through the windows. They'd been knocking these houses down and there was plenty of bricks. I could see all the bottles of whisky on the shelves all being broken. Then they came up here. I followed them. Shouting and bottling, I wondered what it all was. You get mixed up with it. Twenty or thirty or more. They went up Church Street, to a confectioners; they were German. They did the same there – smashed it up. Then they went to a pub near the Cross Keys, but he got ready for them, he had a powered hosepipe and he turned it on them. The pork butcher – everybody liked his food, but he'd gone to Germany and they all said he must have been called back. His wife was an English woman, but they smashed that place up and they had everything out. They started to rob her! I never lifted my hand against any of them. Never touched nothing and I never threw a brick. I didn't like it. He was a good butcher and she was a grand woman – they went too far.[6]

Ernie Rhodes

Afterwards his main emotion would be one of lingering guilt. He was almost certainly not alone in his reaction to such unpleasant incidents.

When the 'boys' went off to war their families were left behind to cope as best they could. In most working-class families the loss of a wage packet would have been a serious issue had the government not taken some palliative measures to help out. Raynor Taylor remembered how this helped keep the family afloat when his brother Albert Taylor joined the 7th East Lancashire Regiment.

The war began to affect us more when the middle lad, Albert, joined up, September 1914. The pay was a shilling a day; it was a shilling for a long, long time. When a man joined the army he could allocate a certain amount to his dependants – if he wanted. You would allot sixpence of your shilling a day so you could draw three and sixpence a week instead of seven shillings – Albert did that. Now the government added some to this three and sixpence to make up for his absence from home. So mother drew that and in some ways they were better off because she didn't have to keep him and she was drawing money – although we never thought of it in that respect. We were proud, very proud indeed when he went to France. My mother always wrote to him but he wasn't a good communicator. When you got a letter from him you could say that three parts of it were standard things that he'd said in his last letter, 'Dear Mother and Father, Pleased to say that I'm getting on all right.' That he'd met somebody we knew, there were one or two people in the same unit, 'Bill McGhee's all right'. They were very short letters.[7]

Raynor Taylor

Once a soldier had gone 'off to war' then his family would not see him very often. Leave was infrequent and it was a significant event for the Taylor family when in 1915 Albert came back to 'Blighty', as it was universally known. He was very much the 'returning hero' to his younger brother.

> He was one of the very first that came on leave in this area. It was in the summer time, we were in bed and a knock at the door. We slept in the back room, my mother and father in the front room. My dad gets up to look through the window and I can hear him now shout, 'It's our Albert!' And there's our Albert on leave from France. If you'd have seen him – he'd got clay up to the eyeballs – he'd just come out of the trenches. My mother says, 'Well, go and let him in.' My dad went downstairs and opened the front door still in his shirt. Of course we wanted to know what it was like, had he brought any souvenirs. And he had, he'd brought the brass spike off the German helmet, which we thought was wonderful! There was no such thing of him glorifying it, or making it so horrible – he just told us as it was – we tended to glorify it. Every little thing he could tell us was wonderful. He was one of the first came on leave in this area and it caused a sensation. Before I went to work, I stood holding his rifle. And I ran all the way to work to tell them how Albert had come home. After breakfast Albert came to the mill – they were all stopping work to come and have a look at him.[8]
>
> Raynor Taylor

Soon the trickle of soldiers back home on leave became part of the backdrop of daily life. People were glad to see them, but they were no longer such a point of curiosity within their community. Sadly, not everyone survived to come home on leave. Ernie Rhodes had an older brother, Sapper Harry Rhodes, serving on the Western Front.

> In 1915 he was reported missing – and we've never heard nothing about him since. We got a telegram from the War Office: 'Missing, presumed killed at Ypres.'[9] We were all deeply upset. He was what you call a good lad, he never smoked nor drank. He always said, 'I'll never get married, Mam, never, I'll always stay home with you and me Dad!' It was a terrible shock. That's what made me join up; I was so bitter to think he'd been killed by a German – I'd lost my brother and the Germans had done it. That's all I could say. I was stupid, must

35

have been. They'd got me you see then; they want you to be like that. All I had in my mind was I wanted revenge.[10]

Ernie Rhodes

The news of these first casualties among the regulars and early volunteers had the biggest impact on local communities. Before that everyone could share the comforting illusion that it was all a great adventure. Allen Short was working as a clerk in East London when one of his older friends died in action.

> The force of the war came when the first boy at the local church was killed at Festubert in May 1915. That was our first casualty as far as we had locally known. His name was Alfred Ernest Cawthorne[11] and he lived in Abbots Road. He was a friend of the family. He was a postman by trade, a very nice man. I knew his two brothers – they took it hard. One conveyed one's sympathy, but everyone was working class, there was no excess of money to be able to support any family that suffered. The church would do what it could in the way of comforting.[12]
>
> Allen Short

As the months turned into years, the lists of the dead in the press became more a never-ending litany of young men cut short in their prime. Their blurred photos still gazed out from the local newspapers and every name still reflected a tragedy to a grieving family. But somehow the communal closeness started to fade. There were just too many of them.

VOLUNTARY RECRUITMENT FLUCTUATED throughout the war, buffeted as it was by a variety of factors. The monthly totals were the summation of hundreds of thousands of individual decisions, each taken and retaken on a daily basis. Yet it was becoming apparent that some element of compulsion would be required to secure the continuous stream of recruits needed. The upper age limit for recruitment was raised from 38 to 40 in May 1915, but this was merely tinkering with the problem. The first step towards conscription was the National Registration Act of July 1915, with the compulsory registration of all men of military age. It was discovered that there was a reservoir of nearly 3.4 million men eligible for military service, with a further 1.6 million in reserved occupations of a skilled and essential nature. On 11 October 1915, Lord Derby was appointed Director General of Recruiting and just five days later he brought in his eponymous Derby Scheme to increase the rate of recruitment. Every man aged between 18 and 40 was offered the choice of voluntary enlistment, or attestation with the obligation to enlist if called up under any subsequent compulsory scheme. The male population was to be divided up into forty-six groups depending on marital status and age. To encourage enlistment among men worried about their responsibilities to their families and dependants, a War Pension was introduced at the same time. Once formally registered, the men would remain in civilian life until called up, but would henceforth be entitled to wear a grey armband emblazoned with a red crown to show that they had signed up.

> They were finding difficulty in getting volunteers. People were realising what an awful time they probably would have and war wasn't going to be a sudden victory. To avoid the white feather idea or chivvying people unnecessarily, if you cared to join up under this Derby Scheme you had a khaki armlet given to you with a crown on it and you could wear that or keep it in your pocket. If anybody said, 'Why haven't you joined up?' You could say, 'I've already joined up and I'm waiting for my call-up.' I think none of us wanted someone else to die for us or do our fighting for us. We felt that if there was going to be a sacrifice we wanted to do it ourselves. I never wanted to be in the army. I never wanted a stripe. I always felt I'd do the right thing but I wouldn't do more. I wouldn't rush out and get killed just for the sake of doing something heroic. I'd just do what I could so that no one else was taking my place as it were.[13]
>
> Victor Polhill

The results of the Derby Scheme were mixed. A further 215,000 men took the plunge and voluntarily enlisted, while 2,185,000 men attested for future call-up if it proved necessary. Sibbald Stewart was one who registered in November 1915, although at that time he was working in a reserved occupation in the 6-inch shell section of the Elswick Ordnance Factory.

We started at 6 o'clock in the morning and we worked until 6 at night. Twelve hours on the machine, then the night shift came on and took over from us. Two twelve-hour days for each machine in the twenty-four hours. Heavy going. It was production lines all through the factory – from one department to another. We started off from the casting. They were rough and ready, but we had to polish the insides of 6-inch high explosive shells. They were put on a lathe and then polished with emery paper so that the fluid going in would run smoothly. They went to a turning lathe where they were finished off on the outside, copper banded on another machine and then the caps were put into the nose of them. Then the percussion cap was put into back end of the shell, the last thing before going to the filling factory. There were Board of Trade inspectors who inspected every branch of the work as it passed through.[14]

Sibbald Stewart, Elswick Ordnance Factory, Alexandria, Glasgow

Nevertheless, despite its partial success in getting men like Stewart to sign up, the Derby Scheme still left some 38 per cent of single men and no less than 54 per cent of married men still unregistered – even though they were not working in one of the key industries.

The scale of the challenges posed by the war was such that there was only one feasible response left: compulsory conscription. In consequence, a series of obligatory call-ups under the auspices of the Derby Scheme began in January 1916, until all the unmarried groups other than 18-year-olds had been summoned by March 1916. At the same time, full-scale conscription was introduced with the Military Service Act passed on 27 January 1916. This deemed that every male citizen who was 19 or over and still under 41 had automatically enlisted for general service and was transferred into the reserve where they were brought under the aegis of the Army Act from the appointed date of 2 March 1916. The only immunities from conscription would be tightly controlled by specially established tribunals who would consider each case individually before a certificate of exemption could be issued. The four main grounds were work of national importance, the threat of serious hardship due to exceptional financial, business or domestic obligations, ill health, or conscientious objection to the undertaking of combatant service. The call-up of each class would be by a combination of public proclamations and individual notices. The compulsion came in the form of severe penalties being imposed on anyone not responding to their call-up or for assisting those evading conscription.

The element of compulsion brought opposition from several disparate groups who objected on a variety of political, religious and intellectual grounds. Within the socialist political classes there was a split between those who supported the war, and anti-war elements within both the Labour Party and Independent Labour Party. Pacifists formed the Non-Conscription Fellowship with a membership open to all political and religious opinions who refused to bear arms from conscientious motives. I never interviewed a conscientious objector, as the bulk of the work had already been carried out for the IWM by first Margaret Brooks and then Lyn Smith.[15] The following extracts from their work illustrate the pressures on individuals who found themselves unable to accept the idea of military service.

> You found the ranks of the Non-Conscription Fellowship were
> made up of men from every conceivable angle of life. You had all
> sorts of religious groups from the Salvation Army to the Seventh
> Day Adventists; Church of England, Roman Catholics; there was no
> limit. It was a sort of cross-section of every type. Then you had in
> addition to that the more politically minded: the Independent Labour
> Party, and different degrees of socialists, and the ordinary political
> parties. Then a very curious group of what I used to call 'artistically
> minded'. There were a lot of men who were not in any way organised
> or attached, but I should call them the 'aesthetic group': artists,
> musicians, all that. They had a terrific repugnance at war which could
> only express itself individually. There were of course splits within the
> NCF and within the pacifist movement. They were some of the most
> argumentative people. You found so many points of view; it seemed
> inherent among pacifists. The thing that brings them to that point
> is that they're all men of strong individuality, and when you get that
> clash of personality coming along you almost inevitably strike strong
> differences of opinion.[16]
>
> Howard Marten

Soon there were over 2,000 tribunals composed of supposedly impartial members of good standing in the community alongside a uniformed military representative. When a conscientious objector applied for exemption the tribunal would attempt to judge his sincerity and motives before deciding one of four options: refusal of exemption; exemption from combatant duty only; exemption conditional on undertaking equivalent work of national importance; and complete exemption. As a result, two generic types of conscientious objectors could soon be identified: 'Alternativists' who were prepared to accept alternative forms of service or work and 'Absolutists' unwilling to accept anything but absolute exemption.

> My first, local tribunal was pretty hostile. They were men of not very great depth of vision or understanding, and although I wouldn't say that I was a complete absolutist, a do-nothing, I wasn't prepared to do anything under military direction, or to be exempted in a very restricted way. I think people get the impression that it was only that people wouldn't fight. It was something more than that; it was an objection to having one's life directed by an outside authority. After I had been rejected by the tribunals, I was committed to a magistrate's court to await a military escort. And then I was handed over to a military escort and taken to Mill Hill Barracks. Then the first thing you had to face was putting on a uniform. You see, you either had to accept uniform and take it, or you had to sit on or lay on the floor and kick. Well, I wasn't prepared to do undignified things. I said to the NCOs in charge, 'Look here. I suppose you've got orders to dress me forcibly. I have no objection to putting on a uniform, but it won't alter my attitude.' And I compromised in that way.[17]
>
> Howard Marten

Of the approximately 16,000 who faced the tribunals, some 9,000 accepted alternative form of service and 3,300 served in the Non-Combatant Corps.

The absolutists found that the state was determined to break them. Usually they were arrested, taken to an army camp and put in the guardroom. Once they disobeyed any order they would be court-martialled and given a prison term, usually 112 days hard labour. Then a warped game of 'cat and mouse' began. When the conscientious objector was released he was almost immediately re-arrested as a deserter and court-martialled again. Francis Meynell was imprisoned in Hounslow Barracks in 1917 and he resolved to go on hunger strike to end the impasse.

> The first few days I put water in my mouth and spat it out thinking that it wouldn't affect things. But then my doctor friend visited and said, not at all, that I would be absorbing it, so I had to give that up. The painful thing was the drying up of my tongue; it was really like a little piece of wood in a decaying barrel of my mouth. That was highly unpleasant and that developed late in the strike – on the ninth or tenth day. Throughout my hunger strike, I had fantasies of flying to heaven and also of walking home – I was certainly not in an ordinary frame of mind. Psychologically, from one's physical condition, one did get into a state of euphoria. There was a danger of brain damage although I didn't know much about that at the time. I don't think that I ever felt that I had to give my hunger strike up, I think that my absolute set of mind became even firmer the more infirm I became. I thought it would be a quick thing – release from the barracks or death. I hope martyrs felt the same, but ridiculous really to think of me as a martyr.[18]
>
> Francis Meynell

Howard Marten also found himself in a terrifying predicament when for a while it seemed that the army intended to treat him as a 'real' deserter.

> I think there was a very definite movement that they would break our resistance by sending us to France. If they could get us into the firing line then they could pass the death sentence, and that was that. The first punishment was stopping three days pay, but as we refused pay under any circumstances, that amounted to nothing. Then we were given twenty-eight days field punishment. Now field punishment can be a very nasty thing. In its most extreme form, a man can be tied up to a gun-carriage, which isn't at all a pleasant thing. But normally he's sent to what is known as a field punishment barracks, and there the prisoners are tied up for three nights out of four. They're tied up maybe on a fence, or to ropes, with their arms extended, and their feet tied together, or they may be tied back to back. It varies in form; and that's done for two hours. Not exactly a pleasant experience. Then we were forever being threatened with the death sentence. Over

and over again we'd be marched out and read a notice: some man being sentenced to death through disobedience at the front. It was all done with the idea of intimidating us. Finally, after our second court martial, we were taken out to the parade ground where a big concourse of men were lined up in an immense square. We were taken to the side of it, and then under escort taken out one by one to the middle of the square. I was the first! Then an officer in charge of the proceedings read out the various crimes and misdemeanours: refusing to obey a lawful command, disobedience at Boulogne and so on and so forth, and then: 'The sentence of the court is to suffer death by being shot.' Then there was a pause and one thought, 'Well, that's that!' And then, 'Confirmed by the Commander in Chief'. That's double-sealed it now. Then another long pause and, 'But subsequently commuted to penal servitude for ten years.' Having the death sentence read out gave you the sort of feeling of being outside yourself. It was very curious. A sort of impersonal feeling; something that wasn't affecting you personally; that you were almost looking on at the proceedings. Very strange.[19]

Howard Marten

By the end of the war some 6,000 conscientious objectors had been given prison sentences of varying durations. Of the hard-line absolutists some 1,300 continued to refuse any form of service or cooperation, with 819 conscientious objectors incarcerated for twenty months or more. During the process some sixty-nine died and a further thirty-nine had developed severe mental problems. In the Great War, conscientious objection was not an easy option.

THE PROBLEMS OF RECRUITMENT ASIDE, it is difficult to exaggerate the scale of the effort involved in converting the British Army from a small regular colonial force to a full-scale continental army capable of matching the might of the German Army. From a standing start they would have to first catch and then overhaul an opponent who was already up and running at full speed. Remember this was not a mere trebling or even quadrupling in the size of the army. By the end of the war some 4 million men were serving, in contrast to the 250,000 original regulars. Officers of every rank were required, all imbued with the military skills and leadership necessary to take inexperienced soldiers into action. There were far too few experienced regular officers and NCOs left over to act as instructors to the influx of young volunteers.

At a simpler level there was a logistical nightmare as hundreds of thousands of men flocked to the colours right across the country. Within a few days in August many more men had enlisted than would normally be dealt with in a whole year. They all had to be housed, fed, clothed and equipped for war. The pressure of numbers was such that the old Regular Army depots and barracks had no chance of coping, and accommodation was extemporised in all kinds of public buildings, empty factories and church halls. Despite all these efforts there were still thousands of men billeted with ordinary families. This could be a very varied experience for the soldiers concerned. Many were treated like one of the family.

> I was billeted on an old farm labourer and his wife and daughter. Two other Royal Marines besides myself were there in a little tiny cottage. He kept pigs and chickens in the garden. It was very, very countrified. He had to go to work on Sundays he said to feed the animals, clean them up and do the milking. He had 12 shillings a week – that was his pay. He served us up with home-cured bacon and parsnips fried in this lovely bacon fat. He really fed us ever so well – I'd never had anything like it. For that he had a golden sovereign for each of us for the week.[20]
>
> Private Thomas Baker, Chatham Battalion

Nevertheless the pressing realities of working-class life came as something of a shock to some of the sheltered young officers who were required to act as billeting officers. Lieutenant Malcolm Hancock found it all a bit much.

> Every week one of my jobs was to go round these various places where my company was billeted and pay these people. Most of them were in little backstreets and terraced houses with very little garden. They were very pleased to see you because you were bringing money. But the atmosphere in nearly all these houses you could have cut with a knife! You see the thing was that whatever happened no

window was ever opened – that was Rule No. 1 – there might be a
fire burning, there might be four or five people in one room – the
atmosphere was pretty thick. So we used to dive in almost holding
our breath, get the thing over with and nip out as soon as we could.[21]

Lieutenant Malcolm Hancock, 1/4th Northamptonshire Regiment

Many of the troops were initially accommodated in tents, but as winter
approached thousands of huts had to be built, and of course that in turn
needed hundreds of skilled tradesmen to build them.

The army had gone to considerable trouble in formulating the programme of basic training that every recruit should be put through and
this had been digested into a series of manuals which encapsulated the
lessons gleaned from the Boer War and subsequent field exercises. Yet
at root there was still a heavy reliance on the time-honoured method
of inculcating discipline and team-spirit into a body of men by putting
them through hours upon hours of foot drill across the parade square.
The troops were also given a course of physical training designed to 'fill
them out'. Many working-class lads were undernourished and the combination of PT, an improved diet and fresh air generally worked wonders
on their overall physical condition. Yet some harboured the deepest
suspicions as to the motivation of their instructors.

We had a Leading Seaman Harris! Oh, a proper swine, really a swine!
We used to go out route marching and drilling, 'Right turn, left turn,
advance, fix bayonets! Keep your rifle at the port!' And every time
we came to some mud, 'Lie down!' Honestly and truly we got wet
through. He seemed to make a point of making us lie down where it
was muddy. I couldn't for the life of me understand why he was such
a so and so.[22]

Ordinary Seaman Joe Murray, Hood Battalion

One of the easiest methods of improving overall fitness was the route
march, which started as a couple of miles and would be built up to long
distances as the recruits' endurance gradually improved. Many of the
men found it hard going.

It was a month of great heat, we sweated tremendously. We carried
about 60 pounds of ammunition and kit and our rifle, we got blisters

but we did about 15 or 16 miles a day with a ten-minute halt every hour. We lay on our backs gasping, water bottles were drunk dry, people in cottages, women in sun bonnets, came up with apples and jugs of water and we passed some of the battalions who had been in front of us whose headquarters were in some of the poorer quarters of London – I remember so well the dead white faces, many with boils, lying completely exhausted, sun stricken in the hedges, hundreds of them.[23]

Private Henry Williamson, 1/5th London Regiment (London Rifle Brigade)

As they marched along the men were often allowed to sing. The songs varied widely, but early on in the war were generally popular tunes of the day, or mildly satirical parodies. Leading Seaman Arthur Watts had joined the Royal Naval Volunteer Reserve in September 1914 and found himself in the Benbow Battalion of the Royal Naval Division (RND) billeted at Crystal Palace.

It was on the route marches that we used to sing to the tune of 'The Church's One Foundation':

We are Fred Karno's Navy,
We are the RND,
We cannot fight, we cannot shoot,
No earthly use are we!
But when we get to Berlin,
The Kaiser he will say,
'Hoch Hoch Mein Gott,
What a very fine lot,
Are the Boys of the RND!'

They all used to give us a cheery wave.[24]

Leading Seaman Arthur Watts, Benbow Battalion

Lieutenant Eric Wolton recalled with great affection the dulcet tones of his men singing as he marched up hill and down dale across the local countryside.

We used to sing marching along, the whole column singing songs. All the windows opened wide and the band and everything. I don't know who started it but the Fifth Suffolks used to sing:

We are the Suffolk Boys, Boys!
We are the Suffolk Boys, Boys!
We know our manners,
We spend our tanners,
We are respected wherever we go,
When we're walking up the tramway lines,
Doors and windows open wide, wide,
We can drink beer or ale,
Out of bucket or a pail,
We are the Suffolk Boys!
'Tipperary' of course and:
We shall have a pint!
We shall have a pint!
We shall have a pint!
Mr Wolton's going to pay!

When I annoyed them by telling them to buck up and be smart, they used to sing:

And a little child shall lead them,
Lead them gently on their way!

Of course it was ridiculous a boy of 18 or something commanding men double his age. We were very friendly; we were all local Lavenham people. They knew me and I knew them.[25]

Lieutenant Eric Wolton, 1/5th Suffolk Regiment

In the circumstances there was considerable latitude in what the men could get away with; some officers would stand on their dignity, but far more had the sense to accept it in good part. And, though never popular, the route marches toughened the men up and got them used to the long distances covered on foot during active service.

Every infantryman had to be taught how to use the rifle. Most were issued with the Small Magazine Lee Enfield Rifle Mark III, an excellent rifle, reliable even under adverse conditions and almost soldier-proof – a crucial feature for any weapon. The swift bolt-action mechanism allowed extremely fast rates of fire in skilled hands. Joe Pickard had finally joined the army at just 15 and underwent rifle training at the buttes with the 21st (Provisional) Battalion, Northumberland Fusiliers.

> Eventually you would be marked up on what sort of shot you were. You got a marker every time you fired a shot: a bull, an inner, or an outer – whatever it was. Like everything there was always rumours on the grapevine. Our thing was to get a Second Class shot – not a First Class shot because if you got a First Class you became a sniper. I remember a sergeant standing behind me while I was firing and he said, 'Keep it up – that's wonderful.' I put the next five over the top. God, he called me worse than dirt, he said, 'I know what you did!'[26]
>
> Private Joe Pickard, 21st (Provisional) Battalion, Northumberland Fusiliers

They also had to learn to use the bayonet – an 18-inch blade attached to the rifle barrel and used to terrifying effect in close-quarter fighting. It may have seemed out of date, but it was taken seriously.

> A red-tabbed and red-faced major gave a gruesome lecture on the use of the bayonet. He said he'd been to examine men who had been killed by the bayonet and how unnecessarily it had been used. Because the bayonet is grooved, if you bayonet a man and try and withdraw, very often it's very hard because the flesh closes – you've got to give it a twist. If you withdraw without giving it a twist, the outside could close and it won't bleed, it will only bleed internally. As the bayonet's grooved, giving it a twist allows the air into it; then the blood flows freely.[27]
>
> Private Basil Farrer, 2nd Yorkshire Regiment

They were also taught how to use the hand grenade, or 'bomb' as it was then known. This old weapon had almost fallen into disuse. But trench warfare gave grenades a whole new lease of life. They offered a sure method of clearing trench bays and dugouts where the close confines amplified the deadly explosive effect. The Mills bomb, introduced in 1915, was the first effective fragmentation grenade with a steel casing designed to shatter into lethal shards.

> You were told the mechanics of the Mills bomb: what it did, how lethal it was and how much care you had to exercise. It was oval

shaped about the size of a fist. Serrated and a loop at the top with a handle. Now this handle looped under some gnarled guards, you pulled it down and pressed it to the grenade. Below that there were two protrusions stuck out with a hole through and a pin fitted through those two holes which held the handle. When you took that pin out, you would still hold the handle down, because immediately the handle was released it started the detonator and in five seconds your grenade would blow up! So if you threw it, you took the pin out, throw it, by throwing it you release the handle, it would fly off and in five seconds it would explode. You stand sideways to your object and throw overarm, releasing the grenade at the top – just like a cricket bowler and immediately ducking down – you didn't wait to see where it had landed you know.[28]

Private Raynor Taylor, 2/1st Glamorgan Yeomanry

At first the tactical training undergone by the troops was of a very simple nature.

An awful lot of our training was based on the Boer War. That was the latest form of military exercise. If we attacked the imaginary enemy – thank God they were imaginary, mind you – they would be lining that bank 100 yards away. So you advanced in extended order, a yard or two between each man across open country in short rushes. You gave the command to, 'Rush' and then, 'Down'. Everybody laid down, so that you didn't get shot I suppose. In the meantime you were in full view of the enemy. You probably had about two of these rushes. The last 50 yards you charged and everybody shouted, 'Hooray!' Whether that was supposed to frighten the enemy to death I don't know, but it must have been absolutely suicidal. That was the basis on which we were supposed to attack – of course it was quite impossible for us to have survived.[29]

Second Lieutenant Malcolm Hancock, 1/4th Northamptonshire Regiment

But as the war progressed and the years went by, the tactical exercises became more progressively sophisticated and specifically tailored to the new trench warfare conditions. The men were taught how to use their weapons in deadly combinations.

We learnt how to clear a trench of the enemy; how to get them out of it. You weren't in the trench, you were on the ground above the trench, with an NCO in front and behind him a bomber with Mills bombs, and a couple of men with bayonets fixed down in the trench. The corporal called, 'Throw' and the man threw his bomb into the trench ahead. As it exploded the two riflemen with their bayonets dashed round the trench – you cleared it bit by bit like that – bomb and bayonet. We practised jumping into trenches with the bayonets fixed and pushing it into a sandbag on the far side of the trench as you jumped in.[30]

Private George Thompson, 3rd Durham Light Infantry

The new warfare required far more of soldiers than rapid musketry. This was a complex war.

Once an infantry soldier had completed his basic course he could be given more specialist training. If judged suitable he might be selected for instruction on the Vickers machine gun. This was a development of the Maxim machine gun first issued to the British Army in the late nineteenth century; by 1914 there were two allotted to each battalion. A reliable weapon, rarely afflicted by serious stoppages, it fired belts of the same .303 rounds used by the SMLE rifle. It was deadly, not only in a direct fire mode, but also for indirect fire with an effective range of up to 4,500 yards. Private Norman Edwards was delighted to have been chosen to be part of what he regarded as an elite team.

It was a rather heavy weapon: water-cooled barrel and there was a separate tripod. No. 1 did the actual firing, No. 2 carried the tripod. Each section was four or five men. They had to carry the belts of 250 rounds. We inherited this song from the Regular Army:

You can talk about your rifle,
You can talk until you stifle,
But it's only just a trifle,
To the gun we have now,
The Maxim of course is,
The pride of all the forces,
So just unhitch the horse,
And let the bugger go!

You caught hold of two handles and with your thumb pressed the lever and the thing went, 'Knock, Knock, Knock, Knock' about as fast as that. You gradually traversed the thing on your target. We had a lecture by an experienced regular machine-gun officer. He told us all about the elevations: how you turned the wheel to elevate it and for each degree of elevation the bullet would go so many feet further on and so on and so forth. When he finished he said, 'Now carry on with the training, Corporal.' The corporal said, 'I'm sorry, Sir, I don't think I'd better take that on – I'm a greengrocer in private life!'[31]

Private Norman Edwards, 1/6th Gloucestershire Regiment

Later in the war the Vickers guns were concentrated together in the newly formed Machine Gun Corps which then provided a Machine Gun Company to support each infantry brigade. After the removal of the Vickers guns, the much lighter Lewis guns were introduced to provide direct machine-gun support within the battalions.

We had a Lewis gun to each platoon. You'd got a No. 1, a No. 2 and plenty of pannier carriers. I was No. 2 on the Lewis gun. The No. 1 gunner was in charge of the gun, the firing and I was the one that loaded the pannier for him: took one pannier off and load the other on. All the rest of the platoon were just loading the drums. There were forty-seven bullets in a drum, they put the bullets in and passed me the complete pannier. They always used to say, 'What happens if you get a No. 1 stoppage?' That was when the gun stopped firing! Well the idea was pull back the cocking handle, rotate the magazine and carry on. 'If it doesn't go next time and you've got a No. 2 stoppage, what do you do then?' Well throw the bloody gun away and get another![32]

Private John Grainger, 5th (Reserve) Battalion, King's Liverpool Regiment

Stoppages or 'jams' were a common problem with the Lewis gun, but the men had learnt their stoppage drills and were generally able to quickly remedy the fault. The Lewis gun would prove itself to be a crucial addition as it massively increased the firepower of infantry platoons that were no longer filled with regular soldiers capable of fifteen rounds a minute.

Perhaps the most desperate need of all was for the legions of new gunners that the Royal Field Artillery (RFA) required. Despite this, there were simply not enough artillery pieces left behind for the recruits to practise on. As a result, many learnt their gun drill on old 15-pounder guns. The men may have grasped some of the basic drills, but gunnery was greedy for specialists: the Royal Artillery needed a copious supply of competent sergeants and junior NCOs to run the gun detachments; it needed officers that could understand the mysteries of trigonometry and the scientific tenets of gunnery and they in turn needed assistants intelligent enough to help in drawing up complicated barrage tables; the artillery also required trained signallers, drivers and riders. Although they tried their best, the batteries sent out to the front in the early years of the war were often lacking at every level and would have to make up the rest 'on the job'.

WHILE THE INFANTRY, CAVALRY AND ARTILLERYMEN were all undergoing their training the army also had to train thousands of new officers to lead them into battle. For far too many this was a case of being thrown in at the deep end and trying to stay just one step ahead of their men. One such was the young Second Lieutenant Norman Dillon. He had been commissioned into the 14th Northumberland Fusiliers in September 1914. His first impressions on meeting his men were salutary.

> When I arrived at Berkhamsted I met the adjutant who said, 'Oh, you're in charge of C Company'. There on the right were 250 men in very worn-out civilian clothing and one or two elderly looking chaps with medal ribbons on their breasts standing about in front of them. I had no idea how to dismiss the company. I walked up to one of them, stood to attention smartly and said, 'Who is commanding the company?' He said, 'I am. I'm Corporal Rubbins, I was in the South African War and these are my medals. Will you please take over the company, Sir?' And he left me standing! I had no idea how to dismiss the company or what I had to do! I unconsciously applied the traditional usage of the army and told this chap, 'Well, let me see how they march; will you carry on and dismiss?' He promptly marched the company off and dismissed them. I drew a deep breath of relief! I went down to W. H. Smith and Co. who had a bookstore at the station where I could buy a copy of the *Manual of*

Military Training. Fortunately it's very explicit and it gave all the drill movements from the beginning to the end. I had a box of matches and put them out on the dining room table to represent sections, platoons and companies and I got one or two movements off by heart. Next morning they went off all right and next day after that I got a couple more movements – by the end of the week I was turning the company inside out, back to front and marching sideways and every way. Delighted with myself. I don't think the troops ever cottoned on for a moment that I was only one jump ahead of them![33]

Second Lieutenant Norman Dillon, 14th Northumberland Fusiliers

Dillon was a determined individual, but less resourceful officers floundered badly. It is a truism that the encouragement of older, wiser and above all more experienced officers was crucial to the proper development of young subalterns. In this respect Lieutenant Eric Wolton seems to have been fortunate to receive excellent guidance which neatly encapsulated what was expected of him.

We had one regular adjutant who was excellent – a man called Lawrence, a captain from the Cameronian Highlanders. He always emphasised again and again that an officer's first duty was to look after his men. And that's what we did. We had to see that our men were fed and housed properly before we had our own food. With the consequence that if you looked after your men, the men looked after you.[34]

Lieutenant Eric Wolton, 1/5th Suffolk Regiment

The intentions may have been good, but for the ordinary soldier in the ranks the officers seemed distant figures. They may have had the best interest of their men at heart, but any communication generally had to be carried out 'through the proper channels'.

There was a great insistence on the proper way to address an officer. If you are standing in the ranks and you are addressed by the officer you must be careful to say, 'Sir' after every ejaculation. You never start a conversation with an officer; if he speaks you answer him – once when the officer asked me a question I answered and I didn't say, 'Sir!' This sergeant major shouted, 'SAY, SIR!' So I had to say, 'SIR!' That satisfied him I suppose.[35]

Private Reginald Johnson, 1/4th Norfolk Regiment

The scale of the expansion was such that the British Army was left lacking in experienced officers at every level of command. The individual battalions had to be welded into the brigades and divisions with all the supporting arms that would actually have to fight the Germans. Individual units could not stand alone in modern war. They were dependent for survival and success on being part of a smooth well-drilled organisation, where everyone knew what he was doing. Far too many divisions would be sent overseas lacking in both basic skills and any real integrated training.

IT WASN'T ALL WORK and the soldiers did have some free time in between their training and the endless 'bull' of preparing for kit inspections. They had the use of canteens which offered the time-honoured 'wad and a char' (cakes and tea), some even were 'wet' establishments where the men could buy a pint of beer. Some of the men were tempted to gamble what little they had.

> Crown and Anchor was a great thing. A big cloth about a yard square. Then there would be a crown and anchor, spades, diamonds, hearts and clubs. Then they'd bet on any of those, put your money on. The fellow would have a dice, throw it and pay whichever one was there. There used to be the old song, he'd start:
>
> *Who'll have a bit on the old dice*
> *Who'll have a bit on the old crown*
> *Come here in rags*
> *Get away in motor cars*
>
> They had their own spiel like the fellows on the sideshows. Some fellows would lose all their money. You'd lose every time – it was a gamble – he had the dice! It would be in some quiet corner of the camp. The Military Police would come around and there would be a scamper then![36]
>
> Private Ivor Watkins, 59th (Training Reserve) South Wales Borderers, Kinmel Camp

Once they could pass as soldiers in their uniforms, the men were usually allowed out of the camps and barracks into the local communities.

Many just strolled round, visiting teashops, cinemas or theatres, but many took the chance to go drinking in public houses. Their wages may have been low, but some men always seemed to find a way to get drunk. Private Thomas Baker remembered watching in awe as a paralytic Marine staggered into Chatham Barracks.

> One night Peter Carr came in very thoroughly tight, singing away just as it was lights out in the barrack room. Peter got into bed and somebody had fixed it – and he went down with a terrific wallop. 'Holy Jesus,' he said, 'I'll shoot the bloody lot of you!' He got off the bed and loaded his rifle – we could hear him loading in the dark – and he fired five rounds, the whole lot, through the ceiling. Fortunately they went through the floor of the upper deck and he didn't hit anyone in bed up there and they went out through the roof and knocked the tiles off. It was a wet night and it started to come pouring down through the top deck, through their beds and down through our deck. Within five minutes the guards collected Peter and took him off in his shirt and put him in the cooler. But he only had five days so he got off very light really.[37]
>
> Private Thomas Baker, Chatham Battalion

Along with the drink came the temptations of the flesh. Many of the younger recruits had little or no knowledge of women. Despite his rank, Sergeant William Davies was just 20 years old and he certainly backed timidly away from any opportunities to broaden his minimal experience while undergoing training with the 8th Cheshires at Brookwood Camp in Surrey.

> Coming back by train, it would stop at one of the stations for quite a time before we got into the station at Brookwood. Whenever it stopped there was always a bunch of girls trying to talk to us. We sergeants were all together in one compartment. There was a girl came up, she had a green dress – she was awful nice. She poked her head through and said, 'I think I'd like to go out with you!' So I said, 'You'll have to ask me Dad!' That was to the elderly sergeant on the other side. She shut up then![38]
>
> Sergeant William Davies, 8th Cheshire Regiment

Other men, such as Private Ernie Rhodes, watched goggle-eyed as more worldly-wise men actually dared ask out the local girls.

> While we were at Scarborough, there was a young lady there we used to see her of a morning on this bridge. Everybody fancied her because she was a bonny girl. Only be about 16 or 17. One night one of the fellows said he'd got a date with this girl – ooh we were all jealous – honest! There he was getting himself dolled up to go and meet her. Anyway off he goes. It wasn't very, very long before he was sick! And he got what is called a 'dose'. He was absolutely rotten I believe. He was taken away and he never came back to us. Now that did me good – because she looked lovely. I always thought, 'Well, listen, if that's the risk you take going with women, having sex – I'm not bothered at all!' I was too frightened for my health.[39]
>
> Private Ernie Rhodes, 5th (Reserve) Manchester Regiment

Of course, given the opportunity human nature could not always be denied, and in consequence rates of venereal disease soared as syphilis and gonorrhoea ran riot among the troops.

The length of the men's training varied, and it often took far longer than the six months recommended by the handbooks. This was inevitable given the manifold confusions caused by the shortage of uniforms, instructors and proper equipment. Yet eventually the men were trained and their battalion was ready – at least in theory – for war. For many the first sign of this was a series of ceremonial inspections by senior generals or even the King himself. Lance Corporal Tom Williamson and the 1/5th Norfolks had to wait for a considerable time under the pouring rain for their meeting with royalty.

> King George V came to inspect the battalion at Colchester. It turned out to be a very wet morning and we were standing on parade I should think two hours. He turned up, just went down the ranks, back and said, 'Dismiss them, they are a fine body of men!' He used his humanity, to make it as quick as he possibly could. He was suffering with us as we were suffering with him. We were glad of course, some of the men were stricken – it's a long while to stand to attention waiting.[40]
>
> Lance Corporal Tom Williamson, 1/5th Norfolk Regiment

As they marched out of the towns and villages where they had become such a feature during their long training, the parting was often an emotional one.

> Come the day we paraded in the main street in St Albans in column of fours with the band leading us to march down to the station which is perhaps three-quarters of a mile down the London Road to the old Midland Station. Well off we went. There were crowds of people on either side of the road, hundreds of people there must have been. As the band struck up they came along on each side of us, shouting to the men in their ranks – probably their wives. It wasn't long before they were in among the ranks, trying to carry the chap's rifle, his haversack, his equipment for them. It was an extraordinary thing. We simply couldn't keep the ranks clear, it was no good trying to do anything. They wanted to show their affection for us – that we represented some of the army which was protecting the country. I think everybody realised that. We just went on and got down to the station.[41]
>
> Lieutenant Malcolm Hancock, 1/4th Northamptonshire Regiment

Although they may not have known where they were going, they knew they were off to the front: whether it be the Western Front, Gallipoli, Mesopotamia, Palestine or Salonika. They were confident in their training, but they also knew they could not all survive. As Sergeant William Davies and the 8th Cheshires marched off he witnessed a poignant scene that affected him deeply.

> When we left Brookwood we had a little send off from relatives of some of the lads. 'Ginger' Harp,[42] my company sergeant major, had his wife and two little children – two little boys. As we walked along to go to the station 'Ginger' said to his wife, 'I won't be long!' I thought to myself, 'I'd like to be able to help him and see he did come back', but of course he didn't.[43]
>
> Sergeant William Davies, 8th Cheshire Regiment

The trains took them to the ports where they embarked on the troopships and ferries that would carry them off to war. Few had ever been abroad and it was an emotional wrench to leave their homeland, all too

56

aware, as they were, that they might never return to see their families again.

> We were packed like sardines. We went down Southampton Water on the 25 September, a beautiful moonlight night. That was the night we sang 'Home Land':
>
> *Home Land, Home Land, Land of my Birth,*
> *The dearest place on earth*
> *I'm leaving you and recall the old song with a sigh,*
> *It may be for years, it may be forever,*
> *Dear Home Land,*
> *Goodbye ...*
>
> I've often wondered how many of the thousands of us on that boat ever saw their country again.[44]
>
> Signaller Jim Crow, B Battery, 110th Brigade, RFA

4

1915: WESTERN FRONT

THE NEW YEAR BROUGHT A DAWNING REALISATION that the troglodyte existence of trench warfare would be the new normality for the foreseeable future. Trench systems were still relatively simple, but effective: they seemed almost impenetrable. From within the trench the defending infantry could shoot their rifles to maximum effect into advancing troops while at the same time being protected from any return fire. The strands of barbed wire strung out across No Man's Land may have been scanty, but they were still effective in slowing the progress of attacking troops, at which point the machine guns added concentrated firepower to the tactical mix, pouring bullets into their helpless targets. The employment of artillery was relatively primitive, yet infantry caught massing in the trenches, or crossing No Man's Land, could be destroyed in a matter of moments.

The Western Front became an impossible problem for the generals on both sides. How were they to break down this integrated system of defence? Ultimately what was needed was a means whereby the defending infantry and artillery could be prevented from firing while the attacking troops were exposed in the open. But this demanded a variety of sophisticated gunnery techniques and developments in armaments technology which would only appear as the 'fruits' of the science of war in the years to come. As a result, separated only by No Man's Land, the great armies continued to sit in trenches that wound from Switzerland to the North Sea.

The Battle of Neuve Chapelle

The British made their first real attempt to break through the German lines at Neuve Chapelle, when the First Army commanded by General Sir Douglas Haig attempted to pinch out the salient around the village. A heavy bombardment was intended to destroy the German front line: no less than 340 guns were concentrated along the 2,000-yard frontage to be assaulted by the IV and Indian Corps – a ratio of one gun for every 6 yards of front attacked. In this low-lying section of the front the German trenches were largely restricted to sandbag barricades, about 5 feet thick. The British guns were brought up in secrecy and registered their targets as unobtrusively as possible. It was also the first operation to utilise properly the potential of the RFC to photograph the sector to be assaulted, using the nascent art of photographic interpretation to reveal German artillery batteries, machine-gun posts and headquarters.

A 'hurricane' bombardment of thirty-five minutes commenced at 07.30 on 10 March. Shrapnel fire was used to cut the German barbed wire into small harmless scraps, while the breastwork trenches of layered sandbags were broken apart by high explosive shells. Many of the defending troops were killed or demoralised – exactly as had been intended. As soon as the barrage lifted the troops went over.

Although in places there were hold-ups, the front line was swiftly overrun. But when the troops tried to exploit their gains everything began to go wrong. Communication problems multiplied alarmingly, leading to a dreadful confusion over pre-arranged artillery schedules, the urgent needs of the infantry and the practical difficulties encountered by commanders faced with life-or-death decisions without sufficient knowledge of the facts. There were long delays before any attempt was made to exploit early successes.

As the British offensive ran out of steam, the Germans capitalised on the delay by moving up their reserves before launching a series of stinging counter-attacks. In the midst of this chaos, Second Lieutenant John Wedderburn-Maxwell was sent forward to man a makeshift observation post.

> I had to go up with the infantry, both supporting them with the fire they wanted, protecting them against the German counter-attacks and seeing what was happening. I went up – it was rather difficult. As you can imagine the place was quite devastated, firing going on all round – some rifle fire, a great deal of machine-gun fire. All of a sudden my little signaller boy, very young, he was suddenly flat: dead. I met a great friend from the 3rd Battery called Alan Hornby. Alan and I sat down and watched these heavy shells coming over from the Germans, who had woken up then to the fact that this was a very serious business. You heard these things coming, 'WWHHHOOOOOOOOHHHH!!' You saw a black thing hurtle to the ground and then a huge flame of black smoke. Later I was up with the 'Jocks', the Cameronians. We repelled several counter-attacks with our SOS fire; every time our infantry moved forward you had to adjust your SOS protection. I was doing the work for six guns. The 'Jocks' found the Germans killing their prisoners or something – anyhow, they absolutely got their rag out and I know they really murdered everything they could get hold off – it was very savage.[1]
>
> Second Lieutenant John Wedderburn-Maxwell, 5th Battery, 45th Brigade, RFA

When the aftershocks had died down it was evident that, although much had been learnt, the operation had failed. The battered remnants of Neuve Chapelle had been captured, but all efforts to push on to Aubers Ridge proved an expensive failure. In all the First Army suffered a terrible 11,652 casualties, the Germans about 8,600. Any chance of a proper breakthrough clearly depended on the British attacking on a wider front, making the resulting gap difficult for the Germans to plug. This, however, would require an unfeasible amount of men, guns and shells. There was one more inconvenient truth for the British: the Germans also had learnt lessons from the fighting at Neuve Chapelle and in the bitter fighting further south against the French. They now realised that just one line with attendant barbed wire was by no means sufficient to secure the integrity of their front. When the British next attacked they would find the German defences very much improved.

Second Battle of Ypres

Germany would be standing on the defensive on the Western Front: their main strategic effort in 1915 would be on the Eastern Front, where they had resolved to knock Russia out of the war. Yet they were still looking for any potential means to break the stalemate and their preferred solution took the form of poison gas. They had already tried various experiments with lachrymatory gas, but had settled instead on a large-scale trial with chlorine gas in the Ypres area. There, the unfortunate 45th Algerian Division in the Langemarck sector and their neighbours of the French 87th Division faced the release of some 168 tons of deadly gas. At 17.00 hours on 22 April, the yellowish-green clouds of chlorine rolled on a slight easterly breeze towards the French lines, promoting first incomprehension, then raw panic and a pell-mell flight. The Algerian and French soldiers had absolutely no gas protection and the chlorine soon took effect, creating a burning and choking sensation as the gas first irritated then flooded their airways and destroyed the tissue of their lungs. It was fortunate for the Allies that the Germans had not expected their experiment to be quite so successful, so had neglected to allocate sufficient reserves to press home the attack. The German infantry themselves had only crude respirators and when they saw what the chlorine had done to the French, this seems to have restricted their enthusiasm to press on beyond their initial objectives.

Two brigades of the recently arrived 1st Canadian Division, part of the Canadian Expeditionary Force, were to the right of the French in the front line and were not, therefore, in the direct path of the worst of the gas. Far more seriously affected were the reserve Canadian brigade who had moved forward and echeloned across in an attempt to close the 4-mile gap vacated by the hapless French.

> We saw this green cloud come toward us, just slowly rolling along the ground, and behind it a grey mass of Germans in grey uniforms and some kind of respirator. They looked grotesque and we wondered,

'Just what is this? This isn't conventional.' We just felt terribly bitter: nobody's going to come through here and if we have to we'll die here fighting. Our officer who was wounded told us to get out and meet them hand-to-hand for Canada. We felt pretty mad about the whole thing and no 'so and so' is going to come through here, even though we weren't equipped to hold them. Then one of our boys who was a chemist got a smell of this chlorine gas and advised us to urinate on our handkerchiefs or pieces of puttee or anything that saved our lungs from getting the gas. Well we knew that we just had to hold there – because up in the front line were our own boys who hadn't broken and run and there was this great gap with the Germans pouring through. We just couldn't leave – so we dug in with our trenching tools and hung on.[2]

Private William Underwood, 14th (Royal Montreal Regiment) Battalion, CEF

The Canadians did well, but they were not left alone in the fight for long, as British reinforcements began to arrive. Among them was the 50th Division.

Oral history does allow interviewers to follow their own interests and in my early interviewing programme, perhaps betraying my north-eastern family roots, I seem to have made a special effort to record the survivors of the 50th Division. This Territorial division was raised across Durham and Northumberland and had been sent out to the Western Front for the men to complete their training in the area to the west of Ypres, where they arrived late on 22 April. When the urgency of the situation became apparent the division was quickly moved forward.

There in the distance the sky was lit up and we could see the German shells dropping on the city of Ypres. Eleven miles it was between Poperinghe and Ypres – full of refugees making their way to Poperinghe. Mainly old men, women and children. Never a sound, just mooching along without a word; their spirit seemed to be broken. They had all kinds of wheelbarrows, some with two wheels, some with one. Some of the wheels weren't even round, just pieces of wood nailed together to make it as round as possible – very rudimentary. They carried mostly bedding and personal things. Children as well were carrying as much as they could. I don't know how they managed struggling along past us, heads down, not a word to each other and not a word to us. We arrived at Ypres in the Market Place. Across the cobbled square was the Cloth Hall blazing, all in ruins. The shells were dropping and shrapnel was flying all over. We thought, 'Well, this is war!'[3]

Lance Corporal Jack Dorgan, 1/7th Northumberland Fusiliers

They would be thrown straight away into the fight against the advancing Germans.

After a further gas attack on the fragile lines, the Germans had once more broken through to capture the village of St Julien in front of Ypres. This then would be the focus of the first attacks by the 50th Division, culminating in a frontal assault by the 149th Brigade on the afternoon of 26 April. The attack that followed would have the dubious distinction of being the first made by a Territorial brigade in the Great War. It cannot be pretended that they were ready for their ordeal.

At noon we got orders to fall in. We were in full marching order with packs on our backs. We didn't know where we were going but we were going in to attack St Julien. Nobody had any chance to reconnoitre the place; we were simply going on blind. We knew nothing about it, nor did the officers.[4]

Lance Sergeant George Harbottle, 1/6th Northumberland Fusiliers

The absence of any proper reconnaissance proved ruinous.

Where the huge casualties arose, it was not by the enemy attack on us, or our attack on the enemy but the fact that there was a great long line of reserve line barbed wire about 10 yards wide and about 4 feet high. There was only a single gap. Garton,[5] a brave officer – he had wire cutters and he was stood there cutting another gap – of course he was killed. My section was through the gap straight away and most of the 1st and 2nd Platoon was through the gap straight away – they hadn't got ranged on us. Then when the rest of the battalion was trying to get through that gap they got murdered by machine-gun and artillery fire.[6]

Lance Sergeant George Harbottle, 1/6th Northumberland Fusiliers

The Northumbrians were amateurs, learning the ugly truths of war in the hardest way of all. Jack Dorgan had a terrible experience.

As we went going forward men were being shot down, wounded and killed. Sergeant Pick lay in the middle of a field shouting for help, swearing and tearing, wanting help. You could see chaps had gone forward to help him because there they were lying dead in the field alongside. Yet he still kept shouting for somebody to help him. We just had to pass on, our objective was St Julien. The stretcher bearers were running around carrying our wounded away, leaving the dead for later. A batch of us lay behind a hedge, resting. We never saw an enemy; never saw anybody to shoot at. A shell dropped right in among us. When I pulled myself together I found myself lying in a shell hole. There was one other soldier who, like me, was unhurt, but two more were heavily wounded, so we shouted for stretcher bearers. The other chap says to me, 'We're not all here, Jack!' So I climbed out of the shell hole and there was two of our comrades lying just a few yards from the shell hole. They had been blown out by the same shell. They had their legs blown off. All I could see was their thigh bones. I will always remember their white thigh bones, the rest of their legs were gone. Private Jackie Oliver[7] was one of them, he never recovered consciousness. I shouted back to the fellows behind me, 'Tell "Reed" Oliver his brother's been wounded.' So Reedy came along and stood looking at his brother, lying there – no legs – who died a few minutes later. But the other, Private Bob Young,[8] was conscious right to the last. I lay alongside of him and said, 'Can I do anything for you, Bob?' He said, 'Straighten my legs, Jack', but he had no legs! I touched the bones and that satisfied him. Then he said, 'Get my wife's photograph out of my breast pocket.' I took the photograph out and put it in his hands. He lay there: he couldn't move, couldn't lift a hand, couldn't lift a finger, but he held his wife's photograph on his chest. And that's how Bob Young died. Today on the Menin Gate memorial their names are recorded as having no known graves. I've seen those names many, many times since the war. Jackie Oliver and Bob Young's names are there. When I've stood and looked at them I've sometimes thought, 'My name could have been there as well'. I think, 'How lucky I am to be able to be there seventy years after!'[9]

Lance Corporal Jack Dorgan, 1/7th Northumberland Fusiliers

It soon became evident that they couldn't get any further.

We then could see our own front line down the hill and the German lines on the slope above. We went down there in extended order. We eventually reached our own front line – they said, 'Well, what the hell's all this about?' They didn't know what we were up to at all. I asked the usual three questions we had been trained to ask as soon as you reinforced anywhere: 'Are you being attacked? What's the range? Are you short of ammunition?' They said, 'Get your head down, never mind where the enemy are, there's plenty of ammunition there.' And he kicked a couple of great boxes of ammunition. They weren't interested. When darkness came we were ordered back again – we never advanced from there at all. It was the wickedest thing going and all these fellows killed for nothing.[10]

Lance Sergeant George Harbottle, 1/6th Northumberland Fusiliers

Thus the advance had spluttered out in the most dreadful of anti-climaxes. The Northumberland battalions were withdrawn from the line that night. They had suffered some 1,954 casualties – nearly two-thirds of the brigade strength – and all apparently for nothing. In his later years, Jack Dorgan certainly felt bitter at the way this terrible incident was written up after the event by his officer.

Captain Watson Armstrong writes about that incident where Bob Young and Jackie Oliver were killed. He writes in his book, 'Bob Young, I understand, was singing "Tipperary" when he died.'[11] Which of course was nonsense. I was there when Bob Young died. He died with his wife's photograph in his hand, he had no thoughts of singing 'Tipperary', his voice was getting fainter and fainter all the time until he pegged out. What the captain was trying to imply was that the morale of the Northumberlands was so high – but it didn't happen that way.[12]

Lance Corporal Jack Dorgan, 1/7th Northumberland Fusiliers

The survivors were recalled to the very field from which they had started. And although there would be many more battles for Dorgan and the rest of his battalion, rarely would they suffer such painful losses.

On 30 April, Private George Ashurst and the 2nd Lancashire Fusiliers were moved forward into the Ypres area as part of 4th Division to relieve the Canadians on the left of the British line. At the same time the British were getting ready for a tactical withdrawal from the exposed salient centred around Zonnebeke to a more secure line some 2 miles from Ypres. By this time the risks of gas attack were understood, but the palliative measures available were still minimal.

> They tell us that we may be gassed when we go in the trenches. So NCOs would be issued with so much red flannelette, a yard or two and so much elastic. We had to fold the flannelette two or three times, attach the elastic and put it round our heads – over our mouth and nose if the gas came. So I got an issue, but it was in the bottom of my haversack. I never bothered. We never cut it up or shared it. 'They'll not send any gas, they'll not gas!' the lads said. They never bothered and I never bothered.[13]
>
> Private George Ashurst, 2nd Lancashire Fusiliers

Despite their confidence, the next German assault would indeed be preceded by another gas attack. On 2 May, after a relatively quiet day, the Lancashire Fusiliers were taking it easy when it happened.

> At about quarter to five I went along to my company headquarters to have a cup of tea. I'd only just poured out my tea when the sentry in front called out, 'Will you come and look, Sir?' So I got up to look and out of the German trenches, about 600–800 yards away, great jets of yellow cloud were shooting up into the air like water out of a hose. As the gas went up into the air out of these jets, it formed together into a cloud and dropped onto the ground and started rolling towards us with a slight breeze behind it. We knew what it was – I didn't get my cup of tea! We had to get busy. A man called Jackie Lynn, a machine gunner with us, was getting his gun out of its proper position and putting it up on top of the parapet and getting up behind it – without putting his so-called gas mask on. I got back to my platoon as quick as I could, warning all the men on the way to get up. The only thing to do was to try and get these flannelette things over our mouths and shoot. We had to wet them and there wasn't very much to wet them on the spur of the moment. I know some chaps dipped them in their tea; some of them had a bit of water in their water-bottle and poured it on – but a lot of us just dipped them straight in the latrines. It was the only thing to do and it wasn't very pleasant.[14]
>
> Second Lieutenant Victor Hawkins, 2nd Lancashire Fusiliers

One of the Fusiliers went a significant step further in his frantic attempts to survive the gas that was swirling towards them.

> I don't mind admitting that I didn't think much of the urinating on handkerchiefs, I didn't think it was sufficient protection, so I went into one of the trench latrines, you know, just a bucket stuck in a hole, and I stuck my head in the bucket – I made sure of it. I stopped down long enough till I couldn't hold my breath any more, came up, took a good breath of air, down again.[15]
>
> Private Alfred Bromfield, 2nd Lancashire Fusiliers

Hawkins tried to keep his men firing into the cloud

> We were very soon enveloped in this thick yellow filthy cloud and could see nothing. We didn't really know whether the Germans were coming up behind it or not so we just let fly with everything we had and went on shooting. I must have been lucky because it didn't seem to affect me as badly as it did my men, but even then I didn't like it. We had a wonderful doctor with us, an Irish rugby international called Billy Tyrrell,[16] and he was going up and down that trench, livid with rage with the Germans for this dirty trick, doing what he could – which was very little at the time – for the men. Trying to make them hold their respirators up and so on. Eventually he came down my end of the trench and just when I was really feeling pretty desperate he came up and said, 'Well, how are you doing, young fellow?' I wasn't doing awfully well and I said, 'I don't know if I can stand much more of this.' Really for something to say. I thought perhaps he'd say, 'Oh, well hold on old boy!' He didn't; he turned on me and said, 'Well, if you can't – give me your rifle and I will!' I was really so angry at him saying this – perhaps he meant me to be – that it pulled me up with a jerk and I thought, 'Well, if you can I can too'. I have no doubt in my own mind that that remark and his example made all the difference to me.[17]
>
> Second Lieutenant Victor Hawkins, 2nd Lancashire Fusiliers

In view of William Tyrrell's robust attitude towards Hawkins, it is amazing to read the evidence he subsequently gave to the War Office Committee of Enquiry into Shell-shock of 1922. Here Tyrrell referred to his own experience of shell-shock after being buried by a burst shell as a result of which he was reduced to a state of utter nervousness and actual tears. His evidence stated baldly, 'I knew the thing was coming on for months before it finally arrived. I was always consumed with fear and it was difficult to conceal that fear. That is the mainspring of my evidence. It is the repression of fear: the repression of the emotion of being afraid that makes the greatest tax upon the man's mind and strength.'[18]

Nevertheless, many of the Lancashire Fusiliers had not waited for the gas to swamp them, but had simply made a run for safety – and who could blame them?

> We were in our trench and in a reserve trench you're not so much on the *qui vivre* as the front, you don't need to be – the fellows in front of you are looking after Jerry. 'It's gas! It's coming over here!' It looked like a brownish-green stuff coming, not too thick, you could see through it. These lads out of the front trench were on their way, jumping over the top of our heads, they were running, hopping it out of the gas, jumping across our trench all together and running away towards Ypres. Well everybody was grabbing their handkerchiefs, coughing and spitting. One or two attempted to get up the back of the trench and the officer was there with his revolver, 'Get back! Get back you! Stand To!' No sooner had he stopped a fellow getting out of the trench there, while he was doing that a fellow was nipping out here – running away. We all thought we'd had it, 'We're bloody poisoned now we are!' But we had to breathe it; it had to go in our lungs. It was nasty stuff to breathe – coughing and spitting! We kept spitting it out and yellow green stuff was coming up our throats. A shout came, 'Retire!' I think it was a bloody soldier that shouted it, it was no one in authority. The officer must have thought it was official, I never saw what happened to him. I jumped up the back of the trench and I hopped it. They were scattering the place with machine-gun bullets and shelling like hell – shrapnel. A little piece hit me in the back of the neck. There was two men with me, us three together running away to get away from this gas as far as we could. Walked and ran; stopped trying to get a bit of breath for a minute. Then off again. We threw our equipment away – our rifles even – threw the damn lot way. We didn't know whether they were attacking or not – we weren't even bothered. If he was coming after us we didn't know and we didn't care. We got into Ypres. Frenchmen were dashing

out giving us salt and water but we couldn't swallow it, it made no difference – it wouldn't go down our necks to make us sick – we couldn't drink it. This stuff kept coming up our throats. It was oozing out – greenish froth.[19]

Private George Ashurst, 2nd Lancashire Fusiliers

There were disadvantages in making a run for it, as the gas stayed with them as they ran, following them with the wind; whereas if they remained at their post then in time the gas would pass over them. Hawkins and a few others stuck it out in the front line. Among them was Private John (Jackie) Lynn whom Hawkins had seen dragging his machine gun up onto the parapet. Although almost overcome by the chlorine gas he stuck it out, continuing to fire and checking any German advance as the gas billowed over him.

We were in that gas cloud about fifteen minutes altogether and then quite suddenly one got a breath of fresh air. It was the most marvellous feeling and one fairly sucked it in. At that moment I turned round and I saw 'Jackie' Lynn.[20] He'd kept his gun going right the way through and he was carried past me on a stretcher, blue in the face, dying. He actually died about five minutes later. I've never seen a chap blue like that. It was the most beastly thing to see. The effect of this gas was to form a sort of foamy liquid in one's lungs – a lot of men died pretty quickly, others were soon down drowning from this beastly foam coming up from their lungs. Out of 250 men we started with at 5 o'clock we were very soon down to about forty or fifty men. Some were dead and some were dying and the others were on the ground.[21]

Second Lieutenant Victor Hawkins, 2nd Lancashire Fusiliers

Private John Lynn would be awarded a posthumous Victoria Cross for his courageous actions.

The battle continued to rage on at Ypres, fought to secure tactically significant features of ground, many just small hillocks or ridges that barely showed on the map, but which offered good observation behind the British lines. Deadly fighting at Hooge and Sanctuary Wood scored these names deep into the memories of thousands of British families. One such vicious battle raged over the 'summit' of Hill 60, which was nothing more than man-made hillock of spoil dug from the adjacent railway cutting of the Ypres-Comines-Lille line. But the view towards Ypres seems have been regarded as beyond price, so when German forces overran the hill following a gas attack on 5 May, a counter-attack was ordered. Private Alex Thompson, drafted in April to join the 2nd King's Own Scottish Borderers, had just arrived. Now he was going into the thick of battle. They were to go over the top at 22.00 – after a twenty-minute bombardment which proved more of a warning to the Germans than assistance to their own side.

> Our fellows were shelling and shelling. But those shells were falling short and missing the wire, yards and yards short of the wire. We were in a front-line trench. You just felt, 'Well, this is it – a case of sink or swim.' We were all ready on the firing step. Just your ammunition and your rifle, all your kit was in the trench. Then we got the order, 'Over the top and charge!' So we were over the top, fixed bayonets and charged. We advanced maybe 5 or 10 yards, some of them never got that length they were killed going over the trench. That was your training you see, to just keep going, making for the German trenches. It was like pie meat for the Germans, near everyone was getting fast in the barbed wire. There was Germans at that side, Germans there, with their machine guns, Germans all over the place with machine guns! They were just cutting us like cutting hay. The fire was rapid, continuous, machine-gun fire and shrapnel bursting. You wonder who's going to be shot next – and I was shot next. I felt myself getting blasted, toppled upside down, 'Oh dear me, I must be hit somewhere!' I'd got an explosive bullet in the left arm, it split my left arm from the forearm, right up to the forearm, another bullet just above my wrist did for my thumb – it cut the sinews. Then I got another one in this side – a shell burst – shrapnel. I got a hole here in the left-hand side of the stomach and that was running with blood. Shrapnel in the shoulder up here. All in seconds, all in a bunch one after the other. I was knocked right upside down. I was sort of dazed and I says to myself, 'Well, I came this way – so I'll go back the same way!' So I crawled back on the one arm, shoved myself along the ground. I knew I was hit but I didn't know what the results were at the time. The fire was going on any amount – helter-skelter. I couldn't see nothing for blood on myself – I was plastered with blood. I

managed to crawl back to the trench and some of the boys pulled me down.[22]

Private Alex Thompson, 2nd King's Own Scottish Borderers

Hill 60 remained in German hands for another two long years.

Still the fighting raged on and on. The frightfulness of modern war seemed unremitting, beyond comprehension. Second Lieutenant Martin Greener, whom I had the pleasure of interviewing in his home under the shadow of Bamburgh Castle, had a terrible experience to recount of an attack on his trenches situated north of Lake Bellewaarde. He was serving with the 1/9th Durham Light Infantry, who had been temporarily attached to the regulars of the 2nd East Surreys to gain experience. On 24 May the Germans began a terrible bombardment culminating in a gas attack.

> At dawn they opened a very heavy fire. Then we heard this sizzling; you could hear this damn stuff coming out. Then we saw this awful great greenish yellow cloud coming over, about 20 feet up. They'd got these nozzles practically right on top of the trench. Nobody knew what to think. Certain men were stepping down off the fire trench; we had to get them back on top. But immediately it got there we knew what it was: you began to choke. A sweet oniony smell. It stopped you breathing. It was very frightening. Word came, 'Whatever you do don't go down!' If you got to the bottom of the trench you got the full blast of it – because it was heavy stuff. They thought the gas would finish us off and then all they would have to do was come over after that. So it was quite a bit before we saw any Germans. We opened fire but this gas affected the rifles – the bolts in the rifle had verdigris – you could use your rifle but you were much slower. We only had one machine gun and that was useless. I lost my voice; I couldn't speak, you just choked. It dulled your brain; you didn't really know what was going on.[23]

Second Lieutenant Martin Greener, 1/9th Durham Light Infantry

Despite it all the Durhams and their neighbouring battalions managed to repel the German attack.

MINE WARFARE, a partially forgotten technique from the age of great sieges, was also resurrected on the Western Front. On 20 December 1914 the Germans detonated ten small mines in the Givenchy sector, with follow-up exploitation attacks on the lines held by the Indian Corps. The British response was rapid, helped by the fact that there were hundreds of coal pits all across Britain. Special appeals were made to get miners to enlist into specially formed Royal Engineer Tunnelling Companies. George Clayton was one that answered the call.

> The Germans started that game. They blew our trenches up first and we were urgently required to go there as quick as possible to give them some of their own back. A fortnight after leaving my work at the collieries at the Charlie Pit, I was at the front-line trenches along with the others that had volunteered.
>
> Sapper George Clayton, 175 Tunnelling Company, Royal Engineers

Tunnels snaked out under No Man's Land as both sides sought to lay huge mines beneath the front lines and redoubts of their enemies. The first British mines were detonated on 17 February 1915 beneath Hill 60. Clayton himself was working on tunnels being pushed out towards the German positions at Hooge Chateau.

> The Hooge Chateau had been a big Belgian house, but there was only the cellars left, the house was all shot away. Our objective was get under them and give them some of what they were giving to us. When Lieutenant Firebrace got us into the front line of trenches in Sanctuary Wood, 'Well,' he says, 'I think we'll sink the shaft here.' We told him that none of us had ever done any sinking. He said, 'You call yourselves miners and you've never done any sinking?' But in our part of the world there's special teams go from one colliery to another. He was an Australian officer and he'd been used to prospecting for gold – only shallow. 'Well, we'll have to make the best we can of you.' We made an inset and started to sink a shaft 4 feet square, timbered sides till we got down about 25 feet. There was a rope ladder, that's how we got up and down. At the bottom there was water: we had to get a pump. It was worked with a handle and there was pipe up the shaft and so far away to a low part of the trench where the water could run away. We had entrenching tools, picks

and shovels. I was the tunneller's mate; his duty was to get away the earth the tunneller was digging out. You had to hold the sandbags for him to fill, drag them out and get them to the shaft bottom. Then they were hauled up by the windlass, two or three at a time, and then carried away to some low-lying ground. We took a straight drive towards the German trenches, the shortest distance between two points. Sometimes we travelled quite quickly. The strata we were working among was easily worked – it was mainly a grey kind of a clay. We had a surveyor, John Warnock, a Glasgow man. He took his bearings and we worked under his instructions. You had candles to get as good a light as you could expect. The candle goes wonky, that's an indication that the air's going slack. Before you notice it yourself you could tell by the way that the candle was burning – a dim kind of a light. There wasn't the oxygen in the air. We were getting away from the natural air: but a blacksmith's bellows put that right! A bellows on the surface and a pipe laid down – it got you plenty of air. As we were digging it out, we were putting our timber in. It was close timbered all the way, bottom, sides and top. You could put it up making very little noise, it fastened itself as the earth fell around it and it didn't need any hammering. Once you'd got it timbered there was no more earth fell in to remove – it was sealed up like being in a box. There was no danger of it falling in on you. We were working three eight-hour shifts, seven days a week, working night and day. We got under the cellars: I've heard them muttering in German, heard the noise of their feet coming down the steps, you could even hear their glasses – they've maybe been drinking lager – hear the tinkling of the glasses with the geophone, it was very sensitive. We had to have our feet muffled and on no consideration were we to speak to one another in case the noise was heard. We got that laid with explosives: ammonal. We carried tons in, packed it in. Then the stemming was very important or it would blow to the line of least resistance. You've got to make the stemming as tight as what there is in front, or above you, or it would blow the wrong way. We'd be on about three or four nights and days stemming it. Filling sandbags, tree trunks, anything we could get – fastening it in. We put a detonator in and the wires came right the way back, up the shaft and away into the support trenches. When the Hooge Chateau was blown up, I would be about 250 yards from it looking from my trench. A dull thud. You felt it! Like an earthquake! You saw the earth go up. It shook the ground and made a hole like a quarry.[24]

Sapper George Clayton, 175 Tunnelling Company, Royal Engineers

The Hooge Chateau mine was detonated at 07.00 on 19 July, creating a 120-foot wide crater that was 20 feet deep with an additional 15-foot high lip of piled up debris and rubble surrounding it. The British infantry charged forwards, achieving complete surprise, and soon managed to consolidate the position.

As such mining operations became more extensive there was also an attempt to capitalise on the experience and skills of mining experts who were already serving at the front. One such was Second Lieutenant Martin Greener who before the war had been training as apprentice mining engineer, and was thus the ideal choice as a brigade mining officer. Both sides had begun counter-mining, driving out tunnels with the intent of exploding a camouflet mine to collapse their opponents' underground galleries.

The Germans started blowing our trenches. We knew if they were mining they had to get rid of the spoil. We used to get the artillery to shell the spoil and see what kind of material it was: whether it was clay. If it was blue clay, well, you knew they were mining. We started counter-mining. We drove shafts down, drifts they were called. The tunnels would be 4 feet high, continuously timbered – boxed in. We saw every shift start and you'd always go down and have a look to see what was going on. The sergeant in charge would be reporting all the time. You drove out and all the time you were listening. Every couple of hours you'd stop everything and use these geophones and you listened – the sounds came through the clay. You put the things in your ear and the machine against the clay face. We'd stop mining, listen and try to locate exactly where a noise was coming from. Then very slowly we'd go towards it. When you think you'd got near enough to it we'd blow in the whole thing. It's a matter of experience. In that blue clay we knew how sound travelled – and it travelled very slowly. Two or three yards of blue clay would be almost a barrier. The explosives came in big cylinders, you had to tank them in with sandbags. You wired detonators to them, took

74

your leads out into the trench onto your exploder. It was a nerve-wracking job.[25]

Second Lieutenant Martin Greener, Headquarters, 151st Brigade

Gradually the old skills of siege mining had begun to seep back into common usage.

The Germans still had one more weapon to unveil, which they duly did in their counter-attack to retake Hooge at 03.15 on 30 July 1915. That night Lieutenant Gordon Carey and the men of the 8th Rifle Brigade had been squeezing through cramped trenches to take their stint in the front line.

We waited for the men to be able to see for the first time this bit of horrid landscape that we were supposed to cling on to. I did not like it as we went on, I felt there was something definitely wrong, I felt something was happening, something was brewing. Well, after the deathly silence, I was at the farthest point away from the crater when the thing happened, so dramatically and so suddenly that I was quite incapable of any sort of consecutive thought at all. The first idea that sort of flitted through my mind was that the end of the world had come and this was the 'Day of Judgement', because suddenly the whole dawn had turned a ghastly crimson. Then, as I began to come to my senses, I definitely saw four or five jets of flame passing across the trench that I had been in one minute before. And it was just out of my reach, thank heavens, at the time. With a horrible hissing sound and at the edge of the flame, there was a nasty sort of oily black smoke, and then I did begin to think with a little sense, and I clambered out on to ground level behind the trench so see if I could see what was happening. And it was then that I realised that the Germans were coming over into my bit of trench. The light was very dim, but I could see the chaps jumping and I had no doubt whatsoever that they must have jumped right on top of my men, who could not possibly have been doing anything but lying in the bottom of the trench until the flame stopped, and it had only just stopped. They must have jumped in on top of them with a bayonet.[26]

Lieutenant Gordon Carey, 8th Rifle Brigade

This was the first use of liquid fire, projected by the German *Flammen-werfern*. It was a terrible surprise and the 8th Rifle Brigade were soon overwhelmed and swept back. But a new line was soon improvised and swiftly consolidated; nothing really had changed. The flamethrower became just another weapon to be dealt with, another addition to the ever-growing arsenal of war.

AFTER THE GERMAN ATTACKS IN EARLY MAY there was little real point to the fighting around Ypres. But the murderous fighting in the Salient continued deep into the summer. Their initial assault had nearly burst through, but they could not exploit what was briefly a very promising situation, since the bulk of their reserves were engaged in attacking the Russians on the Eastern Front. The Germans were tempted by the fragility of the British lines, but no matter how many fresh horrors they unleashed, they were constantly thwarted by the inherent strength of trenches and barbed wire combined with modern firepower. War is about choices and those made by the German High Command ultimately resulted in their failure to achieve a decisive victory on either front. The British casualties in the Second Battle of Ypres, which officially stretched from 22 April to 31 May, totalled nearly 60,000 men with German losses of about 35,000. Ypres may have been a 'soldiers' battle' but in Wellington's day that had meant just a few hours of torment; in 1915 it stretched into weeks, then months of agony. Ypres came to cast a shadow over the lives of almost every soldier in the BEF: little did they know it had only just started.

Battles of Aubers Ridge and Festubert

Once Joffre realised that the main German effort would be centred on the Eastern Front in 1915, he planned a series of major spring offensives to try and wrest back the initiative on the Western Front. The first of these would be an advance in the Artois area, where the French aimed to seize the Vimy Ridge heights before attacking across the Douai plain. The British would be involved in a minor capacity through a subsidiary assault by the First Army on Aubers Ridge on 9 May 1915 – essentially a diversion to pin down German reserves. The BEF had a large number of problems to contend with: they were still somewhat short of shells, the ground in front of them was relatively flat with open defensive fields of fire, and by this time the Germans had greatly strengthened their trenches and the barbed wire blocking the way. Accordingly, Haig planned two attacks as a pincer movement converging on the Aubers Ridge. The infantry would attack after a forty-minute bombardment fired from 625 guns. Though impressive-sounding, this concentration of artillery was nowhere near enough, as by this time the Germans had not just one trench line, but three. When the British infantry attacked at 05.40 on 9 May they were slaughtered by heavy machine-gun fire. Private Patrick Horrigan witnessed the explosion of a British mine in the Delangre Farm sector near Fromelles as part of the northern pincer. Then it was their turn.

> There were little ladders to go up over the top. When the mine went off a great mound of earth came up, 'ZZZZWWWHHHHOOOOF!!!!' These poor Germans were up to their necks in earth. Over the top we went. There's all our regiment all out in the open, I could see them there in little parcels of men. I was in a shell hole looking at the German line. Around me were all these fellows getting shot in the head. I remember the sergeant having a pair of field glasses and I said, 'What can you see, what can you see, give us those bloody glasses!' I started peering to see if I could see where all these bullets were coming from. Just then I got one in the head as well. They were marvellous marksmen. Captain Whitty said to me, 'Go on Horrigan, you'd better go.' I started to crawl. There was no point in me getting up and running – they'd have had me as easy as winking. So I decided to crawl. I'd got my white bandage round my head and the bullets were spitting in front of me – I'd turn the other way. When I was wriggling back I could see our bombers trying to bomb the Germans out of their trench. Eventually I got into a safe area. The colonel was in there with a telephone saying, 'For God's sake send more machine gunners and bombers!'[27]
>
> Private Patrick Horrigan, 1/13th London Regiment (Kensingtons)

In the equally doomed southern attack near Neuve Chapelle, Lance Corporal William Edington of the 9th King's Liverpool Regiment was moved up to the British front line, ready for a possible further assault, but also to secure the line against a possible German counter-attack.

> Our platoon sergeant, he was a fine big man about 6 feet tall, ruddy faced and a very good sort – he'd been a Territorial for years. He led us out. When we got about five or six steps I saw him fall to the ground rigid like a plank falling. I thought for a moment, 'What on earth is he doing?' I wasn't sure it wasn't some new manoeuvre! It was practically instantaneous – it takes me longer to tell you than the thing took at the time. I suddenly realised what had happened – he'd been hit and he afterwards died from his wounds. That gave us a terrible fright, to see this happen so soon. I was lance corporal and I became responsible for the men behind me. Although I was so terribly frightened myself, I realised then that with the men behind me I couldn't stop, so I went straight on walking round this prone sergeant of ours. We went on; we could hear nothing of course with the bombardment. It was just a question of going on because if you were not hit you were lucky; if you were hit – well you could do nothing about it. We had to make our way in dashes up to the next lot of breastworks. There were several holes blown in the breastworks in front of us so we made our way across fairly regular fields. It was spring, May, nice green grass growing. If it hadn't been for the war it would have been a very pretty scene. The Germans had spotted these breaches in the breastworks and then they began shelling them. As we got there a shell burst very near; that frightened us to death again. I had never seen a human corpse before that day and it was a fearful experience. But after the first fight of the morning and carrying the responsibility of being a lance corporal, I gradually got confidence and by the end of the day I was quite calm.[28]
>
> Lance Corporal William Edington, 9th King's Liverpool Regiment

Frantic attempts to organise a new attack later in the day were further disrupted as the Germans commenced a heavy barrage of the British front lines. The attack ground to a halt on 10 May with nothing whatsoever achieved and some 11,000 casualties suffered.

The Battle of Aubers Ridge was an utter failure. This made even more tragic the repeat performance just a week later in the Battle of Festubert, which started on 15 May. Haig had appreciated that the strength of the German fortifications could not be overcome by short 'hurricane' bombardments, as he did not have enough guns or shells to make it sufficiently devastating. Instead, a two-day methodical bombardment would be employed, with careful observation, to maximise the effect of each shell. But a longer bombardment period meant that the First Army had sacrificed the element of surprise; so the Germans, too, were ready for battle. Fundamentally, no matter how the artillery was employed, there were still far too few guns and the shell supply situation was exacerbated by the prevalence of poorly manufactured 'duds' among those they had. When the infantry attacked, even where they had some early success, communication problems and difficulty in timing the deployment of reserves meant that the Germans soon stabilised the situation. Even when ground was gained, it was often only because the Germans had retreated to a new line in a stronger tactical position. The overall sense of failure was such that it leaked into the political arena triggering the 'shells crisis' back in Britain that would prove the downfall of the Liberal government under Asquith and the formation of his new coalition government with the Conservatives. The appointment of a previous Chancellor of the Exchequer, David Lloyd George, as the very first Minister of Munitions showed the seriousness with which the shortage of shells was perceived.

Battle of Loos

Throughout 1915 the BEF had been growing in size and by August Sir John French had some 28 divisions under his command (11 Regular, 6 Territorial, 7 Kitchener, 2 Canadian and 2 Indian divisions), a total of some 900,000 men. Although still very much a junior partner to the French (which had 98 divisions) the BEF was slowly becoming a significant force – at least numerically. Unfortunately, although a rough facsimile of a soldier can be created in six months of basic training, this was emphatically not the case for officers and NCOs. They needed time to absorb the lessons of command, and to gain the required experience and self-confidence to be able to cope under the extreme conditions of battle. In particular, the plethora of new brigades, divisions and corps meant that there was a crippling shortage of qualified staff officers to make all the exceptionally complex arrangements for a modern army in wartime. Inexperience in the whole decision-making and administrative process, combined with a totally inadequate communications system, created a lethal cocktail of delays and confusion in the midst of battle. In essence, these new officers were attempting to learn their trade while in close combat with the awesome power of the German Army. It was a sure recipe for disaster.

As the BEF grew in size it took over more of the Western Front from the French, a section extending south from the La Bassée Canal right down to the town of Loos. This flat landscape, dominated by mining villages and their associated slag heaps, would be the area selected for the next offensive, which was to coincide with the huge French autumn offensives planned for late September in the Artois and Champagne sectors. The British role was relatively minor – six divisions of the First Army under Haig were to attack at Loos to the left of the seventeen divisions thrown in by the French Tenth Army in the Artois. Nevertheless, to the British this was widely seen as the 'big push'. But once again the British were in trouble before they even began: the German front line had been greatly strengthened, their support lines no longer being afterthoughts but carefully planned defence works in their own right. The second line had been placed beyond the range of British field artillery and concealed on a reverse slope with its own integral 15-yard-deep belt of wire. Behind that was yet another line of trenches. The depth of these defences meant that there was little chance of breaking through in one bound, as the artillery would have to be moved forward to overcome the second and third lines. As the Germans would be moving their own reinforcements forward at the same time, it was plain that a formidable task lay ahead of Haig's First Army.

To avoid the perils of attacking on a relatively narrow front, all six divisions were to be in the line in order to maximise the width assaulted. But this merely drew attention to the fact that there were insufficient artillery resources to deliver an adequate bombardment to cover such a breadth of front. It was therefore decided to use extensive smoke barrages to conceal what was going on, and also to release chlorine gas to make up for the inadequacy of the four-day barrage which opened on 21 September. Once again, in the attempt to guarantee the destruction of the German trenches, all surprise would be forfeited. A great deal was being pinned on the gas release, but its effectiveness was dependent on the right wind direction, as in such a large attack there could be no flexibility in the start time.

Dawn on 25 September brought predictable disappointment for the British, as the wind was little more than a breath of air, barely sufficient to carry the gas. Haig had no realistic choice but to press on and hope for the best. The gas was released efficiently enough, but the infantry found it more of a hindrance than a help as they stumbled across No Man's Land. This was particularly the case in the area under assault by Gough's I Corps.

> We opened up with a terrific bombardment to try and break through the wire and then the gas was let loose and our infantrymen went off all clad in those 'Klu-Klux-Klan' helmets; they fitted straight over the head with just a little mouthpiece. Well they had to charge, there was no loitering. The exertion of going almost 800 yards, uphill, loaded with ammunition, rifle bayonets and that, made them think that they were suffocating and they pulled their helmets off. Unfortunately, just at that moment the wind saw fit to change – not only to change but to start to blow back, and the gas, instead of going over the German trenches, remained stationary and if anything came back towards our infantry. It caused terrible execution.[29]
>
> Bombardier John Palmer, 118th Battery, 26th Brigade, RFA

Private Walter Cook was back in the reserve line facing the Hohenzollern Redoubt where the 9th Division had managed to effect a lodgement but were now facing a terrible battle. As the wounded streamed in he was given a special task.

> I was to give tetanus injections to every wounded person who came in. I was told to put a big 'T' on his forehead with indelible pencil. I had one or two rather large syringes and each of the tetanus serum doses was encased in a wooden box. This box was held with a tack; the lid had to be slid away, the phial had to be broken, the syringe filled and the injection given. The difficulty was that I hadn't got enough syringes and secondly these wooden boxes gathered round my feet. There were thousands of men coming and I had no room to

move about, no one to help me get the things out of the way, no one to give me a fresh syringe. In fact, although no one escaped my 'T' on the forehead, I think some of the injections must have been a little painful![30]

Private Walter Cook, 27th Field Ambulance, Royal Army Medical Corps

There were some successes on the IV Corps front, where the 15th and 47th Divisions overran the town of Loos and advanced up the dominating Hill 70. Once on the reverse slope they encountered the almost undamaged German second line and were soon forced back without securing the hill. At this point the battle still stood in the balance, and could have been swayed by fresh divisions of reserve troops. Unfortunately, the only two reserve divisions available were under the direct control of Sir John French and had been held too far back to be able to reach the front before nightfall. When at last they arrived, Corporal Jim Davies and the 12th Royal Fusiliers encountered wounded soldiers as they moved up into the line.

The first thing I saw in the morning were wounded Jocks coming down. Motor ambulances to start with, then horse ambulances, then walking wounded. I never saw so many wounded Jocks. One of the chaps said, 'Is it always like this up here?' And a Jock said, 'Only on Saturdays!' We hadn't got a clue.[31]

Lance Corporal Jim Davies, 12th Royal Fusiliers

The fighting around the Hohenzollern Redoubt grew to a crescendo as new battalions were thrown into the fray.

Our objective was to capture the Hohenzollern Redoubt; a trench system in the form of a loop. The Germans had one side, we were in the other. We marched along to a communication trench which was absolutely stuffed full of walking wounded coming back from the front. People in a dreadful condition – one man holding his stomach out and walking. We turned round a corner from that and into the front line. Our Captain Lucas, waving his sword, said 'Charge!' And I'm very glad we did, because I can say I once charged the enemy. We got up on top, I got my revolver and trotted along towards the redoubt wondering what was going to happen. There was an enormous German ahead of us in the place we were going to take; people were handing him bombs and he was throwing them at us. The man next to me had half his head shot off. But I went on. When we got there the Germans had cleared off. So although we charged, it didn't lead to any bayoneting. I dropped into the trench and found out I was the only officer. Lucas was wounded in the knee and the other one was dead. I started to try and collect people and went along to see what my flanks were like. There we stayed. I spent one night crouching in a dugout with an enormous German, sitting on a box as dead as mutton, others lying down dead on both sides. I'm not a brave man, but I wasn't bothered; I just did what I had to do.[32]

Second Lieutenant William Hildred, 1st York and Lancaster Regiment

Next day, 28 September, the Guards were sent in to attack Hill 70. Private Walter Spencer of the 4th Grenadier Guards gave us a wonderful account of what happened as they completed the capture of Loos and moved onwards and upwards.

There were a lot of dead Highland Light Infantry still hanging on the old German wire – I wasn't very thrilled. We were all a bit despondent – we didn't realise in our young minds that war was so drastic – they were the first dead troops we'd seen. Loos was still occupied by German soldiers at the top end. There was a colliery erection sticking up in the air called Tower Bridge. That was the place we had to march on.[33]

Private Walter Spencer, 4th Grenadier Guards

The battalion split up into companies and advanced through the streets of Loos.

Brigadier Haywood said to me, 'Where is your CO?' I replied, 'I believe he's been gassed, Sir!' He says, 'Gas be buggered!' That was the actual words he said. There were some affected by the chlorine gas and they put their gas helmets on; it was up to them. The old shirt helmet was a hood of cloth with artificial lenses to see through. It also had a nose clip so that you couldn't breathe through your nose and all the air that you breathed had to come through the tube that went into your mouth – not very effective, I'm sorry to say. I didn't put my helmet on, there wasn't sufficient gas about, you could certainly smell it, but it wasn't sufficient to cause any trouble. We were in extended order – about 4 or 5 yards between each man – got among the cellars and threw a few Mills bombs about in case there were any Germans around. If you went down and there were Germans there they'd get you before you got them. But if instead of going down you throw the bomb, you're not involved – and they are.[34]

Private Walter Spencer, 4th Grenadier Guards

The Germans retired up onto Hill 70.

Getting towards night-time it was dark and we were lying in the open just above the village. Jerry was firing these Very lights to see who was moving about and one came down straight on my back. It burnt a hole straight through my haversack and I daren't move in case Jerry put his machine gun on me. Fortunately it burnt out – I couldn't have done much about it. We laid out there for two to three hours. When it was completely dark we made a rush for what had been a German communication trench. The machine-gun fire was very intense but there was no artillery fire. We were on a hill you see and he couldn't get his shells to drop just where he wanted them. The machine guns were mowing us down, you could see men dropping and all you could hope was that you weren't going to be the next. You could hear the bullets whizzing by, but as long as they didn't hit you you were all right. We tried to dig in a bit deeper – it was only about 2 foot 6 inches deep – and we tried to get as much cover as we could. It was a job to dig far with an entrenching tool. We made it about a yard to 4 feet deep. We remained in that position all the next day. We just had to lie there; it was an awful position – to lie for hours and hours and not be able to move. He had so many machine guns on it. They reinforced their front-line trench preparatory to an attack; they didn't actually make it while we were there – the Middlesex got it the next night.[35]

Private Walter Spencer, 4th Grenadier Guards

At this stage of the battle there was almost no chance of any kind of serious success. The Germans had moved up their reserves and the ferocious fighting for tactically significant features like Hill 70 had only local significance. Nothing here was going to affect the outcome of the battle.

As with so many Great War battles it would rage on for weeks, with the Germans counter-attacking in force to try to regain any territory they had lost. By the end of the battle it had cost the British some 61,000 casualties – the 'Big Push' had failed.

A horrific number of the dead were scattered about the battleground.

> The other problem was the disposal of the numerous dead lying all about. This could only be done under cover of darkness. To venture out in No Man's Land in daylight was seeking instant death. The evening burial parties were a feature which went on for several months before the battlefields were finally cleared up. Each battalion had its share of this very unpleasant task. My company commander was Captain J. E. Sloane, who was once a Glasgow Highlander but now with the HLI. One early frosty December evening of 1915, practically the whole of the company, including the captain himself, were on a special burial party to dispose of a large number of the 7th East Surreys who had been killed. Proceeding out of the trenches with caution in small parties, each party dealt with the dead by simply pulling them into depressions in the earth or shell holes. This was not a pleasant task and occasionally the arms disintegrated from the bodies. The bodies were covered over with a light layer of earth, this being dug in by the entrenching tools. Before the bodies were actually covered over, the main task was to retrieve the identity discs found round their necks. These were cut off, collected and in due course sent back to headquarters. All the work had to be done on all fours as to stand erect was courting disaster. In addition, the very frequent Very lights of the Germans necessitated instant stillness while these lights were in the sky. So the work was slow, laborious and difficult.[36]

Second Lieutenant George Craic, 12th Highland Light Infantry

The main French offensives had also failed: it was another debacle for the Allied forces. There was very little indeed to show for the loss of so many men. As the German defensive systems developed in complexity, it became apparent that although with a supreme and painful effort the British could break in – capture a front line, take a redoubt – they could not break *through* the system. More German trench lines, more barbed wire, more redoubts still lay ahead of them. The frustrations this engendered were apparent in the controversy that welled up after the battle over the deployment of the reserves by General Sir John French in his capacity as Commander in Chief. His position soon became untenable. Both politicians and the military abandoned him, and French was replaced by General Sir Douglas Haig on 10 December 1915. The BEF would approach the challenges of 1916 with a new leader.

5

WAY OUT EAST, 1914–18

THE VARIOUS CAMPAIGNS AGAINST TURKEY AND BULGARIA had a terrible similarity. The British Easterner faction, which in early 1915 included both the then Chancellor of the Exchequer David Lloyd George, and the First Lord of the Admiralty Winston Churchill, considered that the trenches reaching across the Western Front offered only stalemate and endless slaughter. Instead, they looked to an older maritime tradition of British warfare, which aimed to snipe away at the outskirts of the conflict, avoiding the main theatre of battle. Their strategy focused on Turkey and the Balkans, but their plans ignored reality, failing to assess correctly the available Allied forces, the logistical situation or the strength of any likely opposition. The campaigns waged against the Ottoman Empire (Turkey) in Gallipoli and Mesopotamia all too clearly reveal the problems of launching over-ambitious operations.

At the beginning of the war, Turkey had been courted intensively by Germany. This was in stark contrast to British insensitivity when Churchill unilaterally appropriated two Turkish dreadnought battleships being built in British shipyards. It was therefore doubly unfortunate that incompetence by the Admiralty and local naval commanders in the Mediterranean then allowed the German battlecruiser *Goeben* and the light cruiser *Breslau* to escape. These two ships passed through the Dardanelles Straits on 10 August 1914 and were promptly 'sold' to the supposedly neutral Turks. Turkish entry into the war thus became inevitable. It was finally triggered when on 29 October 1914, the *Goeben* led the Turkish fleet on a series of raids on Russian ports in the Black Sea.

Gallipoli

Gallipoli was an adventure of staggering stupidity. It began when the British government responded rashly to a request on 1 January 1915 from the Russians, who were under severe (but temporary) pressure from a Turkish offensive in the Caucasus. Instead of a polite refusal, the British War Committee offered the compromise solution of a naval demonstration. This seemingly innocent attempt to utilise naval power in order to assist their ally proved to be the start of a series of events that would ultimately cost the lives of tens of thousands of Allied soldiers. Churchill's eloquence had persuaded his fellow politicians that a force of obsolescent pre-dreadnoughts could blast their way through the Dardanelles Straits and force the surrender of the Turks by appearing off Constantinople. This decision represented a collective inability to focus on the real British enemies represented by the High Seas Fleet and the German Army. They looked for an easier battle, and so the Gallipoli adventure was launched.

From the outset, the campaign proved to be an anticlimax. The fleet first tried to exert steady pressure by grinding down the Turkish forts defending the Straits, but when this proved to be too slow, they launched an all-out assault on 18 March 1915. Private William Jones was one of the Royal Marines manning the secondary armament of the pre-dreadnought *Prince George* as the Allied fleet sailed into the Straits.

> I was a member of one of the 6-inch guns on the lower deck. There were eight of the crew and two by the ammunition hoist. We were in that casement eleven hours. It was about 14 feet wide and 12 feet deep. Inside it was very hot. Some of us were very scantily dressed. I was wearing a bathing costume and a pair of heavy boots in case a projectile dropped on your toe. We were forbidden to go outside

whatever – what we wanted to do we had to do in the casement, whatever it might be! When we loaded the gun it was quite a big job because the shell was about 112 pounds. You open up the breech of the gun, pulling the breech back. Up comes a No. 4. He gets a shell on top of the shell guide, gets a rammer and rams home. A No. 6 comes along with a cylinder and enters the tube, pushes it right home. A No. 2 closes the breech. 'READY!' Immediately you stand clear from the gun and it's fired by the No. 1, the gunlayer. Then open the breech again. Get the extractor on your arm, that fits around the back of the cartridge, and you fling it aside, and I can assure you it's red hot. Then the whole procedure is gone through again.[1]

Private William Jones, HMS *Prince George*

True the British had their big guns, but by this time the Turks had an integrated defence system prepared with heavy guns in the forts, layered lines of minefields across the Straits, batteries of howitzers hidden in the hills and torpedo tubes in the Narrows. And if by some chance the Allied fleet got past the Straits there was still the *Goeben* and the rest of the Turkish fleet waiting for them. The day proved to be a catastrophe when the Allies sailed into an unsuspected extra line of mines that had been laid a few days before. One French and two British pre-dreadnoughts were sunk and several other ships suffered severe damage. Overall nearly a third of the fleet had been rendered *hors de combat* in a single day. After this it became inevitable that there would have to be major military operations to clear the Turkish forts before the fleet had any chance of breaking through.

The unconsidered nature of the drift from a naval to a predominantly military campaign was reflected in the random nature of the units gathered in the Mediterranean Expeditionary Force and put under the overall command of General Sir Ian Hamilton. The 29th Division, the Royal Naval Division (RND), the Australian and New Zealand Army Corps (ANZAC), the 42nd (East Lancashire) Division, a stray Indian brigade and a couple of French divisions were in no way a homogeneous force, but rather an intriguing mixture of nationalities composed variously of regulars, colonial troops, Territorials, naval reservists and raw recruits. Most of the divisions were only half trained and lacked sufficient artillery for modern warfare. Worst of all, there was no understanding of the inherent difficulty of what they were about to attempt; indeed a golden glow suffused the expedition as they looked forward to an easy victory over the vastly underrated Turks. One early shadow was cast by the death from septicaemia on 23 April of the poet Sub-Lieutenant Rupert Brooke, who was serving with the Hood Battalion of the RND. Brooke was buried on the Island of Skyros. Among the witnesses was Private Thomas Baker.

> To me it was lovely – a lot of rocky uncultivated land with bushes growing up – ever so wild – and huge green lizards running around. I'd never seen a lizard before, but on Skyros there was no end of them. It was ever such a lovely natural harbour: a narrow entrance between two high rocky cliffs. It must have been very deep there and that held quite a lot of ships. While we were there Rupert Brooke died and I was within about 50 yards of him when he was buried. Of course we didn't know who Rupert Brooke was in those days. It was just an ordinary little service of a few of his own officers, a few of the men and a firing party provided by the Royal Marines. We were just a few feet away. He wasn't very old anyway – he never saw the Gallipoli show at all.[2]
>
> Private Thomas Baker, Chatham Battalion

There Brooke remains to this day.

Hamilton and his staff decided to try to confuse the Turkish High Command by a complicated series of landings and diversions all around the Gallipoli Peninsula. Of the two main landings, the best remembered today was the landing by the ANZAC Corps just to the north of Gaba Tepe. The first troops ashore were to make a night landing and seize the first three ridges to gain a secure bridgehead. The whole force would then burst forth to capture Mal Tepe, a hill dominating the low ground in front of the Kilid Bahr plateau – the key high ground overlooking the Straits defences. The second series of landings was to be made at dawn around the Helles Peninsula at the tip of the Gallipoli Peninsula, while the French landed at Kum Kale on the Asiatic shore.

The ANZAC Corps night landings, at 04.30 on 25 April 1915, were marked by chaos. Although the first wave of the 3rd Australian Brigade came in slightly to the north of their intended landing place, they were perhaps fortunate to come ashore at a relatively sheltered beach now forever known as Anzac Cove. The first boats pulled in almost unopposed, but the men then found themselves facing an appallingly difficult terrain of randomly fractured ridges and gullies. Behind them the second and third waves ashore faced an increasing amount of fire from Turkish guns based near Gaba Tepe and from snipers lurking in the hills overlooking the beach.

> We lined up on the *Galeka* and waited for the pinnaces and tows to come back. The old bosun of the *Galeka* came along, 'Any of you got any letters to post? Anybody got any of those dirty postcards that you bought in Cairo? If you have, you'd better put them down on the deck because if you get knocked they send them to your next-of-kin.' By this time I was feeling as brave as a ring-tailed possum and I wished I was anywhere but on the *Galeka*. The boats eventually pulled up alongside. We were all done up with rifles, shovels, ammunition and packs – how we got down those rope ladders I just don't know – what with the nervousness and the excitement of not knowing what was in front of us. I just felt washed out. As I got into the boat there were about three chaps of the 9th Battalion who had been killed and they hadn't had time to lift them out, so we had to walk gingerly over these blokes. Then I heard the voice of the little 'Middie' pulling these three boats. It was a child's voice really and I thought, 'If it's good enough for him, it's good enough for me.' Well, we packed in together. The shrapnel was falling. The machine guns were pelting and as the pinnace hit the shore we boats at the back were pulled up into anything up to 3 to 4 foot of water. Somebody said, 'Out you get!' and out we got. Lumbering with this shovel and rifle and pack and ammunition we were loaded like blessed elephants. There were dead and wounded of the 3rd Brigade all around. We scampered as hard as we could to a little bit of shelter and dumped our packs and dumped the shovels and picks. We'd had enough of those. Then somebody said, 'Well, up you go!' And away we went up the slope.[3]
>
> Private Frank Brent, 6th Battalion, AIF

They managed to get up the hill, but only to find that the 3rd Brigade had been held on the Second Ridge rather than pushing on as intended to secure the bridgehead by capturing the Third Ridge. The Turks initially only numbered a company or so, but they fought hard, aided by the broken terrain. Sniping slowed the Australians progress and as the Turkish reserve battalions began to arrive, the whole operation began to fall to pieces.

> I heard somebody say, 'This in no good to us! Come on, heads down, arse up and get stuck into it!' We went into it. We cleared them. Bayoneted them, shot them and the others ran. A little while afterwards a bloke out of the 8th Battalion said, 'Here, look at that bloody bush. It's moving!' We looked at it and it was obviously a sniper and he was done up like a Christmas tree. He'd got branches out of his head and shoulders and he was for all the world like a bush. But he didn't look like a bush when we'd finished with him! One bloke shouted, 'Share that amongst you, you bastards!' The bloke next to me was Robbie Robinson,[4] a corporal in my battalion. He was laughing at the remark and I can see him now grinning all over his face – the next thing his head fell on my shoulder and a sniper had got him through the jugular vein. I really think that was my baptism of fire, because Robbie's blood spent all over my tunic.[5]
>
> Private Frank Brent, 6th Battalion, AIF

While the Australians consolidated well short of their original objectives, the Turks seized the high ground. By the end of the day the game was up; the Turks everywhere looked down on Anzac positions penned back into a bridgehead measuring just 1,000 yards deep and only 2,500 yards long. There was little chance of the ANZAC Corps breaking out; indeed the main question was whether the Turks could break in to throw them into the sea.

On the night of 28 April, Hamilton moved in the Marine Brigade of the RND to allow the exhausted Anzacs a chance to rest. The Marines were mostly recent recruits and many were intimidated by their surroundings as they took up positions on Second Ridge. They had a trickle of casualties, but on the afternoon of 29 April the Turks launched an attack.

> The Turks began to attack in the afternoon in huge numbers en masse. They came out of this scrub like rabbits towards you and – oh my word – we had a tough time repelling that. I'd got two men

loading for me and I kept firing these rifles. They got very hot until I couldn't fire them and I had to wait until the first one cooled off. But by then we'd quelled the attack, otherwise it could have been very, very sticky because when you can't hold your rifle you're snookered and they got ever so hot. I reckon if you missed one you'd probably have the next man. Mind you, you didn't get too much time to aim; you'd got to get on with the job. It was all over in minutes. They were heaped up wounded and dead. They didn't get within 50 yards finally.[6]

Private Thomas Baker, Chatham Battalion

The Turkish attacks came mainly at night to avoid being caught by naval gunfire. Machine gunner Private Joseph Clements was in the front line.

There was flags flying and bugles blowing and they were coming over in droves. I'd got our machine gun fixed up and I sat there and I was shooting, swinging it backwards and forwards, not taking aim but you couldn't miss. No more than 200 yards, there was so many, they weren't spread out because there wasn't the room for them to spread out. I was firing, the No. 2 he was seeing the belt ran and getting a belt out of the box ready. You couldn't see the effects – you were just firing into a kind of a big object. It didn't look like individual people. It finished all of a sudden. They just turned and there wasn't anybody there any more.[7]

Private Joseph Clements, Deal Battalion

The Turkish attacks blew themselves out. The ANZAC Corps and their British reinforcements managed to create a coherent line based on a series of interlocking posts along Second Ridge, each being able to cover the others with a hail of deadly fire. They had not quite given up hope of breaking out, so launched an attack on the night of 2 May. Three Anzac battalions assaulted the head of Monash Valley and when they failed, the British Marines were ordered forward.

Our officer, Captain Richards, ordered us to scale this steep rise and we lay there right at the end of the toe. He said, 'Open fire at 200!' And he stood up there in full view of the enemy, kept shouting, 'Come on men!' Suddenly I saw this huge triangular cut below his right shoulder blade, he was facing the Turks and his back was to

93

us. His shirt opened up. He must have been hit by a dum-dum. He came back and he ordered me to move to the left. He lay down and he was still shouting, 'Open fire at 200!' We lay along there, shoulder to shoulder. We fired away at all the Turks who kept advancing. They were then about 150 yards away and they came up in almost mass formation so we had very easy targets. An Australian came and lay next to me. On his right another man scaled this steep slope and he turned out to be Major Armstrong of the Portsmouth Royal Marines. Captain Richards was next to him and all the way to the right were men shoulder to shoulder lying on the ground. No cover at all, no trenches, just lying on the ridge.[8]

Private Thomas Baker, Chatham Battalion

The Turks began to counter-attack and then the Marines found them-selves under fire from behind.

Suddenly a machine gun crackled away at right-angles to us; he was slightly behind our position and on the right. He had a good view because he was higher up and he could see exactly what he was doing. It was like mowing grass I should think for him. We were firing ahead and it was even behind us. This machine gun went along and killed every man on the ridge except the Australian and me. We were the only two left. The Australian said to me, 'The bastards can't kill me, they've had lots of tries – they can't kill me!' I looked again. The machine gun started barking again behind us. Then it came along – it was knocking the sand up and that covered every man again. Every man, it came right along. When I saw those bullets coming along I knew that it would be the end of me if they came along far enough. They say your past comes up but I can say truthfully that I hadn't got very much past at 19 and all I thought of was, 'Am I going to live?' That's all I thought, that's what struck me, 'Am I going to be lucky?' Because I couldn't see how I could be with all these bullets coming along – and I waited for it – it was inevitable. I felt the bullets thud into the Aussie and he never spoke again. I felt as though I'd been hit by a donkey and I had a bullet through the right foot.[9]

Private Thomas Baker, Chatham Battalion

The machine gun stopped its deadly chatter, but the damage was done. Minutes later the Turks overran the Marines' position along the ridge.

I lay there and I didn't know quite what to do. The Turks came along and prodded various men with their bayonets. Fortunately they didn't poke me, otherwise I shouldn't be here now! I could hear them jabbering away and then they moved away again. 'Well,' I thought, 'I must do something!' So I gave myself a push off and went bumpity-bumpity right down to the bottom of the ravine over dead men, rifles, bush, all kinds of things.[10]

Private Thomas Baker, Chatham Battalion

Baker was lucky enough to be rescued and safely evacuated. His comrades were left rotting for the rest of the campaign on what quickly became known as Dead Man's Ridge. By the time Baker left Anzac Cove it was clear that the landing there had failed. Although the ANZAC Corps could hang on to their positions, they had no chance of breaking out to their real objectives.

HAMILTON'S PLAN FOR THE HELLES LANDINGS on 25 April 1915 was ludicrously complex. The 29th Division were to make two main landings at the well-defended V and W Beaches at the toe of the Peninsula, with subsidiary flank landings at X, Y and S Beaches. It was intended that they were to take the hill of Achi Baba by nightfall and push on to capture the real objective of Kilid Bahr on 26 April. The Turks were relying on just one battalion to hold back the British until their reserves could arrive.

The men of 29th Division who landed on the morning of 25 April are not well represented in the IWM oral history recordings. Not only was there a terrible slaughter at the time, but the fighting then continued unabated for six months before Gallipoli was evacuated. Then they were all dispatched to the Western Front, where the Germans inflicted further grievous slaughter for two more years of hard fighting. Few survived to tell their story. As the 1st Lancashire Fusiliers rowed into W Beach at 06.00 on 25 April, the Turks were ready. Despite being outnumbered, they had every inch of the beach in their sights. Private Sydney Hall recounts what happened next.

There was four boats drawn by a pinnace – about thirty in a boat. The pinnace drew us as far as they could into the land then they let go and the sailors rowed us in. All you could see was the cliffs in front of us. We got fired on because round the top of the cliff was a trench and all they had to do was lean over and shoot us all down. I had no nerves, I didn't know what I was going into. All of a sudden 'Ping, ping, ping!' And fellows all getting knocked out. As we got nearer me and a few more we jumped out of the boat. The water was over my nut, over my head it was! I carried on till I got to the beach and over I went a few times because I think there was trip wires in there. I got to the beach more to the right and there was this barbed wire about 4 foot wide – it hadn't been touched. I crawled under the wire, the old pack getting hooked up. Then up the cliffs and into the trench. I never saw the Turks. The trench was empty; they'd gone back. I didn't see any officers. I looked after myself and kept going forward as best I could. The next day we were all eating our rations but when I came to mine, my bully beef had a bullet in it![11]

Private Sidney Hall, 1st Lancashire Fusiliers

The bulk of the Lancashire Fusiliers had been held back by the barbed wire on the beach. They came under heavy fire and casualties were mounting rapidly before they broke through. By the time Ordinary Seaman Stephen Moyle arrived there was still evidence of the terrible battle.

The Lancashire Fusiliers were still lying there. We had some very tough lads amongst the Naval Reserves and one spotted one of these bodies. He went forward, three or four paces and undid the pack straps of this Fusilier lying on his face. Us youngsters watched, we didn't know what he was up to. When he got the pack straps undone he was quite a time looking at something in his hand. We pressed forward a bit to see what it was, and of all the things in this world in his hand he had a baby's shoe which had been put on the top of the pack. It looked as though the Missus had said, 'Here take this for luck!' That tough stoker just put it back on top of the pack and fastened up the straps again.[12]

Ordinary Seaman Stephen Moyle, Drake Battalion

96

Meanwhile, at V Beach the troops came ashore in strings of rowing boats and concealed deep within the 'Trojan Horse' of the adapted merchantman *River Clyde* which was run ashore off the beach. Luckily for Second Lieutenant Reginald Gillett, he was not required to go ashore with the first waves.

> As dawn approached we were ordered to brace ourselves firmly to take the shock of impact with the shore. As a matter of fact the impact was so slight that we hardly felt it. For a short space there was dead silence. A strong current made the positioning of the barges connecting with the shore a difficult and dangerous job. The Turks held their fire till the foremost of the troops reached the shore. Then hell itself was let loose. We in the holds could see nothing, but the row of bullets hitting the *River Clyde* was deafening. More troops were ordered ashore. I then led my troops out of the *River Clyde* onto the gangway on the starboard side. The sight that met our eyes was indescribable. The barges, now linked together and more or less reaching the shore, were piled high with mutilated bodies and between the last barge and the sand was a pier formed by piles of dead men. It was impossible to reach land without treading on the dead.[13]
>
> Second Lieutenant Reginald Gillett, 2nd Hampshire Regiment

The shattering fire from the Turks on V Beach was so deadly that the troops could only get ashore when night fell, and the Turkish defences above the beach were only overrun on the afternoon of 26 April.

Meanwhile, the battalions that had landed at Y Beach were soon cut off by the Turks and early on 26 April they were forced to withdraw, having achieved nothing. The troops on X Beach linked relatively successfully with the W Beach force, but those on S Beach landing were totally isolated until being subsumed into the overall advance on 28 April, now known as the First Battle of Krithia. This too, though, was a fumbling affair, finally limping to a halt well short of the Turkish positions. By this time the Kum Kale landing had been abandoned and the French were given the task of holding the right-hand side of the Helles lines, which left them vulnerable to Turkish artillery fire from just across the Straits.

On 1 May it was the Turks' turn to attack, buoyed up with fresh reinforcements determined to make their presence felt. Constrained by the presence of the massed guns of the Allied fleet they were forced to attack at night. They flung themselves forward time and again until the attacks collapsed in a welter of blood. The result was stalemate.

The British and French forces were exhausted after their ordeal, but Hamilton decided that they must push on before it was too late. Every day meant more Turkish battalions and trenches between the Allies and their goals. He therefore ordered a renewed attack – the Second Battle of Krithia – which began on 6 May. This proved a chaotic advance to contact and what happened to the Hood Battalion was typical as they probed forward. To them the Turks were completely invisible, but their bullets seemed to be everywhere.

> There were no trenches; it was open fighting. We had to rush along the front of the house and go through this gap. Only four people got through, we had to climb over the dead and the wounded. We got about 10 yards in front, and down we went. The bullets were hitting the sand, spraying us; you were spitting it out of your mouth.[14]
>
> Ordinary Seaman Joe Murray, Hood Battalion

Feeling terribly isolated and not knowing what to do, they decided to keep on trying to push forward.

> I remember, Yates was just a little ahead of Don [Townshend] and me. We crawled up more or less line abreast but the bullets were hitting the sand, spraying us, hitting our packs. So we decided, 'How about another dash?' Off we went. Near enough 15 yards, one drops, everybody drops. We decided to go a little bit further. We'd got to keep bearing to our right slightly, because we seemed to be dodging the line of fire. But it was still winging overhead and flying about, hitting the ground. I think it must have been a machine gun. But there's a tendency for a man, if he's being fired on by two or three men at the same time, to think it's a machine gun. You couldn't see them and there was a rattling going on, not only in our section but all over the place. We decided to go a little bit further and all four got up together. Yates was in front and all of a sudden he bent down. He'd been shot in the stomach, maybe the testicles, but he was dancing

around like a cat on hot bricks, then he fell down on the ground. But as soon as we got somewhere near him he got up and rushed like hell at the Turks and 'Bang!' Down altogether – out for the count. Young Horton, he was the first to get to Yates and he got a hold of him and sort of pushed him to see what was wrong when a bullet struck him dead centre of the brow, went right through his head and took a bit out of my knuckle. Poor old Horton. He kept crying for his mother. I can see him now. Hear him at this very moment. He said he was 18, but I don't think he was 16, never mind 18.[15]

Ordinary Seaman Joe Murray, Hood Battalion

The attacks on 6 and 7 May were an utter failure. Yet as every day the Turks grew stronger, Hamilton felt he had no choice but to press forward. In desperation he brought in two brigades from Anzac to bolster his forces. They met the same fate.

You could see your mates going down right and left. You were face to face with the stark realisation that this was the end of it. That was the thought that was with you the whole time. Despite the fact that you couldn't see a Turk, he was pelting us with everything he'd got from all corners. The marvel to me was how the dickens he was able to do it after the barrage that had fallen on him. I copped my packet and, as I lay down, I said, 'Thank Christ for that!'[16]

Private Frank Brent, 6th Battalion, AIF

Soon the Turkish lines snaked right across the entire Helles Peninsula, forming a fully fledged trench system with redoubts, communication lines and numerous support lines. The British aims shrank from breaking through the Straits and threatening Constantinople to merely gaining control of Achi Baba, the hill from which the Turks could peer down on the entire Allied sector at Helles. Soon even that relatively modest ambition would become an unachievable dream.

With the arrival of summer, the men of Gallipoli suffered terrible conditions of service: sweltering in the blistering heat, enduring a repetitive and unsuitable diet, and lacking enough water. They were surrounded by flies that buzzed randomly between their food, the rotting corpses and the stinking latrines.

There was a narrow trench dug – out in the open. If you'd looked in there you'd have been sickened. You'd think they'd parted with their stomachs or their insides. It was awful. You had to cover it and dig another. It hadn't to be so high or else you could fall down. There were no supports or anything; it was just an open trench, but it was fairly deep.[17]

Private Harold Pilling, 1/6th Lancashire Fusiliers

Disease felled entire units, hollowing them out from within.

With dysentery you keep on trying to discharge something but there's nothing to discharge, it's only slime, just slime, no solids at all.
Then of course we didn't have any toilet paper and you had to wipe yourself with your hand, there's nothing else. Then you'd wipe your hand – originally on the grass, but grass was getting a bit short – rub your hands on the sand and your trousers.[18]

Ordinary Seaman Joe Murray, Hood Battalion

It was deeply degrading and soon even the strongest found themselves helpless.

My old pal, a couple of weeks ago he was as smart and upright as a guardsman. After about ten days to see him crawling about, his trousers round his feet, his backside hanging out, all soiled, his shirt – everything was soiled. He couldn't walk. My pal got a hold of him by one arm; I got a hold of him by the other. Neither he nor I were very good but we weren't like that. It's degrading, dragging him to the latrine, when you remember how you saw him just a little while ago. We lower him down next to the latrine. We're trying to keep the flies off him. We were trying to turn him round to put his backside in towards the trench. I don't know what happened but he simply rolled in to this foot-wide trench, half sideways, head first into this slime. We couldn't pull him out, we didn't have any strength and he couldn't help himself at all. We did eventually get him out but he was dead; he'd drowned in his own excrement.[19]

Ordinary Seaman Joe Murray, Hood Battalion

Wherever they were there was the risk of a Turkish shell landing at any time. Indeed most places were within range of small-arms fire and in the front line there was a vicious battle between the opposing snipers.

> We had an iron plate with an aperture big enough to get a rifle
> through. I was sniping one day – about 300 yards away the Turkish
> trench was. I saw a turban fly off with one shot I made. They must
> have brought down a sniper of their own. I had a jam on my rifle,
> withdrew the rifle and was trying to get the cartridge out, when the
> sniper put a bullet through that aperture – it was only about 4 inches
> square. So I said, 'Right-oh boy, you're a better shot than I am!'[20]
>
> Ordinary Seaman Stephen Moyle, Drake Battalion

A tragic incident underlined the accuracy of Turkish snipers for Private
George Peake.

> This ex-guardsman he jumped and said, 'I'll get that blighter!' He'd
> just put his rifle through the loophole and it was too late, he was
> dead – a bullet hit him in the head and his brains came all over us as
> we sat down in the trench. Mitchell. He had a wife and two children
> – he was showing us a photo of them. He said, 'Oooh, the swine – I'll
> get him!' He moved the body to one side, jumped up and put his rifle
> through the loophole and he was dead! Both their brains came over
> us.[21] You brushed them off, you're so used to it. They say you can get
> used to anything.[22]
>
> Private George Peake, 1/8th Lancashire Fusiliers

The casualty rate rocketed whenever the Allies launched one of their
doomed efforts to break through the Turkish lines. Their chances of
success were always going to be minimal, given that the Turks had equal
numbers, excellent commanders and all the tactical advantages in their
favour. An account from the Third Battle of Krithia of 4 June 1915 will
have to stand for all these futile assaults. The RND went over the top
on the right of the British line. That morning found Joe Murray and
his friends sweltering in the packed front line, ready to go over the top.

> We were standing there; couldn't sit down, couldn't lie down, just
> standing there. The fellow next to me was messing about with
> his ammunition, fiddling about, cleaning his rifle, looking in the
> magazine. Another fellow was sort of staring. The blinking maggots
> from the dead bodies in the firing line were crawling round right

under our noses. Every now and again if a bullet hit the parapet there was a 'Psssst!' Wind – gas – it smelt like hell. The sun was boiling hot. The maggots, the flies – the stench was horrible. Honestly and truly the next half an hour was like an age. Between you and I, I said my prayers, 'Please God, not only for myself but for my parents – may I survive?' Lieutenant Commander Parsons, standing on the ladder, called out, 'Five minutes to go, men! Four minutes to go!' 'One minute to go, men! Now, men!' He blew a whistle and off we go.[23]

Ordinary Seaman Joe Murray, Hood Battalion

A storm of lead cut through them.

There were men falling back into the trench or on the parapet. There was dead all over the place. My platoon commander got through. I followed him up there. Parsons[24] had already been killed. We got into dead ground. The petty officer said, 'Well, come on, lad! C'mon!' We moved again and then lay down to get a breather. He was an old reservist, his bald head glittering in the sun – he'd lost his helmet. He was up on the trench with his rifle and bayonet, 'C'mon! C'mon!' Around his head he'd got a white handkerchief and blood pouring down his face just like the pictures in the *London Illustrated*. He was bleeding dreadfully. I wanted to keep up with him but he was now 20 yards ahead of me. I got to the trench and in I go – it was 10 feet deep! There was one or two dead, nobody alive.[25]

Ordinary Seaman Joe Murray, Hood Battalion

The RND did well, but the French on their right had been given an impossible task against strong Turkish redoubts, and as their advance crumpled, they left the RND right flank exposed.

All of a sudden the right flank started retiring; the Anson Battalion. We were forced to retire, hopped back, jumped over the second trench; then we scampered back to his first trench. I thought, 'Well, now if we can stop here we can hold them here!' I kept on turning round and firing, but there wasn't much opposition from the front. I couldn't understand why we were retiring – we weren't being pressed at all. We were almost near his first trench. I was out of puff, so tired and I thought, 'One more trot and I shall be in the trench.' But when I got there it was full of Turks! So instead of stopping over the trench

102

I leapt over the top and I was helped over by a bayonet stuck right in the posterior – right in the nick! I went falling right in front of the trench into a shell hole, lying flat in there.[26]

Ordinary Seaman Joe Murray, Hood Battalion

Living up to his nickname of 'Lucky Durham' he managed to lie still until nightfall when he made it safe and sound back to the old front line.

This would be the pattern for the rest of the summer at Helles. Time and time again the Allies attacked. The battlefield became covered with rotting bloated corpses and the result was a nauseating miasma that could be smelt for miles. Private Thomas Baker noticed 'a certain something' on his return to the Peninsula after recovering from his wound.

There was a terrible smell in the air and I said to somebody, 'What's that awful smell?' He said, 'That's dead men – in front of our trench.' If you've ever smelt a dead mouse it was like that, but hundreds and hundreds of times worse. Three lines of bodies as far as you could see to the left, as far as you could see to the right. The bodies were black – a terrible sight. The stench was indescribable and you live with that stench. The smell of death – you never get it out of your system. I've still got it – I can still remember exactly how it was.[27]

Private Thomas Baker, 1st Battalion, Royal Marines

Baker went to his grave still haunted by the memory of that disgusting odour.

ALL THE LATER ATTACKS AT HELLES were doomed to fail. Indeed, Hamilton had already decided to deploy five extra divisions grudgingly allotted to him by Kitchener in an attempt in August to break out from the northern flank of Anzac, seize the high ground of the Sari Bair Ridge and simultaneously make a new landing at Suvla Bay. These were complex plans. They depended on everything going right in a series of widely dispersed independent actions which, despite terribly fractured ground conditions, were meant to be closely synchronised. The troops were given tasks that failed to take account of either their experience or their physical condition, and their leaders were often woefully inadequate. And, despite all logic, any Turkish opposition was discounted or ignored.

On 6 August, the Australian 1st Division launched a heroic diversionary attack to set all eyes on the Lone Pine Plateau at the southern end of Anzac. Once darkness fell, the columns marched stealthily along the coast from Anzac before moving up the valleys and spurs leading to the high ground. In the dark, all was confusion and the delays soon multiplied. The New Zealand Brigade advanced up Rhododendron Ridge towards the Chunuk Bair, a key hill behind the Turkish lines that overlooked 'old' Anzac. They then intended to charge down and take the Turkish lines from the rear. Unfortunately everything went wrong: units got lost, commanders failed to press forward and the Turks had time to get just enough troops onto Chunuk Bair to thwart the attack. It was this breakdown in the plan that left the Australian Light Horse to charge to their deaths at the Nek. It is not often realised that a British unit, the 1/8th Cheshires, were meant to follow up as a support unit to consolidate any gains. But as they moved up towards the Nek behind the Light Horse they came under heavy collateral fire. Caught up in the bitter fighting, Sergeant William Davies watched as his popular Company Sergeant Major 'Ginger' Harp was an early fatality.

> Shells, high explosive, shrapnel – they had us – absolutely hopeless –
> we felt it was futile. 'Ginger' Harp[28] was killed. The shell dropped right
> amongst them: Harp and about eight others were killed. They were
> at the front of my company; I was at the tail end. I told them to keep
> close to the side. We carried on until we came to what we knew later
> as the secret sap. It took us into the next gully without taking us over
> the top. We moved into this next gully which was quite a deep one,
> mainly sandy soil you slipped about in. We stayed on the left-hand
> side. The Turks were on top of the hill behind us, Hill 971, so if we
> were on the other side we'd have been seen off. We went down there
> towards what was known as the 'Chessboard'. The Turkish trench was
> all covered in with big logs of wood. We were lined up that afternoon
> and we'd been given two bombs each. We were to attack it. We were
> all lined up, just ready for the off. We'd said our goodbyes. We knew
> it had to be done. There were plenty of us, perhaps about 800 ready

to go over and over again. Our CO, Colonel Drummond Willoughby, he came galloping down over the hill and he said, 'You're not going!' We'd said our goodbyes! We'd have got through probably, but we'd have lost a lot of people. He saved his battalion, he saved us. We turned right round and went back into the gully.[29]

Sergeant William Davies, 8th Cheshire Regiment

A second Australian assaulting column was moving along the coast, while British battalions were to secure their left flank. Second Lieutenant Joseph Napier had been commissioned into the 4th South Wales Borderers.

It was to be a quiet affair as far as possible: no firing of rifles – in fact no ammunition in the rifles – no shouting. We had patches on our backs, coloured ones we tied to our jackets, so that our supporting ships could see where we had got to. We lined up in a nullah called Aghyl Dere. I don't think the Turks were really expecting anybody. When we moved out to assault Damakjelik Bair, which was supposed to be held by the Turks, I don't think anybody had any idea as to what we would come up against. One knew nothing and saw nothing you might say. As far as I was concerned there was no difficulty in getting up; it was a straight run in the dark with my troops. It wasn't particularly dark, but you couldn't see much because the country was so encrusted with nullahs, hills, steep ravines and so on. I was in the left platoon of the whole of the left covering force. We went up this slight rise and there were some trenches at the top. Very indifferent ones, the Turks were not there in any great force. I saw a few Turks but they gave, as far as I was concerned, no trouble. I was standing there in the dark, waiting to see what was going to happen.[30]

Second Lieutenant Joseph Napier, 4th South Wales Borderers

Everything seemed to be going well.

Suddenly a bomb went off, not far from me, which lit up the whole scene around me. I was looking back towards our line and I saw one of my fellow platoon commanders, 'Taffy' Jenkins,[31] charging straight at me with a rifle and bayonet. I remember saying, 'Hello Taffy, what are you doing?' I happened to make this casual remark because his platoon should have been some way off. Some days later Taffy rather

105

hesitantly said, 'You know, Joe, that evening I was just going to bayonet you. If that bomb hadn't lit the atmosphere and you hadn't said, "Hello Taffy", I think you'd have been a dead man, much to my regret!'[32]

Second Lieutenant Joseph Napier, 4th South Wales Borderers

In the later phases of the fighting, on 13 August, when all real hope of success had long gone, Napier suffered a particularly personal loss.

We'd just pushed the Turks out of a line of trenches which were not very deep and I should think at about 6 o'clock that morning some soldier came down the line to my platoon and said, 'Your father's been hit – better come and see him!' So I went down through the trenches and when I arrived I found he was out at the back of the trench which sloped down away from the enemy, being bandaged up. He had his jacket over his head, so they could get at the wound, while the sergeant major, I think it was, prepared a field dressing. There was a certain amount of blood about and I watched a few moments in some interest, not thinking it was serious probably. I finally said, 'How are you feeling?' I got no reply so I took his jacket back over his head and I saw at once that he was completely dead.[33] No question of it. People have asked me what one felt on an occasion like that and it's very difficult to say. I don't think I had any immediate reactions of great sorrow because one had been in the midst of all this sort of thing. One had seen so many dead bodies lying around and being young one had got hardened – when I saw him dead I just accepted it as another of the facts of war. I didn't stay very long. As I walked away I just had a feeling of pride that he'd done his job. I went back to my own trench and as I've told several people my own batman was killed next day and to be quite honest I felt really upset because he knew where all my things were and I didn't.[34]

Second Lieutenant Joseph Napier, 4th South Wales Borderers

In the face of determined Turkish counter-attacks, the breakout from Anzac failed.

The landings at Suvla were to be carried out on the night of 6 August by 11th Division, who would be the first units of Kitchener's New Armies to go into action. They were to be followed up by the rest of the newly formed IX Corps under the command of Lieutenant General Sir Frederick Stopford. The purpose of the operations was to secure a secure base from which to launch the next phase of the offensive should the Sari Bair Range be taken by the Anzac breakout. Speed was essential if the high ground that surrounded the Suvla Plain was to be seized, but Stopford was too old, too cautious and too timid to drive his troops on. They got ashore successfully, but the well-disciplined Turkish defence proved far too much for the inexperienced British troops. None of the senior officers exerted any grip on events, so the British milled about without any real sense of purpose, all the while taking casualties from the fire of the invisible Turks and suffering agonies of thirst as their water supplies failed. The fighting soon degenerated as new units were landed and the troops flung into battle with no order or purpose. Corporal Ernest Haire and the 1/4th Cheshires found themselves advancing across the dry bed of the Suvla Lake on 9 August without a clue as to what they were meant to be doing.

> We set off in artillery formation in echelon, but eventually we had to go in extended order, one long line across Salt Lake, an arid terrible place. We'd gone about 400 yards when we heard a yell, 'So and so's been hit!' 'Is he all right?' 'Yes they've got him, sent him down.' He was a tram conductor, 'Next stop, Tranmere Rovers!' It was sandy, very rough sand, not easy to march on, horrible, about 3 or 4 inches deep. We were very tired because we hadn't had much sleep in the last forty-eight hours. We had a very heavy pack, it was dreadfully heavy with the ammunition, too heavy altogether. It was 102 degrees in the shade, the beating sun – it was terrible.[35]
>
> Corporal Ernest Haire, 1/4th Cheshire Regiment

Early next day they were sent in to attack Scimitar Hill.

> My company commander said, 'All right boys, we'd better go.' It was heavy going and with the rifle and bayonet fixed you were sort of half plunging and stumbling along. We couldn't run, we were too handicapped, the ground wasn't good and we were very, very tired. Only walking, just walking, trying to get further on. We had no cover – we just had to face the enemy. We could see the flashes of the rifles and the machine guns. They opened several machine guns on us and

that did the damage. We lay down. We were too physically tired to go any further. We finally slid back – we went back where we started from.[36]

Corporal Ernest Haire, 1/4th Cheshire Regiment

There was to be little respite for the exhausted Cheshires. Just three hours later they were ordered forward again. Nothing had changed.

We thought it was ridiculous to try again. One fellow said, 'I'm too bloody tired to go.' We had to try to struggle. It was a fruitless thing. We were obeying orders – we had to. I was no more frightened than any others, but we were all afraid. You must be when you're facing machine guns. We did try and make the attack not because we wanted to, but because it was our job as soldiers. We were met by withering machine-gun fire. I was hit and fell. They had to retire again and I was there between the lines in the blazing sun. I was hit at midday. I put my field dressing on, I knew it hadn't hit the artery or otherwise I would have died – blood would have been pumping out – and it missed the bone. I cut the khaki drill off and my knee was exposed and it went black with the sun. The burning was more painful than the wound. What I was afraid of was that the Turks had a habit of bayoneting the wounded and I was scared stiff. Then one of my old Sunday School friends spotted me. He'd been searching the place. I was very weak, I'd been out eight hours. He said, 'I'll stand you up.' Then I fainted and he carried me 300 yards – and I was 10 to 11 stone – until he found a stretcher. He put me on it and said, 'Bye-bye lad. I'll see you again some time!' He was killed at the first Battle of Gaza.[37]

Corporal Ernest Haire, 1/4th Cheshire Regiment

Whole divisions, tens of thousands of partially trained soldiers, were thrown into battle and, without the battle-hardened skills needed to overcome the determined Turkish opposition, in just a few hours were cut to ribbons.

On 12 August, there was a fruitless attempt to clear Turkish snipers from the open spaces of the Suvla Plain. Among them was the 1/5th Norfolks, who were reputed to have mysteriously vanished without trace during this operation. Lance Corporal Tom Williamson saw what really happened.

The enemy line wasn't really known, they just pointed forward. My duty was to just keep them in order – my section and my platoon officer. Advancing in sectional rushes with the others, getting towards the enemy as fast as we could. We were annihilated, there's no doubt. We lost our leaders early on – they were hallmarked by the snipers, Gallipoli became a hell, fire was let loose from all angles. We arrived at a place where we could see the Turks. My officer went over this ridge, he fell down wounded. We had been told not to look after anybody, but I rushed to his side. I took out my field dressing and his: put one on the front, one on the back. He had a wound an inch and a half wide. He said, 'Never mind Tom!' He called me by my Christian name. 'You take the platoon over, what remains; never mind about me!' I went on till we found ourselves through the Turkish lines, only just through, but behind the Turkish lines. I fired at Turks, I actually saw some drop, I did really. But the scrub was on fire, only small fires but you couldn't lie down in the heat. So we stood up. Then I was shot through the right arm. I was firing and it came into the muscle just below the shoulder. I knew I had to get back. I had a section of men but they all lay still, killed. They had surrounded us, we were intermixed with the Turks, they were scattered around us. My only hope was to get back. I knew I was finished. It was then that I noticed about forty men, under a sergeant, sheltering in a barn. I can picture him now rallying his men. The scrub was on fire, the snipers, more or less surrounded by the Turks, a hopeless position for them to be in, really. They were undoubtedly killed or wounded where they were.[38]

Lance Corporal Tom Williamson, 1/5th Norfolk Regiment

By this time it should have been obvious to anyone that the Suvla operations had failed. Yet still the futile attacks went on: ordered by generals too timid to accept their own failure, but willing to sacrifice the lives of others.

There was one last huge attack on 21 August. This was the biggest battle ever fought at Gallipoli. Thousands died and were maimed, but it was an indictment of the generals who ordered the attack that it never, even for a moment, offered the slightest chance of success. Their horizons had shrunk from the high ridges that surrounded Suvla Bay to the foothills of Scimitar Hill and W Hills. During this tragic battle yet another new division, this time the 2nd Mounted Division, were sent forward. They had left their horses behind in Egypt and so the yeomen trudged across the Salt Lake under heavy fire.

> It was salt, pretty firm. God it was slaughter. Terrible! I was stretcher bearing and I was covered in other men's blood. I always remember one officer – he was a gentleman – he was wounded in his thigh. He said, 'Don't worry, I'm all right, there's others worse than me!'[39]
>
> Trooper Arthur Bull, 1/1st Royal Gloucester Hussars

The attack failed and the fighting finally descended into a squabble over the possession of Hill 60, a small promontory which, despite being only 60 metres high, by a curious configuration of the ground offered a view over the tenuous junction between Anzac and Suvla from one side and a tempting vista behind the Turkish lines on the other. The fighting was vicious in the extreme and in the end both sides secured enough of the hill to deny their enemy, but not enough to gain any real advantage for themselves. Hill 60 would remain contested territory for the rest of the campaign.

By a splendid coincidence, two of the most interesting Gallipoli veterans I interviewed, Malcolm Hancock and Eric Wolton, were both part of the British garrison occupying Hill 60 in September 1915, and their interviews give us an interlocking view of what conditions were like.

> A lot of the parapets had been built up with dead bodies which were partially buried under earth – it was a pretty gruesome business. Just as we entered the trench going up into the system there was a body and a hand was sticking out. It was all dried – probably been there a fortnight, three weeks. And a New Zealander said, 'Well, that chap – I've known him for some time. He must have been a dry old stick!' Well, the first time we saw that, it wasn't awfully funny. But you'd hardly credit this: we got so callous that every time that men went by they always used to shake hands with it. It sounds awful but one couldn't give way too much to one's feelings.[40]
>
> Lieutenant Malcolm Hancock, 1/4th Northamptonshire Regiment

British and Turks both tried to patrol in No Man's Land but there was little or no room for manoeuvre in that cramped battlefield. The slightest noise would alert their enemies and provoke a sudden torrent of small-arms fire.

> I remember a Turkish patrol coming and we were very proud because we shot two or three of them. We were very proud of seeing these bodies lying in front. Until – the smell was *so* awful, *too* awful – we wished we'd taken them in straight away. We used to hope that by shooting into these bodies the smell would go, but they kept swelling and swelling, getting worse and worse, making awful smells. It was a very strange thing – however many bullets you pumped into them it didn't seem to make any difference. I thought the gases would have escaped and gone but it didn't appear to, not for a long time.[41]
>
> Lieutenant Eric Wolton, 1/5th Suffolk Regiment

Liberal use was made of hand grenades; especially on the disputed crown of Hill 60 where opposing trenches were within easy bombing range. Hancock was appointed as a company bombing officer and soon became regarded as a bit of an expert. It is fair to say that he threw himself into the task with a great enthusiasm.

> It was my job to use what rather small supply of bombs we had to the best effect – in other words to be as big a nuisance to the Turks as we could. I'd have two chaps with me and they'd have these bombs lined up behind me – I did the throwing always. They were pretty crude sorts of bombs. One was what we called a jam tin into which was put a charge of explosives. It was filled with all kinds of odds and ends: bits of stone, flint, old expended cartridges, bits of iron, nails – anything! Then a fuse was inserted into a detonator. The neck of the detonator was crimped together to hold the fuse into the detonator. It was put in through the top of the lid down into the explosive and then you've probably got 4 or 5 inches of fuse exposed. The thing was that to light the fuse you had to be darn careful not to show a light at night and often I would use the end of my cigarette. Then as soon as you heard it begin to fizz you kept it for two or three seconds: not too long but not too soon either – you tried to get it to explode on landing. It wouldn't be in the air very long and you had to try to get your timing right. You hoped it dropped into the Turkish trench. There were two other kinds I remember. One was what we called the cricket ball. It was about the size of a cricket ball,

a cast-iron round-shaped thing with a hole in the top. It had been previously filled with an explosive. You primed it with a detonator and a fuse down through the hole and threw it, bowling overarm, lobbing it over into the Turkish trench. When it exploded the cast iron broke into little bits and it was the fragments which did the damage. The other was called the hairbrush. It was a flat piece of wood about 6 inches square with a handle at the end. On to that slab of wood was tied a piece of dynamite. You primed it and it was a good thing to throw because you'd got a handle. The explosion was very local but very intense. Another source of bombs was the Turkish jam-tin bombs. They were the same principle as ours but extremely badly done. I should think 30 per cent of them failed to go off. We heard them fall and if they didn't go off we marked that down, 'There's a dud there!' Then at night I used to go out crawling about in No Man's Land collecting these damned things. We were damned short of these things. All I had to do was to take the fuse out which hadn't burnt through; take that out, re-fuse it with a detonator on the end and chuck it back – and they always went off – a highly satisfactory sound.[42]

Lieutenant Malcolm Hancock, 1/4th Northamptonshire Regiment

His enthusiasm was noticed, with the result that Hancock was appointed brigade bombing officer. Here he had access to a 'Heath Robinson' contraption to project the grenades right across the wider sections of No Man's Land.

It was a wooden contraption meant to work on the principle of a catapult. There was a hollow wooden cylinder on a framework which on either side had a strong elastic tape. You primed and cocked the thing by winding a handle. You pulled back the cylinder down until there was a pretty good tension on the rubber and then fixed a catch. You then got the bomb, lit the end of it, dropped it in the cylinder and then released the catch and up she went. Well, it was literally cockshy because there was no question of seeing where it went. You just guessed at what angle you set the thing, high or low and you had to work the tension of the rubber so it didn't go too far. It was a very hit-or-miss affair. It was rather quite fun really.[43]

Lieutenant Malcolm Hancock, 1/4th Northamptonshire Regiment

Lieutenant Eric Wolton watched these catapult activities with consider-able bemusement and no little trepidation.

> The operators were brigade people and as soon as we heard they were coming everybody would say, 'Those bastards have come!' They'd set themselves up and start firing. Not scientific – so amateur – the bomb would go anywhere, sometimes to the right, to the left, you never knew where it was going. Instead of facing the enemy, everybody in the front line and supports would be looking backwards to see the bomb didn't come near them. And laugh! When you'd see this bomb going right smack in the middle of another company. They'd rush left and right to get out of the way of this awful bomb. If you weren't concerned it made you laugh![44]
>
> Lieutenant Eric Wolton, 1/5th Suffolk Regiment

Both Wolton and Hancock received leg wounds and would be evacuated in October 1915.

EVACUATION WAS SOON THE ONLY REALISTIC OPTION at Gallipoli. The failure of the Anzac and Suvla operations, combined with Bulgaria's entry to the war on the side of the Central Powers on 15 October, meant that supplies of heavy artillery and munitions began to funnel through to the Turks, allowing them the prospect of blasting the Allies right off the Peninsula. In the first instance just Anzac and Suvla were to be evac-uated, a process that was completed on the night of 18/19 December. There was great tension, but it all went off without a hitch. Only the gar-rison at Helles remained. Everything was carefully planned, culminating in the final night of the evacuation on 8/9 January 1916. As they walked back, they passed the graves of all the comrades they would be leaving behind. Ordinary Seaman Joe Murray was deeply upset.

> I thought to myself I don't like sneaking away like this after all this bloody trouble. I was really distressed in my own mind, I thought to myself, 'We're stealing away'. We stole away from Blandford, stole away from Egypt and now we're stealing away from Gallipoli. I remember when I came towards Backhouse Post, I thought to myself, 'Oh dear me, poor old Yates and Parsons, all killed and buried here.'

When we first went to Backhouse Post on the 30th April I remember how happy and anxious we were to get stuck into the Turks. And here we were only a handful left.[45]

Ordinary Seaman Joe Murray, Hood Battalion

At last Murray reached V Beach from where he was to embark, passing through the poignant hulk of the *River Clyde* to board a bobbing lighter. By then he was in a foul mood.

We were so packed we couldn't move our hands up at all. We couldn't! I remember the chap in front of me was as sick as a dog. Half of them were asleep and leaning. We were packed up like sardines in this blinking lighter. It was dark, of course – no lights, no portholes. I remember a couple of fellows behind me pushing and shoving, and I thought to myself, 'Do as you bloody well like!' All of a sudden the damned thing started to rock, and it did rock. There must have been a shell – I couldn't hear it – there must have been a shell dropped pretty close, and you know we laughed at V Beach shelling, we laughed, and there we were, no reason for laughing. There must have been hundreds in this blinking lighter, must have been, and every now and again it was rocking. All of a sudden it hit the pier. Those that were asleep were half awake, those that were sick were still being sick and, oh dear me, it was stifling hot, stifling hot! And then another one came along and I thought to myself, 'Why the hell don't we get out of it?' It may only have been a little while, but to me it seemed hours, and then all of a sudden we felt the gradual rock and I thought to myself, 'Well, here we are; we are at sea now anyhow!' We left there like a lot of cattle, being dumped into a lighter and just pushed to sea, and nobody gave a tinker's cuss whether we lived or died.[46]

Ordinary Seaman Joe Murray, Hood Battalion

Despite many alarums the evacuation was carried out without loss; a testament – whatever Murray might think – to the virtues of sound planning and conscientious staff work.

SO THE GALLIPOLI CAMPAIGN ENDED with total defeat for the 'one imaginative scheme of the war'. Far from being a close-run thing, it was a humiliating disaster that never had any real chance of success. The Turks had proved to be tough unyielding soldiers who were generally well led in battle. The Allied campaign had been founded on blind optimism, lacking in any real consideration of terrain or tactical realities. It was a logistical near impossibility. Yet somehow it still fascinates, and indeed Gallipoli was the subject of my first oral history project as an interviewer for the IWM in 1984. The strength of the material above is a tribute to the wonderful interviews given by the members of the Gallipoli Association which in the mid 1980s was still a thriving veteran concern.

Mesopotamia

The Mesopotamian campaign, fought in the Turkish province now known as Iraq, was another disaster that began in a blaze of unthinking hubris. The underlying cause was the desire to secure the local oil supplies required by the Royal Navy for the oil-fired turbines of new generations of warship. After some exploratory probing at the head of the Persian Gulf, in October 1914 the British moved the 16th Brigade to Abadan as a precautionary measure. Following the outbreak of war with Turkey on 5 November, elements of the 6th (Poona) Division, commanded by General Sir Arthur Barrett, landed and advanced, taking Basra on the evening of 21 November. So far so good: the oil fields had been secured and the campaign should then have been placed on a defensive footing – what they have, they hold. Unfortunately, it was decided that Basra would be more 'secure' if they advanced to capture the junction of the Tigris and Euphrates rivers at Qurna, some 40 miles inland from Basra. The Battle of Qurna that followed on 9 December 1914 was a fascinating engagement, redolent of colonial engagements in the nineteenth century.

> We went up with a gun section on these boats overnight, landed at dawn and prepared for an attack. The battery opened out and the observers gave a certain range. Two shots were fired – but nothing happened. After further observation they discovered there was nothing there – it was due to a mirage. When we moved up we saw our own shell holes. Well, we opened up and cleared the village – it was burnt down and the Turks cleared back. I was just a trumpeter

and captain's horse holder – when the guns went into action I grabbed the horses when the people dismounted and returned to the rear with the wagons. I used to hold three horses besides my own.[47]

Trumpeter Jack Callaway, 82nd Battery, RFA

The Turkish resistance was feeble, and in the aftermath the British force took some 1,200 Turkish prisoners and captured nine guns. Here again was the chance to stop, create a defensive front blocking the way to Basra and to bask in well-merited acclaim for a job well done. Yet then temptation reared its head: if the Turks were weak, why not brush them aside and advance all the way to Baghdad much further up the Tigris? So the British were sucked into yet another 'Easterner' adventure.

At first everything went swimmingly. The 6th (Poona) Division was commanded by Major General Charles Townshend, an interesting character, who saw himself as imbued with the genius of Napoleon. Townshend was ordered to advance across flooded plains to capture the town of Amarah in May 1915. History had taught Townshend to pursue defeated enemy – so he did. With brilliant improvisation he led an amorphous collection of river boats in what became known as 'Townshend's Regatta' pushing forward first to capture, with minimal losses, the town of Amarah.

By now the troops were having to get accustomed to conditions of service in Mesopotamia. First of all it was hot, desperately hot, even in the shade. Temperatures reached 120–130 degrees Fahrenheit and life-threatening cases of sunstroke were common. Yet at the same time the nights could be uncomfortably cold. In this harsh climate, basic army rations were hopelessly inappropriate: the usual salted bully beef soon melted into a greasy liquid, the dry 'dog' biscuits were unappetising and there was a chronic shortage of vegetables that the troops would actually eat, as they turned their noses up at local staples like okra. Water was in short supply and sanitation non-existent. Soon dysentery was rife, draining all the strength and vitality from the troops, while the endemic sandfly fever added greatly to the health problems.

As Townshend advanced up the Tigris, communications problems grew worse, for Mesopotamia had no proper roads, no railways and there was not enough river transport. Every step away from Basra lengthened the vulnerable British lines of communication. Still on they went to Townshend's next target, the town of Kut-al-Amara, where the Battle of Kut, fought on 26 September, resulted in another success for the resourceful Townshend. This time the Turks did not retreat far, but dug in at Ctesiphon only a few miles away. It was then that the last vestiges of common sense were abandoned and Townshend was ordered to continue the advance right up to Baghdad. At the Battle of Ctesiphon on 22 November 1915, the British eventually took the Turkish front-line positions but suffered some 4,600 casualties.

> Our orders then were to advance: we opened out in battle formation and advanced towards the lines. Then we could see that the enemy were there. The Turks opened fire at us all of a sudden. I don't know how many things fired at us – rifles, guns and everything – and we had to take ourselves to the ground. They pinned us down. We didn't get near them; their fire was so heavy. We suffered a fair amount of casualties. We stopped there for quite a time; I expect the regiments on our right were trying to get forward. Lieutenant Naylor was collecting wounded off the battlefield, putting them on these bullock carts to shift them down to the river. I was helping them. Anything from three to six people on each cart. We put the serious stretcher bearer cases laid flat on the bottom, the not so serious could sit up in these ammunition carts, iron-bound wooden wheels, no springs, everything they went over was jolt, jolt, jolt, jolt, jolt! They went about 7 or 8 miles to the river bank where there was two of our flat-bottomed boats.[48]
>
> Private William Finch, 1st Oxfordshire and Buckinghamshire Light Infantry

Now the transport difficulties really kicked in and the position of the wounded was desperate. There was a shortage of doctors, medical supplies and ambulances, and it took thirteen days to get casualties back to Kut.

Ctesiphon proved a Pyrrhic victory for the British. Even when the Turks were forced to withdraw, it was apparent that Townshend's own position was hopeless. Bowing to the inevitable, he ordered a retreat back to Kut. Once they realised what was happening, the Turks soon pursued, but as the British fell back they were also under attack from Arab irregulars.

The Arabs harassed us, thousands of Arab all along the river bank pot-shooting at us. They were nearly all armed with these Martini-Henrys: a lead bullet cartridge, a rolled case cartridge, all back-fired of course, no cordite in the cartridges – very old stuff from way back. It wasn't very accurate, but it was dastardly if you got hit by it. These lead bullets would splutter and give you ghastly wounds if you got hit. I remember seeing an officer of the infantry standing with his rifle up and three or four sepoys stood there beside him. And a mass of Arabs – thousands of them. The sepoys had a machine gun and they were just sort of holding them, daring them to fire while we cleared away. That stands out in my mind. I've often wondered who he was and whether he got away. It was bad luck for any wounded – the main thing was to make sure they were all dead. Rotten luck if you accidentally leave somebody – they'd slit your throat you see – terrible. That happened to the wounded a lot.[49]

Trumpeter Jack Callaway, 82nd Battery, RFA

Townshend's forces finally staggered into Kut on 3 December 1915. Here he was ordered to stand fast and a siege commenced. The town of Kut lay within a loop of the Tigris and was thus relatively easy to defend.

The Turks had kept cutting away trenches so as to get up to us to make a final assault on all our positions. I was in the fort with the regiment on Christmas Eve when they started at dawn in an attack. They blew holes in our parapets, got in, and we drove them out again. I suppose quite half a dozen times they broke in at different places and we drove them out. In front there was anything from between 800 to 1,000 left dead and dying. They called off their attack as it was dusk. On Christmas Day the Turks asked for an armistice so they could bury their dead. Everything was going all right; we started to shift their wounded, when a Turkish officer got up on our parapet and started sketching our position. Our colonel sent in to ask General Townshend what was happening and the armistice was called off. Those selfsame people were left there till we buried them in the middle of March. Before they died we gave them water, which we put through our loopholes – tied a can on a piece of string, filled it with water and twisted it down until someone got hold of it and emptied the can, then we brought it back again. We kept them going a day,

day and a half, until there was no more noise down there and we knew they were all dead.[50]

Private William Finch, 1st Oxfordshire and Buckinghamshire Light Infantry

The Turks decided that the cost was too high and both sides settled down to 'sit it out'. Some 13,000 British troops were left trapped behind Turkish lines. What were they going to do now?

THE POWERS IN LONDON belatedly began to realise the looming consequences of the over-ambitious and under-resourced Mesopotamian operations. More and more troops were diverted to the front in an effort to prevent further injury to British prestige in the East, already in danger from the imminent need to evacuate Gallipoli. One of the officers sent out to join the gathering relief force was Lieutenant Joseph Napier, who had recovered from the wounds he suffered at Gallipoli and was with a draft travelling out to rejoin the 4th South Wales Borderers. En route he encountered a somewhat intriguing officer.

At Port Said we took on a number of intelligence officers going on to Mesopotamia, one of whom was put in the cabin next to the one I shared. He was rather an offensive little fellow and we didn't think much of him – we occasionally used to go in and rag him or pull him out of bed, or some silly tricks like that. His name was Lawrence, but that didn't mean anything to us. He came on as a second lieutenant and we thought, 'Well, this is splendid!' There weren't many second lieutenants so he can do duty officer and he was put on the following day. Instead of turning up to do his job, he turned out as a staff captain, complete with cherry tabs. The senior officer called him in and said, 'Well, what are you?' He explained he'd been just promoted and was rather hesitant to show his tabs. Well that was that! On the journey onwards from there he didn't enter into our fun and games at all, he sat at a table on his own, didn't seem to eat much. I had a camera and I've still got a mass of photographs of all my pals that I took – I never bothered with Lawrence because he was such a nonentity we all thought! Of all the astonishing things, we arrived off Basra. A packet boat came rushing up alongside and the first person that was taken off was this little fellow Lawrence.[51]

Lieutenant Joseph Napier, 4th South Wales Borderers

The intelligence officer was none other than Lawrence of Arabia, apparently on a hopeless mission to bribe the Turks in an effort to secure the release of the Kut garrison.

As the reinforcements began to arrive at Basra they formed a new Tigris Corps under the command of Lieutenant General Sir Fenton Aylmer. Still hampered by severe transport difficulties, they pushed forwards to Sheikh Sa'ad, still well short of Kut, where they encountered the Turks amassed in roughly equal numbers. A good indication of the difficulties that lay ahead was given when their frontal attacks were smartly rebuffed with heavy losses on 6 January 1916. Although the Turks fell back, they merely retreated to more entrenched positions. The new arrivals soon discovered the horrors of campaigning in Mesopotamia.

> The hot weather used to knock hell out of me; I couldn't stand hot weather! I started feeling weak, but I hadn't the sense to think I'd started with dysentery. You were that weak you couldn't run to the toilet. Then I picked malaria up at the same time. That was a feeling of hot weakness. Oh I was damned ill. Men were dying, they were carrying them out every day in a blanket – dead! I was damn lucky but I was young – that helped me. A man getting into his thirties and forties he couldn't stand it the same as I did. But it ruined my insides completely.[52]
>
> Private James Snailham, 11th East Lancashire Regiment

Second Lieutenant Ian Macdonald of the 28th Punjabis summed up the conditions of service rather succinctly.

> Wherever you went, the mirage went on ahead of you. The effect is of an inviting stretch of water in a country where the only water is what is contained in the river bed and the occasional oasis, where there is a well. Hot in the day, surprisingly cold at night – almost bitterly cold. A desert march, absolutely flat, absolutely without scenery, practically without vegetation. That is to say, sand, mud, mirage.[53]
>
> Second Lieutenant Ian Macdonald, 28th Punjabis

Groups of Arabs still scavenged round the outskirts of their camps, taking what they could, whenever they could. They proved resourceful thieves and it was difficult to fend them off.

We kept watch to prevent Arabs breaking in and pinching rifles. Looking back over the Tigris it was the most wonderful sight to see the sun coming up behind these 10,000 foot peaks in Persia. You just waited for the moment when the sun would come up over the top of them and then you knew a really hot day was ahead of you. Pickets were very necessary because on one occasion the brigadier lost his horse – they came in and pinched his horse! The order was the men sleeping in their tents had to bury their rifles under them and attach a piece of wire round the trigger and then tie that round their own hands and sleep on their rifles. Even then the Arabs somehow twisted them over and got the rifles away from them, so it was a tricky business.[54]

Lieutenant Joseph Napier, 4th South Wales Borderers

Recreational opportunities were very limited in Mesopotamia, but while they were staying at Sheikh Sa'ad, Napier and his men were treated to a concert party where the troops got a piquant surprise.

Suddenly four women came out on stage to the great excitement of the men who hadn't seen a woman for quite a time. The Arabs were reputed to call us the 'Cockless Army' because of the complete absence of women! After dancing a while, throwing their legs about, they started talking and it turned out they were men dressed as women. You can imagine what the troops felt![55]

Lieutenant Joseph Napier, 4th South Wales Borderers

Many grim battles lay ahead for the Tigris Corps as they tried their best to relieve Townshend and the Kut garrison. The Turks had constructed an impressive series of well-sited defensive positions, culminating in the Sanniyat lines on the left bank of the river and the Dujaila Redoubt along the right. The relief force made a series of desperate efforts to break through, but to no avail.

The conditions suffered by the unfortunate wounded were such that there would later be a government inquiry into who was responsible. It would have been of scant consolation to Second Lieutenant Ian Macdonald who was incapacitated by a back injury and endured five days of hell as he was evacuated.

I was put on board one of these river boats. The boat was crowded with people lying on the deck. I lay next to a Seaforth Highlander, either wounded or very ill. For days upon end he said one word, 'Mother!' He died, so I and the corpse lay side-by-side. No medical care at all. Nothing but the water in your bottle which I rationed myself until someone came along with some water. You simply lay there – and waited – and waited – and waited. Thank heavens I'd had the foresight to buy this blessed haversack full of dates before the advance – the only food available. On that I existed until reaching the hospital ship at Basra. No sanitation: what you had to do you did! So that in the end when you got to Basra everything had to be cut off. It was all one blessed relief to be back to civilisation. You fell into the arms of the Indian Medical Service and from then on everything was civilised.[56]

Second Lieutenant Ian Macdonald, 28th Punjabis

Macdonald would recover, but the long-term damage to his digestive system was such that he could never serve in a hot climate again.

The Turks brought up reinforcements, their morale having been greatly boosted by their recent triumph at Gallipoli where they had learnt a great deal about the art of defensive warfare. During this period of relentless fighting the Tigris Corps suffered a casualty list that rose to 23,000 – far more men than were trapped in Kut. The Mesopotamian campaign was again spinning out of control.

MEANWHILE, INSIDE KUT, the siege progressed in an extraordinary fashion. Back in 1895, Townshend had been besieged at Chitral in the Kashmir, where he and his men were finally relieved after forty-six days. For most of the Kut siege Townshend seems to have been confident that relief would arrive in time and that he could fend off the Turks till then. This would prove to be his undoing, as Townshend initially kept his men on full rations.

Townshend always thought he was going to be relieved within six weeks, and we just used up the rations in that six weeks. After the relieving force had failed to get through, he suddenly found out that by commandeering all the Arab food, the piles of grain and using the mules, he could hold out for another eighty-four days. We had seven weeks of plenty, followed by ten weeks of adequacy, gradually getting less and less, and finally four weeks of starvation which was complete hell. You hadn't got enough in your stomach. You were hungry – you can't get away from that. People would eat all sorts of things. Four ounces of bread is about three small slices and that's got to last you twenty-four hours. By the time we got to the end the bread was all barley, with a lot of sweepings from where it had been stored. You had a morning meal which would have been one slice of bread and mule stew. You had an afternoon meal, which was a slice of bread and ginger tea. Ginger was a ration article of Indian troops and all you did was pour boiling water over it – it wasn't very nice but it was hot! Then an evening meal which was mule stew and any bread there was left over. The meat was good: there is no doubt that mule is quite good, better than horse but you get very tired of meat by itself; it tastes like a bit of chewed tin in the end.[57]

Lieutenant Henry Rich, 120th Rajputana Infantry

There was a plentiful supply of horses in Kut, each artillery battery having over a hundred.

So many horses were killed every day – part of our job. There were always plenty that had to go because in any case we couldn't feed the horses. There was no grain for them, no grass, no hay. We had to give them chunks of date palm to chew. You couldn't exercise them either. When we first were cut off we used to take them round the streets as a little exercise. But that threw up the dust and that was stopped as it drew attention to movement and the Turks always opened up on any movement. Then the horses were too weak to go round. When the rains came in December they were up to their bellies in mud in the streets where they were 'parked'. They suffered terribly.[58]

Trumpeter Jack Callaway, 82nd Battery, RFA

There was ample horse and mule meat, but no means of providing a balanced diet for the men. Unfortunately many of Townshend's men had not been in the best of health when they were first blockaded in, worn down by the rigours of the campaign and the pernicious effects of dysentery or sandfly fever. They were in no state to withstand the rigours of a long siege.

The general fact of starvation and more particularly the absence of vegetables reacted on the health of the men. They got very tired and couldn't do their work; they couldn't dig, not for more than a few minutes at a time. They got so weak. We noticed it ourselves – going upstairs you got out of breath. The scurvy got very bad, so that wounds wouldn't heal properly. We got other diseases like beri-beri. Then towards the end we got a very bad disease – almost cholera-like – and men died very quickly with vomiting and diarrhoea. We didn't know if it was cholera or not, it was very much like it. The last two weeks we lost a lot of men that way.[59]

Private Charles Barber, Royal Army Medical Corps

A bold attempt to break through the Turkish lines with a mass of food stores loaded aboard the paddle-steamer *Julnar* failed, and it was left to the seaplanes of the Royal Naval Air Service to try to bring succour in the first ever air re-supply operation. Second Lieutenant Humphrey De Verd Leigh took off in his seaplane from their base on the Tigris at Sheikh Sa'ad.

We tried to do two trips a day: morning and evening – really it was too hot in the middle of the day. We were carrying four 80-pound sacks of gee, ata, rye or whatever it was, slung underneath with a contraption we had made ourselves. It was very crude but it worked. It was an awful job getting the aircraft off the river because it was a fairly fast-flowing thing. It was a job to get them unstuck. We were not supposed to fly over Kut under 6,000 feet because the Turks had guns waiting for you. Getting up to your height took an hour and forty minutes easily. They were fortunately extremely bad shots and they never hit anybody – but still you'd feel as if they were going to.[60]

Second Lieutenant Humphrey De Verd Leigh, Royal Naval Air Service

In the end there was to be no escape for Townshend and the men of 6th (Poona) Division. On 26 April 1916 he asked for a six-day armistice. The Turks refused, insisting on an unconditional surrender, and on 29 April 1916, after a siege of 147 days, the British hoisted the white flag.

This surrender by over 13,000 men was one of the greatest military disasters ever to have befallen the British Empire. The British and Indian prisoners were in a terrible physical condition and the Turks proved not to be sympathetic captors. Their own soldiers faced hard conditions of service and it was therefore to be expected that their prisoners would suffer privations. Although the British officers fared reasonably well, the other ranks went through a harsh ordeal.

> They gave us some very coarse rough biscuits to eat, and fellows were so hungry they used to eat them and drink the water from the Tigris. We lost about fifty or sixty there through these biscuits; after eating them they used to swell in their insides and kill the person. Fortunately I couldn't eat them – my stomach turned against them. They started to march us on towards Baghdad. There was no transport, just a few cavalry to escort us. We were very weak at the time and just marched as best as we could. All the time they were behind you, hammering you, 'Come on!' Hitting you in the back with a rifle. And if you fell out you were left to lie and die if your comrades did not help you. We went through many Arab villages and the cavalry had to gallop up and down to keep them from getting at us. The Arabs would draw their knives across their throat and say, 'English finished!' The last day before Baghdad I had my boots stolen and I had to walk along with the help of my comrades – I was very weak. When we got to Baghdad there was a mob of Arabs there, throwing mud and spitting on us.[61]
>
> Private Ralph Hockaday, 2nd Queen's Own Royal West Kent Regiment

As the march continued the men were desperate for water.

> They said it would be about two days before we got to the next water. We'd got no water bottles, nothing to carry water with. So when we came to where the water was you had lie down and lap it up. A lot of our fellows died because of the typhoid germs in this water. What myself and a chum of mine did was to make a little hole in the sand and let the water percolate through into this hole – but it was a terrible half-hour waiting for that water to get there. Then you drank it. With thirst your throat swells up at the base, it seemed to choke you. Your lips all turned black and you can't talk. You try and you go, 'Whark! Whark! Whark!'[62]
>
> Private Frank Ponting, 1st Oxfordshire and Buckinghamshire Light Infantry

Over half the prisoners would die during their long years of captivity, either of disease or at the hands of their Ottoman guards.

FINALLY THE BRITISH EMPIRE BESTIRRED ITSELF to take Mesopotamia and the Turks seriously. Over the next two years, hundreds of thousands of men were dispatched to Mesopotamia, each a man who was therefore not present on the Western Front, facing the German Army in the battles that would decide the war. A trivial unnecessary expedition had expanded into a hopelessly overblown campaign being fought largely to retrieve Britain's reputation.

When the British finally renewed their advance up the Tigris in December 1916 they had some 166,000 men, they were properly resourced and had a new commander of the Mesopotamia Expeditionary Force, Lieutenant General Sir Stanley Maude. This time there would be no mistake. Maude won an impressive series of victories and was able to recapture Kut in February 1917. The fighting was still hard, but the Turks were pressed back, falling back first to Ctesiphon and then to a weak forward position on the River Diyali which soon fell, allowing Maude to enter Baghdad on 11 March 1917.

It wasn't all success, as Lieutenant Joseph Napier and the 4th South Wales Borderers discovered when they took part in the further rapid advance which, by establishing a forward defensive line, was designed to consolidate the British grip on Baghdad. On 30 April 1917, after a brief bombardment, they attacked a Turkish position near the River Adem.

> I remember firing my revolver at one of them – probably for the first time in the campaign. I suppose I was a bit excited and bloody nearly hit my own foot. I rather enjoyed that battle: they were running away from us. We captured a large number of Turks and even a battery of guns which they'd abandoned. But to make things difficult, one of these awful dust storms got up which blotted out more or less the whole scene for anybody in support of us. We got very much muddled up; we went too far to the left and the Cheshires too far to the right. We got to a position alongside the Adem and there we sat down and waited for developments. No serious danger – until looking back we suddenly saw, right behind us, what could only have been

a large body of Turks. So Staples,[63] who commanded a company, 'Taffy' Jenkins[64] and I decided the only thing to do was to retire from the positions we were in. We found the Turks were in considerable numbers compared to ourselves. I think there was some resistance here and there, a few people got injured or killed, but the Turks made signs for us to throw down our rifles. In view of the disparity of numbers we did the only sensible thing. We had some Lewis guns with us. I suppose we could have carried on firing at them with these. There was no one commanding or doing anything very much; it was a rather unexpected situation we found ourselves in. I myself happened to get hit through the side and wasn't sure whether it was serious or not and I wanted to put on a field dressing. Eventually I found myself in a small crevice beside the River Adem, lying with a rather badly wounded Cheshire soldier.[65]

Lieutenant Joseph Napier, 4th South Wales Borderers

A very different version of this debacle was rewritten in the Regimental History of the South Wales Borderers as a heroic defence to the last round, 'Captain Staples now tried to get away along the river-bed but was intercepted by more Turks. His men had fired away their last round in keeping the frontal attack at bay, and realizing that an attempt to force a way through with the bayonet would only end in massacre, Captain Staples ordered them to lay down their arms.'[66] Napier was explicit in his interview that this was pure fabrication.

Even after the capture of Baghdad the Mesopotamian campaign was still not over, and Maude himself would die of cholera on 18 November 1917. The last year of the war saw continued advances reaching further and further north towards the Caspian Sea and the Mosul oilfields. By then the campaign had lost all real purpose, but it continued regardless, with a momentum all of its own. In the final phase the British advanced quickly to seize the Mosul oilfields, a further valuable bargaining chip for the post-war world. When on 30 October the final Turkish surrender came, there were some 260,000 British and Indian soldiers in Mesopotamia. In the end it had taken the Allies four years, and at a cost of 80,000 casualties, to drive the Turks out of the Mesopotamian oilfields – something that they had, in effect, achieved at minimal cost back in December 1914. Altogether, some 675,000 fighting troops were deployed in Mesopotamia. Mission creep – the unconsidered addition of extra objectives to an original plan – had overwhelmed all common sense and by the end few could have explained why so many troops were festering in Mesopotamia when the war on the Western Front in 1918 was building to a crescendo.

Sideshows

All of the sideshows were a criminal waste of scarce resources. Gallipoli and Mesopotamia were by no means the only strategic insanities indulged by politicians seeking an easy route to victory. The British also launched major campaigns in Palestine, Salonika and East Africa that would dissipate enormous amounts of effort and sacrifice lives in equal measure. The experiences of the men who fought in these campaigns are no less fascinating, but sadly they were recorded in far less detail by our interviewers, who, when pressed for time in the 1980s, had to make choices that rather weirdly mirrored the strategic decisions made during the Great War. The end result is that Salonika and Palestine were rather shamefully neglected and our collections cannot do justice to the bitter fighting that raged in these theatres.

Salonika

Salonika was another campaign where the Allies drifted into a major commitment. Following the Bulgarian declaration of war on Serbia in October 1915, French and British divisions under General Maurice Sarrail landed at Salonika in Greece. He found a politically charged situation, as the Greeks were officially neutral, but deeply divided into pro-Allied and pro-German factions. As Sarrail advanced into Serbia, he found the Serbian Army had already been overwhelmed. When the Bulgarians pushed forwards, the British and French fell back towards their base at Salonika which would then give the campaign its name. The British wanted to evacuate, but the French were adamant that they must remain – so they stayed. By 1917, Sarrail's L'Armée d'Orient had swollen until it consisted of some twenty-five divisions (six French, six Serbian, seven British, one Italian, three Greek and two Russian brigades) and they managed to create an integrated Macedonian Front stretching across to the Adriatic coast.

Conditions were tough in Salonika, where the climate ranged from freezing winters to baking hot summers. The variable climate caused some adaptations to the uniform they wore.

In the summer we had steel helmets with a khaki cover that came over the helmet and there was an apron that came down over the back of your neck. The steel helmet got pretty hot even with the covers on. At night the mosquito net was pulled over the steel helmet and tucked into your tunic. We were also issued with shorts that turned up and buttoned at each side. At night the order would come, 'Sleeves down! Shorts down!' and you'd let the shorts down and tuck them into your puttees so you had no bare knees for the mosquitoes. In the summer of 1917 we were all dished out in khaki drill uniforms and pith helmet. Of course your pith helmet was not used in the line – your steel helmet was always worn in the line. Also, during summer 1917, we were given an old sandbag and some string. We had to fold the sandbag into a long strip and tie the string round the top and bottom ends. The top you'd bring round your neck and then it would come straight down your spine, to keep the sun off your spine. We also had a blue flannel belt that went round your stomach and tied in front. It was to regulate the heat on your stomach from the heat of day and cold of night. But it used to get full of lice. I think it defeated the object really; whether they were good or bad I don't know, but they were uncomfortable – they were lice traps.[67]

Private Ernest Jones, 8th King's Shropshire Light Infantry

The trenches were further apart than was usual on the Western Front and it was considered crucial to maintain a strong presence in No Man's Land.

There was a lot of outpost work. After I'd been in the battalion a couple of months I was picked for outpost. There was six men and a sergeant and we had a guide to take us out through the wire and through the ravines. We'd get into one ravine; there was a little dugout at the bottom of that ravine. The sentry would climb up the side of the ravine and he'd lie under a bush at the top. You'd have one hour there and you were told if you saw any activity in front you'd roll a stone down to the bottom of the ravine and then the sergeant would come up and have a look. You might see a Bulgar patrol and in some places you could also see the Bulgar lines. You had to keep your eyes open for any concentrations of troops. Each man had 240 rounds of ammunition extra on that post and a box of Mills bombs. Our orders were that, if an attack was imminent, we should keep the enemy engaged as long as possible, use all the ammunition and the bombs and then get back to your trenches as best you could. We'd take our rations for twenty-four hours, the next night we'd be relieved by another lot. Our orders were to never give your post away unless you were attacked.[68]

Private Ernest Jones, 8th King's Shropshire Light Infantry

Both sides engaged in patrolling and these could be fraught affairs. One patrol was taken out by the newly commissioned Lieutenant Ernest Haire (whom we last saw badly wounded with the 8th Cheshires at Suvla Bay in August 1915) who had arrived at the front to join the 12th Lancashire Fusiliers on the Doiran front. He soon found himself playing a dangerous game of hide-and-seek in the mountainous terrain.

At about 11 o'clock at night I took out six men and a sergeant. We were well armed, the men with rifles and me with a revolver. I took a compass bearing on a mark where we wanted to go. We went down into a little ravine and we came out through a smooth road approaching the ruined village of Smoll. The sergeant said, 'I can hear movements, Sir!' Evidently a Bulgar patrol. So I said, 'Lie down!' and watched. It was a patrol of about twenty-four Bulgars with a German officer – we'd have been slaughtered, so I said, 'Not a sound!' We waited. They tramped past; we let them go into the distance. I turned back, went up another ravine. We could see nothing at all. We were approaching the Bulgar lines, a silent night and one of my fellows dropped a rifle. You could hear it clatter – and so did the Bulgars! They didn't know where we were but they opened up with some machine guns. Then our artillery started pumping over a shell or two. When that died down we came back as carefully as possible.[69]

Lieutenant Ernest Haire, 12th Lancashire Fusiliers

The next real British attack would occur with the First Battle of the Doiran between 22 April and 8 May 1917. The offensive was in a mountainous area punctured by deep ravines and dominated by jagged peaks. Here they found the Bulgarians had used their time wisely, digging complex trench systems with reinforced concrete posts, interlocking patterns of defensive machine-gun fire, and artillery registered to the inch. The result was a disaster, at a cost of some 5,000 British casualties.

Sporadic fighting took place on the plain of the River Struma which was the sideshow's sideshow. The low-lying plain was infested with mosquitoes, the resulting malaria being a serious drain on manpower, to the extent that there were 162,517 cases during the campaign.

> The Struma had the reputation of being the most malarial district in Europe. Masses of mosquitoes which started about May and went on till the end of September. When we went there were no precautions, no mosquito netting issued – there was nothing. So the troops just went down like flies. The usual symptoms: a violent shaking ague and a very high temperature. Once you had it you were always liable to a recurrence. We started a quinine parade; every sundown everybody paraded and you had a couple of spoonfuls of quinine thrust down your throat.[70]
>
> Lieutenant Terence Verschoyle, 5th Royal Inniskilling Fusiliers

One interesting aspect of the Salonika operations was the observation work carried out by the RFC kite balloons.

> When I went up I just climbed in the basket. On each side were maps on a wooden frame. On the front and rear were two parachutes hanging outside the basket. They were the 'Guardian Angel' type and were packed in a casing rather like a big fat umbrella. The officer gave me the microphone and an earpiece connected to the telephone exchange through the yards of cable around the drum on the ground. The first thing to do was to test the line to make sure that your communication with the ground was secure. Immediately that was done the officer said, 'Let her go!' The men, hand over hand, would let the ropes go up and before they got to the end of the ropes the winch cable took the strain and the buoyancy of the balloon pulled the cable up. On a good day you could get to about 5,500 feet. Once up, the whole panoramic view lay before you – almost under your feet as it were.[71]
>
> Wireless Operator Walter Ostler, 17th Kite Balloon Section, RFC

Ostler was a witness to a famous incident when British cunning brought an end to the depredations of the German flying ace Leutnant Rudolf von Eschwege who, before he began to prey on British observation balloons, had claimed some sixteen kills.

> We were not troubled until one day Lieutenant Thrower, who was second of the section, was up observing at about 4,000 to 5,000 feet. As a bolt out of the blue came this German Albatros straight down on the balloon and in seconds the whole thing was ablaze. Thrower jumped and the burning balloon passed his parachute on the way down and scorched it. He landed quite safely, looking very white and needing a stiff whisky. That put the wind up all of us! For several days no one went up.[72]
>
> Wireless Operator Walter Ostler, 17th Kite Balloon Section, RFC

Eventually their commanding officer, Captain Charles Gimingham, went up one afternoon.

> Again von Eschwege came down. Although it was standing orders that observers in the basket must be tied on to their parachutes, Gimingham was not so tied. In facing the front of the balloon and tying on his parachute he was shot through the jaw – the bullet had gone clean through the balloon. The balloon was hauled down as fast as the winch could haul it and Gimingham jumped – von Eschwege sheered off. As soon as the parachute took his weight he fell away. The parachute floated down to earth quite gently – he fell like a stone.[73] We all rushed up to close where he fell, but of course he was dead.[74]
>
> Wireless Operator Walter Ostler, 17th Kite Balloon Section, RFC

They then got the advice of a Royal Engineers explosives expert as they planned a trap for von Eschwege. The sapper told Ostler what he planned.

> 'We must make this balloon basket look as realistic as possible – I will have a dummy made to represent the officer dressed in Flying Corps uniform. We will have maps hung from the sides of the basket.' He told me that they were putting 200 pounds of ammonol in the basket and it was going to be fired by electrical contact. Our two observation posts were on hill tops on either side of the balloon.[75]
>
> Wireless Operator Walter Ostler, 17th Kite Balloon Section, RFC

The trap was set and was triggered on 21 November 1917.

> All at once von Eschwege came out of a wisp of cloud. He was very
> clever at finding any little bits of mist or cloud that he could hide in.
> He came streaking down, straight on to the balloon. As he got over
> the top of it the man depressed the plunger. I was standing watching
> about an eighth of a mile from the winch. I have never seen, nor
> expect to see, such a huge ball of fire in the air. It blew the Albatros's
> tail off, one wing, and threw von Eschwege out of the cockpit. They
> all fell in different directions. As soon as we saw it falling in pieces a
> huge yell and cheer went up. We all started to run towards the spot
> where von Eschwege[76] was falling. I saw him lying on the ground in
> his German flying outfit – just a fair-haired boy.[77]
>
> Wireless Operator Walter Ostler, 17th Kite Balloon Section, Royal Flying Corps

The German ace had been killed by a clever ruse – or unsporting cunning,
depending on perspective.

The undercurrent of being a forgotten army is never far from the
recordings of Salonika veterans. The campaign stagnated and the Salonika Force attracted the uncomplimentary nickname of the 'Gardeners
of Salonika'. The last act occurred when the multi-national force, now
under General Franchet d'Espèrey, launched a major offensive in the
summer of 1918. In the Second Battle of Doiran on 15 September, the
British once again assaulted the Bulgarian defence lines along the formidable 2,000-foot-high Pip Ridge and Grand Couronne. The result was
another disaster and a further 3,155 casualties. Fortunately, the French
and Serbian attacks had fared much better. The Bulgarians fell back, not
yet completely defeated, but undermined by the certain knowledge that
the mainspring of the Central Powers – Germany – had been defeated
on the Western Front. Further resistance was futile, and an Armistice
ended the war on the Bulgarian front on 29 October 1918.[78] Salonika
had been a disaster for the Allies, soaking up hundreds of thousands
of troops chasing the flickering shadows of a Balkan triumph. In all,
some 404,207 British soldiers saw some kind of service in Salonika
between 1915 and 1918. There were 23,787 casualties in the fighting,
but these were dwarfed by the hundreds of thousands of cases of non-
battle casualties that reached 505,024 through the horrendous rates of

malaria and dysentery, which (thanks to multiple illnesses afflicting the same patients over the period) actually exceeded the number of men deployed on the front.

Sinai and Palestine Campaigns

An early Turkish attempt to cross the Sinai desert to launch an attack on the Suez Canal had ended in a plucky but comprehensive failure in February 1915. As the link to India, the Suez Canal was an absolute strategic necessity for the British Empire. It is doubtful whether the Turks ever had the resources to pose a serious threat to the canal, yet a huge campaign would result from the British decision to promote a more 'active defence' of Egypt in 1916. After the evacuation of Gallipoli there were thirteen divisions of the Egyptian Expeditionary Force totalling 400,000 troops. The intention was to use them to push back the Turks so that any lingering threat to the canal was removed.

Operations in the desert of the Sinai Peninsula proved difficult as the swirling sandstorms, blazing temperatures and scarce water resources made it an inhospitable landscape. Major logistical preparations had to be undertaken, including pushing forward a railway and a water pipeline. Prominent in the fighting were the Australian Light Horse who, after their dreadful experiences as infantry at Gallipoli, had had their horses restored to them.

> Our biggest problem was monotony. You'd see the sun get up in a big red ball in the morning and he'd go down in a big red ball at night and that was our only sense of time actually. Nothing but sand dunes as far as the eye could see and you had the heat in the day, you were lying in the sand. The glare of the sun, the glare of the desert and your rifle barrels would get that hot in the middle of the day that you couldn't hold them. You had to hold it by the wood. You were lousy from morning to night, continually scratching where you could scratch, with a cavalryman where his trousers fitted tight and his leggings he couldn't scratch. They were full of septic sores: sometimes you wouldn't get your clothes off for four or five maybe six weeks. You were out on patrol camping on the desert, you just lay on the desert like a dog with your horse – it was the only bit of shade you had that your

horse made for you. You had no water for days and you might be out six weeks without a bath, six weeks, one bottle of water a day, a little tin of bully beef and two dog biscuits – army biscuits. It was a monotonous life: the same old faces, same old sand and the same old sun.[79]

Private Lawrence Pollock, 9th Australian Light Horse Regiment, AIF

Little did Pollock and the Australian Light Horse know it, but they were participating in one of the very last successful cavalry operations – thousands of years of mounted warfare were coming to an end as the horse was superseded by armoured vehicles.

After the Battle of Magdhaba on 23 December 1916, the British managed to clear the Turks from virtually the whole Sinai Peninsula. It was then decided to launch an attack on Gaza. The main attack was made by the 53rd and 54th Divisions on 26 March 1917 but the defensive positions were too strong and the attack ground to a halt. They were ordered to try again and the Second Battle of Gaza was fought on 17 April. This, too, was a failure. Captain Eric Wolton was still with the 1/5th Suffolks as they moved up to capture the Sheikh Abbas Ridge. From there they watched as the rest of the 163rd Brigade, under heavy fire, made a frontal attack against the Turkish trenches.

The 4th and 5th Norfolks they were wiped out, the 8th Hants just the same. We were the only reserve left and they sent us into it. I should have thought I should have been very afraid, but strangely enough, instead of being afraid, I was thankful – we were the 163rd Brigade and I was thankful to share in this. I don't know what the men thought. We went ahead and they could see what had happened. We stopped under the shelter of a very small little ridge and there we dug in as best we could. Of course it was a ghastly business because the Norfolks and the 8th Hants they were all crying out for help and we couldn't do anything at all – frightful. During the night we were out there, trying to dig trenches. But mercifully the brigadier general came out and saw the position was hopeless and the 5th Suffolks were ordered back. I remember falling in my platoon, collecting rifles from the dead. Close by me were two or three wounded Norfolks or 8th Hants people. They said, 'You're not leaving us behind are you?' I said, 'Of course not!' But I did.[80]

Captain Eric Wolton, 1/5th Suffolk Regiment

Later Wolton was sent out on a night patrol near Samson Ridge. It was a terrifying experience.

> It was pitch dark. I heard a Turk patrol coming through this bean field. If you go shooting, you get shot at from both sides. The only other way is to go in quietly with the bayonet. So I stayed where I was and trusted they wouldn't! Anyway I knew if they came near me that we had the initiative, we knew they were coming, we should catch them by surprise, but using a bayonet has never been my metier! Mercifully, although they came towards us right close – about 20 yards – I kept quiet and they went past. I suppose I should have gone for them, but it wasn't very pleasant.[81]
>
> Captain Eric Wolton, 1/5th Suffolk Regiment

One of the refreshing things about oral history is an acceptance that not everyone can be a hero all the time.

The failure at Second Gaza led to the appointment of General Edmund Allenby to command the Egyptian Expeditionary Force, which then consisted of the XX Corps, the XXI Corps and the Desert Mounted Corps. He was to reinvigorate the whole campaign and achieve the capture of Jerusalem. Allenby took stock and requested significant reinforcements to guarantee success. His preparations took time, and months drifted by before he was ready to begin moving again. The first step was the attack of the XX Corps and the Desert Mounted Corps on the eastern flank of the Turkish lines at Beersheba on 31 October 1917. This featured a remarkable cavalry attack by the 4th Light Horse Brigade. Private Lawrence Pollock saw it happen.

> Well, we'd taken Beersheba – it might have been midday, it might have been after: time doesn't matter much to ordinary soldiers, only sunrise and sundown. Then the light horse charged on the flat, two – just simply two lines of horsemen at full gallop with fixed bayonets on rifles. They jumped the first line of trenches and the second line was coming up, then the Turks slung it in. The Turks on the whole, right through the whole campaign, didn't seem to like the steel. At 600 yards they were good shots and they'd shoot you; the minute you got in amongst them, well you had them.[82]
>
> Private Lawrence Pollock, 9th Australian Light Horse Regiment, AIF

The main British attack at the Third Battle of Gaza on 6 November 1917 proved a success, as the Turks retired to avoid being cut off.

Although there was still hard fighting ahead, the Turks faced over-whelming British superiority in numbers, artillery and materials. This advantage was hammered home by excellent leadership from Allenby and his subordinates. On 9 December 1917, the city of Jerusalem fell to the British, and much propaganda was made of this timely success in what had been a bad year for the Allies. Still the Palestine opera-tions continued to expand. After the pushing through the Judean Hills and capturing Jericho, Allenby planned to cross the River Jordan before advancing into Syria. He even created a third army corps, the XXII Corps, and the Palestine theatre of war became second only to the Western Front in terms of numbers employed. Then the German spring offensives on the Western Front in 1918 left the British with their backs to the wall, and the most obvious source of reinforcements was Pales-tine, which in comparison was clearly a sideshow. It took months for Allenby to rebuild his forces and only by September 1918 was he able to launch a final offensive. The Turks collapsed at the Battle of Megiddo on 19 September after which, in cooperation with irregular Arab forces organised by T. E. Lawrence, Damascus was captured. Fighting dragged on in Syria, until the Turkish Armistice signed on 30 October brought a simultaneous end to both the war and Turkish hegemony in the Middle East. Overall the campaign had been a success, but it had absorbed enor-mous resources with nearly 1.2 million men serving there at some time. Of these there were 51,451 casualties in battle, a figure dwarfed by the incredible 550,000 casualties from disease.

BUT NOW WE MUST RETURN to the front where in the end the Great War would be decided. The sideshows are fascinating, but they were in the end just that – a distraction from the main event – the battle against Germany. There was no easy way to win the war; no gaping back door to Germany for Britain. Of course there was a very real war raging on the Eastern Front where Russia was engaged in its own titanic battle with Germany and Austro-Hungary. This, too, could have decided the war, had Russia collapsed before 1917, or alternatively had the Tsar's forces swept to victory. But for Britain the Western Front was where the war would have to be fought and won, fighting alongside France (and eventually America) in a battle to the finish. It was there that the German Army must be defeated in the field.

6

1916: WESTERN FRONT

THE YEAR 1916 SAW THE BRITISH ARMY finally begin to play its full part in the war. The BEF had expanded from the first four divisions deployed in August 1914 to an imposing thirty-eight divisions by January 1916, and there were still more New Army, Territorial and Colonial divisions due to arrive on the Western Front. For two years the French and the Russians had borne the brunt of the war at a terrible cost to even their colossal manpower reserves. Compared to the monumental losses suffered by their allies, the British casualties had so far been trivial. Now, for the first time, the BEF was entrusted with a key role in a joint Anglo-French offensive, which would be launched on the Western Front in concert with simultaneous offensives from both Russia and Italy.

General Sir Douglas Haig had replaced Field Marshal Sir John French in command of the BEF in December 1915, but the site of the offensive was chosen by the French Commander in Chief Joffre, who selected the Somme area at the junction of the British and French sectors where he could keep an eye on his allies. Haig was well aware that his New Armies needed more training before they could be relied on. The Allied plans were disrupted by a predictable source of trouble – the Germans. On 21 February 1916, Falkenhayn launched a huge offensive at Verdun designed to drain the strength from the French Army by sucking them into an attritional battle. This titanic fight raged for months and as it drew in more and more French divisions, the character of the planned Battle of the Somme began to change. The French would still attack, but the British contribution became the defining element.

The Fourth Army, commanded by General Sir Henry Rawlinson, was charged with making the attack on 1 July 1916, while a Reserve Army (later known as the Fifth Army, commanded by General Sir Hubert Gough) would exploit any breakthrough. Rawlinson's eventual final plan depended on the raw power of the 1,537 guns and howitzers amassed for the attack. In the end the tactics to be employed were fairly simple, although by no means uniform, as considerable independence was allowed to subordinate formations. The barrage would build to a crescendo while the assaulting troops would move into No Man's Land ready to attack. At the Zero Hour of 07.30 the barrage would lift to the next German line and the attack would go in, usually at walking pace, with long lines of men just 2 or 3 yards apart. The bombardment was the key to success and it was confidently believed that it would crush any German resistance.

As the troops moved up there were many scenes that now seem unutterably sad, given hindsight of what was to befall them.

> Down in the valley near us there was a brigade of men. One evening they struck up that Scottish song, 'You take the high road and I'll take the low road and I'll be in Scotland before you.' This song was taken up by everybody and there must have been three or four thousand men singing it – most touching. It was a beautiful evening, with a setting sun over on the hill, shining through some trees. It would have livened the heart of Turner to have painted that scene. But over it all there was this rumble of guns going on the whole time.[1]
>
> Corporal Norman Edwards, 1/6th Gloucestershire Regiment

In the last few weeks hundreds of guns had to be covertly moved up into the line. Most of them were the field artillery made up by the 18-pounder guns and 4.5-inch howitzers, though more of the heavier gun batteries were also beginning to appear. The 36th Siege Artillery Battery of the Royal Garrison Artillery (RGA) was equipped with the impressive 8-inch howitzers. Moving such monsters was a difficult task.

> They were improvised howitzers, because they were old 6-inch Mark Is, cut in half and the front half was thrown away. The rest was bored out to 8 inches with rifling and given a modern breech mechanism mounted on enormous commercial tractor wheels. They were monstrous things and extremely heavy, but the machinery of the guns was very simple. One was the very first ones to be made was marked, 'Eight-inch Howitzer No. 1 Mark I' so we called that gun, 'The Original'. It was marvellously accurate. We moved to a splendid position near Beaumetz. The guns were dug into an enormously deep bank about 10 feet deep by the side of a field. The digging we had to do to get into that gun position – 10 feet deep and about 40 feet in length – was simply gigantic. We camouflaged it extremely well by putting wire netting over it threaded with real grass. We had to manhandle these enormous monsters – they weighed several tons. We had to push them – couldn't pull them – push them into their positions. When they were there they were very well concealed, so much so that a French farmer with his cow walked straight into the net and both fell in. We had the most appalling job getting this beastly cow out. The man came out all right, but the cow! It was one of those delightful moments when you all burst out laughing.[2]
>
> Second Lieutenant Montague Cleeve, 36th Siege Artillery Battery, RGA

Once safely in position the massed guns still needed hundreds of thousands of shells to be brought up and concealed. It was another huge task. After all this hard graft the bombardment finally opened on 24 June 1916. To the men watching it seemed an awe-inspiring display of artillery power. They could not believe that any German could survive what seemed a veritable deluge of shells.

> We were just standing looking at the German lines and we could see the bursts of the shells – all over – big ones in the distance. We could see the dirt from the sandbags dancing up and down. Then you could turn about and all along the skyline you would see flashes: big flashes, little flashes, hundreds of them all along the skyline. Over the top there was a roar like a score of trains going all at once over the top of

141

your head, you could hear them whizzing over. I thought, 'This will certainly shift Jerry, he'll never stand up against a thing like this.'[3]

Corporal George Ashurst, 1st Lancashire Fusiliers

Ashurst sums up the popular perception, but it was unfortunate that the spectacular appearance of the bombardment flattered only to deceive. It was spread out along 25,000 yards of front and also had to reach back beyond the three trench lines that made up the German front-line system to include their equally strong second-line system. This fatally diluted the power of the guns. Although there were more guns than could have been dreamed of in 1914, the vast majority of them were field artillery; there were still relatively few heavy or medium batteries ready for action. As a result most of the shells lacked the sheer brute force to smash deep dugouts or concrete reinforced positions. In addition, the required gunnery skills were not yet possessed by the recently trained swathes of gunners manning the British guns. The theory of gunnery had not been properly assimilated and few officers grasped the vital importance of accurate meteorological data to allow for the fine adjustments that made all the difference between missing and hitting targets.

The senior subaltern said, 'I'm going to the major in his dugout, to ask him if I can put on the "meteor" corrections on the gun.' When he got there the major, who was a regular, mark you, an Irishman, he said, 'My boy, this is war, this is practical stuff, forget all that nonsense they taught you at "the Shop" – if it's cold cock her up a bit!'[4]

Lieutenant Murray Rymer Jones, 174th Brigade, RFA

The 'wise' old officer with his 'commonsense' aphorism was in point of fact utterly wrong: the 'dull' technical gunners at the Royal Artillery School at Woolwich had it right. The Great War would be a technical and scientific war. The British Army still had a lot to learn before it could harness the monstrous power of the guns.

Slowly the clock ticked down towards the moment when men would have to charge out into No Man's Land.

We got so fed up – to the point that we thought, 'The quicker the bloody whistles go for us to go over the top the better.' We always said to one another, 'Well, it's a two to one chance that we either get bowled over or get wounded and go home!' Doing your bit and hoping for the best.[5]

Private Ralph Miller, 1/8th Royal Warwickshire Regiment

AT 07.30 ON SATURDAY, 1 JULY 1916, the British infantry went over the top. The 46th and 56th Divisions made a diversionary attack on Gommecourt, intended to attract attention to the north of the front, but although the 56th Division succeeded in breaking deep into the German lines they were soon cut off by a barrage of German shells. Private Frederick Glanville of the 1/16th London Regiment never got that far.

We were the second wave. We were ordered to lay down about 25–30 yards from the barbed wire entanglements. While I was there I was the victim of a machine gunner – I got a bullet in the top left leg, which came out halfway down my right leg – I was lying in the firing position. You feel the thump and you don't feel any pain from the bullet going through. After I'd been hit I took four or five shots at the man with the machine gun on the German parapet, but I didn't hit him – why I don't know – I'm amazed to this day I didn't hit the man. On the Sunday morning there must have been a truce and during that time one of our officers came and stood by me shouting, 'Stretcher bearers! Stretcher bearers!' but none came. He gave me a handkerchief and said, 'Wave this and I'll send them over to you.' But no one ever came. Later on that day our people started shelling the German front line again and I got hit three times on the chest with small bits of shrapnel. They weren't serious. I was lying on my back. I decided that if I got a bigger one and it hit me on the stomach that would be the end of me – so I turned over. No sooner had I turned over than it happened and a much bigger piece of shrapnel hit me on the left hip bone. Not really serious but a big open wound. I was unconscious for hours on end. What I think saved my life as I lay there – I put my hand down between my legs when I felt something there and my hand came up covered in maggots. I think they ate the bad flesh. I was very pleased to find them there because I realised they

143

were helping me. On the Monday somewhere near midday a couple of Germans came out. I saw them coming and I'd got one bomb in my hand, which I threw as far away as I could. I didn't know what attitude they were going to take towards to me! I got rid of my rifle about a yard away – I was virtually unarmed when the Germans reached me. I was taken in and laid on the German firing step.[6]

Private Frederick Glanville, 1/16th London Regiment (Queen's Westminster Rifles)

Although Glanville was captured, his incapacity was such that he was later included in a prisoner exchange and ended up interned in Switzerland from 1917 to the end of the war.

Much of what we remember as the first day of the Somme comes from the dramatic story of the 'Pals' Battalions in the doomed attack of the 31st Division on the village of Serre. They went forward in their waves, but the attack broke down when they were caught up in uncut German barbed wire in No Man's Land, where they were mown down by machine guns and lashed by the devastating 5.9-inch shells of the German artillery. Private James Snailham of the 11th East Lancashires was hit early on.

There was a mad scramble to get over. You're making for safety. You're thinking, 'Shall I get there!' You've no thought only getting cover, no thought of anything. Men were lying over the damned show. Shell fire was doing all the damage. I hadn't run far before a shell burst above me, I was knocked to the ground and when I looked there was this lump of steel sticking through that leg. I was done then. I had to get in a shell hole and lie there. I'd got almost to the Jerry wire. I could hear movement in front of me. I lay there until 7 o'clock at night – I daren't move, the German fire was so dense. I kept dozing over, wakening and dozing over. At times popping my head out to see. Lads were lying all over the place shouting for help; nobody could get to them at all, nobody. I'd lost blood, I was exhausted. I had no idea of time at all. I had so much pain that I must get back to my own trenches, I was ready to take any risk. At 7 o'clock I made my mind up I was going back. I started crawling back. Men were moaning all over the show, 'Get some help for me!'[7]

Private James Snailham, 11th East Lancashire Regiment

Snailham managed to crawl back to the lines and would later serve in Mesopotamia, but for the rest of his life he had problems with the wounded leg.

Corporal George Ashurst was in the attack from the White City towards Beaumont Hamel.

> Over the top! It was partly blown down and I'm just stepping on top, there was a corporal lying there, all of his shoulder was gone – all blown away, I think he'd been hit by a whizz-bang. He looks up at me as I passed him, 'Go on, Corporal, get the bastards!' Well I daren't stop so I just said, 'Okay', and buggered off as fast as I could run. There seemed to be bullets everywhere. Run – that was the only thing in my mind. Run and dodge. Expecting at any second to get hit, to feel a bullet hit me. I was zig-zagging, holding my head down so a bullet would hit my tin hat, I seemed to be dodging in between them – I must have been to get there. There was gunsmoke knocking about. You could hear when a bullet hit somebody, you could hear it hit him. Hear him groan and go down. It was mainly machine guns that cut us up. I was thinking, 'I've got to get forward!' That's all.[8]
>
> Corporal George Ashurst, 1st Lancashire Fusiliers

The IWM Sound Archive does not have many interviews with battalion commanders from 1916 as most of these older men had died before the interviewing programme commenced in the 1970s, but the interview conducted with Lieutenant Colonel Alfred Irwin, who commanded the 8th East Surreys in the attack on Carnoy, gave an insight into a legend of the Great War.

> Captain Nevill was commanding 'B' Company, one of our two assaulting companies. A few days before the Battle of the Somme he had come to me with a suggestion that as he and his men were all equally ignorant of what their conduct would be when they got into action, he thought it might be helpful – as he had 400 yards to go and knew that it would be covered by machine-gun fire – it would be helpful if he could furnish each platoon with a football and allow them to kick it forward and follow it. That was the beginning of the idea and I sanctioned that on condition that he and his officers really kept command of the unit and didn't allow it to develop into a rush

after the ball, just if a man came across the football he could kick it forward but they mustn't chase after it.[9]

Lieutenant Colonel Alfred Irwin, 8th East Surrey Regiment

While it might seem like jingoistic hubris, Captain Wilfred Nevill was motivated by his very real concerns about how his men would face the machine guns that awaited them. After I had catalogued the interview I remember walking round the museum to see for myself the football kicked that day towards the Germans. Sure enough there it was – proudly emblazoned with the legend, 'The Great European Cup-Tie Final. East Surreys v Bavarians, Kick off at Zero!' Overall, the objectives on the 18th Division front were achieved, but it seems particularly tragic that Nevill[10] himself was killed as they approached the German line.

Their neighbours of the 30th Division also achieved their objectives in the southern sector adjacent to the French, where the ground configuration was less favourable to the German defenders, and the British bombardment had been significantly augmented by French artillery. The 30th Division performed well that day, sweeping through Montauban and consolidating against German counter-attacks. Private Albert Hurst of the 17th Manchesters clearly remembered what they carried over the top with them.

> We had two extra bandoliers of rifle ammunition, a rifle as well as Mills bombs in two of our pockets, a full-sized pick, panniers of Lewis-gun ammunition in water buckets. Men were carrying barbed wire, posts for the barbed wire to go on, cutters for barbed wire. Every man had some extra load. We had to put up barbed wire and dig ourselves in when we got there. You could just about walk. On the back of our packs we had a yellow cloth to distinguish us as being Manchesters and a blank metal plate to reflect the light so that the aeroplanes could see how far we had got in our advancement.[11]
>
> Private Albert Hurst, 17th Manchester Regiment

What the men carried weighed approximately 66 pounds, which has long been criticised as excessive, yet it is difficult to see what should have been left behind. They had to take their personal weapons, while the bombs and Lewis-gun ammunition were essential if they wished to have any chance of holding back a German counter-attack. They needed picks, shovels and barbed wire to consolidate the ground they had won. They needed food rations for the day or so before supplies were sorted out. Strangely enough, the load carried by troops into battle even today is much the same, despite the intervening years.

Although the 30th Division managed to overrun and consolidate their grip on the German first-line system, the German second-line system still lay inviolate ahead of them, up on the ridge extending from Bazentin le Grand through to Longueval. Once more the British had broken into but not through the German defences.

Despite such partial successes, taken as a whole, the British offensive on 1 July was a disaster. Some ground had been gained in the south, but for the most part nothing worthwhile had been achieved; any temporary successes were swiftly reversed or neutralised by the Germans. The 57,470 casualties suffered are unimaginable to the modern mind: some 19,249 men were killed that day – husbands, fathers, uncles, brothers and sons. Sergeant Stewart Jordan was sent up to a crossroads to guide back the London Scottish after the debacle at Gommecourt. Here he saw a depressing scene that must have been repeated many times that night, as the shattered remnants of the assaulting battalions came stumbling out of the line.

> I heard marching feet and after a bit in the darkness I could see that they were wearing kilts and guessed that that was our regiment. When I could distinguish them I noticed about a hundred men I suppose and the adjutant was leading them. So I said to him, 'Which company is this, please?' 'Company?' he said. 'This is the regiment!' About eight hundred men went over and about one hundred came back.[12]
>
> Sergeant Stewart Jordan, 1/14th London Regiment (London Scottish)

Later in the battle, Corporal Norman Edwards looked out at the serried ranks of the dead lying in No Man's Land in front of Serre.

> The devastation was ghastly. A lot of dead men lying around. The night we got up to take over the ground I looked over the parapet to find a place to put my Lewis gun. I saw all these little twinkling

lights everywhere as the flares were going up from the German lines. Twinkling all over the whole area of ground. It was pieces of tin that had been put on the backs of the haversacks of the division that attacked on the 1st of July. These were all men that had been shot down, lying with their face down, with their packs showing up.[13]

Corporal Norman Edwards, 1/6th Gloucestershire Regiment

The underlying weakness of the British 'pals' recruiting system had been cruelly exposed. The opportunity to serve with their friends may have encouraged mass enlistment, but at the same time it invited mass tragedy. Localised recruitment meant that when things went wrong the losses in a small community were unbearable. Towns like Accrington and Sheffield were hit very hard.

There were sheets and sheets in the paper of dead and wounded with photographs, where they could get them, of the men. Of course everybody rushed to the paper every day to see if there was anyone they knew. When we got to know of anybody at the school, the headmaster announced them if they had been old boys. I was brought out of class to be told that my cousin had been killed. There were numerous services in churches. It was a very, very sad time – practically everybody was in mourning. People were in deep black, the men if they couldn't wear black wore black armbands as a mark of respect. The city was really shrouded in gloom. They were very, very sad and nothing seemed to matter any more.[14]

Miss Llewellyn, Sheffield schoolchild

Yet something most 1916 veterans understood was that despite all the infamy, 1 July was not the end of the Battle of the Somme. Despite the fact that it has become, for the British, a totem for the maudlin who feast on the casualty figures, the French had already suffered a far worse mauling on 22 August 1914, when as many as 27,000 French men were killed in a single dreadful day. Continental war was brutal. The Somme would be the major British effort of 1916, a sustained assault on the German Army that was designed to help the French, still embroiled in the long torture of Verdun, to wear down the German strength to the point where defeat became inevitable, and in the hope that they might be successful in breaking through to victory. Nothing would be served by stopping the offensive. It simply had to go on. There was no alternative.

Haig moved the focus of the offensive to the south, where the greatest successes had been achieved. These efforts were designed to secure tactically significant 'jumping off' points such as the Mametz and Trônes Wood prior to the next big attempt to advance which would take place on 14 July. This marked a considerable improvement in British tactics, with a far more intense barrage of around 1,000 guns concentrating some 500,000 shells on just 6,000 yards of front. It was also a night attack, preceded by a final hurricane bombardment just five minutes long as a *coup de grâce*. When the troops went over at 03.25 they overran the shattered remnants of the German front line and gained a firm grip on the whole length of the Bazentin Ridge. At this point the cavalry moved forward to advance on High Wood, but battlefield conditions made progress slow and they were vulnerable to ambush. Signaller Leonard Ounsworth, from his forward observation post, saw the 20th Deccan Horse have a lucky escape.

> A Morane Saulnier, a French aeroplane that we had at the time, kept diving down on to the corner of the field on our left front. I saw this Indian cavalry, the Deccan Horse they called them, and this plane was diving down and up again. Suddenly the officer in charge of the cavalry cottoned on. He stood up in his stirrups, waved his sword above his head and just charged across that field – like a shot out of a gun, like bats out of hell. The two outer lots split, so they made a pincer and encircled them – it was all over in a matter of seconds. The next thing we saw was thirty-four Jerry prisoners, some with heavy machine guns. They had been waiting while the cavalry got a bit nearer – my God, they'd have slaughtered them. The plane was trying to draw their attention, just diving down on top – I suppose distracting these machine gunners, because a plane coming down close above your head is enough to draw your attention.[15]
>
> Signaller Leonard Ounsworth, 124th Heavy Battery, RGA

In the end the line reached the corner of High Wood, which for weeks to come became one of the focal points of the bitter fighting.

There were far too many localised attacks made by lone brigades or even a single battalion. If attacks were not made on a wide front then the unengaged Germans on either side could divert all their guns onto the assaulting troops. Corporal Norman Edwards of the 1/6th Gloucesters participated in a night attack in the Ovillers sector on 21 July. Edwards was part of the third wave led over the top by Second Lieutenant Arthur Smith.

> The whole battalion were going to attack the line in front of John Copse. I know I offered a prayer to God that I might be preserved and do my duty. This was it! This was what we had been all trained for; there was no question of not going: we just had to do it. At dawn that morning little 'Gunboat' Smith, a newly promoted officer from the ranks, gave the most important order ever used at war – that was, 'Follow me, chaps!' We crawled over our own parapet, out into the wire and went over the top. We hadn't gone more than 20 yards when German machine guns opened fire and we had to flatten down. We tried to crawl forwards but this machine-gun crossfire all across this area was completely devastating. You felt completely crippled if you started to move. 'Whizz! Whizz! Whizz!' Sparks would appear on the barbed wire. We were just crawling about in the deepest shell craters we could find to save ourselves. A feeling of intense rage went through me. I wondered if the right thing to do was just fix your bayonet and just go in and try and clear them out of it. But as soon as you started to move, 'Br-rr-rr-rr!' This awful crossfire from machine guns. I found 'Gunboat' Smith – he was wounded. I got dragged into this deep shell hole where we were dressing his wounds. A senior officer said, 'Try and get him back to the front line!' I said, 'I'm in charge of two machine guns!' He said, 'Your job is to get this man back; you can't do anything with this crossfire going on!' Smith was able to crawl. That was an awful trip. Everything was banging away. I started to get him back and I got hit, the bullet went through above my left elbow. It was as though someone had hit me with a crowbar – 'Bang!' With all this I was useless. I somehow crawled up to our front line. I was pulled in by two of our own men and I told them about Smith being in a shell crater.[16]

> Corporal Norman Edwards, 1/6th Gloucestershire Regiment

Second Lieutenant Arthur Smith[17] died of his wounds. And so it went on. The recordings are a reflection of the hopeless nature of much of the fighting. Corporal Richard Trafford of the 1/9th King's Liverpool was wounded before he even got over the top at Guillemont on 8 August 1916.

> There were four of us: one was dishing the rations out. A loaf between four and the jam and cheese was being shared out. I'd got my bread in my right hand and I was holding my dixie lid out in my left hand for my jam, when a shell burst right overhead. A lump of shrapnel went right through the jam and the dixie lid, three or four bits got me all round my hands. The chap that had handed the bread over – he got a lump through his back; he was killed instantly. The other fellow Joe Shaw, he jumped over the trench! Luckily for him he went opposite the German lines, down our lines – shell-shocked, screaming his head off! We shouted him back but he took no notice, kept on going. The fellow dishing the jam out he was the only one that wasn't hit![18]
>
> Corporal Richard Trafford, 1/9th King's Liverpool Regiment

Private Harold Hayward was another victim of the fighting in the Guillemont sector. On 3–4 September, he was acting as the colonel's runner.

> I was talking to the colonel, as near to the old man to him as I am to you, listening to what he was saying and I was hit by a bullet that came up from the captured German trenches. No doubt what it was, it was a German left behind in one of their deep dugouts that hadn't been bombed had come up, seen the colonel, let fly at the colonel – and hit me! As soon as that had happened the German would have walked on down towards our reserve lines and given himself up as a prisoner of war and nobody would have known. I was wounded in the scrotum. The bullet had come up off the ground and carried dirt with it, went through a cigarette tin and went through me. I was carried by Lieutenant Fitz to the dugout. I never lost consciousness. Lieutenant Fitz put my field dressing on me and he reassured me that nature provides two – like it provides two eyes. Well I'm now a father![19]
>
> Private Harold Hayward, 12th Gloucestershire Regiment

The much reassured Hayward was evacuated back to England and admitted to Lincoln General Hospital. Here he began to resent the intrusive questioning into the nature of his injury by one of the hospital visitors.

> In this ward there was a lady from one of the county families who used to come once a week. She was rather nosey – wanted to know everything. Her first visit after I was there she said, 'Where was I wounded?' because of course she couldn't see any bandages and I just pointed down under the bedclothes hoping that would be sufficient. The next week she came she said, 'Where were you wounded?' I knew what she was after and I said, 'Guillemont!' It wasn't the particular place she wanted to know but where the wound actually was, which being under the bed clothes she couldn't see. Finally, the next week she pointed and said, 'But where are you wounded?' I was a bit fed up with this continual questioning and so I said, 'Madam, if you'd been wounded where I've been wounded; you wouldn't have been wounded at all!' All the rest of the fellows in the ward guffawed somewhat loudly and she stalked out of the ward not to come back again while I was there.[20]
>
> Private Harold Hayward, Lincoln General Hospital

By this stage, the battle had degenerated into desperate attempts to get a better 'jumping off' position for the next 'big push' which was planned for 15 September 1916. Typical of this was an attack on Ginchy on 9 September made by the 6th Connaught Rangers commanded by Lieutenant Colonel Rowland Feilding. The battalion had already been severely battered.

> The commanding officer had been killed; the second-in-command had been killed. Various other people had been killed and we were sort of reforming under a new CO – a Guards officer. There were a whole lot of senior majors, who if a CO got killed, they sent regardless of his regiment. We got this Colonel Feilding, then a major, an elderly gent in the Coldstream Guards who was not a regular soldier, but a nice man. He was a Roman Catholic and they thought, 'Ah! Send him to the Connaught Rangers!' So Feilding turned up, a very large rubicund man.[21]
>
> Second Lieutenant F. W. S. Jourdain, 6th Connaught Rangers

One of the pleasures of oral history is finding that an interviewee had met the author of autobiographical books one has already read, rather like recognising a friend in a crowd of strangers. This Colonel Rowland Feilding was the author of an old favourite, *War Letters to a Wife*.[22] Jourdain never forgot Feilding's terse instructions before the attack on Ginchy on 9 September.

> All I knew was, 'We are going over the top tomorrow afternoon! You, F. W. S. Jourdain, are the signal officer!' When the battle started it was all very horrifying, shells shooting over the trench and knocking the sand off the parapet. The troops went forward and they very soon came back; they were really knocked to bits by the Germans. I did not take part in the actual movement because it wasn't my business to do so. I was there in the front-line trench looking after whatever signal communications there were: D3 telephone and lines which kept on being broken. The only useful communication was back to brigade. I had one or two NCOs and soldiers with me trying to keep a line going down the communications trench. One single [telephone] wire on which everything depended. That kept on being bombarded and the thing got cut and several brave men kept on mending it. The whole thing developed into some glorious muddle and there wasn't anything very coherent sent back. In the middle of the battle the adjutant decided to go sick with trench fever! He retired from the war, in fact, and was never seen again. Feilding, who took a certain liking to me, thought I was reasonably intelligent and made me the adjutant on the spot. I was militarily speaking of no height and only 18. The point was I was there! The thing finished as a shambles.[23]
>
> Second Lieutenant F. W. S. Jourdain, 6th Connaught Rangers

I found when re-reading Feilding's book that he actually mentioned young Jourdain's sterling efforts, referring to his, 'wisdom far beyond his years'[24] and saying, 'The boy Jourdain is still acting-Adjutant and is doing it marvellously well, in spite of his extreme youth.'[25] Even though Jourdain was then 92, this was a strangely personal direct link with the long-dead Feilding.

By this time a rumour had circulated among the troops fighting on the Somme concerning the statue of the Virgin Mary holding aloft the baby Jesus which adorned the basilique church in Albert. A shell had caused it to lean precariously and many soldiers were reputed to believe that the war would end if it should finally fall to earth. However, few, if any, took it seriously.

> The legend was that the day this Madonna fell that the war would finish. I was always a bit of a comic like and I says, 'Why, we'll sharp rectify that!' One fellow says, 'How's that?' 'Let's knock it down now – then the war will finish!'[26]
>
> Signaller George Cole, C Battery, 253 Brigade, RFA

But the British had more realistic new hopes for the future. It was becoming evident that the BEF was learning its trade. The Royal Artillery was gradually mastering the power of the guns and the set-piece bombardments no longer shifted to the rear lines just as the British troops emerged into the open. Creeping barrages now preceded them across No Man's Land, forcing the Germans to take cover, thus suppressing their ability to fire on the assaulting troops. Standing barrages could be dropped down in front of newly captured trenches to break up any attempted counter-attacks. Counter-battery fire was taking increasing effect by making good use of the RFC, and new techniques like flash spotting were being used to locate the German guns. There was also a secret weapon in the wings ready to be introduced into the tactical mix: the tank.

THE GENESIS OF THE TANK is a fascinating story of brainstorming initiatives by several individuals. Their work culminated in the arrival on the Western Front in the late summer of 1916 of a new behemoth: the lozenge-shaped Mark I tank. It came in two varieties: the 'Male' tank armed with two 6-pounder guns with an additional four machine guns; and the 'Female' tank armed with five machine guns. Their tracks allowed them to cross rough ground and their armour offered some protection to their crews, but at the same time they were dreadfully slow, proceeding at no more than walking pace, were difficult to steer and were excessively prone to mechanical breakdowns. The tanks would first trundle into action at the Battle of Flers-Courcelette on 15 September 1916. No one really knew how best to deploy them, and few understood their capabilities or realised their crippling restrictions. But it was at least a start. Signaller George Cole had a chance to witness the elemental power of the newly flowering bombardment techniques, and he and his friend Billy Fielding were also able to get a close-up view of one of the tanks in action at Martinpuich.

> It was as quiet as the grave. There wasn't a shot fired. And then, just in the twinkling of an eye, it was hell let loose. Every gun fired at the precise second, hundreds of guns. Just about 50 or 60 yards to the right of where we were, we saw this tank come forward. Our infantry, the 5th Yorks, were alongside and behind him. Billy Fielding, he said, 'A sight for the Gods! A sight for the Gods!' Which it was. Mr Wilson said, 'Come on, never mind about the sight for the Gods!' So we got out, following, running this [telephone] wire out. I think the Germans were startled. They opened out with everything they had, but you couldn't hear a shell – what I mean was it was noise. You didn't know if it was our shells, or their shells, our guns, or their guns. There wasn't a great lot of small-arms fire; it was mainly shell fire, you see. We went forward following this tank, running the wire out, and we were relaying corrections back to our guns. One time the wire broke and we went back to repair it. I was on my knees, fastening the wire together, tying a reef knot in it, pull it tight, clip the ends short and wrap it in insulation tape. Billy says, 'Look at them buggers there!' I just turned to look and here was a fellow with a cinematograph taking photographs of me mending the wire. I turned and looked; I waved my hand to him.[27]

> Signaller George Cole, C Battery, 253 Brigade, RFA

One of the most promising of the tank attacks was carried out by the D-17, commanded by Second Lieutenant Stuart Hastie in the Flers sector.

> Having crossed the front German line I could see the old road down into Flers, which was in a shocking condition having been shelled by both sides. At the other end of this road, about a mile away, which was about the limit of my vision from the tank, I could see the village of Flers, more or less clouded with smoke from the barrage which had come down on top of it and the houses, some of them painted white, some seemed to be all kinds of colours. Across the front of the village, we could see the wire of a trench named Flers Trench and this formed a barricade in front of the village on the British side. We made

our way down the remnants of this road with great difficulty. Just as we started off our steering gear was hit and we resorted to steering by putting on the brake on each track alternately and trying to keep the tank following the line of the Flers–Delville Wood road. When we got down to Flers Trench and passing into the village, there was a great deal of activity from the eaves, under the roofs of the cottages and also from a trench which appeared to be further through the village but which we couldn't just locate at that point. Having steered the engine by using the brakes up to this point, the engine was beginning to knock very badly and it looked as if we wouldn't be fit to carry on very much further. We made our way up the main street, during which time my gunners had several shots at various people who were underneath the eaves or even in the windows of some of the cottages. We went on down through the High Street as far as the first right angle bend. We turned there and the main road goes for a matter of 200–300 yards and then turns another right angle to the left and proceeds out through towards Gueudecourt. But we did not go past that point. At this point we had to make our minds up what to do. The engine was really in such a shocking condition that it was liable to let us down at any moment. So I had a look round, so far as it was possible to do that in the middle of a village being shelled at that time by both sides. I could see no signs of the British Army coming up behind me. So I slewed the tank round with great difficulty, on the brakes and came back to Flers Trench and turned the tank again to face the Germans.[28]

Second Lieutenant Stuart Hastie, Tank D-17, D Company, Heavy Branch, Motor Machine Gun Company

Overall, the attack on 15 September could be considered a success: High Wood was finally captured, Flers was overrun and all in all it was clear that the Germans had been hard hit and even forced into a localised retreat to the Le Transloy Ridge. But the tanks had been hampered by their own mechanical unreliability and the manifest complexities of integrating them successfully into the tactical mix. Haig, however, retained faith in their potential and the tanks would be back at the front in greater strength and to far more effect in 1917.

The Fourth Army followed up with another successful assault on 25 September, yet no matter how much the Germans were suffering they still had sufficient resilience to cling on. As the weather began to break the Somme turned into a dreary swampland. The fighting in October and early November was dreadful; a slogging match in which there were plenty of losers and no winners.

The final act of the long-drawn-out campaign came with an assault on Beaumont Hamel and Beaucourt sur Somme on 13 November. Here the Royal Naval Division (RND) were flung into action for the first time since being evacuated from Gallipoli. Ordinary Seaman Joe Murray gave us a wonderful account of the run-up to the attack and events of the day. From the start the RND were extremely dubious about any chance of success.

> We've got in mind what we got to do. We know we're for the slaughterhouse. We know that the 29th Division, the Newfoundlanders, the Essex and everybody else got slaughtered. We know that. We knew that since then there'd been five attempts all beaten back – five![29]
>
> Ordinary Seaman Joe Murray, Hood Battalion

Murray was in a mood to complain as they moved up into the line facing Beaucourt on 12 November.

> Cups hanging here, a mug hanging there, entrenching tool at the back beating a tattoo on the backside, you've got your haversack on this side, you've got a sack of bombs round your neck, like a blinking Christmas tree. Lousy things, coming up the communication trench, you got tied up with this telephone wire, you pull like hell, then you trip over and the sack would fall in the mud. A wet muddy sack is an uncomfortable thing. We were the front line attacking troops, we were ahead of everybody, every time all the time. It was still daylight, round about 5 o'clock. We couldn't go forward because of the observation balloons and planes flying across the top. We hid in these trenches just outside Hamel. We'd been given a tin of jam each and a glass jar of piccalilli – never seen the damned stuff before. We opened and ate the jam and we ate the piccalilli. Well whether the piccalilli didn't agree with the jam, or the jam didn't agree with the piccalilli, I don't know, but we knew the results afterwards![30]
>
> Ordinary Seaman Joe Murray, Hood Battalion

It was a long cold wait in the freezing November cold with no shelter, no hot food and very little hope to keep them warm. At least they had a distinguished soldier as their commanding officer: Lieutenant Colonel Bernard Freyberg.

> We of the Hoods, under Colonel Freyberg, were right on the right flank, almost on the river. In fact the river was our boundary. It was dark, misty, there was a slight drizzle; it may have been the mist. So I was lying in this hole, the next man to me was about 5 or 6 feet away. I've got a sack of blinking bombs for my head; that was my pillow. It must have been about midnight, but I saw someone come along. I thought to myself, 'Ooooh blimey, who's that walking about in front here?' Normally you would fire, anyone in front of me was an enemy unless you were warned. I heard this fellow talking and I find out it's Colonel Freyberg. He'd come along to inspect his troops before the attack. The generals do it 10 miles away, quite safely, but Freyberg he was coming along. He went past me eventually and went on to see his old pal Kelly[31] of 'B' Company. Freyberg said to me, 'Oh, you here!' He was quite cheerful, wondering how we were getting on. 'Do try and get some sleep.' I suppose we did sleep; exhausted sleep I suppose.[32]
>
> Ordinary Seaman Joe Murray, Hood Battalion

Frozen to the very bone, it would prove a truly miserable night, harrowing for men who knew that they would go over the top before dawn.

> In the early hours of the morning, round about 5 o'clock, we were all woken, perishing cold. About 05.30, most of us started getting warmed up a bit, dancing about, quietly. Then we had to fix bayonets. There's always a noise with fixing bayonets, a clink, a metallic noise, so you put your tunic round it to deaden it. At 5.45, all of sudden, behind us, the whole sky was red, it reminded me of home a couple of miles across the valley from Consett Iron Company, when they used to draw the furnaces there. Immediately afterwards you could hear the shells going over your head and you could almost feel the shells. Then you heard the sound, the light was first, the shell was next and then the sound. There was a lot of them falling short. But at the same time, you know, were it not for the artillery barrage then we'd all have been slaughtered – we wouldn't have advanced at all. So it was the lesser of the two evils. We accepted they were doing a brilliant job. We knew

we had seven or eight minutes, then the Germans would retaliate, they would bombard beyond the front line to the reserves coming up – which they knew would be there. So the quicker we got out of our positions towards the barrage, the safer we were.[33]

Ordinary Seaman Joe Murray, Hood Battalion

Freyberg led the Hoods on to attack the shattered ruins of the Beaucourt railway station.

There was firing going on all over the place: our own shells falling short, the Jerries firing from left and right, our left flank was vacant. They say run, but you stumble, there's shell holes, you can't go direct, you go this way and that way, picking your way round the shell holes. Sometimes there was two or three of you together, sometimes there was nobody. They'd got behind or blown up, you don't know. All the time there was this fumes and the shelling going on. We get to this point on the other side of the sunken road and we capture it. I was almost near the station. We had to go down this road and up the side. There was a lot of dugouts there. Well we got our 'P' bombs out and chucked them down there. As you went along you could smell these phosphorous bombs – a rotten lousy smell. I saw some crowd over here, I thought they were our men, but they were really prisoners. We started talking to these fellows, they couldn't understand, we couldn't hear there was so much bloody noise, but a soldier knows what the point of a bayonet means, 'Quick, quick, quick! Get back!' Some of them wouldn't behave themselves and we shot them. No doubt about it. You'd tell a bloke, some of them wouldn't behave themselves, wouldn't take any notice, or making threatening gestures – 'BANG' – you had no time to fool around with them.[34]

Ordinary Seaman Joe Murray, Hood Battalion

In the total confusion that prevailed in front of the village of Beaucourt, Murray was wounded.

We were at least three or four hours ahead of our time. Somebody realised: 'Look the barrage hasn't lifted.' It was there or thereabouts that I got blown up. I can remember thinking, 'What to do?' And: 'BANG!' The next I knew I was in Mesnil, lying on a stretcher and somebody was washing the mud off my face. There was a shell burst very near; it hit me crouched down and I got a wounded in the abdomen, little bits of shrapnel in here and a bit of a shell took off the skin and pubic hair, nasty.[35]

Ordinary Seaman Joe Murray, Hood Battalion

The Germans on the Western Front had laid low 'Lucky Durham' where the Turks had failed. Murray was invalided back to Blighty but would return to the Western Front in 1917. Meanwhile Second Lieutenant Martin Greener of the 175 Tunnelling Company was pressed into service, checking for booby traps all around the Beaucourt station.

At Station Road especially there were a lot of very good German dugouts. We had to get in there, make it safe and make new entrances into it. It was booby-trapped. We'd been told what we were likely to find and how to find it. For instance these fuses with acid in them: the striker was held back by a spring held back by a piece of wire. The acid according to its strength ate through the wire. Once it ate through – 'BANG' went the detonator. There was one case where a dead man's foot was wired up to a bomb. If he was moved away that would have gone off! Hidden things all over the place. Sometimes they would leave a revolver lying on the table and that would be wired up. Steps were always booby-trapped – if you were going down steps into a dugout you never went down straight away, you rolled something down first because there'd be a bomb under one of the steps. We found several of them that way.[36]

Second Lieutenant Martin Greener, 175 Tunnelling Company, Royal Engineers

Although they were held up just short of Beaucourt, the RND had made a notable breakthrough, while the 51st Division had equal success at Beaumont Hamel. The German defences had been severely breached, but nothing more could be done until 1917. The onset of winter forced the British to suspend their offensive and the battle was officially closed on 18 November 1916.

THE BATTLE OF THE SOMME was brutal; an inevitable consequence of British involvement in a continental war. There was no easy route to success against the might of Imperial Germany, and millions would have to die before they would accept defeat. Any tactical objectives were therefore of minimal importance. The only objective that really mattered was the destruction of the German Army.

The British Army had learnt a great deal during the battle. Lessons had been learnt that laid the foundation of tactics that would eventually be refined to create the 'All Arms Battle' which would win the war. But this was still some way off: tanks were not yet properly integrated and the art of suppressing return fire during an attack had not yet been mastered – that would require two more years of bloody mayhem. Battles in the Great War are rarely measured by dint of the crude measurement of ground won or lost. Far more important is whether they damaged the enemy. On the Somme the Germans suffered greatly, and ultimately the loss of the Pozières Plateau and Thiepval Ridge during the Battle of the Somme would force them in early 1917 to fall back nearly 40 miles. The hundreds of square miles surrendered then was vast in comparison to the ground directly captured in 1916, but it was nevertheless a direct result of the Somme battles. In the end, much had been achieved, but the price was almost unbearably high: the British suffered in total nearly 420,000 casualties – far more than the total strength of the BEF in August 1914. Of these some 131,000 were dead. It was almost incomprehensible, but this was continental war, in which previously unparalleled degrees of savagery were witnessed at every level.

7

ALL AT SEA, 1914–18

THE ROYAL NAVY WAS THE BACKBONE of the British Empire: across the centuries, it had fought the series of battles that had overwhelmed all naval challengers. It had been the gun that 'fired' the diminutive British Army to the point where it would do the most damage, whether on some outlying peninsula, or on a mission to wrest colonies into British hands. Unlike the Army, the Royal Navy was granted sufficient funds to allow the operation of the 'two-power' standard which had given them global supremacy. The Germans, who were the leading military power on land, sought to create a navy with the potential to damage the Royal Navy sufficiently to render it vulnerable to other enemies. To counter this threat, the First Sea Lord, Sir John Fisher, undertook a thorough review of the navy: non-essential ships with little or no function in modern war were scrapped and a new 'All-Big-Gun' class of ships was introduced, beginning with launch of the *Dreadnought* in 1906. These ships were better armed, better protected and faster than the multifarious classes of 'pre-dreadnoughts' all around the world. This development triggered a new and more intensive naval race with Germany, but the British gritted their teeth and maintained their lead. Shortly afterwards, in 1908, Fisher introduced the first battlecruiser *Invincible*, which was essentially a cruiser armed with eight 12-inch guns. By the time war broke out, the Grand Fleet of the Royal Navy could deploy some twenty-one dreadnoughts and four battlecruisers against the thirteen dreadnoughts and five battlecruisers of the German High Seas Fleet.

The Royal Navy was ready for war and the nation was confident that the old naval traditions would see them through to victory. Boy Seaman George Wainford was on the pre-dreadnought *Albemarle* and his view typified popular opinion.

> Everybody was cheering – they thought it was a great joke! We didn't realise what was coming. We were still thinking in Nelson's way: ship against a ship, close up, perhaps 100–200 yards away, knocking seven bells out of each other! Fighting hand-to-hand and all that business. We thought we were so much better than the Germans that it would be a cakewalk.[1]

> Boy Seaman George Wainford, HMS *Albemarle*

However, the Germans had no intention of seeking a great decisive battle at sea, instead maintaining a 'fleet in being', i.e. keeping the German fleet safe in harbour where it could continue to contest the 'command of sea' without actually risking all in battle. At the same time they could send out commerce raiders to disrupt the sea lanes. Faced with this, the Royal Navy was forced to adopt a cautious approach. It was recognised that a close blockade was not feasible given the need for regular refuelling of modern coal-fuelled ships, but that it would also play into German hands, allowing their destroyers and submarines to erode British supremacy. It was therefore almost inevitable that the Admiralty would settle for a distant blockade: the Harwich Force of cruisers and destroyers, backed up by the more modern pre-dreadnoughts at Sheerness, would guard the Channel; while the Grand Fleet under the command of Admiral Sir John Jellicoe was based in the huge Scapa Flow anchorage in the Orkneys, alongside the 1st Battlecruiser Squadron under Vice Admiral Sir David Beatty. Facing them was the High Seas Fleet commanded by Admiral Friedrich von Ingenohl, based at Wilhelmshaven.

At first the Germans believed that the Royal Navy would appear off the German coast as soon as war was declared, but the Grand Fleet spent much of the first month of the war sweeping up and down the North Sea to protect the BEF troop convoys. The first naval action of note occurred when a raid by the Harwich Force, supported by their big brothers of the 1st Battlecruiser Squadron, pushed deep into the Heligoland Bight on 28 August 1914. A confused mêlée with German light cruisers resulted, which was decisively won by the dramatic intervention of the British battlecruisers. The final moments of the German light cruiser *Koln* had a mingled horror and nobility.

> Our last salvoes were fired into her at about 400 yards range. She was on fire. Some of them were jumping into the water on bits of wreckage so as to try and get to us, but the seas were icy cold. The sea was not calm then; it was a choppy sea with a rising mist spray. We tried to save some, we hauled some aboard, but they were too numb; they eventually died and we simply put them back into the drink again. There was no time for any ceremony. We didn't know whether there would be any other German ship about, so we had to keep on the lookout and be ready for anything else. Eventually we saved a baker's dozen, hauled them aboard. I shall never forget seeing that ship go down. She sank at about 7.30. We all had the impression that those Germans were very, very plucky people – I actually saw one man pull out the flag that was aft, he got hold of it and as he was sinking under the water he was still waving that flag as the ship went down. Much as if to say, *'Deutschland still über alles!'*[2]
>
> Engine Room Artificer Ernest Amis, HMS *Kent*

Three German light cruisers and one destroyer were sunk. The Battle of Heligoland Bight was considered a great success in Britain, but at the same time it had been a risky undertaking that exposed the British battlecruisers to potential danger from mines and torpedoes. Shortly afterwards the Germans ceased patrolling in the Bight and filled it with mines to deny the area to the British.

The naval war then quietened down in the North Sea, but even so, Jellicoe's notional superiority was gradually eroded. When his ships were undergoing their regular refits they could not be available for battle, and matters got worse when the dreadnought *Audacious* was sunk by a mine on 27 October 1914. Jellicoe was convinced that the blockade would gradually strangle Germany, cutting off trade, and preventing the import of essential raw materials and foodstuffs. He therefore adopted a cautious policy which curtailed the activities of the Grand Fleet – he commanded the world's oceans, so no risks would be taken just to secure control of the contested North Sea.

Meanwhile, Admiralty attention switched to the hunt for the German East Asia Squadron, which was still at large under the command of Admiral Graf Maximilian von Spee. While the light cruiser *Emden* rampaged about the Indian Ocean to great effect (until she was sunk by the Australian light cruiser *Sydney*), the main body of the armoured cruisers (*Scharnhorst* and *Gneisenau*), accompanied by the light cruisers (*Nurnberg*, *Leipzig* and *Dresden*) crossed the Pacific for the South American coast. Here they encountered the British South Atlantic Squadron, commanded by Rear Admiral Sir Christopher Craddock. Craddock's force consisted of the armoured cruisers *Good Hope* and *Monmouth*, the light cruiser *Glasgow*, the lightly armed merchantman *Otranto* and the venerable pre-dreadnought *Canopus*. Craddock had been ordered to engage only in the company of the *Canopus*, but she was left far behind as he moved round the Cape of Good Hope and into the South Pacific. The situation was further complicated when the two squadrons finally met off Coronel on the coast of Chile at 16.40 on 1 November 1914, as intercepted wireless traffic had led both sides to believe they were about to encounter just one cruiser. What followed was a brave but entirely hopeless fight.

> I saw a shell enter the foretop of the *Good Hope* and blow a man completely out of the top into the sea. I went on the starboard side of the ship thinking the man might float by there, because there we had a life buoy and I was going to slip that life buoy if he was near our ship, but there was no visible sign of any man. Shortly after that, a shell pierced our foretop and took off the signalman's arm, bending his telescope, and there was great difficulty in lowering that man from such a height to the deck of the ship on a rope. It was not long before the *Good Hope* veered to port out of position and the *Monmouth* had started to list. These two ships were really out of control and eventually, a few hundred yards on our port side, there appeared to be a fire in the fore turret of the *Good Hope* followed by

a tremendous explosion. The *Good Hope* disappeared, but *Monmouth* battled on under terrible conditions – the sea was running very high – until darkness – in those latitudes it comes on you very rapidly. We approached the *Monmouth* and asked what condition she was in and she made a reply to say that she was making water very rapidly for'ard and 'I must get my stern to the sea!' With that we left her and shortly afterwards we saw a terrific explosion – that was the end of the *Monmouth*. The battle was over. We were in a very bad condition ourselves, we'd been holed several times. One of our mess decks was flooded, one bunker flooded.[3]

Carpenter Sylvester Pawley, HMS *Glasgow*

There were no survivors from the *Good Hope* or *Monmouth*, with a loss of nearly 1,600 officers and men. The *Glasgow* and *Otranto* managed to escape in the confusion. The defeat at the Battle of Coronel was a humiliation for the Royal Navy, and Fisher took immediate action to secure revenge by dispatching the battlecruisers *Invincible* and *Inflexible* (under Vice Admiral Doveton Sturdee), which would duly accomplish the grim task of sinking the *Scharnhorst* and *Gneisenau* at the Battle of the Falklands on 8 December 1914.

Meanwhile, back in the North Sea, Ingenohl launched a series of helter-skelter raids on the British east coast designed to draw the Grand Fleet into a newly laid minefield. The Germans were endangered by the fact that by this stage of the war, a combination of cracked German signal codes and the astute use of directional wireless interception stations meant that the Admiralty often had a considerable degree of forewarning of their movements. Despite this, the German battlecruisers managed to escape unscathed from their raid on Yarmouth on 3 November 1914, while Scarborough and Hartlepool were bombarded on 16 December. This led the Admiralty to move Beatty further south, to Rosyth in the Firth of Forth, to allow a more rapid response.

On 23 January 1915, the Germans tried again when Ingenohl sent out the 1st Scouting Force under Admiral Franz von Hipper in an attempt to ambush British light forces that might be patrolling in the Dogger Bank area. Forewarned, Beatty leapt into action with his flagship the *Lion*, accompanied by the battlecruisers *Tiger*, *Princess Royal*, *New Zealand*, *Indomitable*, a squadron of pre-dreadnoughts and the 1st

Cruiser Squadron. On the morning of 24 January, the two sides collided as Beatty sighted the German battlecruisers, *Seydlitz, Moltke, Derfflinger* and the hybrid heavy cruiser the *Blücher*. Hipper ran for home and a long chase began. The British ships were marginally faster and began to overhaul the fleeing Germans. Midshipman John Ouvry described the action from his vantage point on the *Tiger*.

> My first sight of German vessels really was smoke on the horizon and then masts. The captain was in the conning tower and I was outside looking for submarines. At about 9.20 we sighted the Germans – they opened fire on us and we on them. The first salvo blew my hat off. Then to my relief the captain sent a messenger to say, 'Come inside the conning tower now!' Which I did. The weather conditions were quite good. The annoying thing was that the Germans made a certain amount of smoke and that obscured us as far as gunnery was concerned. The Germans concentrated on our flagship – that was the *Lion* – ahead of us. So for the first part of the action we rather got away with it! We were firing at them without being fired on ourselves. It meant the *Lion* was bound to get hit sooner rather than later. I could see the smoke and flame of shells hitting her. After a while she was very heavily hit on the water line, the port side. A shell penetrated to the engine room and put her port engine out of action. She had been elsewhere and two of her turrets were put out of action. *Lion* slowed right down and dropped astern our starboard side. That meant the Germans concentrated on us because we were the leading ship. We had a pretty hot time. But meantime we were hitting the enemy. We knew that, because one battlecruiser was on fire. Two of our turrets were hit, one was put out of action. We had a hit very close to us as a shell burst under the deck of the conning tower on which the captain and ourselves were standing. It shook us very badly and killed some men on the decks below. There was a certain amount of smoke in the conning tower. I think on an occasion like that you're sort of pulverised. You carry on automatically doing your duty – you're frightened but you don't say. You're very tense; very tense. You do your job completely and efficiently; at the same time your nerves are all tense. The captain turned round and said, 'Keep steady, boys.'[4]

Midshipman John Ouvry, HMS *Tiger*, 1st Battlecruiser Squadron

Beatty had to leave the *Lion*: while he was between ships there was confusion over signals and, instead of pursuing the German battlecruisers, they turned on the already crippled *Blucher*.

> We turned to port to cut off the *Blucher*, the *Tiger* leading the other three ships. We blasted away at the poor *Blucher* which had stopped. We fired two torpedoes at her at point-blank range. I saw one hit. I saw the foremost turret blow up and the mast came down. She had stopped and was listing. She turned over and disappeared, leaving a number of sailors struggling in the sea. One of our destroyers went alongside and picked up a few, then a Zeppelin appeared overhead and dropped a bomb and the destroyers made off.[5]
>
> Midshipman John Ouvry, HMS *Tiger*, 1st Battlecruiser Squadron

The German Navy used Zeppelins for reconnaissance purposes. Nearly the whole of the *Blucher* crew of some 800 men perished in the freezing cold North Sea, some of their last moments immortalised in an unbelievably emotive photo of them scrambling desperately across the side of the ship as she turned turtle. While the battlecruisers finished off the *Blucher*, the rest of the German ships escaped.

The Battle of Dogger Bank was a British victory, but it exposed serious problems within the Battlecruiser Squadron. The gunnery standards were poor and the communications systems could not cope with the stress of battle. Worse still, it had not yet been realised that poor cordite-handling arrangements within the turrets rendered them vulnerable to cataclysmic explosions if their armour was penetrated – and their armour was too thin to keep out German shells. The Germans had found this out the hard way, when the *Seydlitz* had a cordite explosion in the aft turrets which flashed down into the magazine-handling room, and only the immediate flooding of the magazine prevented the destruction of the ship. Even so, some 159 men were killed. The Germans introduced anti-flash precautions to stop a re-occurrence, but the British battlecruisers still carried the seeds of their own destruction deep within them.

The Germans chafed at the defeat at Dogger Bank and Ingenohl was replaced by Admiral Hugo von Pohl. For now, the High Seas Fleet would lapse into passivity while the possibilities of commerce-raiding using

U-boats were explored. These had already proved their effectiveness but were hampered by the internationally accepted 'rules of war', which specified that neutral ships could only be 'stopped and searched'. Even Allied merchant ships could not be sunk without warning or measures to secure the safety of the crews. These rules rendered submarines almost impotent as they lost their best weapon – the cloak of invisibility. The Germans would have to increase their efforts if they were to strangle the British economy, and so from 18 February 1915, they ordered an unrestricted submarine campaign which threatened the sinking of any Allied merchant ship encountered in the 'war zone' surrounding the whole of Britain. Neutral shipping was sternly warned that their safety could not be guaranteed if they entered the zone.

This campaign was double-edged, for it risked alienating the unattached neutrals around the world. Accidents or controversies abounded, most memorably on 7 May 1915, with the torpedoing by a German submarine of the liner *Lusitania* while it was carrying American passengers. Over a thousand lives were lost. However, the British had their own dirty tricks in the war at sea: the 'Q' Ships. I only interviewed one Q-ship veteran – George Hempenstall – but he had served on the most notorious of them all, the *Baralong*. When the crew joined the ship in April 1915 they were given thirty shillings each to buy civilian clothes and sent out on patrol into the North Atlantic. There was the usual merchant seamen crew, but also two naval officers (Commander Godfrey Herbert and Lieutenant Gordon Steele),[6] two concealed 12-pounder guns crewed by naval ratings and a party of Royal Marines. The idea behind the Q-ship was simple: having the appearance of a normal merchantman it would pose no threat to a U-boat and could then trick the submarine into surfacing to use gunfire rather than expend the limited supply of torpedoes. At that point the Q-ship guns would be unveiled and the submarine dispatched. Considerable care was taken to maintain the disguise of the *Baralong*.

> Two imitation lifebelt lockers with lifebelts painted on them and
> made in two sections so that they could fall in two – one half would
> fall outboard and the other half inboard when you gave them a
> heave. We had boards with different ships' names on them – the one

we had when we went into action was USS *Grant* with the American flag flying. We had other flags, Spanish and Greek as well, which all accorded with the waters we were operating in, what name we were using. Different name boards for each flag. During the night-time we would put the stageboards up and paint the funnel different colours. We never picked a [harbour] pilot up. Wherever he went, Herbert took the ship in himself; he was well qualified. We had to go ashore in civilian clothes. We were told to keep quiet and not to mention anything to anybody. You'd get a white feather given to you – it happened to me on the Liverpool landing stage, 'Kitchener wants you! Why aren't you in khaki?' We had a button, 'On War Service'; you'd show them your button on your lapel and they'd apologise.[7]

Able Seaman George Hempenstall, HMS *Baralong*

The crew were motivated by a very real desire for revenge against U-boat crews, whom they regarded as nothing less than murderers.

We were anxious to get hold of some of them. You hear about them firing on women and kids in the lifeboats. They had no consideration for any survivors and they would get the same treatment from us. We had no compassion about 'poor Germans' or anything like that – they knew what they were doing and they knew what to expect.[8]

Able Seaman George Hempenstall, HMS *Baralong*

On 19 August 1915, the *Baralong* responded to a call from the sinking British liner *Arabic* which had been torpedoed by the U-24. Shortly afterwards they received a further distress message from the *Nicosian,* a freighter carrying mules and munitions, and they hastened to the scene. That day Hempenstall was crewing a concealed gun.

They got a signal that some ship was in distress, being shelled by a submarine and we were put on the alert. We were going to approach the vicinity so we were expecting something to happen. When the alarm bell rang we went up, got close to the gun, laid down under cover where we could see without being seen. But you couldn't see very much – not much further than the deck. We waited for the signal to open fire; we couldn't open fire until we were within 600 yards and we were a couple of miles away. He had to get his ship within 600 yards before he could expose his guns. That was the trouble. They hoisted a signal to the submarine, 'Coming to your assistance to save life!' and kept on steaming ahead. We got up close to the *Nicosian*, she was stopped and the crew were in lifeboats. The ship was lying there blowing off steam and the submarine was firing at her. We crept up behind the *Nicosian* and, while we were behind the *Nicosian*, he managed to get within range and gave the order to clear away the guns. As soon as we got the signal to open fire, down would come the 'Stars and Bars' and up would go the White Ensign and the board with the name USS *Grant* would be dropped at the same time as we cleared the gun away. As soon as we cleared the *Nicosian* we could see the submarine. He fired a round across our bows to stop us – that was the last he fired. We opened fire on him and the first round hit him – 12-pounder lyddite right in his conning tower. The Marines opened fire with their rifles and scattered their gun's crew away, stopped them shelling the *Nicosian*. They all dived over the side. That was all I saw of them. The Marines were firing all the time, but what they were firing at didn't bother us – we'd got our own job to do. We fired away at the submarine: as long as there was anything to fire at we fired at it! It didn't last long against 12-pounders, nose-fused lyddite. Soon put a stop to him. When we ceased fire there was nothing left of the submarine.[9]

Able Seaman George Hempenstall, HMS *Baralong*

Afterwards a Royal Marine boarding party was sent aboard the *Nicosian* where they hunted down and brutally murdered the few Germans that had reached the ship. This was not witnessed by Hempenstall, who remained aboard the *Baralong*. When they got back to the United States, some of the crew of the *Nicosian* reported what they had seen and the '*Baralong* Incident' became an international *cause célèbre*. In fact, both sides indulged in virulent propaganda, denouncing the misdeeds of the other – and indeed there was a simultaneous scandal raging over the forty-four fatalities (three American) suffered during the sinking of the *Arabic* on the same day.

Following the sinking of the U-27, Herbert was replaced as captain by Lieutenant Commander Wilmot Smith. Within a month the *Baralong* was in action again when on 24 September they found the merchant-man *Urbino* under attack from the U-41.

We got there and all I ever saw was one empty lifeboat where the action had happened. No survivors from the ship he's sunk. The submarine came to periscope depth, had a good look at us, steamed around. Apparently he was satisfied and came to full buoyancy. As soon as he broke the surface we opened fire on him. The first round hit him and he did an emergency dive. Flooded his tanks and went down quickly. He had an internal explosion and blew his tanks again and came to the surface. He didn't get time to get out before we hit him again. But as he was going down two of them managed to get out of the conning tower; they swam towards the lifeboat and clambered into it. Apparently we were told to steer for the lifeboat and sink it. That was when the captain sang out to the Marines, 'Don't fire!' We steamed around for a while, a couple of times we tried to hit the lifeboat and they dived over the side again. At last the captain sang out to them, 'If you want to be saved, come alongside!' They pulled the boat alongside and they put the ladder over the side for them to come aboard. I was at the top of the ladder when they came up and the submarine captain was the first one up the ladder, I helped him overboard. He said, 'Thank you very much; I only did my duty!' The other fellow would be his coxswain – those two would be in the conning tower and just managed to get out. They were taken away and we put the captain in the sheep pen. He'd been hit by a splinter or something in his head – I got blood off him on my shoulder.[10]

Able Seaman George Hempenstall, HMS *Baralong*

It seems that this surviving officer was actually Oberleutnant zur See Iwan Crompton, who had indeed been badly wounded; he would later allege that the *Baralong* had deliberately run down their lifeboat before he was rescued. This was denied by the crew – but Hempenstall's account supports Crompton's version of events.

The sea war was a ruthless affair on both sides, but in the end the Germans could not withstand the level of condemnation they received from the neutrals. The German 'mistakes' of sinking passenger liners, such as the *Lusitania* and the *Arabic*, killed far too many American citizens. With the US approaching the point of war, the Germans backed down, and in September 1915 the submarines were withdrawn.

Meanwhile, as the High Seas Fleet remained in harbour the surface sea war stagnated, until a new spirit swept through the German Fleet with the replacement of Admiral von Pohl in January 1916 by Admiral Reinhard Scheer. This gave the High Seas Fleet a vigorous leader who sought to provoke the Grand Fleet into a tactical error which might enable a significant number of British ships to be destroyed, either by submarine ambush or by a partial fleet action. Scheer recognised that the Grand Fleet was simply too strong to take on in a head-to-head battle. At this time Scheer had 16 dreadnoughts, 8 pre-dreadnoughts, 5 battlecruisers, 11 light cruisers and 61 destroyers to face Jellicoe's 28 dreadnoughts, 9 battlecruisers, 8 cruisers, 26 light cruisers and 73 destroyers. Neither side knew it, but *'Der Tag'* – the decisive battle that would decide the naval war – was almost upon them.

Battle of Jutland

Scheer's plan for action was hardly subtle. In many ways it resembled the approach of the earlier 'tip and run' attacks on the east coast of England. Originally Scheer planned a raid by Hipper's battlecruisers on Sunderland, intending to lead Beatty's Battlecruiser Fleet into first a submarine trap and then into the arms of the whole High Seas Fleet. Problems with the Zeppelin reconnaissance arrangements forced a change in plan and instead, Hipper was directed to swoop down on Allied light forces and shipping that might be abroad in the Skagerrak Straits between Norway and Sweden. This was an exercise in 'trailing his coat' in front of Beatty, trying to provoke an intemperate response. Unbeknown to Scheer, the British were still decoding German signals and the full might of the Grand Fleet actually put to sea before the High Seas Fleet had even left harbour. However, this would be the last intelligence triumph for the Admiralty, as a series of misunderstandings then left Jellicoe and Beatty with the impression that the High Seas Fleet was not really at sea. As the fleets converged on the afternoon of 31 May 1916, no one knew the real situation.

The British Battlecruiser Fleet should have been more than capable of dealing with the German battlecruisers (*Lutzow, Seydlitz, Moltke, Derfflinger* and *Von der Tann*). Beatty, in his flagship the *Lion,* was accompanied by the 1st Battlecruiser Squadron (*Princess Royal, Queen Mary* and

Tiger), the 2nd Battlecruiser Squadron (*New Zealand* and *Indefatigable*) and the super-dreadnoughts of the 5th Battle Squadron (*Barham*, *Valiant*, *Warspite* and *Malaya*), which was standing in for the 3rd Battlecruiser Squadron (temporarily attached to the Grand Fleet for extra gunnery practice). But when Hipper and Beatty's outlying forces made contact at 14.28, a combination of poor initial dispositions combined with signalling confusion led Beatty to lose contact with the 5th Battle Squadron, which was left nearly 10 miles behind. Nevertheless, Beatty still outnumbered Hipper by six to five battlecruisers. As Beatty attempted to close with the Germans, Hipper turned his ships onto a south-easterly course, leading Beatty straight under the guns of the High Seas Fleet.

The British guns were of slightly higher calibre, but nagging problems with range-finding meant that the Germans were able to open fire first at 15.48. In fact, the British gunnery was not good, generally shooting well over their targets, while the German battlecruisers soon began to make their mark. At the rear of the respective lines the *Von der Tan* was engaging the *Indefatigable*. Just before 16.00, Leading Signaller Charles Falmer was ordered up the *Indefatigable*'s mast to clear some signal flags which had become entangled.

> We closed nearer the enemy and the message came up for someone to go aloft to clear the flags. I went up, took my sea boots off first, climbed out the foretop, went up the 'Jacob's Ladder' right to the very top. I unfurled the flag and I sat on the wireless yard looking around, naturally watching the firing.[11]
>
> Leading Signaller Charles Falmer, HMS *Indefatigable*, 2nd Battlecruiser Squadron

At 16.02, two salvos ripped into the *Indefatigable*, penetrating her magazines and triggering a mammoth explosion. Falmer was still up in the foretop when disaster struck.

> There was a terrific explosion aboard the ship – the magazines went. I saw the guns go up in the air just like matchsticks – 12-inch guns they were – bodies and everything. She was beginning to settle down. Within half a minute the ship turned right over and she was gone. I was 180-foot up and I was thrown well clear of the ship, otherwise I would have been sucked under. I was practically unconscious, turning over really. At last I came on top of the water. When I came up there

was another fellow named 'Jimmy' Green and we got a piece of wood. He was on one end and I was on the other end.[12]

Leading Signaller Charles Falmer, HMS *Indefatigable*, 2nd Battlecruiser Squadron

Shortly afterwards Green was killed by a shell and Falmer was all alone, surrounded by the flotsam and jetsam that was all that was left of the *Indefatigable*. He was one of just two survivors; in all 1,017 men of the ship's company had been killed.

Behind the battlecruisers, the four mighty *Queen Elizabeth* super-dreadnoughts of the 5th Battle Squadron were struggling to catch up. At last, by assiduously cutting corners, they managed to close sufficiently to open up on the rear of the German line, and this accurate fire would soon begin to have an effect.

Meanwhile, towards the front of the line the *Queen Mary* was under heavy fire from both the *Seydlitz* and *Derrflinger*. One of her turrets was penetrated and she blew up in an utterly cataclysmic explosion.

The *Queen Mary* – we heard the explosion but what it was I couldn't say. Her fore turret started to dip and the forward part of the ship. She dipped down that way and was turning over. As she got abreast of us she was right over. There was a few men that had jumped off the stern into the water onto a Carley float. She went up with a terrific bang, there was debris flying all over the place. The gunnery lieutenant said, 'Look out for debris!' And we did.[13]

Able Seaman Alfred Blackmore, HMS *New Zealand*

As these dramatic events were unfolding, the British destroyers went into action between the lines, the action swirling round too fast for anyone to assess and control. Amid the fray the *Seydlitz* was torpedoed and unluckier destroyers were left crippled between the fleets. Petty Officer George Betsworth was aboard the doomed *Nestor*.

We got tin fish at them and our gunner reported, 'We got a torpedo left in the tube, Sir, shall we get it off?' Bingham said, 'Right, turn 16!' to get this other fish off. As we turned, one of their light cruisers got a 6-inch right into our forward boiler room. This shell came right through, hit the whaler, through the steel deck, into the boiler room to the bottom of the ship and exploded. I was up to my neck in salt water, boiling water – all the lot! We couldn't do much about that. Norman Roberts, the engineer officer, went down the engine room and found out then that they'd got a packet in the engine room. Then they got the range proper – the engine room, the bridge – most of it was in the fore part of the ship. The sub-lieutenant left the bridge, went aft and ditched some books, he knew it was going down. When he got down there they got a couple right on the aft part and blew her stern right off. She began to sink. 'Abandon ship!' I went over and saw some of the lads come up out of the engine room, most of them got away in a whaler and a few Carley floats. This kid, he'd only just joined the ship before we left the Forth, he was smothered in blood and silicate cotton from the lagging of the steam pipes. It was awful to see this kid, he hadn't been left home five minutes – quick bit of training and sent to us. I got hold of him in all the hurry and scramble and this kid died in my arms. I couldn't do anything else with him. Everybody else had more or less left the ship. I thought, 'Well, there's only one thing for it now – over the side!' I dived over and swam away from the ship or what was left of it as she was gradually sinking. I swam out to a bit of sunken wreckage I spotted, it must have been the bow of a boat or something. I got hold of this and stopped on that. They didn't pick me up till midnight.[14]

Petty Officer George Betsworth, HMS *Nestor*, 13th Destroyer Flotilla

Throughout the destroyer engagement, Beatty and his battlecruisers were unknowingly drawing closer to the High Seas Fleet. Hipper had performed his reconnaissance and entrapment role to perfection. It seemed that Scheer's plan to ensnare an inferior section of the Grand Fleet was about to reach fruition.

Scouting ahead of Beatty was the 2nd Light Cruiser Squadron. At around 16.30 they sighted the High Seas Fleet coming up from the south. Now everything changed. Beatty was no longer the pursuer; he had become the prey. But he, too, had a secret, for Scheer and Hipper were unaware that the Grand Fleet was also at sea. The roles had reversed, and it was now Beatty's task to lead the Germans under Jellicoe's massed guns. At 16.40, Beatty issued the signal for an about turn to the north. Due to yet another confusion over signals, the 5th Battle

Squadron delayed their turn until they were under heavy fire and only then turned to take up position at the rear of the battlecruisers.

As the super-dreadnoughts ran to the north they were exposed to threatening concentrations of fire, but their magnificent armoured protection kept them safe from any real harm. At the same time, their huge 15-inch shells were causing significant damage to the German battlecruisers and to the leading dreadnoughts that opposed them. All the while they were drawing closer to the six columns of Jellicoe's dreadnoughts, which were steaming down from the north. Ahead of the Grand Fleet and screening their approach from the Germans were the 1st Cruiser Squadron and the 3rd Battlecruiser Squadron. But as Jellicoe stood on the bridge of his flagship the *Iron Duke,* he had little or no clue as to where the German fleet actually was. It was only at 18.14 that Beatty signalled their location. Jellicoe reacted immediately. He deployed his vast fleet of twenty-four dreadnoughts on to the port column, hoping to gain the best of the fading light for his gunners and to 'cross the T' of the German line. This would enable his whole line to fire at the Germans, while none but the forward guns of their leading ships would be in a position to return fire.

> That I suggest to you was a tremendous moment in anybody's life. At last the two main fleets were in action. I remember thinking to myself, 'Well, we've lost a lot and we're going to lose more. But we don't mind losing this and that as long as the two fleets meet.' This moment had arrived and there was a feeling of extraordinary relief – rather patriotic relief perhaps. It was absolutely wonderful to see the battleships opening fire. I thought, 'Well, this is the end!'[15]
>
> Midshipman John Ouvry, HMS *Tiger*, 1st Battlecruiser Squadron

Midshipman Brian de Courcy Ireland and the crew of the *Bellerophon* 'Q' Turret were making their last minute preparations to open fire.

> We thought, 'This is it, this really is something.' We weren't nervous, you'd got so much to do, you get on with the job and that occupies your mind. The shellroom and the magazine, opening everything up and getting it all ready, getting the first few rounds up into the gunhouse ready for loading. I was on this Dumaresq. It was a round metal thing with various things you could set the course and speed of

the ship on. What it did was you put on the course and speed of your ship; you then put on your estimated course and speed of whatever you were going to engage. You made some allowance for wind. The object of the thing was to work out the amount you had to deflect the guns to fire ahead of the ship you were engaging, so that by the time your shells reached her, she was there! All the data would either come from the bridge or from the captain of the turret who would give his estimations. I could stand up and have a look through the telescope and get my own idea. You'd be altering it the whole time you see, if your own ship altered course, or you thought the enemy had altered course, or increased or decreased in speed. It was very bad visibility – you could only get rough silhouettes. It was very worrying to try and guess their speed and course.[16]

Midshipman Brian de Courcy Ireland, HMS *Bellerophon*, 4th Battle Squadron

As the 5th Battle Squadron turned to join the Grand Fleet battle line there was a brief period when they had to pass through the concentrated fire of the High Seas Fleet at what would become known as 'Windy Corner'. In the course of this, the super-dreadnought *Warspite* was hit by a large number of shells. One shell damaged her steering and for a few terrible minutes the ship was left circling between the lines under heavy fire. Midshipman William Fell found it a terrifying experience.

There was the most monumental crump – it sounded like all the tin tea trays in the world – full of crockery – being dropped on our heads. The whole ship shook and rattled. We realised we'd been hit by something pretty big. From then onwards about every minute we caught a packet from somewhere: 'Crash! Rattle! Bump! Thump!' Eventually there was an even worse one than usual which knocked us all off our perches; we were up on stools doing these various plots. We were all knocked flat on our backs down onto the deck. I frankly don't know much of the next few minutes – I think we were dazed. Everything was in almost complete darkness. There was a faint guttering light over in one corner from the emergency lights, everything else was out – gone. Worst of all was the complete silence: no sounds of engines, no sounds of action, or anything going on at all. The most horrible silence except for swishing water. After a moment or two I noticed that down all the voicepipes was coming a good old sluice of water, squirting down into the Transmitting Room and we were slowly flooding up. I suppose we all began to come to at about the same time. Round the far side of the table were two young boys who had only joined the ship a week or two before, who were frightened. They were scared and beginning to whimper enough. Scurne climbed to his feet, went round the plotting table, took their two heads together and he went, 'Bang! Bang! Bang!' Well that sorted that one! Then we all began to get going, trying to do our jobs. Of course there was nothing coming down. This horrible silence got broken by the sound of engines again so that was much more hopeful and we got a few lamps going. At last Scurne climbed back to his voicepipe and called up to the foretop, 'What another one gone up – oh splendid!' He was talking up a smashed voicepipe to a mythical foretop and he restored morale completely down below. After that it was just a case of waiting. We waited for an hour and a half until we heard banging on the armoured hatches above us and somebody let us out. I didn't recognise the ship when I came out; she was just a shambles.[17]

Midshipman William Fell, HMS *Warspite*, 5th Battle Squadron

The wounded *Warspite* was ordered to return to port and made it safely back.

With the Grand Fleet deployed into line, the High Seas Fleet found themselves sailing into the path of total destruction. But even then there was one more catastrophe for the British battlecruisers to endure: the *Invincible*, the very first of its kind, found that speed could not make up for the lack of armour protection and she blew up at 18.34. Yet again, the thin armour of a British battlecruiser had been found wanting. The *Invincible* broke in two at the middle and the pieces protruded grotesquely from the waves.

I felt quite sure it was a German ship. So I passed to my 6-inch gun crews, 'The wreck of a German ship is now in view on the starboard side!' and the 6-inch crews gave a great cheer. Two minutes afterwards the signal bosun on our bridge rang me up. He said, 'Did you see that ship on the starboard side?' I said, 'Yes I did.' He said, 'Did you read the name of the ship on the stern?' I said, 'No.' He said, 'It was the *Invincible*!' I was terribly depressed.[18]

Midshipman John Ouvry, HMS *Tiger*, 1st Battlecruiser Squadron

Of the *Invincible* crew of 1,032 men, just six survived.

But this was scant relief to the High Seas Fleet, who found themselves in an awful situation, as shells rained down from the Grand Fleet. Scheer had to act quickly and ordered the splendidly named '*Gefechtwendung nach Steuerbord*' or battle turn to starboard – whereby each of his ships would turn individually, starting with the rearmost ship, followed by each ship in turn towards the front of the line. The effect of this was that the High Seas Fleet seemed to disappear into the misty haze. Jellicoe had no intention of following a dangerous foe into the mists, so he changed to a southerly course to place himself right across the line of the German retreat.

During this period the destroyers of the 12th Flotilla came across the badly damaged German destroyer *V48*. Like a pack of dogs they casually tore her to pieces. Watching from aboard HMS *Onslaught* was Able Seaman George Wainford.

> She'd been damaged, but she was still operative and firing her guns. So we engaged her. There was a couple of German seaman, despite the fact the ship was badly damaged, they were still firing their gun. I said to a pal of mine, 'God, I hope them blokes don't get killed! I feel really sorry for them.' Anyway she was sunk: we had to, she was still flying the German ensign and whether they were saved I don't know. You could see lots and lots of wreckage. I'll always remember the amount of dead fish there were floating about. I think they'd been killed by concussion when ships blew up. There was fish everywhere floating about on the surface.[19]
>
> Able Seaman George Wainford, HMS *Onslaught*, 12th Destroyer Flotilla

There were just three survivors from *V48*.

As the Grand Fleet settled on a southerly course, at around 19.10 Scheer's next manoeuvre led him straight back into the maw of the thundering guns of the Grand Fleet. Serious damage was inflicted on the leading German ships, but Scheer proved himself to be up to the crisis and at 19.03 he ordered his battlecruisers and destroyers to attack the British lines while his main fleet executed another '*Gefechtswendung*', to allow the main dreadnought fleet to escape. Shell after shell plunged down onto his already battered battlecruisers which, nevertheless, somehow stayed afloat. Then the German destroyers launched their torpedoes and Jellicoe turned sharply away rather than risk severe losses which would have handed victory to the Germans. Despite this, however, things looked bleak for the Germans, who still had the whole Grand Fleet between themselves and Wilhelmshaven. But night was falling.

With considerable determination, Scheer then headed directly for safety by the shortest feasible route. In doing so he passed astern of the main body of dreadnoughts and straight through the layered lines of British destroyers. A number of small-scale but increasingly deadly actions followed. The Grand Fleet had neglected night-action training and lacked shuttered searchlights or star shells to illuminate suspect vessels swiftly. This proved unfortunate. As the dark shapes of the German ships appeared out of the night, torrents of fire burst upon those British destroyers and cruisers unwise enough to ask for identification signals. Many officers did not understand what was going on; they wanted to leave the decision making to someone else. But worst of all, no one had the presence of mind to wireless contact reports to Jellicoe. They had held the High Seas Fleet within their grasp, but had let it slip through their fingers.

Aboard the *Onslaught*, Able Seaman George Wainford was involved in one of the final contacts, as the 12th Flotilla investigated a mysterious line of ships that had appeared ahead of them in the misty darkness.

> You could just see in the sea mist some big ships coming down. We thought they were our own ships. We went past them in the opposite direction. We didn't know what was going on. I was down by the torpedo tubes. My job as a torpedoman was to load the torpedoes into the tubes. There was a sort of derrick with a little chain on it. You lifted it up and you pushed it in, made certain that the warhead was on correctly and then the chief petty officer, he'd do the actual firing. You had to get a direct bearing on the ship with a direction-finder: you had to get the speed of your enemy, your own speed, the angle of the enemy, your angle – all coinciding – before you fired. He did all that. There was a pistol grip there and it was used to detonate a charge, which blew the torpedo out into the water and then the propeller started.[20]
>
> Able Seaman George Wainford, HMS *Onslaught*, 12th Destroyer Flotilla

Having belatedly realised the ships were German, they turned and attacked as a flotilla, partially covered by a smokescreen, but the *Onslaught* was badly hit by return fire.

> We fired our torpedoes and of course other ships in the flotilla did the same. There was a terrific explosion and a German ship blew up. 'Cor!' I said, 'We got her!' That was the *Pommern* we sank. The moment I said that, either one shell, or a salvo, hit our bridge. There was a terrific bang, and a fire started the port side of the foc'sle where all the hammocks underneath the foc'sle deck were stowed. You could hear a lot of crying and shouting. I went to go up there and Sub-Lieutenant Kemmis said, 'Where you going, Wainford?' I said, 'On the foc'sle, Sir, to help!' He said, 'Get down below and send a senior hand up here!' I gave a hand down below pulling out all the debris. I found out later that it was a bit of a shambles: the forward 4-inch gun and the upper part of the bridge was demolished. I saw one chap who was horribly wounded – his whole stomach was hanging out and he was trying to push it back.[21]
>
> Able Seaman George Wainford, HMS *Onslaught*, 12th Destroyer Flotilla

The shattered *Onslaught* was ordered to return to port. Their captain, Lieutenant Commander Arthur Onslow, had been mortally wounded and was taken below decks.

> The skipper[22] died in the crew's foc'sle, on the mess table. They laid him on there. I'll always remember his last words, he said, 'Is the ship all right?' I said, 'Yes, Sir, the ship's all right!' He said, 'I'll have a little sleep now then.' And that was it. I was there when he died.[23]
>
> Able Seaman George Wainford, HMS *Onslaught*, 12th Destroyer Flotilla

Despite rising seas the *Onslaught* made it back in safety.

On the morning of 1 June 1916, Jellicoe and the Grand Fleet woke to the fact that the High Seas Fleet had escaped. Although the Germans had been forced to scuttle the sinking battlecruiser *Lutzow* and the pre-dreadnought *Pommern* had been sunk, the fleet as a whole made it back to Wilhelmshaven. At first sight the Battle of Jutland seemed a defeat for the British, who had lost 3 battlecruisers, 3 armoured cruisers and 8 destroyers, while the Germans only lost 1 battlecruiser, 1 pre-dreadnought, 4 light cruisers and 5 destroyers. The British suffered 6,094 fatalities as opposed 2,551 German losses. There was a feeling of depression around the fleet as the Royal Navy collectively felt they had failed to deliver the 'knock-out blow' that their country expected from them. The British losses had been painful, exacerbated greatly by the calamitous explosions aboard the three battlecruisers. Had their German opponents blown up so easily the German casualties would have been much higher, for their losses were spread out among several very battered ships that only just managed to limp back to port.

A more realistic assessment of the battle shows that not only had the Germans totally failed in their main objective of significantly reducing the margin of superiority possessed by the Grand Fleet over the High Seas Fleet, but they would never again seriously contest the command of the seas. The main question of the naval war had been answered – and answered in Britain's favour. The Royal Navy had suffered painful losses, but they had more ships in harbour ready to join the fleet than they had lost in the battle: they would continue to exercise command of the seas around the globe beyond the North Sea.

On to Victory, 1916–1918

Scheer tried just once more to suck Jellicoe into a submarine and mine trap by attempting to carry out his original plan of bombarding Sunderland on 19 August 1916. Jellicoe was forewarned by Admiralty intelligence, but the ensuing sweeps proved abortive for both sides. In the aftermath, when Scheer realised from reports that he had once again unwittingly risked total disaster, he turned against the idea of further operations in the North Sea. All that was left to try was a renewal on 6 October 1916 of the attempt to strangle British sea lanes with unrestricted submarine warfare. With the U-boats unleashed for commerce raiding, they were not available for fleet operations, so the High Seas Fleet remained moribund in harbour. The morale of the fleet gradually leached away as the men realised that 'Der Tag' would never dawn.

The British struggled to understand and react to the lessons of the Jutland fighting: work was undertaken to improve armour protection and cordite anti-flash precautions were greatly improved; new more efficient armour-piercing shells were introduced; Jellicoe revised his tactical ideas to allow a slightly more flexible approach; and more emphasis was placed on the duty of all ships to accurately report and maintain contact with German ships. Jellicoe was posted to take over as First Sea Lord on 28 November 1916, but was replaced by Beatty who pursued almost exactly the same policies as his predecessor. He did, however, attempt to encourage still more flexibility among his subordinate commanders, but he never had the chance to test his ideas in battle.

THERE WERE MANY DIFFERENT ROLES that the Royal Navy was called upon to perform: many were routine but that did not diminish their importance. For example, the English Channel had to be kept open to preserve the logistical lifeline to the BEF on the Western Front. Ordinary Seaman Sid Bell soon got used to the routine of night patrols aboard the destroyer HMS *Mermaid*.

> The Dover patrol! We went out from Folkestone, to the lightship in mid-Channel then across to Cap Gris Nez, then patrol back again. You relieved other ships as you carried on with your patrol. On watch you did so much on lookout, so much as messenger, or standby. The officer used to be standing up on the bridge and I used to be lookout on the port side, with the depth charge lookout on the starboard side. You reported from right ahead, right round aft on your side. You used to keep sweeping with your glasses or your eyes – sometimes you could distinguish better with your own eyes. You reported everything: a bit of wood floating, a box or anything, it didn't matter what it was; you reported it, 'Object on the port bow, Sir!' If you could distinguish what it was then, 'Ship, one funnel two masts!' In seamanship you were taught picking out different classes of ships. My action station was on the 12-pounder on the foc'sle. You used to get ready, clear your gun, get ammunition and the racks ready. When fired, the gun recoiled, the breechloader opened the breech, the gun was loaded again, the block was shut and he used to shout, 'Ready!' The gun was loaded and ready for firing. There'd been a lot of trouble with German U-boats getting through the Channel from Ostend and Zeebrugge. They used to come down at high tide, come over the

minefield. Admiral Bacon he made a barrage net across the Channel.
Every so often these drifters and trawlers were stations. They'd put a
calcium flare over the side; it used to light the Channel up and the
patrolling destroyers could see. You went so far and you had to turn.
We had just turned and were coming back from Cap Gris Nez when
the officer of the watch says to the leading hand on the searchlight,
'Switch on, Turner!' When the searchlight flickered on there was a
great big German submarine right alongside of us! You could throw
a stone at it! There was one of the German sailors on the upper deck
with a white jumper on! 'Action stations!' We slewed around and
the submarine dived. When we got to where he dived you could feel
our bows rising, we just skimmed over the top of him. We went past.
The signalman sent the Very light up and all the other destroyers
converged – the *Manly*, the *Meteor*, *Manxman* – all of them came in.
When we intercepted him he'd dived, and with other ships coming
he dived to get clear. The Channel isn't very deep you know! Not long
after we heard a thump – we felt it. The submarine crashed into the
minefield beneath the barrage net and that was the thud we heard.[24]

Ordinary Seaman Sid Bell, HMS *Mermaid*, 6th Destroyer Flotilla

The task of the patrols was unending.

The Royal Navy had their own submarines, but their work was both
hard and dangerous. This was particularly the case with the 'K' class of
large submarines intended to operate alongside the Grand Fleet under
battle conditions. Their very size – they were 338 feet long – restricted
their speed, so that their oil-fired steam turbines could only give them
a maximum of 19 knots; too slow to accompany the fleet. To some
extent this rendered the whole class redundant. Furthermore, they were
extremely difficult to handle whether on the surface or submerged. They
had a disastrous service record and of the eighteen constructed, six sank
in accidents. Wireless Operator William Piggott served aboard the K5,
which was based at Rosyth.

Everything was damp, every nut and bolt dripping water. You
always felt damp, it's a wonder you never got rheumatism! When
you opened a tin of biscuits if you left it till the next day they went
mouldy. If you left a piece of bread out when you went to sea, five
hours after you got out it began to go mouldy. There's forty-seven

men breathing with no outlet when you're underneath so there's damp everywhere. It was a very sparse life, it really was, a terrible life. Two heaters: one in the stokers' mess and one in the ordinary mess where I was aft. You were at your diving station and that's it – you don't move, not when you're underneath. You can't go wandering about on a submarine when you're underneath – you'd tip the boat – you were just balanced. When you stood up you were always nearly bumping your head. You had a diesel engine running all the time when you were on the surface to charge the battery – there was a terrific noise all the time – you couldn't hear. The turbines were quiet underwater. Always the smell of oil fuel – it was on the bare steel plates.[25]

Wireless Operator William Piggott, HMS *K5*, Grand Fleet

When they were ashore people could recognise the submariners by the stench of oil that clung to their uniforms.

The Royal Navy also launched occasional special operations, of which one of the most daring was the Zeebrugge raid of 22 April 1918, designed to make it difficult or impossible for German submarines to use the port as a base. The plan involved sinking three blockships filled with concrete (the *Thetis*, *Intrepid* and *Iphigenia*) across the navigable harbour channels and the Bruges Canal that led to the U-boat base. An obsolescent specially protected cruiser, the *Vindictive*, was to launch a diversionary attack, landing a party of marines to attack the Zeebrugge harbour mole. Meanwhile two submarines – the C1 and C2 – had been filled with high explosives, ready to run into the viaduct that connected the mole to the mainland. It was hoped that this would prevent the arrival of German reinforcements.

The specialist ships and covering light forces made their way across the Channel, their final approach then being covered by a special smokescreen.

Before entering the harbour it was my job to open up for artificial fog to cover all our movements. When all the bottles are open this fog is very dense, you could hardly see through it. The captain steered away from the *Thetis* towards the canal although visibility was nil. We just had to feel our way, knowing what the distance was, we had to estimate the position of the channel. The captain nosed the bows of the ship up the canal, ran into a barge, sank it and then manoeuvred his ship in an endeavour to block the channel.[26]

Petty Officer H. Clegg, HMS *Iphigenia*

The smokescreen may have blinded the ships to some extent, but the German batteries could still see well enough to open heavy fire on the blockships. The *Thetis* was scuttled prematurely, but the others managed to sink themselves in the canal itself.

We got into position and the order was given to abandon ship, all hands to repair to upper deck. The captain then blew the bottom out of the ship. She sank, and as she sank she was a solid wall of concrete, the ship was absolutely filled with concrete – everything except the engines and the boilers were taken out and the remainder of the ship was filled with concrete. I don't think anything could have moved it. Now the difficulty was getting away. We only had one lifeboat, as the other one had been smashed to smithereens. The fog was still very dense and we were subject to terrific gunfire from all quarters – heavy machine-gun fire, shells were bursting all round us. How the lot of us weren't killed I don't know. Eventually we got over the side into the cutter. Our job then was to row that boat out of the harbour and we started to pull away from the ship. Pulling a heavily laden cutter with only a few oars was a difficult task.[27]

Petty Officer H. Clegg, HMS *Iphigenia*

In the event, the blockships failed to fully obstruct the canal, and the Germans were soon able to create a channel which enabled them to get their U-boats in and out of Zeebrugge. As such, the operation was a complete failure. Yet the truth should never be allowed to spoil a good story and the British achieved a considerable propaganda coup over their portrayal of the raid, boosting the dramatic effect by awarding some eight Victoria Crosses.

IN ALL MY INTERVIEWS on the naval war, one story stands out for me in illustrating the true horror of men trapped below decks as their ship slips slowly beneath the waves. Sub-Lieutenant Brian de Courcy Ireland was serving aboard the destroyer *Pellew* when she was hit by a torpedo in the North Sea on 19 July 1918.

> We were escorting a squadron of minelayers and they were laying a barrage of mines across the top end of the North Sea to try and close it off to German ships. I had the morning watch and I'd come down and had my breakfast in the wardroom. Then I went to my cabin for a bit of shut-eye because I'd got the afternoon watch, and told the steward to call me at a quarter to twelve so that I could have lunch before going on watch. So I was actually asleep on watch. I think the torpedo probably struck the starboard propeller which was just a little bit further aft of where my bunk was. I didn't know much about it – there was a hell of a bang! When I sort of collected myself, I was on the deck with most of the cabin on top of me. I lay there for a bit, then I thought, 'Well, I don't think I'm hurt really' and so I struggled up. We – me and the chief engineer – didn't know quite what had happened. We couldn't get out: the hatch had jammed. The explosion had set off one of the depth charges on the stern and that made an awful mess of the upper deck and stern of the ship – we were trapped – no other way out! We were the end cabin, that bulkhead seemed to be more or less holding, but she was settling and most of the stern had gone. She was on fire – abaft us, down below somewhere, some petrol stowed for the motorboat had caught fire – I could hear it. I was frightened it would go to the after magazine and so I tried to flood the magazine, but the two valves were completely smashed up and wouldn't work. Then of course the water was rising; the cabins were getting flooded coming from below somewhere. That was very unpleasant because an oil tank had burst as well, so it was half oil and half water. More or less pitch black. I was trying to get out – she was sinking. Then we heard them working above us on the hatch. I yelled out, 'After magazine! I'm trying to flood it and I can't!' That raised a laugh because there was no after magazine! It had all gone; gone to the bottom! About then we felt her lifting a bit because the stern fell off. The engine room was next to our flat and we could hear them shoring up the engine room bulkhead. That was holding. By the time they got us out the water was up to mid-chest.[28]

Sub-Lieutenant Brian de Courcy Ireland, HMS *Pellew*

The crew managed to put the fire out and they were towed back by six tugs the 100 miles to Aberdeen. They had been incredibly lucky: despite losing their whole stern, only three had been wounded. Young de Courcy Ireland had lost his sea chest and all the rest of his possessions, but at least he had survived. Yet the experience certainly left its mark.

> I never saw a doctor. They just said, 'Are you OK?' and I rather foolishly said, 'Yes!' I didn't feel OK. I think I'd swallowed oil fuel so I was sick. They gave me a week's leave then they appointed me straight away to another destroyer – the *Westcott*. Then I had an awful shock because when the buzz got round, all my buddies in the other destroyers all came on board to hear all about it – and I found I didn't know who they were, their names or anything. My memory had simply gone. They realised something was wrong and they all shoved off. I didn't know what the hell to do so I went down to my cabin and there was a young probationary surgeon, a medical student, he'd seen this and he came down, had a chat and said, 'I think it's delayed shock.' Which it was. I couldn't remember my youth. It was funny, it came and went; I had a couple of blackouts, passed out. I just took it – I got away with it. It got better.[29]
>
> Sub-Lieutenant Brian de Courcy Ireland, HMS *Pellew*

When the war finally staggered to a close in 1918, the High Seas Fleet mutinied rather than emerge to fight. The Royal Navy had achieved total victory without having triumphed in any great naval battle. Their success was marked by the humiliating surrender of some seventy German ships under the terms of the Armistice agreements on 21 November 1918. Able Seaman George Wainford saw it all from aboard the *King George V*.

> We went out and met the German fleet. The Grand Fleet was to the port and starboard of them. The *King George V* was to the port flank. Our instructions were, 'Nobody allowed on open deck unless on duty. No standing about. Everybody's got to be below decks, everybody's got to be at their station!' Well my station was in the engine room! But there was a flat above the engine room where I knew there was a little port hole. I went up there and I could see through this port hole everything that went on. There was all these German seamen – there

was no discipline – waving flags, bits of uniform, old shirts and that, trying to attract attention. Nobody took a bit of notice from aboard our ships – there was no response, everything was shipshape in a proper naval fashion. All their guns were trained fore-and-aft; all our guns were trained in on them! The most imposing thing I saw in the war, all these ships, the German battleships, battlecruisers, then the cruisers, the torpedo-boat destroyers, submarines, a lot of auxiliary stuff, all coming up. There was our ships each side of them – like sheepdogs – making sure they went the right way.[30]

Able Seaman George Wainford, HMS *King George V*, 2nd Battle Squadron

8

LIFE IN THE TRENCHES

THE TRENCHES BOUNDED THE HORIZONS of the infantry, restricting them to a worm's eye view glimpsed over the sandbags. The classic configuration had a wide sandbag and earth parapet measuring about 3 feet high and 6 feet thick in front of the trench, which was at least 3 feet 6 inches wide, with behind it a similar parados. The trench would be over 6 feet deep, so it had to have a fire step 2 feet high and around 18 inches wide for the soldier to stand on when firing over the parapet at an approaching enemy. Where possible the walls were revetted with wire, timber or corrugated iron to prevent collapse, while drains and duckboards attempted to hold back the water. A further sophistication was a system of 'fire-bays' with intervening traverses of solid earth which minimised the impact of shells bursting directly in the trench and reduced the occupying troops' vulnerability to enfilading fire. As the war wore on there were a variety of developments: early on, barbed wire was erected to prevent a 'rush' attack, communication trenches were carved out to allow safe approach and a plethora of support and reserve lines appeared. In the end there would be a complex trench system layered back for several miles, all defended by rifles, machine guns and massed artillery fire – the most deadly form of military hardware, responsible for over 60 per cent of total casualties. Between the lines was No Man's Land, the stretch of ground that both linked and divided the trench systems of the opposing forces.

When the men of the BEF first took to their trenches they little guessed they would still be there four years later. But very soon a way of life developed, which although there were many incremental changes, was still recognisable by the end of the war. Just digging the trenches was an amazing engineering effort, involving copious amounts of hard physical labour which few men escaped, especially in the pioneer battalions.

> It was like digging a grave! When we were on digging you always had 6 foot long, 6 feet deep, and 3 feet across. The NCOs had these measurement rods. It was usually soft ground unless you were a bit unlucky getting on some rocks. We used to help one another. There was a chap who had a shop selling musical instruments – you ought to see his fingers – he never knew what a spade was. So you helped him out, you see. There was two of you on a stretch of 12 feet, so you had to be getting at it a bit.[1]
>
> Sergeant Alfred West, 1/1st Monmouthshire Regiment

Sandbags packed tight full with earth were a crucial part of trench warfare. Bonded together in much the same pattern as traditional brickwork, they granted a flexibility of design and strength not possible with loose earth, and were much less likely to collapse through shell bursts or wet conditions. Indeed, in flat lowland areas afflicted by poor drainage, sandbags would be layered up to form thick breastworks in front and behind to create an artificial trench which stood above ground level.

In the front lines, especially early on in the war, it was unusual for the ordinary British soldier to have any kind of deep dugout; most of them just dug into the side of the trench and did the best they could.

> The ordinary dugout you dug into the side and then put a cover over the top. There was tons of metal and tin knocking about, corrugated iron, stick that over the top. We used to fill the sandbags and put them on top of this dugout. You had a blanket over the front to stop gas. They'd also cut you seats, going round, through cutting the earth

out. It might hold five men, might hold two men, it just depends. Some were what we called cubby holes, dug into the side of the trench just to hold two men. You'd crawl in! If you walked along the trench at night you'd come across somebody's feet! He'd be sleeping in his cubby hole and his feet were out in the trench.[2]

Private Donald Price, 20th Royal Fusiliers

In summer many of the men would just sleep out in the open, lying all along the firestep.

When a battalion first arrived in the front they were attached to an experienced regular unit for a few days to learn the ropes. Once they had settled down, then the routines of trench life enfolded them. If they were collectively to master the business of maintaining armies of men outdoors in the proverbial 'holes in the ground' for days, weeks and years on end, then certain things had to be done, various difficulties overcome. One obvious problem was the necessity to supply the men with enough sustenance to keep them fit for the task at hand. The amount of foodstuffs eaten by the assembled millions of men of the BEF was almost inconceivable and represented an industrial-scale harvesting of provisions from all over the world. The official ration amounts were clearly laid out and added up to a total of between 4,193 calories (if fresh food was available) and 4,111 calories (when it was only feasible to provide preserved meats, biscuits and dried vegetables). Where possible a battalion would try to locate its field cookers somewhere close to the line to allow one hot meal a day. The dixies of food, normally stews, would be placed in a hay box lined with straw or hay which acted as an insulator to keep the food warm. But operational difficulties meant that it was far more often tinned rations that would be collected by the company quartermaster sergeants, who would then have to organise ration parties to carry the food to the men in the front line.

You had to have a strength record of all the platoons and sections. You had to make up the rations: you would draw the rations from the regimental quartermaster sergeant according to your strength. We'd have a sandbag for each section and they could sort it out themselves. When you've done all that the transport would assemble at night, your sandbags would be put onto the limbers and you had to walk with your limber up to the line. When you got up to the dump, the carrying parties would come down from your own company and they would carry the stuff up. You would go up with the ration party: take any mail and newspapers there happened to be; you would see the company sergeant major; see if there were any letters to collect; see the company commander; get a list of any casualties. Then in the early hours of the morning, sling your rifle over your shoulder and get yourself back again to the transport lines.[3]

Quartermaster Sergeant George Harbottle, 1/6th Northumberland Fusiliers

The ration parties would stumble along the communications trenches.

The quartermaster's group would bring the rations up in a sandbag by night. There'd be a whisper over the top, 'Rations, boys!' The sandbag would be there. There couldn't have been more than nine or ten in my section – a couple of loaves of bread, bully beef and Maconochie's. You could always tell when there was a load of casualties because instead of being four to a loaf there'd be two to a loaf. Everything was cold because we couldn't cook.[4]

Private Ivor Watkins, 15th Welsh Regiment

One eagerly awaited ration was the tea. The soldiers made a veritable cult of tea, drinking it with condensed milk and lashings of sugar. It is perhaps not surprising in the bleak environment of the trenches that any comforting hot drink was to be treasured.

Cold food was the norm for many troops in the front line. One staple of their daily diet was the standard army biscuit.

Always plenty of biscuits: about 3 inches square and half an inch thick. They were as hard as nails! You had to get a stone and break it down into small pieces. Then you'd soak it with water or tea. These ship's biscuits were worth having; everybody carried them. If you ran short you could always say, 'Have you got a ship's biscuit?' And somebody would always have an extra one, there were always plenty. More than a standby, they were a staple food.[5]

Sergeant Jack Dorgan, 1/7th Northumberland Fusiliers

Dorgan was being charitable in his nomenclature, for most men referred to them as 'dog biscuits' and with considerable justification!

The other most commonly remembered of the foodstuffs issued was the ubiquitous corned beef, better known then as bully beef. One of the things that most linked soldiers of the Great War with my own undistinguished student existence was the near-universal difficulty encountered in opening Fray Bentos corned beef tins when the 'key' was lost or broken. We used to turn to a humble kitchen knife, but Great War soldiers frequently went a step further! It was amazing how many men I interviewed had injured themselves on this relatively mundane task in amid all the bedlam of the battlefields.

> We had a tin of bully beef. At the side of this thing was a key which you used to turn the top off. Mine didn't act and I got this jack knife to open this tin. Unfortunately it slipped and my hand was jagged – see this – it's still there! A great jag and of course I bled like a pig. The boys bandaged me up.[6]
>
> Private Donald Price, 20th Royal Fusiliers

There were other tinned foods which would be quickly warmed through on a brazier or Tommy cooker. Among these was Maconochie's – a meat and vegetable stew of variable quality – or pork and beans, which consisted of a tin of baked haricot beans into which a somewhat unappetizing lump of fatty pork had been placed. Tinned bacon was popular, for although it looked unpleasant it tasted all right when it was fried up, and the fat was used to give a bit of flavouring to the biscuits. With mass catering on this scale the choice open to the soldiers was bound to be almost non-existent, but they did get fed with enough to maintain their health and military efficiency, which was all that really counted to the army.

With the prevalence of tinned food, one curious partial indication of a unit's overall character in action was its chosen method of disposing of the thousands of empty tin cans. In the best units they were generally incinerated, buried or even stored and then removed to the rear areas.

> We collected the rubbish and buried it in a shell hole at the back. Some units didn't seem to bother and they threw the empty tins over the wire. That's where you got your rats roaming around at night feeding in the tins. We were instructed and always told to bury your rubbish.[7]
>
> Private Horace Calvert, 4th Grenadier Guards

Certainly less conscientious men had a rather more casual approach.

> When we'd emptied out jam tins we used to throw them over the top – in front of us – between us and Jerry. If Jerry was coming they rattled the cans – it was quite full of cans. It told us if anybody was moving about.[8]
>
> Private George Ashurst, 2nd Lancashire Fusiliers

In this Ashurst also exposes the fact that at this time his unit were not seeking to dominate No Man's Land by aggressive patrolling. This may have been understandable, but it was strictly against the instructions from higher command who wished to prevent the line 'going soft'.

There is no doubt that the casual or inefficient disposal of food tins and uneaten rations also helped attract unwelcome visitors. Rats could become a real nuisance, scavenging in among the detritus of No Man's Land and as often as not venturing into the trenches.

> The following day's rations came up about midnight and each man had his share, which he put in his haversack which he hung on the wall. We used to put our bayonets through the wall of the trench and hang our haversacks on that. That didn't stop these rats, which would run along, drop on to the haversack, eat their way through the top and then consume the food. I thought it was adding insult to injury when two of them fell fighting one another over the last bit of my next day's rations – they came through a hole in the bottom of my haversack on to my face.[9]
>
> Private Harold Hayward, 12th Gloucestershire Regiment

The rats were not the universal pest portrayed in some accounts, but some areas were more seriously afflicted than others. One sector liberally endowed with rats was alongside the Yser Canal near Boesinghe to the north of Ypres. Private Horace Calvert had moved into a reasonably comfortable dugout in the canal banks which was deemed capable of holding eight or nine men. There was one drawback.

> There were holes in the corners where rats came in. The first night we were hoping to get a good night's sleep – somebody shouted out, 'There's rats!' We woke up and there were rats all over the place, they were after the food. We had to get some candles and in the

candlelight we took turns to sit up with an old entrenching tool handle. Every time we heard them, 'Thud!'[10]

Private Horace Calvert, 4th Grenadier Guards

A horrible thought lingering at the back of many soldiers' minds was that the rats had recently been feasting on corpses; it was not a pleasant image.

If anybody had to be buried, it wasn't long before you could see where they'd been at each end of the grave going down to the body. They would eat human flesh if they'd the chance and that didn't go down very well if it was one of your pals who'd just been buried. They were loathsome were rats. They'd every facility there, because it was a charnel house.[11]

Private Horace Calvert, 4th Grenadier Guards

THE DAY IN THE TRENCHES always began with the morning 'Stand To' in case the Germans should attempt to use the half-light just before dawn to launch a surprise attack. Early in the war this was the most common time chosen, although in later years assault times became far more unpredictable.

Activities of every description stopped entirely an hour before daylight. There was no whistle blown, no signals given, but quietly every working party finished what they were doing, every patrol was brought back into the trench, all of the sentry groups were put on the alert. That was called 'Stand To!' Over the whole of the front-line trenches there was a silence. In that hour you just stood there quietly, every man out, officers and men all in the front line, bayonets fixed, one in the breech and an ample supply of ammunition for whatever might occur.[12]

Sergeant Jack Dorgan, 1/7th Northumberland Fusiliers

This gave officers and NCOs the chance to visit their men and ensure that all was well. The day proper would begin with breakfast, and the men would then usually begin cleaning their Lee Enfield rifles ready for inspection.

You had to clean your rifle, because that was the only protection you had really. So you made sure that it was clean, oiled and working – that you had five rounds in the magazine. Made sure that it was in good order.[13]

Private Horace Calvert, 4th Grenadier Guards

The men then spent their day attending to the routine tasks designated to them by their officers, or more often their NCOs. The role of the sergeants in maintaining discipline and general good order was absolutely crucial in the British Army.

I always think that a good NCO is the backbone of any regiment. From a corporal right up to regimental sergeant major. They've been through the ranks, they know the problems you can face; they also know more about life than the officer, who has probably been brought up with a silver spoon. They can give you instructions and confidence which the officers couldn't. You've got more trust in the sergeant with you than the officer above you. Because you see more of him, you're with him more and you trust him more.[14]

Private Horace Calvert, 4th Grenadier Guards

When George Ashurst was made a sergeant while serving with the 16th Lancashire Fusiliers later in the war he was certainly very confident in his own role and inclined to be somewhat critical of his officers.

The men preferred me any time to the officers. They believed in me – they'd have followed me anywhere, but they wouldn't have followed the officers anywhere, you know. They could see I was more used to the damned job and I knew what I was doing. Some of the officers had just come out – they didn't. There was quite a lot of cowardice amongst the officers. Quite a lot. Not doing their duty, palming it off to somebody else. I've been out on night patrol, crawling about in No Man's Land. I've had an officer's flask of whisky in my pocket – but he should have been there with the whisky – he should have been there with me. I used to go and do the patrol and he used to hand my report in. It was better really than him coming with us, because he'd only be a damned nuisance. He'd be windy, more windy than the men probably. That war was fought with NCOs not officers. There were some good officers, right enough, but there were some poor officers too.[15]

Sergeant George Ashurst, 16th Lancashire Fusiliers

However, some NCOs were detested by their men. Private Edward Race certainly loathed a bullying sergeant that he encountered in the 18th Durham Light Infantry. He was evidently not alone in this.

They blew the bugle for breakfast and we just used to go ordinary, you know! When we got to the canteen, this sergeant was standing there and he says, 'Come on, you're not properly dressed, go back and get dressed, get your shoes cleaned!' We had to go back. As a rule you had free time off, for writing letters, if you could find a river you could go and have a soak in the river. Well he wouldn't allow that – he had you on parade, forming fours, rifle drill. Hey – he's for it! They were going to get him when he went up the line. Oh aye, I'd have shot him if I'd had the chance! Harry Pattinson said to him, 'You know what, you might be in charge now but when you go up the line, you'll find that we are in charge – not you!' He said, 'Are you threatening me?' Harry said, 'No, I'm not threatening you!' We went up, the Germans attacked and we had to counter-attack. Harry Pattinson said, 'Now, you take charge, Sir!' The sergeant said, 'I don't know what to do! You take charge, there's my stripes!' Harry says, 'I don't want your stripes!' He said, 'I'm dead scared, I didn't think it was like this!' A lad called Kelly, he was the oldest soldier, he took charge. We never heard from the sergeant again, they found him dead. They didn't know how he died – but all the company knew how he died – and they knew who did it! Kelly told us himself. He followed him back and said, 'You've got a yellow streak!' The sergeant turned round, pulled his revolver out and Kelly just shot him![16]

Private Edward Race, 18th Durham Light Infantry

A great deal depended on the individual character of an NCO and there were as many different types of NCO as there are personality types. Oral history shows that they weren't all loved or hated; it all depended on how they behaved, the overall morale of the unit and the situation they were facing collectively.

The status of the subalterns, particularly the second lieutenants, was a moot point, for although they had a leadership role, they were also effectively officers under training. Their platoon sergeant was expected to exert a kindly and wise overseeing eye to tactfully prevent them from making mistakes born of inexperience. This could be a difficult relationship if the officer was arrogant or the sergeant tactless. But generally speaking this time-honoured system worked, with the officer being schooled until he was ready to take over the 'real' command of his platoon – at which point he was often promoted. As the subalterns were expected to lead their men into battle, the casualty rates among junior officers were terrifyingly high.

There were clear class issues evident in the selection of officers. At the start of the war a large number of officers were drawn from public schools. But as the war took its heavy toll, the strata of society from which officers were drawn was slowly widened. First, more officers were commissioned who originated in grammar schools, the world of commerce and clerical personnel. Then experienced NCOs were being commissioned, and by 1918 the whole character of the officers' mess had changed radically.

Throughout the war the men generally accepted that their officers would have the benefits of superior conditions of service. Officers would almost always have access to a proper dugout, often an alcove dug out from the company headquarters.

> The dugouts were very good, deep with good stairways down.
> I imagine they were built by miners because they were so well
> supported by timber. I would imagine the floor of the dugout was
> probably at least 12 feet underground – you had 6 feet to move
> around in and 6 feet of solid earth above you. An area of 10 to 12 feet
> square would be a company dugout, about four, five or six officers
> sharing. The cooks used to prepare the food in a portion of the room
> and we used to live quite well. We had a good table and the mess
> down there.[17]
>
> Lieutenant Charles Austin, 12th King's Royal Rifle Corps

The officers also often had enough private means to allow them to top up their basic army rations to produce a slightly more toothsome menu than the mundane fare given to their men.

We used to take an officers' cook in the line with us who had a
primus stove, a frying pan and one or two cooking utensils. Even in
the dugout we'd have a three-course meal at night. Usually tomato
soup out of a tin warmed up, a few chops used to come up from
the quartermaster, potatoes, tinned peas and that was our meal.
Sometimes we'd have a tin of something for our sweet. Of course
coffee, and a whisky and soda. We always made sure we had that! We
used to get rations, but all these extra things that the cook used to
buy we used to pay for.[18]

Second Lieutenant Jim Davies, 8th Royal Fusiliers

Each officer would also have a servant. He was responsible for keeping
the officer's kit clean, making sure he had somewhere to sleep and was
properly fed. To modern ears this sounds dreadful, but it was the officer's
job to make sure that all his men were properly looked after and his
servant merely performed the same function for him. The servant would
also act as a 'runner', carrying messages as required to the headquarters. Many officers and their servants established a warm and mutually
caring relationship; indeed after the war was over some wealthy officers
employed their servants in a personal capacity as chauffeurs, gardeners
or butlers.

The subalterns and captains commanded the platoons, majors
commanded the companies and a lieutenant colonel ruled over the
whole battalion. The colonel could be remote figure, even to some of
his own subalterns. One memorable character was Lieutenant Colonel
Roland Bradford, encountered by Second Lieutenant Charles Gee when
he joined the 1/9th Durham Light Infantry in 1917. By this time the
youthful Bradford had already been awarded the VC for his leadership
and courage under fire on the Somme in October 1916.

Bradford liked young people – he was young! When we were in the
trenches and the old second-in-command left behind, the average age
of people at headquarters was 20! It's unbelievable but it's true: three
of us 19, one of 20, the colonel 24! I think young people could get
used to anything; older people it's a strain. He was rather frightening
and very impressive. If he was punishing anybody he always gave
them the maximum punishment – twenty-eight days – but he knew

them all by name and spent a lot of time talking to them. Certainly in the trenches he spent all day with them. He ticked me off an awful lot. He was jolly rude! If he was cross about something else, he probably took it out on me. He was difficult, but very nice.[19]

Second Lieutenant Charles Gee, 1/9th Durham Light Infantry

In November 1917 Bradford was promoted to brigadier general commanding the 186th Brigade, only to be killed by a random shell on 30 November ten days later at Bourlon Wood.[20] At the time of his death he was still only 25 years old and the youngest brigadier general in the whole British Army. He was actually four years younger and senior in rank to Lieutenant Colonel Bernard Montgomery, and with Bradford's death the British Army lost one of its future military leaders.

THE STANDARD KHAKI UNIFORM proved highly suitable for the rigours of everyday trench life.

Big strong heavy leather boots, in England they had to be polished when on parade, but when overseas they had to be greased. They were tied with strong leather laces. We wore puttees, long khaki cloth about three inches wide, one for each leg, starting at the boot and wrapping it around your leg up to the knee. Then it had the tape at the top which you tucked in underneath and held it. Khaki trousers with braces. All army issue. Two shirts: a body shirt and the khaki shirt to cover. Your tunic stretched from the neck, right nearly down to the knee. Two breast pockets with a flap over buttoned. Two side pockets, very wide, they could hold your pipe, matches and all your personal belongings. We had a cloth cap, with a peak in front. The uniform was made of very strong khaki cloth: very serviceable.[21]

Sergeant Jack Dorgan, 1/7th Northumberland Fusiliers

The two tunic breast pockets were for a pay book and personal knick-knacks, two smaller pockets and an internal pocket where the soldier kept his field dressing. Added to this was a greatcoat. The harness worn was the 1908 pattern of waterproofed and pre-shrunk cotton webbing which, although it looked complex, was actually a master-piece of functionality. Full marching order allowed the soldier to carry two ammunition pouches each containing seventy-five rifle rounds, bayonet, entrenching tool, water bottle, mess tin and a small haversack with the separate large pack and straps. The webbing was easy to wear, being donned in one piece somewhat in the fashion of a waistcoat before being swiftly buckled up. All told it was a beautifully balanced piece of kit: stronger and more weather resistant than leather, distributing the load evenly about the body and reasonably comfortable to wear even on long marches.

One development forced by the nature of trench warfare was the introduction of the steel helmet to protect the head from shrapnel bursting above the trenches. These began to be distributed in late 1915, and by the time of the Battle of the Somme were nearly universal. The design resembled an upturned steel soup bowl with a leather lining and chin strap. At first the soldiers regarded the helmets as being strangely 'Chinese' in appearance, but gradually their very ubiquity meant that they were accepted with little comment.

When the troops were first in the line in the winter of 1914–15 it was bitterly cold and some effort was made to keep the men warm by the issue of extra clothing in the form of sheep or goatskin coats. These proved to be a mixed blessing!

> We were issued with our sheepskin coats. Oh dear me! You could wear them inside out or the right way. Now if you wore them inside out, you had the lining on the outside and all the wool was inside next to your body – but you were absolutely covered – you had millions of lice on your body. They were creeping out of your neck. If you wore it with the wool outside when you walked up and down the trenches; climbed in and out – all the wool used to get thick with blobs of clay – extra weight. They were warm – that was one thing.[22]
>
> Private George Ashurst, 2nd Lancashire Fusiliers

Lice were endemic in the British Army throughout the war. They never seemed to go away, managing to thrive in any weather conditions.

> They didn't hurt – they were just itchy. You would be sat talking to a chap and you would see one come up out of his shirt and walk up his neck. There was only one thing to do – burn them! That was the only way – get your shirt off and get the flame going along the seams. We

used to run a match – or a candlelight better, it lasted longer – up the seam and burn every egg. You could hear them crack, crack, cracking. You just run the flame up – not to quickly, just nicely so that it didn't burn your shirt, but still it would burn all the livestock in the seam.[23]

Private George Ashurst, 2nd Lancashire Fusiliers

Some of the men found their own weird amusements with the lice.

When you're in the trenches all day long, time takes a long time to go. What we used to do was we had a length of trench with eight men. We used to get a penny out each, take a louse out from under your arm and put it on your penny. So you got eight of you in the line with eightpence involved. And the first louse to get off the edge of the penny wins the eightpence, you see. And the excitement that that caused you would never have believed. I used to wonder what the hell the Germans used to think of us. We used to go blooming daft, the noise we used to kick up. You'd see one, he'd look over the edge and you'd say, 'Go on, go on!' Of course he doesn't, he goes round again, especially if there was a newish rimmed coin. All those worn out ones were banned. I've seen these lice going all round and round on these pennies for quarter of an hour or more before one just goes over. That was great fun![24]

Sergeant Alfred West, 1/1st Monmouthshire Regiment

The lice were also held to be responsible for spreading trench fever among the troops. Typically it meant a raised temperature and a general feeling of malaise among those afflicted, but it was not particularly serious.

We had cases of men coming down with a temperature and I noticed that the Medical Officer marked them all with the same letters, 'PUO' – 'Pyrexia of Unknown Origin' – that was just a fever they couldn't attribute to any particular source. It was the conditions no doubt that caused it. They all had temperatures round about 100 degrees and they went down as casualties to hospital. The only treatment they had would be to have five or ten grains of aspirin three times a day.[25]

Sergeant William Collins, No. 1 Cavalry Field Ambulance

The discomforts of trench life could manifest themselves in other relatively trivial complaints which, in the case of Corporal Donald Price in the winter of 1915, had most amusing consequences – or at least they were amusing from any other perspective but his own.

> I developed a boil on my thigh. You've got to understand how we were dressed: I'd got my equipment on – fighting order, an overcoat, a goatskin, a leather jacket and my waders on. I'd got my boil down here. The doctor came along in the morning as usual and he says, 'Anything doing?' I said, 'Yes, Sir, I've got a boil.' He said, 'Let's have a look at it.' Well now I've got to get my trousers down. Imagine it: an overcoat and all my equipment. Raining like hell. I struggled with all this; I opened my coat and got me pants down. He says, 'Bend down!' Well I bent down and my arse touched the firestep. Well the firestep was sodden and as soon as I put a little bit of weight on it it gave way and I went with it. With my bare arse and my boil in this muck. The doctor looks at me and he says, 'Well, get up!' I got up: my trousers and me covered in crap – and my boil had burst![26]
>
> Corporal Donald Price, 20th Royal Fusiliers

It is this kind of anecdote which most tests the will of even the most professional of interviewers not to laugh out loud!

The trench drainage was often overwhelmed by the rising waters in the low-lying areas and the men spent much of their day up to their knees in freezing cold water. The result was trench foot, where the feet took on a spongy texture or even developed frostbite. George Ashurst was an early sufferer in January 1915.

> I get in my hole in the side of the trench. It had been raining. I'm in like this, my ground sheet over me and my feet down there. After a while I wake up and the ice, thin ice, was round both my ankles. I said, 'Look here, I'm frozen up.' Just as a joke. I broke the ice and pulled my feet out – they didn't feel so bad or 'owt. So I carried on. On the fourth night relief came. I walked out across the ploughed field. I thought, 'Oh, I'm picking up a lot of thick clay stuff off this field.' I got on the lane, so I started kicking it off, but it never went. I walked on – I thought, 'It's like walking on sponges.' When I got to the village I'm asleep all night, when they waken me up! 'Oh hell! My feet are that big!' Both of them. Swollen. I can't get up; can't stand

on my feet. We cut my shoes off with a knife. A lad had to carry me down the street to where we had sick parade.[27]

Private George Ashurst, 2nd Lancashire Fusiliers

He was sent back to hospital for treatment.

They put me in a room with three others with frozen feet. Our feet were uncovered in bed, sticking up at the foot of the bed. They were just bathing them, powdering it and drying – no massage. The doctor used to come round in the morning and just feel at your toes and feet. 'How are you this morning?' 'Not so bad, Sir!' All the time he had a needle – we didn't know that for quite a while – and he was shoving it in your toes. You didn't move – you didn't feel it! The doctor knew when you jumped your feet were getting right. He knew life was there again. Then – 'Ooooh!' – terrible, horrible pain, just a touch of anything and you'd scream out. You used to go to the toilet on your hands and knees with your toes cocked up. A fellow would be coming back and when you got together, 'Woof! Woof!' A bit of a dogfight – the nurses used to laugh at us.[28]

Private George Ashurst, 2nd Lancashire Fusiliers

The best method of avoiding trench foot was to try and keep your feet dry and regularly change your socks – which of course was not always possible in the wet trenches. Everyone was issued with whale oil which was supposed to be rubbed into the feet every night.

If you soaked your sock in it that lasted longer. I used to pour some into my sock and rub it with my hands so that it all went into my sock and then put the sock on then. That would last practically a week. I found I didn't get the frostbite.[29]

Sergeant Alfred West, 1/1st Monmouthshire Regiment

The use of whale oil was compulsory and later in the war cases of trench foot were considered a 'self-inflicted' wound and a disciplinary offence, the incidence of which was regarded as a key indicator of poor battalion morale and discipline.

One obvious concern of trench warfare was the necessity for toilet arrangements, if standards of hygiene and hence the men's health were not to suffer. With so many men cramped together in a limited area for long periods of time, it was crucial to maintain good latrine discipline. Men could not be allowed to urinate or defecate anywhere at will. The latrines themselves were primitive and unsavoury places, which, although not as bad as those at Gallipoli or Mesopotamia, were still fundamentally repugnant. They was usually either a simple bucket, or a deep slit trench with a pole suspended above it. Few men dawdled overlong about their business as there was a particular horror of being hit in such undignified circumstances.

> A hole: everybody had to go in there, officers and all. No paper, we had to do the best we could. We couldn't be bothered about anything else, the quicker you did it and got your trousers up to be ready, the better. It would be an awful thing to be caught with your trousers down. It was a quick move.[30]
>
> Private Ivor Watkins, 15th Welsh Regiment

DAY-TO-DAY FIGHTING was a deadly routine that varied depending on the situation. Sentries would be set, but they would have to be very careful about how they looked over the parapet in daylight. Sometimes periscopes were used, or cautious peeks taken to check the situation if something untoward was heard, but the fear of German snipers was real. At first the British seemed to have been disadvantaged in the 'sniper war', sometimes as much by the ground configuration as by a lack of expert shots and the shortage of quality telescope lenses. The Germans had dug in on high ground best suited to defence, and therefore had a much better chance of getting a glimpse into the trenches of their adversaries below them. German sniping was a potent menace, with sudden and tragic deaths to remind the survivors not to expose themselves unduly above the parapet.

> One of our lads, Charlie Reid,[31] he was a great little fellow. He stood up one day outside a trench dugout, pulled out a German helmet and put it on his head. There was pair of spectacles attached to it, so he put the spectacles across his face, stood up and said, 'Ho, boys!' He folded his arms and stood up there and a German sniper sniped him right away – he was gone – through the head. You had to watch every

movement you made, keep your eyes open to see there was nobody watching you.[32]

Private Sibbald Stewart, 238th Machine Gun Company

Tall men were particularly vulnerable and Sergeant Alfred West explained how taller German soldiers certainly needed to take more care in his presence.

> I used to go to the fairground in England and have a go at the shooting galleries – you know, these balls going up and down on the water. I used to love having a go at those. Funnily enough it happened during the war: one morning there was a German chap with a long handled bowl scooping water and throwing it over his shoulder. I noticed that as he threw it, just a little bit of his head showed above the parapet. I watched this for a bit and I timed it for when he was coming up and when I shot there was just a couple of inches showing at 400 or 500 yards; I must have got him because his tool went out of his hands and up in the air.[33]
>
> Sergeant Alfred West, 1/1st Monmouthshire Regiment

Vulnerable points in the line were marked down by snipers on both sides: perhaps where a bay had been blown in by a shell and not yet properly repaired, or any point where the Germans could get a good view into the British lines. Sniping plates were produced, although many preferred to conceal themselves in a 'hide' in No Man's Land, or just behind the front-line trench.

> If you get a little gap about as square as a matchbox, you get a good view in front of you. The least thing you see move; you let go, you'd be aiming at anything that bloody moved. Sometimes you'd strain and strain. You'd see tree trunks that had been shattered, you'd look at that and you could see it move. The more you stare the more it moves. But you've got to be very careful, because if you let go at a thing like that there might be one of their snipers watching where the shot comes from and have a go at you. But you can see things move in the dark. If you get trouble with a sniper firing occasionally, you just mark and weigh up what position he comes from. Then you fire at that – if you don't hear no more after that you know you've done your job.[34]
>
> Private Ralph Miller, 1/8th Royal Warwickshire Regiment

Sniping was important as, like raiding and patrolling, it helped establish a 'command' of a sector. If snipers got a grip, then all the activities of their opponents were made correspondingly difficult. It wasn't just the men they killed, it was preventing sentries from being able to look out into No Man's Land, and the difficulty in improving or repairing trenches.

Gradually the British got themselves organised and by 1916 had set up a series of sniping schools, which then disseminated the best practice throughout the army. It was a specialist task, but eventually every battalion in the line would have a section of trained snipers who operated in pairs, one 'spotting' a target with a telescope, and the other taking the killing shot. Snipers and sniping were an unavoidable necessity, but the snipers themselves were often looked at askance, even by their own side. It was considered a cold-blooded task that needed special 'qualities' not normally acceptable in polite society.

In truth, the ordinary soldier rarely fired his rifle when in the line. Unless involved in making or repelling an attack he was unlikely to ever even see a German. Few had the inclination to expose themselves to danger by aimlessly firing their rifles, not only because it might provoke a deadly response from the Germans, but also because it meant more work afterwards, as the British .303 rifle cartridges left a black powdery residue in the barrel after firing.

For the first two years of the war the Maxim or Vickers pattern machine guns were still allotted to the infantry battalions. They were valuable weapons, lethal in action and for this reason intended machine-gun posts had to be kept concealed from the Germans.

> At 'Stand To' we used to take the Maxim gun down the trench and fire a belt to make sure the gun was working properly and let the Germans know we were there – but not from the battle positions! We weren't very popular with the rest of the battalion, because when we were going down there early in the morning, the chaps would say, 'What are you going to do with the bloody thing?' 'We're just going to test it.' 'Well, go and do it somewhere else because if you fire it from here we shall get all the retaliations!' The machine gun was supposed to give confidence to the ordinary infantryman, because of

the increased power, but these chaps didn't like us testing it anywhere near them![35]

Private Norman Edwards, 1/6th Gloucestershire Regiment

Even in the trenches the machine gunners had to run through their drills, and soon the humble sandbag found yet another role. Private Albert Hurst was part of a Vickers gun team practising their trade in the Somme sector in the spring of 1916.

No. 2 would run forward first with the tripod and he had a manner of throwing the tripod so that the forward legs go front-ways with the rear leg behind. There is a knack in throwing this tripod! Then No. 1 would run out and mount the gun, he'd carry the gun. No. 3 had the spare-parts bag – he was a very vital man. Each of us was supposed to be interchangeable on the gun. We used to practise loading and reloading. The practice was to get a wet sandbag and put it on sticks in front of the machine gun firing, so that the flash of the gun wouldn't be observable and the sound of the firing was deflected to the flanks. You sighted the gun prior to putting this sandbag up. You couldn't always get water to do this and in one instance the blooming sandbag got on fire! We used to shoot on the Vaux village when we heard the rattle of the German transport, aiming at the road, the houses, but no definite target. We'd hope somebody would get the benefit of being shot![36]

Private Albert Hurst, 17th Manchester Regiment

The long-range indirect fire capability of the Vickers machine gun was of increasing practical importance as they were used to fire a torrent of bullets at targets well behind the German lines.

The ordinary infantryman seems to have truly admired only one of the multifarious skills possessed by the more experienced Vickers machine gunners – at least so far as Private Ivor Watkins was concerned.

One particular machine gunner had the knack of going: 'Pom-diddley-om-pom! Pom-Pom!' He'd wait a few minutes: 'Pom-diddley-om-pom! Pom-Pom!' Jerry would reply: 'Pom-diddley-brrrrrttt!' It may seem silly and amusing now but he could never follow that sequence.[37]

Private Ivor Watkins, 15th Welsh Regiment

German machine-gun fire was a constant threat to anyone exposed above the parapet or out in No Man's Land, but as long as the men stayed in their trenches it did not feature as a great source of casualties.

One new addition to the infantry armoury was the rifle grenade, which provided additional firepower with which to deal with German strongpoints or machine-gun posts that were out of the throwing range for the normal Mills bomb. Corporal Joe Fitzpatrick had attended a training course so was given the responsibility of firing a 'battery' of rifle grenades aimed over at the German trenches.

It was just like a bicycle rack. There was room for four rifles leaning and they had a cup on. There was a box of grenades and they had a rod, not quite a foot long screwed into the base of the Mills grenade. Next morning, as dawn was breaking, I peeked and there was a junction of a trench about 150 yards away. I thought, 'Right!' I adjusted it with sandbags to prevent it moving, then I loaded up with a special kind of blank ammunition. It had an iron rod that you put through – two on the left, two on the right – the triggers. There was a string hanging from it, 10 yards long, so that you could get almost round the corner before you gave it a big jerk and they all go off together. You took the pins out of your bomb and that cup restrained the lever from springing off and igniting the bomb. I got it all set, round the corner, dead on, I sent him four lots – quickly. During the day I cleaned up the rifles and the next morning, four in again and I extended the elevation a bit. Banked it up: 'BANG!' Only afterwards I heard the 'Plop'. You could always hear a *minenwerfer* being fired off. It came through the air, just like a big sausage turning and when it dropped it made a crater bigger than this room. It dropped just behind me, so I said, 'Ta, ta for now!' I went further away. It went 'Plop' again and it dropped right on my rifles and blew them sky high. We never did it again.[38]

Corporal Joe Fitzpatrick, 2/6th Manchester Regiment

The clear lesson to be drawn was that whenever the stakes were raised in the levels of fighting, the Germans would nearly always either respond in kind or worse still, raise the stakes still further.

Throughout the war the greatest menace to the British trench dwellers was German artillery. This threatened men from the moment they began to get near the front. The first shell burst heard by a new soldier was terrifying, the very noise alone suggesting an elemental power that could – and would – sweep them away as so much dust in the wind. Second Lieutenant John Mallalieu was approaching the line in the Neuve Chapelle sector in December 1915 when he had his first traumatic experience.

> Two shells burst behind us, about 20 yards or so – made a lot of noise and did no damage. But of course I had no idea then of the way shells burst; the majority of the impact was forward, especially with shrapnel which came down all forward. If you were behind them you were perfectly safe. Nobody had ever told us that in England, or had given us any instructions – the result was I was completely scared stiff. I learnt very shortly that I needn't have worried very much. I never in the whole of the war experienced as much sheer fright as I did on my very first experience near the line.[39]
>
> Second Lieutenant John Mallalieu, 9th Cheshire Regiment

They soon learnt to distinguish the different characteristics of the varying types of German shells. One distinctive type was the shell fired by the German 77mm field gun which was given the evocative nickname of 'Whizz-bang' from its distinctive sound signature as it arrived and burst. Another much dreaded shell was that of the 5.9-inch German field howitzer which, when it burst, emitted heavy black smoke that gave rise to its common nicknames of 'coal box' and 'Jack Johnson' after the world heavyweight boxing champion. These 5.9s were the scourges of No Man's Land, firing the air-burst shrapnel that riddled attacking soldiers, or high explosive that blasted them to smithereens. As a soldier gained experience, he learnt to judge the likely arrival point of a shell and would only take cover if it seemed that it was going to land close by. But this ability was useless in any real barrage. Private William Holbrook remembered a close escape and the awful aftermath while in the Sanctuary Wood sector in May 1916.

> There were six in my bay. It was my turn on duty for a couple of hours. They said, 'Let's go in the next bay; they've got some cards in there – we can have a game of cards.' Away these other five went. That made about twelve in their bay and only me in this one. All

of a sudden there's one – God, honestly and truly I'll never know what happened – it was such a bloody explosion and it blew me, the sandbags, the barbed wire all in a bloody heap. I just don't know what happened, it must have fallen quite near me. While I was trying to get myself together a young officer came along, he says, 'You all right?' I said, 'Yes.' I was a bit dazed. I said, 'Where did that shell fall then?' He said, 'You should see your next bay, all dead, all of them!' He said, 'Can you help me dig them out?' I was half dazed myself! He got another man, but when we got round the bay he put his hand to his forehead and said, 'Oh Sir, I can't look at them, I can't touch them! It makes me feel ill to see them!' We got down to it and did the best we could. Pulling bits and pieces out. We got hold of a fellow's neck bone – his head was off – to pull him out of the loose earth and all it was was his two legs and his backbone. Next one the shell had scalped him, so that all his skull was peeled white, a hole in the skull. As I tried to get my hand under his chin, all his brains shot out all over my arm. Hell of a state! The officer got his water bottle out, got some rum and we had a good sip. He said, 'How long you been out?' I said, 'Two years!' He said, 'Two years in this! God almighty! Do you know how long I've been here – ten days and I'm bloody well sick of it!'[40]

Private William Holbrook, 4th Royal Fusiliers

It was not only in the front line that death could reach out to the British soldier. Men were frequently killed or wounded before they even got to the front. Equally often they were hit when marching back towards rest and safety after a dangerous tour of duty in the front line. Such casualties were inevitable, as the Germans knew which routes they had to take.

It must be remembered that it was not just the British that suffered from shell fire. All the while, the men of the Royal Artillery were replying in kind and meting out similar, or indeed greater, punishment to the Germans. It was a cruel impersonal business where a man's survival in the trenches depended on luck: not only on the calculations of a distant gunner, but also on the vagaries in flight of any shells. And to survive unscathed an individual had to be lucky every single time one of the hundreds of shells was fired in his general direction. It only took a moment of bad luck to kill or maim a man.

A further refinement in the technology of war brought the advent of effective gas shells following on the heels of the cloud gas releases at Ypres and Loos in 1915. At first the Germans dominated this aspect of warfare.

> There's no great noise about it because there's only sufficient explosive in the shell to open it up. The shell itself is filled with liquid gas. The nose is spigoted into the cylinder part and held on with either lead rivets or wooden pegs, then in the bottom there's a bursting charge which compresses it enough to sheer those rivets and allow the gas to come out as liquid and it evaporates. There wasn't any great danger from splinters or explosives or anything like that. All that happens is that round you hearing these thuds and plops and the clouds of vapour rolling about.[41]
>
> Signaller Leonard Ounsworth, 144th Heavy Battery, RGA

The shells were filled with various noxious substances: lachrymatory gases causing helpless weeping and temporary blindness, chlorine/phosgene mixes that would incapacitate or kill, while mustard gas caused terrible burns. The real objective of a gas attack was to make men put on their gas masks – for if they didn't, then of course gases like phosgene would indeed prove fatal. But once the mask was on, any soldier's ability to fight was significantly reduced: his vision was badly impaired, he could barely hear any orders and his breathing was so impeded that any prolonged physical effort was difficult. After the grim warning of the German cloud gas attacks at Ypres, British gas masks steadily increased in effectiveness. By mid 1915, cotton pads soaked with water or urine had been replaced with the Hypo mask made of chemical absorbing fabric which fitted over the entire head. This primitive type of mask was superseded by the British Small Box Respirator in 1916. This was a truly effective counter-measure with a close-fitting rubberised gas mask with goggle eye pieces, which was attached by a flexible rubber tube to a separate box-canister which contained the gas filters and was carried in a bag on the chest. The beauty of the design was that it allowed upgraded filters to be easily fitted to counter any new German gases. The trenches had gas alarms, normally an empty brass shell case that would be struck vigorously with an iron bar when gas was detected, so that men could don their gas masks as quickly as possible. Although nowhere near as deadly as shrapnel or high explosive shells, the terror of gas was very real, as encapsulated in Wilfred Owen's poem 'Dulce et Decorum Est', a poetic tour de force that sums up the whole concept of gas having overwhelming power. The reality was rarely that sudden or deadly, but the prospect still clawed at men's nerves. Overall, less than 3 per cent of British gas casualties died during the war and of the total British fatalities on the Western Front, only 1.2 per cent were due to gas. Yet it is also undoubtedly true that gas severely damaged the lungs of thousands of men, and there was a significant element of deferred mortality in the post-war years as they later fell victim to serious chest and lung complaints such as bronchitis and tuberculosis.

Another German weapon that caused widespread distress among the British was the *minenwerfern* (trench mortars), used by the Germans to lob shells into the British front line. One of the main reasons for this was the near impossibility of predicting where the rum-barrel-shaped shells were going to fall as they wobbled through the air.

> You could watch these things and you could swear they were going to drop on you. It doesn't matter what part of the line you were in, you got your eye on it, you'd think the blinking thing was following you all over the place. There was one fellow he got the wind up – my God he was bad! Somebody eventually hit him and put him down.[42]
>
> Private Joe Pickard, 1/5th Northumberland Fusiliers

The British also developed mortars although they were slow to introduce an effective model.

> Trench mortars were invented really out in France; they didn't exist in the British Army. The Germans started using them against us, and in the division I was with, the sappers produced the first trench mortar made out of drainpipe, and those were the sort of things which we produced in these workshops that were set up. It was the only way of directly attacking German troops holding the front-line trenches. Troops in a deep trench cannot be got at by rifle or machine-gun fire, and they're normally too far away to lob a hand grenade if thrown by hand, and you daren't shell the front-line trench if it's too near your own front line at the risk of your shells dropping in your own front line. Therefore the trench mortar is the safest way of attacking

the enemy's front line or his communication trenches if you think he's sending up reinforcements by the communication trench. And obviously, when the Germans had a skilfully made trench mortar to attack your own trenches with, we felt we had to have something to reply to him with.[43]

Lieutenant Philip Neame, 15th Field Company, Royal Engineers

After a while they came up with the 2-inch trench howitzer firing 50-pound 'toffee apple' bombs, which gained their name from their spherical shape mounted on a steel stick. By 1916, the Stokes mortar had reached the front, which proved the perfect trench-warfare weapon. Simple and quick to operate, it involved dropping bombs into the barrel, and could soon generate a mini-barrage of mortar shells falling in the region of a target. For big offensives the British also deployed the Livens Projector, essentially a simple mortar used for firing large bombs that contained huge quantities of inflammable liquid or poison gas into the target area.

THE EFFICIENT TREATMENT AND CARE of the wounded was essential to maintain good morale among the troops. At any moment they could be wounded, so it was essential that they knew they had a chance to survive. If a soldier was hit in the front line, he would be collected by stretcher bearers and taken to the regimental aid post.

There are four regimental stretcher bearers per company – that is two stretchers per company. He doesn't have the Red Cross, he's still an infantryman, he's not covered by the Geneva convention. He goes over the top with the regiment and is liable to be shot just like they are. All he has on is a brassard 'SB' (stretcher bearer) to distinguish him in the regiment itself. It is one of the most hazardous tasks in that those troops who are successful in attaining their objective, they dig in, whereas a stretcher bearer is going backwards and forwards all the time, collecting wounded, gives what help he can, gets them on the stretcher and he carries them to the regimental aid post as quickly as possible. He's moving on the top all the time. The communication trenches are full of troops going up and walking wounded coming down. They get congested.[44]

Private Basil Farrer, 2nd Yorkshire Regiment

At the aid post they would be quickly assessed by the medical officer and his orderlies. At some point a simple triage would be performed to decide which people were to be given priority of treatment. In essence, those with wounds that would probably be fatal and the walking wounded suffering minor injuries were given much lower priority than the seriously wounded who appeared to have a reasonable chance of survival. From the aid post the wounded would be collected by stretcher bearers from the nearest Royal Army Medical Corps unit.

> We got this call to say that a poor fellow had been shot through the head. It was the first wounded man I'd carried out. I felt sorry because he looked a mess with his head all bandaged, so I took my tunic off and put it under his head. We found that the trenches were too narrow and we couldn't carry the stretcher at the full extent of the arm with a sling round like we normally did, we had to carry him with the crook of our elbows, because lower down it was too narrow for the stretcher to pass through. There were four of us – you take it in turns because of the distance you have to carry it. We carried him for about a quarter of a mile. One of us was walking behind because we found that people with their heads wounded badly had a tendency to rip the bandage off. We put him down when the trench got wider to change hands because of the strain. As we did so he snatched this blooming bandage off. All his brains and blood went over my tunic – he vomited also and there was this awful mess. We got the poor devil down to the dressing station; we never heard anymore what happened to him. I very much doubt from the extent of the brains on my tunic that he got through. My pay book was in the tunic pocket – it got all bloodstained round the edges and I carried that all through the war. When I got back our colonel called me a bloody fool for putting my tunic under and he said, 'If you do it again we'll make you pay for a new one!' But I felt so sorry for that poor fellow.[45]
>
> Private Joe Yarwood, 94th Field Ambulance

One man stuck out in the memory of Sergeant William Collins, when he was working in the Vermelles sector in early 1916.

> Then came a day which I shall remember as long as I am alive. I was walking up Hulloch Alley and I came across a stretcher party of the 9th Division. Four of them carrying a man on a stretcher. I stopped

them and said, 'Is there anything I can do?' They looked at me and said, 'Well, have a look at him.' I looked and he was very badly wounded. He was pock-marked on his chest. I said, 'Well, come down to our aid post because we're the nearest point here.' I took them down to our hole in the ground at Vermelles and we put him on the crate, took his jacket off him, stripped him down. I think it was Captain Graham who leaned over him; he'd got multiple wounds. He gave a little sigh and died. Captain Graham looked at him and said, 'Well, there's nothing we can do. You go through his pockets. What he has we'll send home to his next of kin.' I looked at his chest and saw the ribbon there, 'That's the Victoria Cross, Sir!' 'Yes, so it is!' I took his document out and he was Private Robert Dunsire VC, Royal Scots.[46] There was a letter from home so I got his address. In his pockets there was an envelope with a document telling him he'd been promoted and in the envelope was a lance corporal's stripes. He'd never had time to put it on his sleeve. It was a most tragic thing to me. I sent his things home to his next of kin.[47]

Sergeant William Collins, No. 1 Cavalry Field Ambulance

The early stages of medical treatment would often be restricted to disinfecting the wounds and re-bandaging.

Iodine – which had been the good old standby for treating all wounds – the first thing you did was do the edges of a wound with iodine or if it was not very large you could paint iodine over the whole surface. Iodine caused a bit of shock; it burnt. Put iodine on a cut and it's like a burn because what iodine does is to burn the nerve endings. That's why when you apply iodine to a cut on your hand you get a burning sensation for a very short time. It's almost like putting a hot iron to them. It induces a certain amount of shock – you couldn't apply it to a large open wound area. Someone invented a substance called Eusol which had no such bad characteristics. It was much more bland – you could apply Eusol and get no burning sensation and just as powerful an antiseptic action.[48]

Sergeant William Collins, No. 1 Cavalry Field Ambulance

It was noticeable that the wounds caused by high explosive shells, which spat out great chunks of steel shell casing, were markedly different from bullet or shrapnel ball wounds.

The Germans had begun to use high explosive shells instead of shrapnel. Very different, much more severe wounds. A shrapnel wound was a nasty wound, but nothing compared to the great jagged pieces of metal that were flying about making nasty wounds. One of the worst I had to deal with was a private of one of the Yorkshire regiments. An HE shell had dropped right in among them and blown off both his legs, halfway up the thigh, leaving the femur exposed as if they were two crutches. He sat upon the stretcher, looked down at his legs and the bone sticking out and said, 'If only my Missus could see me now! Give me a cigarette!' That was the guts and courage of those men. I took him down, got Captain Rogers to look at him. All we could do was to cover the wounds up with gauze, to keep the dirt and air away as much as possible, a bit of wool over the gauze, bandage them and put him on the first ambulance away. The greatest danger to that man was shock. The wounds could be dealt with, but the shock to the body and the brain was the greatest danger. In seven or eight hours time he'll get the reaction – the shock to the frame of the body and the mind. The reaction would be immense. If he was exceptionally strong he might survive it.[49]

Sergeant William Collins, No. 1 Cavalry Field Ambulance

Eventually they would get back to the advanced dressing station run by the field ambulance attached to every brigade. Here again treatment was mainly palliative although if necessary some operations would be carried out. With men hanging on to their lives by no more than a thread, the medical orderlies often had to make life-or-death decisions.

The dead were prepared for burial in the nearest cemetery and any salvageable equipment would be removed before they were interred.

The mass graves, you couldn't have individual graves, you put twenty, thirty and more in graves. We had identity discs, one was red, the other was a kind of green. You buried the man with one and the other went back with his effects. So that when the chap was eventually dug up and reburied he'd still have this green disc.[50]

Private Basil Farrer, 2nd Yorkshire Regiment

Of course many of the bodies were in a terrible state and assignment to a burial detail could be an awful ordeal.

A pal of mine, Arthur Hill, had the job of sewing up the dead in blankets. This poor fellow had been in a dugout, a gas shell had burst, he got the full effects and he died. Arthur asked me to give him a hand fix this fellow up. As he did so the gas was bubbling out of his mouth! A dreadful sight it was; an awful death.[51]

Private Joe Yarwood, 94th Field Ambulance

Often the padres were intimately involved in the final stages, helping identify the dead and collecting personal effects for return to the grieving families before mumbling the appropriate religious obsequies. Finally, someone had to write a letter home to the relatives. This could be an emotional business, but as the letters tended to reassure the family that the deceased had 'suffered no pain', they bore little resemblance to the grim reality.

If they survived, patients were then moved by ambulance or wagon to a casualty clearing station. This was also usually tented, but it would be a well-equipped medical facility that equated to a hospital, and here complex operations and procedures could be carried out. More serious cases were evacuated to Britain, or Blighty, as everyone called it. Nurse Bird saw the convoys of the wounded coming in.

The convoys were coming in day and night. All the time. The men were just roughly cleared up at the casualty clearing stations. We were all rather young then and it was difficult to imagine how terrible it was. They were so glad to be back. I went round the wards at night and the men were so grateful to talk to someone. So happy to be warm and comfortable and well fed. Those with superficial wounds made a terrible fuss about them, but any that were severely wounded, and so many of them were, they were marvellous, absolutely marvellous. One had one leg off below the knee, one leg off above the knee, the right arm off and the left eye out – and he was the life and soul of the ward! Kept everyone very amused. At night, they were very talkative because they couldn't sleep unless they were heavily sedated. Many were looking forward to going home and not having to go back to the front again.[52]

Nurse Bird, Colchester Hospital

For both nurses and patients it was a terrible ordeal.

TRENCH WARFARE had a strong nocturnal element. In most units the onset of dusk triggered another 'Stand To' after which, especially in winter, the men were given a rum ration, although this varied greatly between battalions.

> The ration would come up in a rum jar: about 14 inches high, a stone jar with a handle and a stopper. It had to be issued by an officer and an NCO. Being one of the only teetotal sergeants in the battalion, I was invariably the rum sergeant! We went along from sentry group to sentry group, dugout to dugout at the beginning of the night. Everybody would be up and waiting for it. Word soon spread, 'The rum ration's on the job!' The officer would carry the rum jar and I would have a large spoon and the ration consisted of one spoonful. The rum we had was much stronger than the rum we have today! Although you may think a spoonful of rum is not much, it was both beneficial and ample. The spoon was always licked by the fellow when he received his ration. That cleaned it ready for the next man![53]
>
> Sergeant Jack Dorgan, 1/7th Northumberland Fusiliers

Generally speaking the issue of rum had to be very tightly controlled as it represented a terrible temptation to some men. However closely something is monitored, there is nothing more certain than that somebody will always find a way to circumnavigate rules to their personal advantage.

> The officer used to give you a spoonful. I had a friend called Dick Westmacott[54] who was very fond of his rum. Dick says to me, 'What about your rum, do you want it?' He gave me sixpence for my rum – I used to give it to him. Then he'd go to somebody else. By the time he'd finished, Dick had had his fill. The next thing we knew he was on the top of the parapet shouting, 'I'll kill the buggers!' Shouting his head off and dancing about on top of the trench. All of a sudden these bullets came flying round. The old Jerries started firing – having a go. Of course we pulled him down. He was well away, old Dick! The officer came round and Dick was on the floor, the officer says, 'What's the matter with him?' 'Well, he's not very good, Sir!' 'What's all that row been going on here?' We had to pick him up and put him on the firing step. When we got out Dick was court-martialled

for causing an affray – he got seven days Field Punishment No. 1 – tied to the cooker, his arms and his legs outspread! He didn't mind – he'd had his rum![55]

Corporal Donald Price, 20th Royal Fusiliers

Scientifically it is now accepted that alcohol lowers the body temperature, but at the time it was a truism that a tot of rum had a warming effect that helped them endure the freezing cold. Even ardent teetotallers were sometimes tempted into indulging, and Gunner Sidney Taylor always remembered his first 'tot'.

I was on duty and one night the mud was so thick you couldn't walk. It took you all your time to lift your feet up. It was very, very cold. There was another lad with me, and a corporal – three of us on duty. Up to then I'd never tasted alcohol, but after you were relieved, the other two always used to go to the officer's dugout and get their rum ration. And they used to go straight to sleep. It used to warm them up. I would lie there frozen stiff. Then when I did get warmed up I couldn't get to sleep for the lice biting. This one night I said, 'Well, I'm going for the rum ration!' The lieutenant looked at me – he knew it was the first time I'd ever been. He had a fuse cap and he filled it to the brim. I just got a hold of it and I drank it like a drink of water, 'Ohhhh!' I stood there and I couldn't do a thing! The lieutenant, the corporal and this gunner were laughing their heads off, laughing like billy-ho. I was stood there for quite a while, I couldn't speak. I went into the dugout and I could feel my inside getting warmer and warmer – I went straight to sleep and I had a real good night.[56]

Gunner Sidney Taylor, C Battery, 250th Brigade, RFA

The rum became the subject of much gossip and humorous conjecture among the men – with the general opinion being that the NCOs got far more than their fair share.

As dusk gave way to night and blackness, there had to be heightened defensive precautions in case of German raids. This certainly placed extra responsibility on the sentries posted in every fire-bay along the line. Inexperienced sentries were haunted by fears of Germans filled with malicious intent creeping about in front of them in No Man's Land. Paradoxically, at the same time simply staying awake was a real problem for men exhausted by the accumulated privations of trench warfare. Most were also conscious of the theoretical threat of the death penalty for being caught asleep on duty. Some men even placed their bayonet under their chin to prevent them dozing off.

To help prevent surprise attacks and to gather intelligence on German activities there would often be forward posts established at the end of short saps, or listening patrols just lying out in No Man's Land as close to the German wire as they dared to go. Private James Snailham[57] was asked to go out on such a mission on the Somme in the spring of 1916.

> Colonel Rickman says, 'Snailham, you are to go out to the German wire and anything you see report to me in the morning!' I went out and I would lie in a shell hole and look across there. I was frightened at first. I stuck as near as I could to our wire and never told them – till I got used to it. Then when I'd been a night or two you knew where to get. Where there was a shell hole or two, or three. There would be a German not 100 yards away on the same job – we never clashed – he never bothered me and I never bothered him. Sometimes I would get as far as the wire and I could hear them. Their trenches were far better than ours: tidier, cleaner. I was to report whether the guns had done their job in blowing the wire away. I was looking for openings in the wire so we'd know where to make for. Some nights it would never have been touched; odd times you'd see a break in the wire. I would report back the movement of troops in the German trenches, or where there was signs of light, which meant there was an officer.[58]
>
> Private James Snailham, 11th East Lancashire Regiment

Darkness provided a cloak for various activities that would not have been feasible in the broad daylight. One common task was that of wiring parties to improve the barbed wire defences.

> We were supplied with wooden posts with pointed ends and a big wooden hammer. The posts had to be driven into the ground. Fellows used to wrap sandbags around the head of the hammer to deaden the sound of when the blow was struck against the post to drive it into the ground. Even with the sandbags, the sound of that hammer would stretch out in the quiet night. You would hear the sniper's

bullet come winging across, or a machine gun. You only got a couple of blows or so to drive it in and then you had to duck down. Then when the machine-gun bullets had passed by, you had another few strokes. The barbed wire was single strand wrapped on a pole carried by two men, very awkward in No Man's Land in the dark. You'd stretch your wire between one post and another, back and forward to make an entanglement. Before the summer was over, that wooden post was abolished and we had a 3-foot steel twisted bar with a loop at one end and at the other end it was sharpened. All you had to do was put a piece of stick in the loop at the top and turn it down into the ground. It made a very effective post. The single strand had been disregarded and barbed wire was in coils – about 2 foot 6 wide – that would stretch about 8 yards and could be compressed into a foot or so. One end could be attached to the steel bar and then stretched to the next bar. It made the erection of barbed wire entanglements a much easier job. A second line of barbed wire would be erected a few yards beyond. There was gaps laid, but they never had to be in line with each other or the Germans could pick them out.[59]

Sergeant Jack Dorgan, 1/7th Northumberland Fusiliers

The barbed wire would be about 20 to 50 yards from the British front line. This would soon be augmented by a parallel fence, with the gap filled with coils of barbed wire. There was a frequent need for improvements and repairs by the wiring parties. Private Harold Hayward had an unfortunate experience on his first wiring party, that greatly amused his comrades.

The first time we went over wiring, of course everything was, 'Schhh, schhh, schhh! Going out over the top tonight. Go quietly!' Not a word to one another. We were going to make a proper continuous line. I just happened to step to one side and I went up to my neck into a French latrine. I said, 'Help, Help!' They said, 'Schhhh! Schhhh!' I thought, 'I'm not going to die like this!' When my parents asked, 'What caused his death?' 'That he fell into a latrine and was drowned!' So they pushed their rifles down and I caught hold of two of them and they pulled me out – but no one would come near me for the rest of the time in the line![60]

Private Harold Hayward, 12th Gloucestershire Regiment

In front of the wiring party would be a covering party to protect them from any German patrols that might surprise them in the course of their labours. Theirs was another dangerous task and Sergeant Jack Dorgan remembered one exciting incident.

I was out in No Man's Land and one of the companies had a covering party out in front of their own barbed wire for a working party repairing the barbed wire and the front-line trench. As I approached them, one of the covering party – Private Somerville – received a sniper bullet right through the body. He began to make a lot of noise. Arriving on the spot I said to the corporal in charge, 'Send your men back. Because with this noise the Germans are going to know that something's happened!' The corporal and I were left with this man, out in No Man's Land in front of three lines of barbed wire. We started off. We never bothered to look for where you could creep through the outer line of barbed wire. We got a hold of Somerville and we flung him on top of the barbed wire and we climbed over afterwards. Somerville shouting all the time and me clouting him to keep him quiet. It didn't keep him quiet! The Germans used a couple of machine guns sweeping back and forward along the length of the trench. Then an officer from the trench, Major Walsh, came out, and he says to the corporal, 'You go back and the sergeant and I will bring the wounded man in!' We were then in between the second and third lines of barbed wire. We bent down to pick up Somerville and a bullet came and hit Walsh in the shoulder, it must have just passed my face. He dropped the wounded man and left me. Away he went back. So I got a hold of Somerville, pulled him up, shoved him on top of the barbed wire, climbed up over him and rolled him off the wire. The machine guns were then firing to hit the exact top of our trench, which deterred anybody else coming out to help me. The wounded man still shouting! I got him onto the first line of barbed wire and tumbled him over. This had all taken time, and my worry was that daylight would catch me out in No Man's Land. Then I had about 8 or 9 yards to haul him to our trench. I had to get him up the front of the trench to drop him into the trench. The fellows in the trench were shouting encouragement, but nobody could come out and help me. Eventually I got him laid out at the bottom of the heap of soil and sandbags which was the parapet of the trench with my feet. When I thought there were no machine-gun bullets striking the top of the trench, then with my feet I rolled Somerville up the front of the parapet and soldiers inside the trench picked him up.[61]

Sergeant Jack Dorgan, 1/7th Northumberland Fusiliers

Dorgan would be awarded the Military Medal in 1917 for this incident. By then he had been wounded and was back home when it arrived in the post. However, news of his exploit had already spread and he had been presented with a commemorative watch by his home town of Ashington on 8 November 1916. He would proudly show that watch to me in 1986. It suddenly brought the story much closer to home.

Another common task was carrying out reconnaissance patrols designed to extend the battalion's knowledge and control of No Man's Land. It was generally accepted that regular patrolling was the very best security against a German surprise attack. The basic procedure was fairly simple.

The whisper would come through, 'There's a patrol going out tonight!' You'd be numbered off, 'You, you, you, you! You rest now during the day, you're going out on patrol tonight!' It wasn't voluntary, you take it in turn. At night we'd gather together, we were given our orders and we were given a password. We were going to reconnoitre a certain area in front of us, to the right or the left. The troops would have been warned beforehand that there was a patrol going out, so that if they saw anything moving they wouldn't be daft enough to open fire. You'd be in fighting orders with your rifle. Keep low. We'd got through these passages through the wire, zigzagging, only we knew the way through. We'd go perhaps right up to the German wire in extended order about a hand's breadth away from each other. Stoop, crawl in the last, it all depends on the terrain. Star shells would light up a good area, mostly a red glow: you'd have to lay down and keep your face down – it would reflect you see. The terrain, the position of their wire, whether there were any gaps, any traps or obstacles that hadn't been there before: anything like that we were looking for. You may hear a voice; you may hear a rattle. We'd stay out for about three or four hours. Get back the same way; then when we come back over the parapet we had to whisper the password.[62]

Private Ivor Watkins, 15th Welsh Regiment

It was only when they went out into No Man's Land that the sheer foolishness of throwing tin cans willy-nilly out in front of the trenches became evident!

> The only thing I used to worry about was fellows used to throw out empty tins. Maconochie's, corned beef and pork and beans tins thrown out in between the lines. They threw them about 5 to 10 yards outside the front line. Well, at night-time you had a hell of a job in the dark and if you kicked one, you'd get machine-gun bullets from the other side – they'd be listening you see. I used to go with a fellow he was always kicking them. I said, 'Can't you move about properly without kicking those bloody tins!' He was one of those clumsy fellows – he couldn't miss them![63]
>
> Private William Holbrook, 4th Royal Fusiliers

The men on the patrols were usually armed with rifles and grenades but some vicious-looking improvised weapons were taken out.

> I carried my knobkerrie. I didn't carry a pistol or rifle in No Man's Land. It was my entrenching tool handle, about 16 inches long, like a heavy hammer shaft. At one end it had a steel covering. I got from our transport people a big steel nut and I slipped that on the end. It was a very effective weapon.[64]
>
> Sergeant Jack Dorgan, 1/7th Northumberland Fusiliers

One problem was that every so often the gloom of No Man's Land would be brightly flooded by light from star shells, flares or signal cartridges.

> A Very light is fired from a short broad-mouthed pistol. You put this cartridge, very wide, about 2 inches wide, about 5 or 6 inches long. You could fire it up into the air, it would go up about 50 or 60 yards – they floated in the air, lighting up No Man's Land. Not like daylight, but difficult light, like intense twilight. You could stand still in No Man's Land and if you tip your head down, with your white face down towards the ground and put your hands close to your trousers, you could stand still and 15 or 20 yards away you couldn't be seen. But if you moved you could be seen.[65]
>
> Sergeant Jack Dorgan, 1/7th Northumberland Fusiliers

The Germans used a great number of star shells fired at random intervals – or when suspicious of what was going on – to illuminate the ground in front of their trenches. For men caught in No Man's Land it was a real test of nerve to stand motionless while these floated down to earth.

An even more dangerous pursuit was the trench raid, carried out with the aim of capturing a live prisoner to identify the unit garrisoning the trenches. These raids were also sometimes carried out for tactical purposes, to destroy mortar or machine-gun posts, disrupt mining activity or just to be a general nuisance. It was considered that raids helped inculcate the right aggressive spirit among the troops and prevented them from drifting into an attitude of 'live and let live' with the Germans. Although raids were usually carried out at night, they could on occasions be made during daylight – as Private Jack Hepplestone found to his cost.

> When headquarters wanted some information they called for volunteers for going out on a daylight raid. You hadn't a chance to say, 'I'll go!' It was, 'You, you, you and you in the captain's dugout!' He'd have a map there, a photograph and drawing of that section of the German trench. What kind of terrain it was you were going over and a good idea of where to jump in and where not to jump in. Where there was a deep dugout; when there was a bit of bother going off, the Germans used to nip down there and only leave one man up top. It was him you used to have to get – take him prisoner. You had to get him alive; he was brought back for information. The night before we used to put a Bangalore torpedo under their wire: tubes about a foot or 18 inches long. They used to screw into one another like a sweep's brush and we used to shove it under their barbed wire. Two Royal Engineers would fashion a wire to it and take it back to our trench. Next day the artillery would open out and put a horseshoe barrage round the dugout at a certain time and our men in the front-line trenches used to open out. The engineers would blow this Bangalore torpedo and it used to sweep the barbed wire away as though you'd gone over with a brush. Then we used to run in and grab this German sentry at the top; it didn't matter how you got him so long as you got him back. We always carried a couple of Mills bombs. When we got in, the Royal Engineers used to chuck a full petrol tin with a detonator on top down the dugout. As that went down it exploded and fastened

in all those that were down in the dugout. The trick was getting back. By the time you got the prisoner, the Germans would have woken up, the horseshoe barrage would have stopped, they'd be coming out and they'd open up with machine guns. Usually it used to be about a 20-yard sprint to get him back![66]

Private Jack Hepplestone, 7th York and Lancaster Regiment

Trench raids were not the sole province of the British and the Germans carried out similar raids on the British lines. The 18th Durham Light Infantry had no sooner moved into the line when they experienced a sudden night attack on 5 July 1916 at Neuve Chapelle. The German raid proved a failure and Private Frank Raine helped mop up the few survivors that managed to get into the front line.

The first night in Neuve Chapelle, we'd no sooner got in, than he started to belt stuff over at us and he raided us – what he was after was prisoners for identification. We were firing at them as they came. God knows how many we hit on the wire. I felt elated, 'Take that! That's for so and so!' He got through into our trenches and we give them the mauling of their lives. We chased them about, shot them. We killed them all – we didn't take any prisoners. I never used the bayonet, I couldn't bear sticking a bayonet into anybody. I was safer shooting them. I always used to say, 'If it comes to bayonet fighting, I'm having a bullet in the breech!' Instead of going near enough to use your bayonet you could kill him from 2 or 3 yards with a bullet and there would be no personal contact. Not that they were very particular about standing up to us; all they wanted to do was run away or give themselves up! I shot them! Let the buggers have it! In fact I worked quite a bit off on them that night; I was quite happy. It did me the world of good instead of thinking they were world beaters. They became ordinary mortals. We just vented our anger at all that had happened. We didn't lose a man that night. They had about thirty dead, they laid these dead ones all out behind us. The bloody generals said, 'Leave them there!' They were all laid our regimental fashion. In the middle of very hot weather they stank like nothing on earth. These generals were about three days coming to see them! There they were decked up like Christmas trees saying what a wonderful sight the bodies were.[67]

Private Frank Raine, 18th Durham Light Infantry

Although raids were often bitterly resented by the troops and seen as a waste of human life, nevertheless the information secured could be valuable as the staff were able to learn a great deal from tracking the movements of German units in, out and along the line. Captured documents and letters also provided basic intelligence that provided a picture of what the Germans were up to and their state of morale. It is true that raiding was a costly enterprise when things went wrong, but this merely reflected the grim nature of the Great War. Battalions could not be allowed to sink into inactivity, or cede control of No Man's Land to the Germans.

THE TRENCHES WERE A BLEAK ENVIRONMENT where discomfort and death were inextricably linked. If the troops were not to descend into a morass of malingering and general unreliability it was essential that their morale was kept up to the highest level. Yet in the dreadful circumstances this was a hard task. Comradeship was at the heart of the matter; together men could endure trials that would tear individuals apart. The British Army aimed to instil the sense within every man that they were part of an elite unit more than capable of dealing with the Germans. Such was the case when Private Victor Polhill's draft joined the 1/5th London Regiment at Laventie in late 1916.

> We marched into the square and Colonel Husey[68] addressed us and said we'd joined a wonderful regiment, the best in the British Army and the first in the City of London. He said, 'As far as the enemy goes, people say there are good Germans and bad Germans; there's no good Germans. The only good Germans are dead ones – all the rest are bad!' The impression he gave us was he'd prefer that we didn't take any prisoners; that we should shoot them all off.[69]
>
> Private Victor Polhill, 1/5th London Regiment (London Rifle Brigade)

When after six months of training a new battalion went out to the front for the first time, the men were proud of their status as soldiers and quick to take offence whenever the honour of their unit was impugned. Private Tom Bracey remembered their 9th Royal Fusiliers song, written specially for them by a more than usually literate American serving in their ranks.

James Norman Hall came from Boston. He was on holiday in Wales and he joined up. He used to write for the *Spectator*. He was quite a gentleman really, quite a character. We went on fatigues one day and when we come back he'd written a song up on the board:

We're bombardier blighters, we're all day and nighters,
An Army Corps all on our own!
Two thousand a minute, is far from our limit,
We never leave Fritzie alone!
Our officers blind us, the Germans don't mind us,
But when work's to be done they send Colonels to find us!
We're Bom Boms, Pom Poms, the pride of the 9th Fusiliers!
So we're worked to distraction, with this satisfaction,
We've only signed on for three years![70]

Private Tom Bracey, 9th Royal Fusiliers

Hall had feigned that he was Canadian when he enlisted and was eventually discharged in 1916 when his US nationality was uncovered. He would subsequently write a well-known book, *Kitchener's Mob*, of his experiences.

In the newly raised battalions, close links had been forged among the men who had enlisted and trained in tandem. Now they were in the trenches together. As the long months passed, this band of brothers was gradually eroded by the drip-drip-drip of casualties, which suddenly accelerated to outright slaughter in their first real battle. Inevitably personal relationships became far more transitory as men came and went with distressing regularity.

When things were nice and easy you could keep your friends, but as soon as you got casualties you'd got to make another friend and as the war went on, the casualties were so enormous the turnover of friends became – every other month you'd probably get a new pal because your friend previously had been killed or something. The fellows I've slept with, divided my bread with, divided my butter with. Then all of a sudden they're killed – gone. Now I've got to make new friends. You've always got to have somebody: you've got to have

231

a pal to dig with you, to share your rations, to do everything with –
he relies on you and you rely on him.[71]

Corporal Donald Price, 20th Royal Fusiliers

Given the hurly-burly of military life it would have been strange if soldiers had not developed personal enmities based on real or imagined
grievances within their close-knit world. Private William Holbrook's personal *bête noir* in the 4th Royal Fusiliers was a certain Private William
H. Podmore.

I was very friendly with Grant, who was a conscript; he came in from
Hitchin and his father was a builder. He was about my age and very
small. Another fellow in my company was named Podmore – he was
a burly, gloating sort of bighead. I never did like him, he never liked
me! I always felt as though I could put my fist in his face! He was
always getting on to Grant, 'You bloody conscript!' Whenever he
could he insulted him. One day we were in a Nissan hut and we'd got
a brazier. The fellows were standing round it, about half a dozen, and
the others were scattered about the hut. Young Grant was there near
me and Podmore started getting on to him, 'Bloody conscript!' All
that! I said, 'Why don't you leave him alone and get on to someone
your own size!' He said, 'What's it got to do with you?' I'd got an
old French coffee pot on top of this brazier, Podmore picked this
up – shoved it right on top of my head, the grouts, all that burning
coffee. It ran down my neck! Cor blimey! I was so mad – I hit him
and knocked him the length of the Nissan hut! He skidded along the
polished floor. I chased after him and before he could get up I got his
head between my hands – I know I'd have killed him, I was hitting
his head on the bare boards and they pulled me off! You see my finger
– that's what I got from hitting Podmore – it's never got straight, I
could never do anything with it. All those years! So I must have hit
him pretty hard![72]

Private William Holbrook, 4th Royal Fusiliers

Long after the war William Podmore[73] would be brought back to Holbrook's attention when he opened his newspaper to discover that his
old adversary had been tried for murder. In January 1929, the decom-
posing corpse of Vivian Messiter, the proprietor of the Wolf's Head Oil

Company, had been found behind some boxes in a lock-up garage. During the war Messiter had served as an officer with the Northumberland Fusiliers, but now his skull had been shattered by several brutal blows and a bloodstained hammer was found nearby. It was discovered that Podmore had been employed as one of his oil company salesmen – and had been claiming commission on sales to non-existent customers. It was speculated that Messiter had uncovered this fraudulent behaviour and had been murdered during a confrontation with Podmore. To the modern eye the evidence was circumstantial, but Podmore was eventually convicted and duly hanged at Winchester Prison on 22 April 1930.

The things that all these men experienced and witnessed in the trenches hardened them to the manifold horrors of war. First, men masked their feelings with cynicism, but they soon began to be so numbed and detached that nothing much seemed to shock or disgust them.

> There was a little stream running down through our trench at Hill 60. That was our drinking water. One foggy day somebody went scrounging round in No Man's Land and they found a Scotsman and a German that had bayoneted each other and they were lying in the stream we were drinking out of. That was just a laugh![74]
>
> Quartermaster Sergeant George Harbottle, 1/6th Northumberland Fusiliers

On the same battlefield, but two dreadful years later, Captain Norman Dillon had a terrifying experience while taking shelter in a former German dugout close to the Menin Road.

> I went out on the Menin Road with a section commander, Basil Groves. We'd got part of the way up the road and the Germans started to get nasty, put a few over at us, so we dived into a shelter which was just at the side of the Menin Road, half underneath it. We were sitting there in the dark and our eyes got accustomed to the gloom and I said to Basil, 'Hello, there's some Jerrys here!' There was a double-tiered bunk and on the top bunk was a dead German. We were sitting talking and smoking, waiting for the 'storm' to abate up above when all of a sudden the dead German on top flung out his arm which came round and caught my friend a clip on the head – which frightened him considerably. I think what had happened was that

233

these two had been put in there and *rigor mortis* had set in. I suppose
the heat of our presence had just turned the temperature enough to
release the dead man's arm. We looked at them closely and examined
their eyes and so forth but they were as dead as mutton – an amusing
experience.[75]

Captain Norman Dillon, B Battalion, Tank Corps

This kind of emotional detachment was commonplace.

There were two dead Germans, one lying on his face and the other
leaning against a wall. He was a handsome bloke, he reminded me
of my father a bit. A shell had dissected him nicely; it had taken the
whole of the front off his chest down to his stomach. Neatly cut
aside and laid apart as if he was in an anatomy school. I said, 'What a
fantastic exhibition of anatomy!' It sounds heartless but then you're
in an area of suppressed emotion so your mind tends to take over.[76]

Corporal Edmund Williams, 19th King's Liverpool Regiment

Many of the men became resigned, accepting that they had little or no
control over their fate, particularly before they 'went over the top' in
an attack.

I was apprehensive – I wondered if I'd be alive that night, I wondered
whether I was going to be killed. I accepted the fact as a soldier;
the thing was, you had to be a fatalist. We often said, 'If it's got
your name and address on it; it will find you – so what's the use of
worrying!' So you've just got to go and you hope for the best.[77]

Private Basil Farrer, 2nd Yorkshire Regiment

Given their circumstance this was not an unsurprising, or indeed inappropriate, reaction. At times the war seemed an unending torment, with
no honourable way out other than a serious wound or death in action.

When you looked ahead you had nothing to look forward to. You
couldn't look forward to the end of it, because all you had in front of
you was a front line, No Man's Land, a lot of enemies who were going
to stop you. Well, you had nothing else to look forward to.[78]

Private Joe Pickard, 1/5th Northumberland Fusiliers

But it was helplessness in the face of shell fire that most undermined morale. Most had recourse to desperate prayers for divine intervention.

> Good God, yes, you were nervous, because you expected at any moment one would be for you. You knew it was quite possible. In a heavy barrage you could hear them coming. I've been on a heavy barrage when there were that many going over that you couldn't speak to your pal – the noise of the whistle of the shells. Oh, it was shocking. Well, you prayed to God, oh yes, definitely! If a man tells you he hasn't then I think he tells lies. I did! I was always a little bit religious, but that was the time when you really prayed hard to your 'Maker' to save you.[79]
>
> Private Ernie Rhodes, 21st Manchester Regiment

There was nothing they could do. A move to the left or right, into or out of a dugout, could save their lives from the next shell – or just as likely condemn them. All they could do was cower down and hope.

> I felt flattened and frightened. I was a fighter by nature always – if I could fight back. But when you had to grovel on the ground at the bottom and you could do nothing – that's when it hit you. When I was firing back at them and it was a fair fight I thoroughly enjoyed it. But being shelled and being able to do nothing about it was terrifying.[80]
>
> Private Frank Raine, 18th Durham Light Infantry

Many found that cigarettes were a very real aid to maintaining morale. Second Lieutenant Ernest Millard was a gunnery officer but he summed it up neatly.

> I found it was a great relief to have a cigarette in action. If you've got a job to do a cigarette was very mellowing. It's quite extraordinary. That's why, when I had a barrage at 4 o'clock in the morning, I had whisky and a cigarette before I went out – that was fine, that was my breakfast. A cigarette was a great satisfaction – it was a meal in itself.[81]
>
> Second Lieutenant Ernest Millard, D Battery, 95th Brigade, RFA

At this time most men smoked and cigarettes or pipe tobacco were issued as an official ration. Smoking was something to do with their hands and perhaps a stray Freudian might point out that the oral component inherent in smoking was in itself an aid and comfort in stressful situations.

The nature of fighting was such that many men could not always cope with the enormous physical and mental traumas inflicted upon them. One result of this was the combination of medical symptoms and psycho-neuroses that were generically described as shell-shock.

> I think it was a shock to the brain and people reacted differently. Some people would think that they were still fighting – throwing a bomb – that sort of thing, break out in a sweat. The sound would affect the brain, a shock to the system just as if you'd had a punch on the jaw. It's physical – you're jarring the brain. I think it largely rests in the brain. You can't help it if the shock is loud and big enough. But in the normal way you take a philosophic view, say 'Well, it's just too bad!' and adjust to it – use a bit of brain power to help to overcome it. But with a weaker man he'd almost give in to it. Mind you, some of them used to put it on. I've seen them do it – doing the act – going through the movements.[82]
>
> Private Joe Yarwood, 94th Field Ambulance

Yarwood's attitude verged on the unsympathetic, for there is no doubt that many of the symptoms were nigh-on impossible to feign and were triggered not necessarily directly by the blast of an explosion, but more from the endless stress of having to remain in such excruciating circumstances. The effects of shell-shock were totally unpredictable: mutism, stammering, deafness, temporary blindness, loss of senses of smell and taste, uncontrollable tics and spasms, loss of use of limbs, phantom wound symptoms, loss of memory, delusion and the collation of cardiac symptoms collectively known as 'soldier's heart'. Any one or combination of such symptoms could reduce the strongest man to a shambling ruin. The symptoms sometimes cleared up after a period of rest, or sessions of hypnosis, but some had caused serious long-term mental disorders that seemed incurable.

> We had quite a few shell-shock cases. They hadn't any clothes on. The NCO in charge would be able to look through a letterbox to watch them in padded cells; they weren't allowed any implements.

One beautiful man, he was so handsome and well proportioned, would kneel all day, all night. He thought he was Jesus Christ come to deliver mankind. He prayed all the time and he had a beautiful voice and one was inclined to want to listen to him. Others were in various stages of shell-shock. Some who were reliable were allowed to go out and have tea in the town or do a bit of shopping. One boy used to like to come down and talk to us. The sergeant in charge knew this and didn't attempt to stop him in any way. But one day he was missing and of course the Military Police had to be called out. Eventually they found him and that put an end to his little journeys out and his visits to us. He was quite reasonable to talk to but one never knows how exactly they are going to behave. Suddenly they could take off, get excited or become a nuisance.[83]

Nurse Bird, Colchester Hospital

Shell-shock patients such as this could be institutionalised and trapped in asylums for the rest of their lives.

BACK IN THE FRONT LINE some men, driven far beyond their personal limits, would be willing to seriously injure themselves in order to escape their ordeal. Self-inflicted wounds were a measure of the desperation of the individual; of just how far they were willing to go in order to get away from the front.

This fellow he was fed up with everything. He was a likeable chap, a rosy-faced young-looking boy, very likeable. He said, 'I can't stick this, I can't do it, I'd sooner be dead than stick this!' I said, 'Don't be so damn silly, you'll get over it!' One morning there was a hell of an explosion at the back of my trench. When I went to see, there he was – he'd gone round the back of the trench, put his hand under a steel helmet, pulled a pin out of a Mills bomb and blew his hand off. He got no pension at all, nothing, he lost his arm. He was only about 22.[84]

Private William Holbrook, 4th Royal Fusiliers

It was far more common for a man to wrap his foot, or hand, in a sandbag and shoot himself with his own rifle, hoping that the sandbag would prevent the tell-tale traces of cordite powder on the wound. Self-inflicted wounds were frequent enough for several of those we inter-viewed to have had close contact with men who had resorted to that desperate expedient.

> They used to take their puttee off and wrap it round the foot or the toes and fire the rifle into it – self-inflicted. They would do anything to get out of there. They were crippled for life. I've had some tight corners but I never thought of doing a thing like that.[85]
>
> Private James Watson, 9th Northumberland Fusiliers

However, the wounds that resulted were difficult to 'control' and most men preferred to take their chance with the Germans.

Another way out for the desperate, nerve-shattered or generally broken soldier was to desert. This was in direct contravention of the Army Act and was punishable by death.

> We had a man deserted to the enemy. A month or so before, out of the line, he'd not gone on parade. It wasn't an important parade and he got court-martialled and he was charged wrongly. He was charged with repeatedly disobeying an order and we couldn't prove he'd had more than one order and he was acquitted. He felt he was unpopular with the other men and he went over to the enemy in the dark. His corporal, who'd seen him running over, was given twenty-eight days for not shooting him. The deserter got thrown in the duck pond after the war back home.[86]
>
> Second Lieutenant Charles Gee, 1/9th Durham Light Infantry

The army authorities did not have a consistent response to cases of desertion, cowardice in the field, or soldiers going absent without leave (AWOL) when battles were imminent. Some men were charged on the very first offence, but others were given several chances. If cases got as far as a formal court martial and the wheels of military justice began turning, then the accused were effectively playing for their lives in a rather grim lottery. Of the 3,080 men sentenced to death during the Great War, some 90 per cent would be reprieved and 'only' 306 were actually executed. Of these, 266 were for desertion, 37 for murder, 27 for cowardice, quitting their posts or casting away their arms in the face of the enemy, 11 for striking their superiors or disobedience, 3 for mutiny and 2 for sleeping at their post. Of those shot by firing squad, no less than 91 were already under a suspended sentence from an earlier conviction. Private William Holbrook was a close friend of Private William Roberts, whom he had to watch being executed at Renninghelst on 29 May 1916.

> We had a nasty case of desertion. His name was Roberts.[87] I knew him very, very well. He never hesitated to go on any raid. But if there was any French girl behind the lines he'd get with her – go away and desert with her. Leave the front line and be away for months. The time before last he got caught, he was put in a tent and we had to guard him. We let him out – everybody liked him! It was some months before he got caught again, in the south of France. He was tried, court-martialled and sentenced to death. The troops were upset about it, but a lot of the troops that knew him had gone, died, wounded and away. It was a place called Renninghelst, we were out at rest and we were in some old barns. We were called out one morning, early, no reason and when we got there in this meadow behind the village, there was Roberts, sitting on a chair. General Potter read out a statement, 'The man you are going to watch has been sentenced to death. He is not a coward, he is a very brave man, but it is beyond my powers, I can't do anything about it, the sentence has to be carried out.' They placed an envelope over Robert's heart there. They put a bandage round his head. He said, 'Take that off, I don't want a bandage round my head, I'd sooner die with a British bullet than a German!' he said. They pulled out six men and he was executed.[88]
>
> Private William Holbrook, 4th Royal Fusiliers

Unlike the French Army, where in 1917 massed mutinies spread like wildfire and many regiments refused to obey orders, mutiny was not a problem in the British Army. The closest thing to outright mutiny occurred at the Infantry Base Depots at Étaples on 9 September 1917.

> I went into Paris Plage, had a few drinks and dinner. I came back with another officer – we came into Étaples and it was full of troops. I said to this bloke, 'What's happened?' I never thought for a moment that there'd been a mutiny. There were crowds coming over the bridge.

I should have asked the troops what was going on, but I thought, 'We'll get back to the Infantry Base Depot!' We got back and they were all standing to, the Fusiliers were loyal. The adjutant saw me and said, 'Right, you'll take forty men down to the bridge and hold the bridge! Stop them getting into the town!' I went to the sergeant and said, 'Are they armed?' He said, 'They've got five rounds, but they're not loaded!' I said, 'No, they won't be!' I got a few catcalls and jeers from the troops as I was marching down the road and I took up position on the bridge – and fixed bayonets. I thought, 'At least we'll do that to show we're armed!' We were probably about three or four deep in line across the bridge with our backs to Étaples. There was an accumulation of troops in front of me, 20 or 30 feet away gradually forming up en masse: Scots, New Zealanders and all other regiments. Perhaps a hundred, perhaps two hundred – I don't know, it was a bit dark – just a mob – like a football crowd. A Babel going on, they were shouting out, 'We're coming through!' I said, 'Don't be stupid, you can't get through, go back to your units, settle down and it'll all be over tomorrow – you've had your fun!' Words to that effect. They said, 'We'll get machine guns – we're coming through!' This I think was from an old sweat. I knew they could get machine guns from the armouries. I looked at my troops, half of them were boys, I was certain they wouldn't fire on the troops – I wouldn't either. Anyway they were not loaded. I was never taught how to handle a mutiny. There was nothing in *Infantry Training, 1914* on 'How to Handle Mutinies'. I remembered a thing a senior officer had said to me, 'Never give an order that you know won't be obeyed.' I thought, 'To hell, I've had enough!' I said, 'Right, go through!' There were troops down in town anyway. Fundamentally, I didn't want to see any more trouble! There would have been bloodshed, which I didn't want to be mixed up in. I told my troops to unfix bayonets and I marched them back. I didn't report to anybody. I thought I was walking into a court martial.[89]

Second Lieutenant Jim Davies, No. 17 Infantry Base Depot

After three days of unrest a mixture of common sense and the forcible re-establishment of discipline managed to end the mutiny without serious bloodshed.

THE BEAUTY OF THE BRITISH SYSTEM was that the troops were regularly rotated between the front-line trenches, support lines and the relative safety of rest periods well behind the line. In this they had a considerable advantage over the German and French units who were held in the line for much longer. Although it varied according to the situation, a typical brigade would have two battalions occupying the front and support lines on their frontage, which in turn had two companies in the front line and two in the support line. The result was that the ordinary soldier would normally spend about three days in the front line before being moved back into support, reserve or rest. This allowed men to have something to look forward to – the end was always in sight.

When the troops were in the reserve positions they were usually held in billets or dugouts and would only actually occupy the reserve trenches in moments of high tension. Although free of the front lines, it all depended on the attitude of their officers and NCOs as to how much the 'spit and polish' or 'bull' (short for 'bullshit') they had to endure. Private Ivor Watkins chafed at the lack of allowance made for the appalling conditions under which they had been serving when he came out of line in the Ypres Salient.

> We came back to Canal Bank and had to bed down wherever we could. We had to have a damn good clean up when we came out. Our officer inspected us and apparently two of us had some mud left between the sole and the upper of our boots. For that we had to wash one of the battalion limbers down, the spokes and the rims of the wheels, as punishment for not cleaning our boots properly. I felt a bit irked because then there was a hell of a mess on our boots, but there we are, that is it, you have to get it clean.[90]
>
> Private Ivor Watkins, 15th Welsh Regiment

Best of all was when they were brought right out of line as their division was relieved and sent off to rest, away from even long-range shells. One thing they certainly found they could not leave behind them in the trenches was the plague of lice and fleas. Where they could, the officers would arrange for the men to have a bath at whatever facilities could be found in the locality. Many men remembered visiting old brewery premises.

The platoon commander said, 'Fall in for baths, bring your towels.' We fell in and we marched off down the country lanes. We came to an old wine place for brewing wine. 'Now strip off and put your clothes all together.' We went inside the building then and there were two big round vats about a yard deep. 'Get in!' They threw some blue soap at us and there we were. It was hot enough, just nice to get in. But you can imagine: fifteen or sixteen in one tub. We couldn't move round, we had to wash each other's backs and all that sort of game, you couldn't bend down to do your legs or feet – there were too many in the tub. You can imagine the fun we had, a tremendous lot of joking. A proper soaking. We dashed out then when the officer said and ran back to our clothes. They were all steaming hot and when we put them on we looked like old tramps. Everything was as creased as they possibly could be. They'd had them in a fumigator while we were in the baths, killing all these lice. But as soon as you got them on and your body got them warm again they came alive – they were there.[91]

Private George Ashurst, 2nd Lancashire Fusiliers

Out at rest the men were billeted in a variety of factories, cottages, farm outbuildings, old barns, purpose-built huts and tents.

The rear areas were teeming with troops and it was a logistical challenge to try to fit such an excessive extra load within the often primitive local infrastructure. One example of these stresses was the problem in obtaining sufficient water. The French farms would have their own wells but they could rarely generate sufficient water to feed the extra thousand men from a battalion. This often caused friction with the thirsty men who were not disposed to accept these restrictions.

You go in with a quart of water in your bottle; you take it from the water cart. You're not supposed to drink the French water because there was only enough water for French people – you get a whole army come in and they'll drink all the water. Of course we'd got to their pumps when they were asleep and then the blooming pump would go 'Wheee-hewww'. The door would open, out they would come jabbering and we'd run off like a lot of schoolboys, because if you got caught you were on orders.[92]

Private Tom Bracey, 9th Royal Fusiliers

The better types of accommodation were usually reserved for officers. As in the trenches, they lived a far more comfortable life than their men. Second Lieutenant Jim Davies was newly commissioned from the ranks when he reported to the 8th Royal Fusiliers behind the lines in early 1917.

> They were out at divisional rest so I joined them in a little village. We were greeted by the second in command, Major Sam Saunders. Most immaculate: points to his collars with press studs, a monocle and beautiful field boots. He said, 'I don't think I have anything to tell you. I don't know if you boys are used to drinking, but they drink in this battalion! But there's one thing the colonel insists on, if you can't get drunk as a gentleman, you mustn't get drunk at all!' I always remembered that! He said, 'You report to D Company – Captain Nicholson!' I went down there, nervously banged at the door and they were playing bridge in a cottage. I said, 'Davies, reporting for duty, Sir!' Nicholson said, 'Come in, have a drink!' That was the first thing he said. I said, 'Thank you very much!' He said, 'Two fingers, four fingers of whisky?' He said, 'If a bottle of whisky is open it has to be finished, but as I shall be around most of the time it won't bother you!' I thought how nice and friendly it was. We used to buy whisky from the Expeditionary Canteen for sixty francs a case. That's five francs a bottle. I took to it very well – it suited me.[93]
>
> Second Lieutenant Jim Davies, 8th Royal Fusiliers

When the men had settled into their billets they would still be required to do a certain amount of training. Drill sessions and parades would be held to ensure that their general discipline did not go to seed. Sometimes they were sent out on route marches, and it is noticeable that their songs were often more pessimistic than those they had sung as raw recruits. Stretcher bearer Basil Farrer remembered the change in mood.

> The soldiers had their own songs. One in particular:
>
> *I want to go Home,*
> *Don't want to go in the trenches no more,*
> *Take me over the sea,*
> *Where the Allemand can't get me,*
> *Oh my I don't want to die,*
> *I want to go home!*

That's the kind of song we'd sing on the march – we'd become a little more cynical. There was one which our officer commanding would stop us singing. The medical officer had been captured – the Jerries attacked the medical post [which] was overrun and he was captured and we'd composed a marching song:

Hey ho, Poor old Number Nine,
Hey ho, Poor old Number Nine,
Down in the quarries,
Down in the quarries,
And they left old Number Nine down in the quarries,
And the Stretcher bearers helped to do him in!
Hey ho, Poor old Number Nine!

The medical officer – we used to call him 'Number Nine', because whatever ailments you got it was always Number Nine – that was a purge![94]

Private Basil Farrer, 2nd Yorkshire Regiment

But many of the songs were still essentially good-hearted.

You would sing parodies mostly. The sergeant or officer, they couldn't stop you. 'Stop that noise!' Then someone in the back would start again. There were all sorts of parodies – we used to make them up you know. Somebody would give a line, say something; then somebody else would put another line on; then someone else would build on that and then the whole lot – you had a verse. Then they would pick a tune, try the tune on to the verse and then you had a parody. They weren't really respectable – they were rough and ready. There was a music hall song where the thing was, 'With my shirt on fire, I walked along the wire, with my little wiggle waggle in my hand!'

With me little bombing bucket in my hand
I went up to the trenches
With a big flare pistol
A compass and a map
They gave me six bombers
And they chased me down a sap
I was shaking and quaking
For by the block I knew I had to stand

When Fritz he came across
He was fairly at a loss
When he saw the bombing buckets in our hands.[95]

Private Joe Pickard, 1/5th Northumberland Fusiliers

Behind the lines the troops were often put through exercises to practise the latest tactical innovations, lectures would be given and numerous cadre training courses run for prospective NCOs, the signallers, Lewis gunners, bombers and all the new specialist trades required as the war grew in complexity. Having been taught by experts, they would return and act as tutors to the men of their battalion, thereby passing on their new expertise. This cadre system was an effective means of disseminating training in an army that was often still under strain from rapid expansion, while at the same time experiencing constant erosion of 'stocks' of experienced trained personnel.

Although they had their military duties to carry out, the men did get considerably more free time when they were out at rest. One of the common occupations was catching up with their correspondence. The postal system was efficient and many men wrote home every day. There was a variety of types of letter, of which the simplest was the field postcard.

I wrote a field postcard every day. On one side you would put the address. On the other side was a printed list: I am well, I am not well; I am in Hospital, I am not in Hospital! You crossed out 'nots' and so on! I have been wounded or I have not been wounded. I have received your parcel; I have not received your parcel. I have received your letter; I have not received your letter. You crossed out what didn't apply. I sent one every day to my mother. Occasionally to my girlfriend.[96]

Sergeant Jack Dorgan, 1/7th Northumberland Fusiliers

Then there were ordinary letters which would be censored by their officers locally. These letters were often written in an almost formulaic manner and researchers in the IWM Documents collection soon became familiar with letters which follow the general pattern of: 'Dear Ma, Hope this finds you as it leaves me in the pink' followed by a series of amiable platitudes which gave little away as to what was really happening to them in the front line. This wasn't just because they were afraid of upsetting the censoring officer. The more common reason was that it was generally seen as bad form to inflict extra pain on relatives who were already suffering agonies of worry on their behalf.

> This officer said, 'When you write home don't be mournful and miserable; try and write home as bright and cheerful as you can!' I made that my motto. I tried to write more or less every day home and I always said something cheerful – normally about a parcel, because mother sent me a 7-pound parcel every week.[97]
>
> Private Victor Polhill, 1/5th London Regiment (London Rifle Brigade)

Some of the men were illiterate and needed help to communicate. Sergeant Jack Dorgan remembered acting as intermediary for one of his men intent on plighting his troth with a girl back home in Northumberland.

> You rest, slept and wrote your letters. We had a fellow in our Company who couldn't write, Private Billy Bacon. He couldn't write or read, he was a big feller, six foot one or two – real good soldier. I was dishing out the post, I says to him, 'Bill, you're never getting any letters!' He just turned away. Afterwards I said, 'What was the matter?' 'Well, I can't read and I can't write – I never learnt at school!' When I found out, I took on the job of writing letters. I wrote home to his girlfriend as if it was him writing the letter. The letter he got back he used to bring to me and I used to read the letters to him from the girl. Her father was a publican; he had a pub in the village of Choppington. When I passed after the war I often thought of calling in; but I never did.[98]
>
> Sergeant Jack Dorgan, 1/7th Northumberland Fusiliers

There was another special type of letter which was available if men wanted to have at least the illusion of privacy in writing on family or deeply personal matters.

> I had a supply of green envelopes. An ordinary letter with an ordinary white envelope, it had to be censored by your own officer. Well nobody liked that, letting your officer know what your intimate

family life was. Now a green envelope meant that it would be censored but not by your own officer.[99]

Sergeant Jack Dorgan, 1/7th Northumberland Fusiliers

The men would get letters back in return, normally in rough proportion to the number that they had written themselves. The arrival of the post was a highlight of the day, whether at rest or in the line.

> I'd been doing a bit of courting – she worked at the cotton mill. I'd got a girl, I thought it was wonderful. I used to get some very nice letters from her. When I came home on leave during my training I used to go out with her every night. I'd even got to the extent that I'd been invited to go to her house for my tea – which was a step forward! I thought I was in love with her – I really did. Now if this sounds daft and you want to laugh – laugh by all means because I do now! But I was always pleased when I got a letter from this girl. I treasured these letters. Full moon, not a sound, you're on sentry duty in the front line. You're thinking about home. Me – I was thinking about this girl! Thinking that same moon would be shining on her that was shining on me. I'd been there a while, we came out of the line and I got a letter from her. At the same time I got one from me mother. I didn't open me mother's, I opened my girl's first to see what she had to say. What she had to say it was devastating! She didn't want to go out with me again because she was going out with somebody else. Honestly, my world fell apart! I'm 18 years old, this was the first girlfriend I'd had and she'd ditched me! A lad that I knew who I thought was a good friend – he'd pinched my girl off me. I was really upset, I thought it was the end of the world. Even today, with all the experiences I've had I can't think of anything that upset me more than that did emotionally.[100]

> Private Raynor Taylor, 24th (Pembroke and Glamorgan Yeomanry) Battalion, Welsh Regiment

Such disappointments were not uncommon and merely reflected human nature in a time of war. Women could not be expected to wait for an indeterminate number of years for a man that they had perhaps barely known before exchanging ill-considered promises in the heat of the moment. The *coup de grâce* would be given in what became known among the soldiers as a 'Dear John' letter. But however the news was revealed, it could cause real bitterness to young men who had staked all their post-war hopes and dreams on a single fragile relationship.

> I was married when I first joined the army. The time I was away my wife was unfaithful to me. The first leave I came and she'd had a baby. I took the pension book off her and I stopped paying. I had to allow her sixpence a day – it was only a shilling a day wages: she got three shilling and sixpence a week and I got three shilling and sixpence a week. So I stopped it. I went and told the quartermaster that they had to stop it. That went on for years and years. I thought there would be a lump sum when I finished but there wasn't a penny – he'd never done it – I lost all that money.[101]
>
> Anon

Although little spoken about in interviews, this kind of situation was all too common.

The men often spent their free time during the day resting and engaging in the kind of meaningless conversation and banter that has always existed in the services. Some would go for walks, exploring the local countryside and generally relaxing. In the evening, groups of pals would often go out to the local estaminets. These café bars were run by local French or Belgian civilians, who seized the opportunity to capitalise on the vigorous demand. Private George Ashurst recalled many nights in one such Le Bizet estaminet.

> It was a cottage, with a bit of a counter inside as you walked in, and there's where they served the beer. It wouldn't have made a sparrow drunk the beer. It was nothing only brown water! We drank *vin blanc* mostly – white wine. Two or three glasses that's all. It would perhaps be full, everybody sat down at tables. They'd be standing round. You get your drinks and you'd be chatting away with other English soldiers. There'd be an old French man or two inside; not a lot of women there, probably a woman or two behind the bar.[102]
>
> Private George Ashurst, 2nd Lancashire Fusiliers

When they could afford it many of them would get drunk. In the circumstances there was no real shame attached to it, and indeed for some it was regarded as a badge of honour. The estaminets served simple food – normally egg and chips – that provided a welcome break from the monotony of army rations. Other men had more basic needs that were catered for by a variety of brothels.

> We decided to go on the booze, and the first place we came to was a brothel. There was I knowing nothing about this! All these lads were sitting down at filthy tables covered in beer. There was a stairway and these men were going up regularly to see the girls, coming down again. I was very keen and I said to one of these fellows, 'How much is it?' He said, 'How much you got?' 'I've only got a sixpence!' 'Well, that's no good – it's a shilling!' I didn't go up because I hadn't got the money. That was my first experience of a brothel – I was quite merry with the drink I had. The next day we went into the trenches.[103]
>
> Private Donald Price, 20th Royal Fusiliers

It is a golden rule of oral history that it was never the men you interviewed who had availed themselves of the services offered by the women in brothels. But one thing that is certain is that – wherever it came from – there was always a copious demand for sexual relief no matter how sordid the circumstances.

> They were all wanting women and the women knew that. They used to put in the window 'Washing done here for Soldiers'. I've passed by one of those premises and I've seen twenty men in that front room and probably the other one's upstairs with a woman. They told me that the woman used to sit on the end of the bed and they had some fluid, brownish stuff. They used to sit there, open their legs out and they used to flick all around their privates ready for the next one. And there they are all the way up the stairs waiting their turn.[104]
>
> Sergeant Alfred West, 1/1st Monmouthshire Regiment

Private George Ashurst certainly knew a lot of details 'from his friends' as to what went on upstairs at an Armentières estaminet brothel he and his friends patronised.

> We were drinking *vin blanc*. It was absolutely crowded and there were five women in there and it was five francs a time if you went with them up the stairs and in the bedrooms. Fellows were going in and

coming out; going in and coming out the bedrooms with the girls. I didn't fancy them at all! Tom said, 'Are you going up there?' I said, 'No, not with them things!' They were all sorts of ages, the women. Fellows would tell you what it was like going in, 'She's there, the first thing she does is grab your five franc note! Then she unfastens our flies and has a feel, squeezes it, see if there's anything wrong with it. Then she just throws this cloak off and then she's on the bed, ready for you! Then when you've finished, she has a kettle boiling there with some herbs in, she just gives you a bit of a swill with it – for safety's sake for disease!' But I didn't go up there. One night the padre walked in the estaminet and the stairs leading up to the bedrooms was full – a man on every step waiting his turn to go in with a woman. He came in and me and Tom, a couple more, were sat at the table. You can imagine how he dressed us down, 'Have none of you any mothers? Have none of you any sisters?'[105]

Private George Ashurst, 2nd Lancashire Fusiliers

The military attitude to brothels was ambivalent. At one level there was an underlying disapproval which revealed itself in frequent calls for moral restraint and abstinence. This is perhaps exemplified by Kitchener's appeal, which was stuck in the pay books of every man going over to France in 1914. 'Keep constantly on your guard against any excesses. In this new experience you may find temptations both in wine and women. You must entirely resist both temptations and while treating women with perfect courtesy, you should avoid any intimacy.' But at the same time there was a practical recognition that some opportunities for sexual contact were necessary to help maintain morale. It took no particular empathy to realise that naive young men facing death might have a yearning for female company and an underlying wish not to die as virgins. The less innocent knew well enough what they were missing and were determined to satisfy their lusts wherever possible. Past efforts to stamp out prostitution had failed, and as a result there was a reluctant acceptance of the need to establish a system of semi-regulated brothels. As France already had a scheme of regulated prostitution there was little or no obstacle locally. The larger villages or towns would have two kinds of brothels: those with blue lights which catered for officers and the more traditional red light establishments for the other ranks. These were inspected on a regular basis by doctors, although poor medical hygiene may have rather undermined their efforts. As a further complication, although the symptoms of syphilis could be discerned in the women afflicted, it was far more difficult to identify gonorrhoea. Outside the 'official' brothels there was a thriving network of 'amateur' unlicensed prostitutes who were largely unmonitored, hence allowing an even greater danger of infection. In consequence the British authorities encouraged attendance at special disinfection stations after any sexual contact. Unfortunately the moral climate meant that the issue of prophylactics to the troops did not start until late in 1918.

In spite of the de facto three-pronged approach of moral appeals, licensed brothels and medical prophylaxis, VD rates were still far too high in a war where manpower was an increasingly scarce resource. Indeed, at one point VD cases rose to a level that amounted to no less that 18 per cent of total casualties, and in 1918 alone there were 60,099 hospital admissions – each of which involved an average of just over a month of treatment in the wards. In these circumstances it is not surprising that the army authorities resorted to punishment, whereby any soldier hospitalised with VD was liable to suffer not only a stoppage of pay but a significant loss of leave.

THE BIGGEST AND BEST REST OF ALL was to get home on leave. Technically this was not something that was his by right; it was granted as a privilege. Units were allotted a certain amount of 'Blighty leave' which in turn would be granted to men of good character, with a further preference given to those who had served longest in the field. This lack of precision led to large variations in the number of days given to individual soldiers, which caused considerable disquiet. Some seem to have received just one period of up to ten days in all their years of service, whereas officers seem not only to have had more leave but also enjoyed far greater opportunities to take shorter local breaks. A further grievance was that little notice was taken of the travelling time necessary for soldiers from the more remote areas of Britain to get back home. Nevertheless, it was something that the men looked forward to with great relish. Many became more edgy as the great day approached, nervous that they might be killed or wounded, or otherwise prevented from going – this was generally known as 'sweating on leave'.

Sergeant Jack Dorgan was one of the first of his battalion to get home leave in June 1915. He was determined to take full advantage of his status as the 'returning hero'!

> I took off my army issue hat on the bank side and I put a bullet through it. So that when I went home back to England, wearing a hat with a bullet hole through it, I could say, 'That was a near one!' Members of my Scout Troop were all trying the hat on with the bullet hole so that they could say, 'That was a near one!'[106]
>
> Sergeant Jack Dorgan, 1/7th Northumberland Fusiliers

One mistake made by Signaller George Cole was to send a telegram home warning of his imminent arrival. For a wartime working-class household with a man serving at the front, an unexpected telegram could only have one meaning.

> I got my first leave in June 1917, and when I got to Folkestone I sent a telegram, 'Home tonight!' That's all I put on it. Sent it away. My mother got the telegram and my father was out somewhere – she daren't open it. The insurance man happened to call and he could see she was upset, he said, 'What's the matter?' 'I've got a telegram here – I daren't open it.' So he opened it and told her I was on leave![107]
>
> Gunner George Cole, A Battery, 250 Brigade, RFA

When they got home soldiers found that many of the unwelcome 'friends' they had acquired in the trenches had accompanied them on their journey. Joe Fitzpatrick remembered his arrival back in Manchester.

> When I knocked at the door somebody looked through the window upstairs, 'Our Joe! Our Joe!' My twin sister happened to be at home – and me mother. She soon had the fire going; the old egg and bacon going. My sister picked up the jerkin, 'Oooh what a lovely fur coat!' So I said, 'Don't put it on – I'll show you!' I opened it out and had it near the fire. I said, 'Have a look at these!' There was millions of lice! The old lady said, 'Put it in the yard!' So it hung in the yard all the time I was home on leave.[108]
>
> Lance Sergeant Joe Fitzpatrick, 2/6th Manchester Regiment

Some men burnt the candle at both ends, drinking to excess and roistering the nights away, but most seem to have spent their precious few days enjoying some semblance of normality, visiting old haunts and friends. Of course, most of their contemporaries would themselves have been away serving. The leave would be over in a flash and it was with heavy hearts that the men made their way back to the front. At the major railway stations, the same traumatic scene played out again and again, as innumerable men made their sad farewells to their families and loved ones for what would very possibly be the last time.

9

1917: WESTERN FRONT

EARLY IN 1917 the Allies were confident that they had a reasonable chance of defeating the Germans before the year was done. At the Chantilly Conference in November 1916, it had been agreed to launch a series of huge spring offensives on the Western Front. The BEF would strike north of the Somme, between the River Ancre and Vimy Ridge, while the French would attack between the Somme and the Oise before launching an assault along the Aisne. At last the British Empire had its shoulder fully to the wheel alongside the French, and this, coupled with coordinated offensives by Russia and Italy, would surely bring the mighty German Empire to its knees. There was even some justification for this optimism, for the Somme and Verdun campaigns had taken a grim toll of the German Army. The new German supreme command team of Field Marshal Paul von Hindenburg and General Erich von Ludendorff were well aware of the military threats, exacerbated by the draining effect of the Royal Navy blockade on their wartime economy.

By the end of 1916, the Germans, forced to rethink their defence tactics to take account of the increasing power of the Allied artillery, had introduced a new system of 'defence in depth': instead of a system of continuous lines that would be defended to the death, the Germans adopted a more elastic system, using concrete pillboxes and strongpoints as the focus of resistance in the front-line battle zone. They combined this with a more sophisticated use of barbed wire to deny ground to any attacking troops while 'channelling them' inexorably towards interlocking machine-gun posts. If a position was clearly about to be overrun, then retreat was considered permissible in order to conserve troops for battles that they could win. A counter-attack would only be launched by divisions held back beyond the killing range of the mass of Allied field artillery. All these lessons had been utilised during on the construction of the Hindenburg Line behind the Somme front.

In December 1916, the replacement of the French Commander in Chief Joseph Joffre would significantly change the Allied plans on the Western Front. His successor, General Robert Nivelle, was committed to the idea of a massive French offensive in April 1917 on the Chemin des Dames above the River Aisne. Rather unexpectedly, all he required from the BEF was that they take over responsibility for a further section of the Allied front line to free up more French troops, and to launch the diversionary Battle of Arras a few days before the French offensive. After his successes at Verdun in October 1916, Nivelle was certain that he had cracked the secret of victory on the Western Front. To him it was simple: after a devastating bombardment, two French armies would smash their way through the German lines by sheer brute force, after which a third army would rush forward to exploit the breakthrough. Haig was dubious of these somewhat grandiose plans, but he was left with no choice when Prime Minister David Lloyd George, in thrall to the eloquence of Nivelle, directly subordinated Haig to the French general for the duration of the offensive.

The Battle of Arras

The Battle of Arras may have been a diversion, but it was still a major undertaking. Two armies were involved: the First Army, commanded by General Sir Henry Horne, was to capture Vimy Ridge, which lay 3 miles north-east of the city of Arras, while the Third Army commanded by General Sir Edmund Allenby was to push forward into the Scarpe valley towards Monchy le Preux. There was an emphasis on the new artillery techniques that had been hammered out during the Battle of the Somme. Sophisticated creeping barrages forced the defenders to keep their heads down, while great attention was paid to the identification of German artillery batteries using aerial observation, flash spotting and sound ranging. Even wire cutting was becoming more effective, thanks to the gradual introduction of the new 106 fuse which burst instantaneously on contact. Yet amid the planning process the situation radically changed when the Germans decided to withdraw to the new Hindenburg Line fastness from the lines tactically compromised during the Somme fighting.

The German retreat began in late February 1917 and fell back some 40 miles, thus illustrating the utter irrelevance of taking ground in a Great War battle. The Allies were far better served by having the Germans in tactically suspect positions than in a strongly defended shortened line.

As they retired, the Germans destroyed the entire infrastructure of the area, creating a wasteland. The British sent out cavalry patrols to feel their way forwards into this void. Since late 1914, the cavalry had had few opportunities for mounted action on the Western Front, and although visions were fast fading of the *armeé blanche*, of desperate madcap charges using sword and lance, cavalry still had a vital role in modern warfare. Tanks and armoured cars may have been in existence, but they were still slow, with a minimal range and were, above all, mechanically unreliable. Cavalry were the fastest moving units available, whether exploiting brief opportunities, acting as mounted infantry plugging unexpected gaps in the line, or probing ahead as scouts as when following up the German retreat. Trooper John Fell was on a four-man patrol following up the Germans towards Vermand.

> Everything had been devastated. There wasn't a building that wasn't a heap of brick rubble, trees had been cut down and were lying across the road, telegraph poles cut down, any major road intersection had been mined and blown up. We rode in the shape of a diamond, one man in the front, two on each side and one behind. The officer in charge would be in the middle. It covered the ground and gave us the best lookout. We were approaching a village and right in the middle of the road was a lovely German dress helmet, all shiny-black with

metal facings. Just the thing to pick up for a souvenir! But we had
been warned that things like that would be booby-trapped – so I gave
it a wide berth.[1]

Trooper John Fell, 1st Surrey Yeomanry

Later on, Fell found himself briefly isolated from the rest of the patrol as
he entered a wood. Now his nerves were really jangling.

Whether it was the spooky atmosphere, but I suddenly had a
premonition that something was going to happen. It suddenly
occurred to me that the most likely thing was that we could run into
a patrol of German cavalry, Uhlans, armed with lances. It suddenly
struck me that I'd never had any instruction about defending myself
against an attack with a lance.[2]

Trooper John Fell, 1st Surrey Yeomanry

As he left the wood he was hit by a bullet.

Suddenly something smacked into the back of my left arm. It wasn't
painful particularly, but it was a pretty hard whack. At that same
moment the horse sprang up in the air on his hind legs, twisted
round and set off at a mad gallop. The bullet went right through the
back of my elbow, went right up the arm and came out of the wrist
– severed all the muscles and nerves – a hell of a mess! My arm was
completely paralysed, I looked down and saw a mass of blood, over
everything – my forearm, britches, tunic, the saddle and the horse's
shoulders. Then I began to feel faint; I suppose it was the loss of blood
or sheer fright.[3]

Trooper John Fell, 1st Surrey Yeomanry

Trooper Robert Cook was part of another cavalry patrol and he gave us
an insight into the origins of the photographs so lovingly cherished in
the IWM Photograph Archive as a record of the patrols.

No cameras were allowed and none were concealed so there were
no photographs at all. The official photographer came along to us
and we had to redo it for his benefit. They arranged everything very
nicely; they put the odd German helmet about and we did what we
could to make it as 'live' as possible![4]

Trooper Robert Cook, 1st Surrey Yeomanry

Coming up behind the cavalry were the infantry and the sappers, with the dangerous role of detecting and defusing the deadly booby traps left by the Germans.

> We were responsible for every bridge and every culvert – because they were all mined. If the infantry were blown up you were in for trouble. We'd say a bridge was 'Not to be used' until it had been examined. You began to know exactly what the Germans were likely to do: being Germans they were very thorough and they always did the same thing. You'd come to a little road bridge and you would find that part of the bridge had been dismantled and a shell – a 5.9-inch as a rule – had been put in, no wiring or anything like that; it was one of these acid traps. They were all timed and the acid eating the wire away was varying in strength. One would go off in say twelve hours, one in twenty-four hours. You just had to get them out and hope for the best.[5]
>
> Second Lieutenant Martin Greener, 175 Tunnelling Company, Royal Engineers

When the retreat was at an end the Germans were safely ensconced in the Hindenburg Line, which joined the existing German trench systems south of the River Scarpe.

Despite the changed situation, it was decided that the British would still attack on 9 April 1917. In all, 2,816 British guns and howitzers opened up in a four-day preliminary bombardment that dwarfed anything seen on the Somme. More guns firing on a much shorter frontage meant that the German trenches were deluged by shells. When the time came, the creeping barrages would create a wall of bursting high explosive and shrapnel shells in front of the advancing troops. Tanks, too, would play their role, crushing paths through any remaining barbed wire and taking on surviving German strongpoints. As soon as the assault divisions had taken their objectives they would be leapfrogged by fresh reserves to maintain the pace of the advance.

It had been realised, by this time, that eradicating or neutralising any German batteries that might slaughter the assaulting infantry at Zero Hour was of critical importance.

> The counter-battery organisation was extremely well run and very complex. You had a counter-battery officer at Corps who kept very

complete records and maps, which were circulated regularly. Every gun position seen firing was entered on the map and it was given a number, so that an aeroplane seeing it fire could send down the signal 'GNF' which meant 'Gun now firing'. The counter-battery staff would know at once that that battery was in action and they would get someone on to it. The majority of the 4.5 howitzers were gas shelling. On the actual night before the attack, we fired more than 500 rounds per gun of gas shell at German batteries.[6]

Lieutenant Kenneth Page, 130 Battery, 40th Brigade, RFA

At 05.30 on Easter Monday 9 April, in terrible weather, the troops went over the top. On the left, the Canadian Corps of First Army were charged with the capture of Vimy Ridge, an imposing objective that offered an observation platform overlooking the Douai plain. The French had already weakened the German positions and left little room for them to deploy defence in depth. The Canadians charged forward, assisted by the detonation of two huge mines, a devastating creeping barrage and a dense smokescreen.

Instead of the long preliminary bombardment, the barrage only lasted about a minute on the front line and then lifted, and the troops immediately moved forward. I myself was struck by the number of men going, you could see them right and left. We had to thread our way amongst the shell holes because the ridge itself had been so pounded it was nothing but a mass of shell holes. The German trenches were almost obliterated. We carried on there; our first objective was the German main line. From then on we went on to the final objective which was just over the eastern crest of the ridge. When we reached the top of the ridge a remarkable sight was unfolded: we saw before our eyes all the German occupied villages around Lens; the mining villages, with their slag heaps and mineshafts.[7]

Private George Hancox, Princess Patricia's Light Infantry

The Canadians achieved a notable success, managing to take control of the whole ridge.

To the south the Third Army accomplishment was perhaps even more remarkable as it pushed forwards in the Scarpe valley. The German artillery may have been neutralised, but conditions were terrible for the poor foot soldier.

> It was snow and sleet and God knows what. Wet, sloshy underfoot. My pal was using his rifle to get along because he couldn't make headway. We had these great big panniers we were carrying on our backs. No overcoat, because when you were in an attack the first thing you gave up was your greatcoat. It was frightfully cold. We passed the Middlesex coming out. Wretched weather, terrible weather.[8]
>
> Private Victor Polhill, 1/5th London Regiment (London Rifle Brigade)

Despite this, the Third Army advanced almost 4 miles. But the more they advanced, the further they were from the support of their field artillery, which could only cover their progress for the first mile or so. The British almost got through, but the Germans had calculated correctly and still had trenches to spare in their deep defence zone. Over the next two days the British attempted to follow up, but were thwarted by the wilderness of the former No Man's Land and the terrible weather. The Germans managed to re-establish their line and the offensive began to stagnate. All eyes were now on the French offensive on the Chemin des Dames, to be launched on 16 April.

The French assault proved a disaster. Although gains were made, Nivelle's optimism faced reality as casualties mounted. The situation was so dire that on 23 April it became necessary for the British to renew their diversionary attacks at Arras. This became known as the Second Battle of the Scarpe; it was a travesty of the methods that had succeeded just a couple of weeks before. This time the artillery preparations were inadequate, the troops were tired and the Germans were familiar with the new British tactics. The German artillery had been pulled further back, so that they were out of range of most of the British guns but could still lash shells down onto the advancing British infantry. Among them was Leading Seaman Joe Murray, who little knew that this would be his last battle with the RND, which by this time had been assimilated into the army as the 63rd Division.

> It was almost daylight. The barrage opened. Major Asquith[9] came along and we were given instructions. We were not supposed to move

until the barrage lifted off the German front line immediately in front of Gavrelle. Any old campaigner knows that to wait until the barrage moves and then have a couple of hundred yards to walk is just simply murder. But Asquith, instead of waiting until the barrage lifted, he took us forward – we went forward to within about 50 yards when it lifted. His judgement was perfect and we were on top of his line before Jerry knew anything about it. We men who survived that battle owe our survival to Asquith ignoring orders. The ground in front of us was not pockmarked with shell holes – it was quite level really – open. Ideal territory for tanks, but we didn't have any. As we got to the first objective it wasn't so bad, we seemed to be organised. When you got in the village it was a different kettle of fish because Jerry was in the cellars.[10]

Leading Seaman Joe Murray, Hood Battalion

Street fighting was a dangerous game and the village seemed to be under fire from all sides.

It was now quite light and being in the open we were perfect targets. There were bricks flying about, rifle fire, machine-gun fire, there was shelling. You couldn't keep in any sort of formation at all. Sometimes you got underneath a half-blown-down house; sometimes you went over the top. The wire that was in front was piled up in heaps as it usually is by our artillery bombardment. We had to keep gathering together to get through a particular place. You couldn't climb over 10–15 feet of bricks. All the time we were being fired on. There was no sort of line, no sort of direction, you couldn't see any officers, you couldn't see any men. Sometimes there were three or four; sometimes you were on your own – where has everyone got to you don't know. You don't like to be alone! We were quite close to the road and I came across an officer lying flat. I tried to undo some barbed wire round what was left of one of his legs, a sub-lieutenant. I turned him over and he had a sort of grin on his face. His face was red – there was red brick dust as well as blood.[11]

Leading Seaman Joe Murray, Hood Battalion

Murray pushed forward along the main road, feeling his way into the very centre of Gavrelle.

I was fooling round trying to get over an old door of a house. As I stood on the damned thing it went over and it went forward. As I slipped, I saw a rifle, from a cellar; I could only see the barrel. I saw it move – instinctively I turned quickly round to the left and I fired. I didn't need the smoke from his rifle to know that I'd been hit. My hand was in my pocket and it went through my wrist. I couldn't get me hand out of my pocket, paralysed. The rifle was swinging and I crawled forward to where the rifle was, 3 or 4 feet. The Jerry was firing out of the entrance of a cellar and I'd shot him, blown half his head away. I got in there, I've got him for company – he's dead of course. A shell burst very close – there were doors and window frames flying about. I thought to myself, 'I'm going to be buried here in a moment!' The blood was running down my trouser leg, excruciating pain. I tried to get my rifle off but I couldn't get my hand out of my pocket. I thought I've got to get out of here somehow. The shells were banging all the time, the rifles going, bricks, sulphur, noise.[12]

Leading Seaman Joe Murray, Hood Battalion

That was the end of Joe Murray's war. He would be rescued and safely evacuated back to Blighty.

By this time the French situation had spiralled out of control as their troops began to mutiny, a contagion which, after three years of incredible casualties and suffering, spread rapidly through the French Army. Haig and the BEF had little choice but to step up their diversionary efforts to conceal their ally's weakness. The result was more disastrous attacks that had little or no chance of any meaningful success. Yet what was the alternative? On 4 May the Arras offensive finally came to an end. It had been a terrible experience for the British Army after the heartening successes of the first day. Most of all it hammered home the lesson that, although the British had greatly improved their attack tactics, the Germans had simultaneously developed their own tactics for defence. The unplanned prolongation of the battle to cover the French disaster had exacerbated the situation, with British and Canadian casualties totalling some 158,000: indeed, it was the highest daily average rate of losses suffered by the British for any battle in the war. As the French mutinies spread, Nivelle was soon discarded, to be replaced by General Philippe Pétain, a more cautious general, keen to conserve the lives of his men. It was also becoming apparent that the Russian Revolution in 1917 had severely destabilised their Eastern Front ally. Doing nothing seemed not to be an option and, following the suspension of the Arras offensive, Haig's attention switched to Flanders where a new major offensive was planned.

The Flanders Offensive, 1917

Prologue: The Battle of Messines

Haig had always been convinced that Flanders would be the best arena for a major British offensive effort on the Western Front. Here there were real strategic objectives. There was a compelling need to push the line further away from the Channel ports just 25 miles behind Ypres, while a relatively small advance would also put the German naval bases of Ostend and Zeebrugge within their grasp. This was considered vital by the Admiralty, who feared the depredations of German submarines and destroyers marauding in the English Channel. There was also the glittering prize of the highly significant Roulers railway junction just 5 miles behind the Passchendaele Ridge. Finally, Haig hoped that a sustained offensive at Ypres, where the Germans would be unable to make a tactical withdrawal, could give the Allies an opportunity to inflict the sustained battering that might at last bring victory, if not in 1917 then early in 1918.

First, it was necessary to eject the Germans from their vantage point up on the Messines Ridge immediately to the south of Ypres. Although only 260 feet above sea level, it provided a wonderful observation platform over the Ypres Salient. The attack was to be carried out by the Second Army commanded by General Sir Herbert Plumer, who decided on a four-day artillery bombardment by some 2,266 guns and howitzers, augmented by a series of devastating mine explosions beneath German lines.

> Spanbroekmolen was the largest mine which I had helped to charge. It was driven 1,707 feet from its entrance, finished off by 171 Tunnelling Company who chambered, charged it and detonated it. Its depth, according to the ordnance map, was 92 feet. The Germans

were down below at 130 feet and every now and again caused us trouble. The essence of mining in a clay area was silence and secrecy. We wore felt slippers, rubber-wheeled trolleys, wooden rails and we spoke in whispers. When the Germans 'blew' us we never answered back; we suffered casualties and did nothing, tried not to give away where we were. We listened for them with very delicate instruments, the geophone and the Western Electric. One of our officers was once so near to a German sinking shaft that he recorded and translated a series of anecdotes that the German NCO told his shift![13]

Lieutenant Bryan Frayling, 171 Tunnelling Company, Royal Engineers

Once they were completed, the mines lay dormant, ready for use when required.

Everything was in order. The commanding officers had been called back to headquarters and each one had been issued with a synchronised watch. They were sent back to their units and we went up to the line. Then we were definitely told when it would be: which was 03.50am on the 7th June. Well, everyone was in a bit of a jitter that morning; we didn't know what was going to happen. The night had been absolutely calm, fewer shots than I'd ever heard.[14]

Lieutenant John Royle, 1st Australian Tunnelling Company

There were nineteen mines in total underneath the German lines. The tension was unbelievable for the engineers as they checked their circuits for one last time.

There we were, all waiting and ready. We manned our posts about quarter of an hour before the time. I don't know whether any of you have had to wait a quarter of an hour in a dentist's room – well this felt four times as long as that. Fifteen minutes to go. We started talking about what we'd do on leave, how was 'Mademoiselle of Armentières', anything we could think of! Then 45 seconds, 30 seconds, 15 seconds, 10 seconds, 5 seconds, 4, 3, 2, 1, GO![15]

Lieutenant John Royle, 1st Australian Tunnelling Company

At exactly 03.50, the tunnelling officers connected the circuits that triggered a series of artificial volcanoes beneath the all-unaware German garrison. Royle's mine was underneath Hill 60.

The whole hillside, everything rocked like a ship at sea. The noise
from the artillery was deafening, the thunder from our charges was
enormous. The infantry dashed forward under a barrage and kept
sending back thousands and thousands of prisoners, I couldn't tell
you how many. They came back through our dugouts, we saw them
and they were absolutely demoralised. We were all so happy that we
didn't know what to do! We thought the war was over![16]

Lieutenant John Royle, 1st Australian Tunnelling Company

Further south there were some even bigger explosions. It must have
been an incredible sight.

After the tremor we saw the flames. I think Kruisstraat was the first,
Spanbroekmolen almost simultaneously with it. A sheet of flame
that went up higher than St Pauls – I estimated about 800 feet. It
was a white incandescent light; we knew that the temperature was
about 3,000 degrees centigrade. The Germans there went up as gas.
The biggest bit of German I found afterwards was one foot in a boot.
When the mines went up, the first remark made by anybody was the
chaplain, who said, 'The earth opened and swallowed them up!'[17]

Lieutenant Bryan Frayling, 171 Tunnelling Company, Royal Engineers

The infantry had been waiting, ready to attack.

The sky was a lurid red all the time with the flashing of the shells and
the guns. It was a bit of a nightmare really. I don't know how long
we stood with our bayonets fixed and a second lieutenant in front of
us. Then there was a terrific explosion that shook the ground we were
stood on. A cylinder of yellow and red flame shot right up in the air
to a terrific height. This was our Busshouse Sap going up underneath
Wytshaete village which the Germans had turned into a fortress.
Then our own guns started a terrific continuous barrage: thundering,
thundering, thundering, Over our heads we could hear the hissing of
our machine-gun bullets; our machine gunners were plastering the
ridge with bullets. Then the whistle went and we went forward. It was
light enough to see by then and the opposition was nil. Our objective
was the sunken road. It had been quite a fortress but our own guns
had hammered it to pieces. The concrete places were all smashed in,

the road itself was chewed up and the banks were chewed. We planted our Lewis gun in a shell hole on the edge of the sunken road.[18]

Private George Thompson, 20th Durham Light Infantry

The power of the creeping barrage that chaperoned them every step of the way forward was deeply reassuring for the infantry.

To the south, Private Frederick Collins was a gearsman in a tank advancing in support of the Australians.

I was the second driver so the other chap was driving. I sat there pulling the gears in for when they wanted to turn. We were sailing along nicely when all of a sudden there was a tremendous thump right in the belly of the tank, outside. A shell had hit our tank. The place was full of smoke, gas and everything else – but the shell didn't come through. The bottoms of the tanks were steel – it bent up about 2½ feet. This chap on the 6-pounder, he stood there, he'd got hit and it had fetched two great lumps out of his hand. The next chap standing with the machine gun his leg was black. The officer shouted, 'See if you can get any stretcher bearers!' We didn't know where we were. It was all smoke, terrible inside the tank, we didn't know who else was hit. But that's all the damage it had done – if it had gone through I shouldn't have been here now. It hit like a glancing blow, bent it up. We couldn't open the door, we tried, we were in a trap until another man came and we opened it. There happened to be stretcher bearers and they came and took these two chaps out, put them on the stretcher. We closed the door again and the officer said, 'See if we can start the engine, we're going to carry on!' They started the engine again. I was as white as a sheet – so they told me. I should think I was as well! We carried on, quietly. The Germans had run like rabbits when the mine went up. At last we came to the mine, we were about 20 yards away. Everywhere was quiet. Thompson said, 'Well, get out and have a look!' We all got out of the tank and walked over to this huge crater. You'd never seen anything like the size of it; you'd never think that explosives would do it. But I saw about 150 Germans laid there, in different positions, throwing a bomb, a gun on their shoulder, all laid there dead with their eyes open.[19]

Private Frederick Collins, B Battalion, Tank Corps

The Messines operation was an excellent demonstration of the virtues of the well-planned set-piece battle. In all the men of Second Army took some 7,354 German prisoners and captured forty-eight guns. Sadly, the attempts to exploit the rapid capture of the ridge by pushing on to take the Oost-taverne Line on the reverse slopes were less successful, and led to bitter fighting that continued until 12 June and cost 24,562 British casualties.

The Third Battle of Ypres: Passchendaele

The Third Battle of Ypres was a titanic battle that now figures in popular memory under the title of its last phase at Passchendaele. In Flanders the Germans had both the time and space to put into effect their new defensive arrangements. Their pillboxes and blockhouses littered the low ridges and reverse slopes, a fearsome prospect for any attacking force. Responsibility for the assault had been passed from General Sir Herbert Plumer to General Sir Hubert Gough of the Fifth Army, as Haig considered that Gough, a 'thruster' by nature, would evince more urgency than the more cautious Plumer. The British still had a series of tremendous tactical problems to solve. If they concentrated all their artillery resources on the German forward zone, before long they would crash up against the undamaged German second-line system, thus restricting the amount of ground that could be captured. Indeed, the majority of the Royal Artillery guns were still field artillery, unable to hit targets more than 1½ miles behind the German front line. The length of the bombardment was also a moot point. A hurricane short bombardment was favoured, but in that case who, or what, would cut the wire and destroy the pillboxes? Yet a longer bombardment simply warned the Germans of what was coming. The technology and techniques available for offensive operations had not yet caught up with the advantages that trenches, bolt-action rifles, barbed wire, machine guns, massed artillery and pillboxes bequeathed to the defending forces. The fissure between attack and defence was closing, but it still remained.

One touted partial solution was the tactic of 'bite and hold'. This surrendered any real thought of a breakthrough in return for seizing just the German front line, or forward zone, and consolidating it into the British lines before preparing for the next 'bite'. The trouble was that this tactical method was excruciatingly expensive in resources and was by its very nature slow. In addition, as it offered little more than a series of pitched battles, the expected casualty rate was still high. In the end, it was not unreasonable for Haig to try to maximise the return for his huge investment of military resources. As a result, he and Gough resolved that they would take the more ambitious course and try to vault the German second-line system as well when the main attack went in. It would almost work; but not quite.

The bombardment began on 16 July and in all the Royal Artillery amassed some 2,092 field artillery guns, 718 medium pieces and 281 heavy guns in the Ypres area – a total of 3,091 guns. The barrage was on a truly mammoth scale, building on all their accumulated experience. It had now been fully recognised that counter-battery fire was crucial – the German guns had to be suppressed – and the German batteries were targeted remorselessly, before being thoroughly drenched with gas shells in the final day. The creeping barrage would be carefully tailored to the progress of the advancing infantry, and a standing barrage would then create a wall of shells in front of them to destroy any German counter-attack before it got anywhere near the new British front line. The noise of the bombardment was almost beyond belief.

> As the barrage opened it was terrific. One person he broke down, he started screeching, like a pig. You've heard a pig screeching – well, he screeched like a stuck pig. He was sent back. It was no fault of his, it wasn't cowardice. His nerves just went. We knew the fellow, he wasn't the type of boy who played football or roughed it up a bit. He was temperamental, a brilliant pianist, and in fact he shouldn't have been in the army at all.[20]
>
> Private Ivor Watkins, 15th Welsh Regiment

The troops went over the top at 03.50 on 31 July 1917. The assault was stunningly successful in the north, where two French divisions met minimal opposition in reaching the outskirts of Bixschoote. Next in line were the divisions of the British XIV, XVIII and XIX Corps, who crashed forwards, breasting the low rise of the Pilckem Ridge, pushing forward into the Steenbeek Valley and capturing the village of St Julien, lost in April 1915. The infantry had tank support, in one of which was a very nervous Lieutenant Horace Birks who was trundling towards Mousetrap Farm.

This was the first time I'd actually commanded a tank in action and I was petrified. I hoped the whole way up that I should sprain my ankle or something like that so that we should never get there or that the whole thing would be called off. We had no luck at all and the ghastly hour got nearer and nearer. The worst moment of all was when we started up our engines and they would backfire – we got a sheet of flame out of the exhaust – everybody calling each other a bloody fool and waiting to know what was going to happen. However, nothing did happen and we climbed into the tank. The gearsmen got into their places, then the side gunners, then the driver and then the officer gets in through the top. We started off.[21]

Lieutenant Horace Birks, D Battalion, Tank Corps

The range of the tank was small, and even that short journey towards the Steenbeek was torture for the crew.

We had to close down because we were within very comfortable machine-gun range and once we were shut down we were completely isolated from the world, we had no means of communication at all. The thing got hotter and hotter and hotter. The only ventilation was concerned with the engine and not with the crew. You could only see forwards through a little slit in the front visor, and if you wanted to see out of the side you looked through steel periscopes which gave you a sort of translucent outside light, all distorted. The tank inside was just steeped in stygian gloom – gloomy, hot and steamy. My particular tank never went until the engine had boiled: once it had boiled, you kept it boiling and it was jolly good. The noise inside was such that you could hear nothing outside at all and people made little gestures to you, rude or otherwise, that was all you could do, your sole means of communicating. When this barrage came down you could distinguish that quite easily because any shell bursting within a few yards of the tank, you got tremendous back pressure and you felt it all the way through. In fact, a shell bursting between the horns of the tank seemed to lift it up in the air. And then the machine guns started. They were quite easy to discern because they were just like peas in a tin can rattling away.[22]

Lieutenant Horace Birks, D Battalion, Tank Corps

The troops reached the 10-foot-wide Steenbeek and the low ridge beyond, when progress began to falter as they approached German defences, which had been less affected by the opening barrage.

Further south, the II Corps had been given the difficult task of attacking the Westhoek Ridge and Gheluvelt Plateau. This was clearly the key to the Ypres Salient as it represented the high ground in a land of hillocks. The Germans were well aware of its importance and had layered trenches, pillboxes and fortifications across it, defending the way to the Passchendaele Ridge. Sadly, Gough had underestimated the strength of these positions and he failed to devote the extra resources required to crack such a tough nut.

Facing the Westhoek Ridge, on the left of the sector was Lieutenant Ulrich Burke. Here things at least started well.

> When you get out on top you try and keep as straight line as possible. You were spaced at 3 to 4 yards interval, going forward at the high port, that is with the rifle diagonally across your chest with the bayonet pointing up at the sky. We reckoned to do a minute to a minute and a half per 100 yards. We knew we could run it in nine seconds. But with the shell holes, the men had to go round them, at the same time being fired on and trying to keep their distance between one another and to keep their alignment.[23]
>
> Lieutenant Ulrich Burke, 2nd Devonshire Regiment

When at last they reached the German trench they took their revenge for the men they had lost crossing No Man's Land.

> It was only when you got to within 20 yards of the trench that you said, 'Charge!' They then brought their rifles facing the enemy and charged into the trench, killing and bayoneting. It only lasted a few seconds. If there weren't many troops about you knew there must be more, so you threw bombs down the dugouts; that wasn't so much to kill them, it was to keep them there.[24]
>
> Lieutenant Ulrich Burke, 2nd Devonshire Regiment

On they pushed, moving slightly to the left of Bellewaarde Lake. But then their attack ran out of steam. Burke was wounded in a particularly horrible manner.

You jump into the trench. This German put his bayonet up and I'm afraid I caught it in the right shoulder, right across my back and just missing my spine – I was impaled on this. My only fear was that he would press the trigger which would have made a hell of a mess. My sergeant, who was near me, saw me, he came in close, shot the fellow and then hoisted me with the help of another man off the bayonet because I was on top of the German – he was dead and it wasn't pleasant. A bayonet wound hurts directly it goes in and the withdrawal is more anguish than the 'putting in' because the 'putting in' is instantaneous. If you get hit by a bullet or bomb splinter it's so hot that it cauterises the wound and you don't feel anything for a minute or so.[25]

Lieutenant Ulrich Burke, 2nd Devonshire Regiment

Just south of them, the troops directly facing the Gheluvelt Plateau had the hardest task: advancing across a wilderness of shell holes, barbed wire and concrete pillboxes in splintered woodland. The appalling ground conditions negated their tank support, and they also lost touch with the creeping barrage. Although the first objectives were taken, the troops were soon cut off from support by retaliatory German artillery barrages.

Meanwhile, the Second Army made a series of supporting attacks between Gheluvelt Plateau and Messines Ridge to the south.

Everybody got into trouble that morning. The first, second, third wave, all the lot of us, because of these pillboxes. Concrete emplacements with a machine-gun slot in the front of them. There wasn't much artillery fire there. These pillboxes were so built that one covered another. If you were busy attacking one, you came under fire from another one, they all covered each other. The only way to really clear them was to creep underneath the machine-gun slot, and put a Mills bomb through – one bomb was sufficient as a rule to clear the inside of them. We hadn't gone much further forward before I was hit, I saw the blood running down my hand; it was painful of course – and that's as much as I know of that battle.[26]

Private George Thompson, 20th Durham Light Infantry

Overall, it seemed as though the offensive had a chance of significant success, but then the Germans counter-attacked, crunching into the unconsolidated British positions, regaining St Julien and forcing the British back to the muddy Steenbeek, before the line bent back towards Westhoek Ridge and the much smaller gains on the Gheluvelt Plateau. The first day of the new offensive had been hard fought, with the Germans losing around 30,000 casualties in the day's fighting and the British 32,500 men. A long and painful struggle lay ahead.

It was essential that the British should maintain momentum and resume the attack as soon as possible, particularly on the Gheluvelt Plateau, but luck was against them as the difficulties of moving guns and ammunition forward were exacerbated by the onset of bad weather. It had started to rain on the first day of the attack and it would continue to rain throughout August. There were only three days that month without rain, giving no chance for the ground to dry out between showers and rainstorms. After three years of shelling, the battlefield already suffered from suspect drainage, and now shell holes filled with water and shallow streams, like the Steenbeek, spread to create dismal swamplands.

Because of this, nothing much happened for ten days. This was a catastrophic delay. Even when serious operations resumed, Gough failed to concentrate his resources to tackle the underlying threat of the Gheluvelt Plateau. The floundering Gough then ordered a general attack in the Battle of Langemarck, launched at 04.45 on 16 August. Although the French did well, gaining more ground to the south, British divisions struggled. They managed to jump the Steenbeek and seize both the fortified village of Langemarck and the rubble of St Julien, but the attack then ground to a halt. Further south, the failure of the attacks on the Gheluvelt Plateau left the 2nd Royal Berkshire Regiment isolated as they moved forwards onto Zonnebeke Ridge. Lieutenant Colonel Alan Hanbury-Sparrow took shelter in an old trench, but it seemed hopeless.

> There was a gun ranging on this particular trench. It had obviously seen us go there and I imagine it was one of four guns in a battery. I knew that once that battery got the range and opened fire we were done. At the same time a machine gun, which seemed very much

closer than I liked, swept the top of our parapet and killed three men in that process. They'd got the position exactly. I knew we were in a very parlous situation.[27]

Lieutenant Colonel Alan Hanbury-Sparrow, 2nd Royal Berkshire Regiment

Hanbury-Sparrow was powerless to change their situation but he could at least try to demonstrate the natural insouciance expected of an officer and set a good example to his faltering men.

Well, I sat down of course, nothing to be done and I did what I generally did on those occasions – I played chess with my adjutant; I always had a little chessboard with pegs! We played on, rather aimlessly it's true, but it steadied the men. Then suddenly a shell fell into the trench. I thought to myself, 'Now our time has come, you've had a long run for your money and I wonder what it will be like to be dead?' At that moment I realised that whatever happened I wasn't going to be killed. Now it's impossible to describe this consciousness, it's not like ordinary consciousness at all, it's something like a prophet of old when the Lord spoke, something quite overwhelmingly clear and convincing. I wasn't very proud of myself, because I didn't care what happened to the others – I was going to survive. I took a rifle and I began shooting. I hit two Germans at 600 yards and made a third skip for his life. The extraordinary part was this. That machine gun never fired again. That was the last shell that that gun fired; there was no reason why it should stop, and the attack on our front, but not on the flanks, petered out and never came near us. It was as though for a moment I got a glimpse of time coming towards me. That was a great and strange feeling that I had.[28]

Lieutenant Colonel Alan Hanbury-Sparrow, 2nd Royal Berkshire Regiment

Overall, the battle was a disaster. They had failed to gain ground where it mattered and the minor gains made were all but irrelevant to the necessities of the tactical situation. The cost was another 16,000 casualties.

From this point on, the August fighting degenerated into chaos, and all Gough could come up with was a series of local attacks designed to secure a good starting line for some future attempt to sweep up onto the Passchendaele Ridge. This echoed the similar mistakes made on the Somme during the August and early September fighting in 1916.

Localised attacks merely allowed the Germans to concentrate their fire, with predictable effects.

The conditions in the Ypres Salient vied with the worst of the Somme and Verdun. Between the Pilckem and Passchendaele Ridges the British were trapped in a series of swampy marshlands. Any remains of the former infrastructure had been blasted apart and they were forced to build new roads as they went.

> We used to have to go up on working parties carrying sawn tree trunks, about 2 inches thick, to lay a road through the mud for the Royal Engineers. These logs were coming up with GS wagons and they were dumping them down. We were carrying them up, two men to a log and the REs were putting them down. We laid about 100 yards or so. Jerry waited till we got that done, then he started to blow it all up again – and he reduced it to splinters. The next day we went up again, we got a bit further. When we went next morning that was all in splinters.[29]
>
> Private Alfred Griffin, 9th King's Royal Rifle Corps

Wherever a man was, whatever he was doing, he was still vulnerable to shelling in the Ypres Salient. Lieutenant George Horridge, who had recovered from the wound suffered at Gallipoli, was detailed to supervise a ration party. Here he had an experience that shook him to the core.

> The ration party consisted of two parties and we'd arrived at this trench. At the side of the trench was a steel plate about 9 feet long by 3 feet wide which somebody had put up. The first party were dumping the rations against this steel plate. I was on one end of it, another officer was in the middle and another at the left. We were watching the rations being dumped. I happened to look up to the right and I could see shadowy forms coming. I said, 'Hello, here's the second ration party, I'll just give them a shout, tell them where we are!' I took two steps – not more – and a big shell fell on the plate I'd been leaning against. A tremendous flash and I was blown down against the side of the trench. I picked myself up, realising that, as far as I knew, nothing had hit me. There was a dead silence. I said, 'Are Mr Mashiter[30] and Mr Hudson[31] here?' They were the two officers

who'd been with me – no reply. Then a sort of hubbub broke out. This shell had not only killed the two officers, it had killed four of the ration party, one of whom had both legs blown off, and wounded eight others.[32] The whole thing was a terrible shock. We had to get the wounded away, in the dark, and we knew the gun was pointing at the same place and might fire another shot at any time. I think I had a certain amount of shell-shock because when we got them away and everything had gone quiet again I went and found an old pillbox and lay down in a corner. I stayed there for twenty-four hours more or less asleep or out. I don't remember very much about it – it was a terrible shock.[33]

Lieutenant George Horridge, 1/5th Lancashire Fusiliers

The ground was rendered almost featureless by constant shelling. Only the squat pillboxes seemed to survive and a few blasted tree stumps. Villages were reduced to reddish patches of brick dust in the mud. Private Sibbald Stewart remembered being sent out one night as a runner. This simple mission turned into a nightmare.

I had to take a message out to a machine gun in No Man's Land, beyond the barbed wire. I lost my way that night; I couldn't find the normal entrance to get through to the machine gun. In the end I go underneath the wire and that's when the German spotted me. They put a star shell up and the whole place was exposed like daylight. Oh, it was terrible! This was 1 o'clock in the morning. After the star shell the Germans started plotting left and right until I was right in the middle. I saw the tracer bullets going off over my head. I couldn't get away with it. I was blown up by a shell. The only thing that was left above the mud was my right shoulder, right arm and my head. If it hadn't been for that mud I would have been blown to pieces, but the mud really it dulled the explosion in such a way that the shell itself did not come through, otherwise I could have been riddled. Sergeant Weir jumped out of the emplacement. I shouted, 'Sergeant, firing orders!' I gave him his new firing orders and he pulled me out of the mud. I was shaking like an aspen leaf – I got an awful shock that night! The next twenty-four hours I don't remember anything about it. When I came to I was lying in one of the dugouts.[34]

Private Sibbald Stewart, 238th Machine Gun Company

To make matters worse, just before the battle had started, the Germans had unveiled their latest 'advance' in gas warfare, which was soon known as mustard gas due to its distinctive smell.

> The yellow cross gas shell, mustard gas as it was called, was particularly nasty. The shell used to burst with a 'PLOP', that's all you heard. The shell burst open and the liquid came out – the moment it met the air it became gaseous. Of course it soaked the ground where the shell had fallen and if some unfortunate soldier happened to sit in that small shell hole he'd have everything burnt away very quickly. Mustard gas attacked all the vesicular parts of the body. The underarm, between the elbow, by the ear – all where the lymphatic glands are. It was a very, very nasty gas, a very bad invention that. It was the one the Germans used most, because they could saturate a place. They would fire hundreds sometimes thousands of shells full of mustard gas, to make a place impossible to hold if they were going to attack.[35]
>
> Sergeant William Collins, No. 1 Cavalry Field Ambulance

Men took shelter where they could. Often the British colonised the captured German pillboxes. A future British Second World War general never forgot a night spent sheltering in Ferdinand Farm in front of Langemarck.

> It had very, very thick concrete walls but it was a curious sort of place to have a headquarters. It had been built by the Germans and so the entrance faced the German lines. It had enormously thick concrete walls, but inside it was only about 5 foot high. At the bottom of the pillbox there was about 2 foot of water. The water was simply horrid: it had refuse in it, old tins and indeed excreta. Whenever shells burst near it the smell was perfectly overpowering. Luckily there was a sort of concrete shelf the Boche had made which was about 2 foot 6 inches off ground level. On this four officers and six other ranks spent the night. There wasn't room to lie down, there was hardly room to sit upright and we more or less crouched there. At the outside of the pillbox there was an enormous shell hole – across this was a plank because there was about 6 feet of water in the shell hole. The only way you could get into the pillbox was over the plank and inside the shell hole was the dead body of a Boche who had been there a very

long time and who floated or sank on alternate days according to the atmosphere. It was also lousy. It was not a place I would enter now for a great deal of money – but we were extremely glad to be in it that night.[36]

Lieutenant Douglas Wimberley, 51st Machine Gun Company

Over everything there was a powerful stench that blended together the essence of explosive fumes, mustard gas, faeces and death.

Ooooh, a horrible smell! There's nothing like a dead body's smell. It's a putrid, decaying smell, makes you stop breathing, you think of disease. It's a smell you can't describe unless you've smelt rotten meat. You've got the smell right under your nose all the time and if there's one at the bottom of the trench and you keep walking over it the black slime comes out – and that's not pleasant.[37]

Private Alfred Griffin, 9th King's Royal Rifle Corps

Few men who served there could ever forget the Ypres Salient.

GOUGH'S FLOUNDERING finally forced Haig to decide that a new broom was needed if the campaign was to make any progress. He acted relatively swiftly and on 23 August Plumer was recalled to take over the offensive, his Second Army being expanded north to take in the Gheluvelt Plateau. With Haig's acquiescence Plumer resolved to take his time: nothing would be left to chance. This was a situation where the tactic of 'bite and hold' could really come into its own. The Second Army would advance across the Gheluvelt Plateau in four carefully defined short steps of just 1,000 to 1,500 yards. Each time the intention was to seize only the German forward defence zone, not to penetrate any deeper. The Second Army alone would deploy some 1,295 guns and howitzers, of which 575 were now medium or heavy pieces.

Nothing was easy for the gunners in the Ypres Salient. When their guns were moved into position they had to make sure that they were not only protected from the German shells, but also that they were as near invisible as possible.

They used to have to lay a platform because the guns were very heavy – 5 tons – and the ground was a bloody bog. Consequently we had to get tree trunks and make a platform. For each of the four howitzers we built a platform. You wanted the gun in a pit but at Ypres you very often couldn't do that because the water level was too high. So we used to make a double sandbag wall round the edges of the gunpit and hope they didn't get too close a round. They would stop a splinter, but of course nothing would help if you got a direct hit. Normally we used to have some posts and camouflage netting over the gun. But in the Ypres Salient the ground was so devastated that the camouflage netting might give you away. What we did was to 'untidy' the position. We used to throw about bits of old sack cloth, packing, sandbags and half a rum jar. Instead of putting the battery handspikes and levers and things in neat order we used to throw them about. We were told to do this by the planes that used to help. They said, 'For God's sake, don't have any kind of order. Have your battery positions as untidy as you can make it and that will do more to defeat the Germans than anything else! Never allow men to approach the guns the same way all the time, or they will make tracks and that will be visible from the air.'[38]

Second Lieutenant Cyril Dennys, 212 Siege Battery, RGA

While the gunners were fighting an unending duel and Plumer's methodical preparations were under way, a number of futile small actions were taking place on Gough's Fifth Army front further to the north.

AT LAST PLUMER WAS READY, and the first step of his odyssey across the Gheluvelt Plateau began with the Battle of Menin Road on 20 September 1917. In one thing at least he proved to be a lucky general, as he was blessed with a period of dry weather and battlefield conditions greatly improved. The final awe-inspiring barrage, augmented by streams of machine-gun bullets, was fired from 05.40 on 20 September.

Our shells were firing over our heads on to the Germans, our machine guns raining lead into them. I've never experienced anything like it in my life and I don't want to experience it again. It was terrible. Solid metal going through the air. Our company had a machine gun posted every 30 yards – we were the advanced section of the light artillery you might call it. The artillery behind us and the infantry in front of us. We had to cover the infantry while they went forward and we followed them forward.[39]

Private Sibbald Stewart, 238 Machine Gun Company

The attack on the Gheluvelt Plateau proved a triumph, as at 05.40 the infantry lunged forward, ejecting the Germans from Nonne Boschen Wood, Glencourse Wood and Inverness Copse. Having achieved their objectives they consolidated and awaited the German riposte – ready and confident in the support of their massed artillery. Now it was the Germans that had to attack in the open. Lieutenant Charles Austin found the experience most exhilarating.

Although the troops were very tired I got them to clean all the German rifles that were there because if we ran short of ammunition we'd have German rifles and ammunition to use. Which, as it turned out, was exactly what happened. The next morning the Germans did counter-attack. We weren't expecting it because a counter-attack is usually preceded by a bombardment. They just got up out of their trenches and came at us. The sentries spotted them, then the shout went up, 'FIRE!' That was all – you hadn't got much time to do anything else. They came over absolutely shoulder to shoulder. We had our rifles, we had the German rifles, we used both and we just fired and fired and fired. We had mud to help us which slowed them up, they could only plod. I used a rifle, it was more accurate. I picked targets, they were never more than 70 to 80 yards away so it wasn't difficult to take a man and fire at that man. I am sure that I must have personally killed four or five or six Germans that morning. It was really the closest I ever came to looking eye-to-eye with a German. It was very exciting – it was them or us – they got to within 20 yards of us. I was told afterwards that we left 166 dead Germans on our company front. I know we took twenty-three prisoners.[40]

Lieutenant Charles Austin, 12th King's Royal Rifle Corps

All along the line the British this time managed to hold onto their gains. The battle had been a great success, but the cost was still terrible, with some 21,000 casualties.

Preparations now began for the second step forward in what would become known as the Battle of Polygon Wood on 26 September. The fighting followed a similar pattern, but for Corporal Donald Price, who was acting as a company runner, it proved a grim business.

> It was hell. There was not a soul about, not a tree, not nothing. All these Very lights up, the whole place looked dreadful, it looked evil. Pieces of equipment, pieces of mules, pieces of men. We were going over and I'd got to take another message. The sergeant major said, 'Take this back to the officers' dugout!' 'Jock' was with me and we had to run along one of these duckboards on top, because there was no path, no nothing. More often than not the shelling had tipped them up and you had to find where the next one was to scramble to it. We were running down this in the dark and he started. Poor old 'Jock'. A shell came and knocked him out, killed him behind me. I dashed on with this message to the dugout. I slid down this dugout and I was absolutely knackered and poor old 'Jock' had gone west behind me. This bloody officer, I gave him this message and this officer said, 'Right – get back as quick as you can!' I could have shot him. I was bloody exhausted and he'd got his whisky and his candle down there and he says, 'Get back as quick as you can!' I scrambled up from the dugout and found my way back to the trench. The sergeant major was there and he says, 'What's the matter with you?' I said, 'I'm tired!' Absolutely knackered. All of a sudden, 'BOOM!' the German shelling started again. I got a real beauty, shrapnel burst above and I got a real smack above the left knee. Then a mustard gas shell burst on the back of the trench and it plastered my back with mustard gas. The sergeant major said, 'Off you go!'[41]

Corporal Donald Price, 20th Royal Fusiliers

The British managed to take the village of Zonnebeke and completed the capture of Polygon Wood. Price was one of some 15,500 casualties. For now Plumer's plans were working and the Gheluvelt Plateau had been burst open.

EVERYTHING DEPENDED ON THE ARTILLERY, but the gun batteries would have been impotent without hundreds of shells reaching them on a regular basis. Although there were ships, railways, light railways, lorries, wagons and limbers to bring the shells in the early stages of the journey from the munitions factory, once they reached the battlefield proper there was usually only one way forward – by pack-horse. On 1 October the ammunition situation was considered so urgent for B Battery, 245 Brigade, that an ammunition party was sent forward during daylight hours.

> This corporal came and he says, 'You, you, you, you!' We had to try and get some ammunition through to the guns. It was just horses, about twenty or thirty, each driver had two horses with this pack you put round the horse with eight shells – four at either side. There was a ring of German observation balloons connected to batteries and they were watching for anybody that came through. Every time we tried to go through they started strafing. Of course we all turned round and galloped back, then we re-formed and Sergeant Emsley said to me, 'Look, Towers, I want you to come at the front about 5 or 6 yards behind me, and when I give the signal to gallop, we gallop and they'll follow you!' The sergeant went off, he says, 'Follow me, give me 5 yards.' He had just his own horse, he hadn't a lead horse. He gave me the signal and I shouted, 'GALLOP!' and we set off. They dropped a shell right between the two of us and that was it. All I remember was going up in the air and landing on the floor. My leg was stiff out. I never saw the horses, I never looked for the horses! There was a shell hole and I rolled down that. When I looked up over the shell hole top there was not a soul about, 'Oh God, am I'm going to be left here?' The other horses had scarpered. My leg was stiff, the shrapnel had gone right into the knee cap. I was looking to see if there was anybody to help me. All of a sudden these two RAMC men appeared from nowhere. They said, 'Now then, what's up?' I showed him. He got a bottle of iodine and he poured it in the hole – Ohhhh! The pain was terrific, I had more pain then than ever. They ran some bandaging round and put me on a stretcher. But what they did was lift me up on their shoulder – and I was covering them. I said, 'Oh, for God's sake put me down!' 'No, you're all right, you'll be all right!' So off we went. But I couldn't see where they were going – it was open barren land. All of a sudden they stopped and put the stretcher down. I said, 'What's up? Aren't you going on?' They said, 'You're all

right, don't worry!' They cleared some stuff away and there was a trap door. They lifted it up and there was a slide, they put the stretcher on, fastened a rope and lowered it down, it was a proper hospital underneath – it had been a German hospital underground. There was a full staff of hospital people there. They took me down into a theatre and I always remember them giving me anaesthetic, it was terrible. They had a white mask that fitted on your face – they pressed it on and when the drops went on you fought. They held you down. 'You're all right, stop it!'[42]

Driver William Towers, B Battery, 245 Brigade, RFA

He woke up to find himself aboard a hospital train on the way back to a Canadian hospital at Étaples.

I had a Thomas splint which was a round wooden ring with iron bars down and a foot rest. You were all strapped in that, but it was uncomfortable and the pain from my knee was getting terrible. I was looking down this marquee and there was an officer coming up with two sisters, he had his arm round them and he was laughing and talking. I never smelt a man smell more like a distillery in my life – he stank of whisky – they'd been drinking. I thought, 'Well, if that's an inspection, he isn't inspecting much!' He came past me and I said, 'Excuse me, Sir, could you have a look at my knee, it's driving me crazy – the pain!' 'Right!' So they took the bandages off and he said, 'Oh, there's a fluid there – we'll tap that tonight'. So they came for me to go to the theatre and I thought, 'Thank God for that!' I woke up in the early hours of the morning and there was nobody there. I said, 'What's the matter here?' My hand dropped off – I thought, 'Oh, my God, my leg's gone!' They'd taken it off – guillotined it off – and never said a word. I thought, 'Oh my God, what am I going to do now?' Because the only thing I knew was the men on crutches with a tin can begging. I'll never forget that day – I prayed to die – what a shock. I'd never given it the first thought.[43]

Driver William Towers, Étaples Hospital

If they could, things got worse. The treatment was excruciatingly painful.

They'd guillotined: they just cut all the flesh round there, saw through the bone, put some gauze on then leave it. Then a nurse came up and she took the blanket off and started to take the gauze off. Tearing this gauze off, it was dried on and she was pulling it. It was like pulling a toe out – I was in agony. I think I called her every name I knew. I said, 'You're inhuman woman!' She wouldn't take any notice – I'm damn sure she was deaf. She just pulled it off, she could have wet it and it wouldn't have been as bad, but she wouldn't. I was very bitter about it. When I'd got wounded, I'd thought, 'Thank God for that. I shall be out of it now!' It was a joy. We thought that a nice little wound would get you to Blighty – but I'd never expected this. I'd rather have stopped out than lose my leg, I'd rather have been killed.[44]

Driver William Towers, Étaples Hospital

Whatever his initial reaction, Towers would prove himself an indomitable fighter in campaigning for limbless ex-servicemen in the post-war years.

THE GERMANS WERE STRUGGLING, as their tactic of defence in depth was considerably undermined by the British seizing only the forward zone. When the British creeping barrage opened up at 06.00 on 4 October for the assault on Broodseinde Ridge, it caught the Germans cold, massed in their front-zone positions. Among the attackers was Captain William Bunning of the 22nd Australian Battalion.

To our surprise as we went down the slope we could see Germans running about in our barrage. We met some in No Man's Land and it transpired that they were attacking at exactly the precise moment that we were! There was not much fighting as far as that was concerned; they were soon devastated by our barrage. We went on, past the big pillbox near the lake – that sort of mopping up was done by the waves behind us. We went on and took what was called the Red Line. It was just 40 yards below the actual top of Broodseinde Ridge. There we dug in and consolidated. The barrage waited for us and the battalions behind waited there for half an hour or so whilst we consolidated our position. Then, at the psychological moment smoke shells came over which indicated to them that the barrage was about to creep forward. The 24th Battalion went through on to their objective which was the Blue Line. My casualties in my company were not really heavy. After we'd consolidated, I moved forward just to check up and see the fields of fire suitable for our men – siting our positions. When I got to the top of Broodseinde Ridge it was really surprising to see before us the green fields of Belgium. Actual trees! Grass and fields of course churned up a good deal by barrage shells – but as far as we were concerned it was open country! Then to look back from where we came – back to Ypres there was devastation. Then I could see why our own gunners had had such a gruesome time. You could see the flashes of all the guns, from Broodseinde right back to the very Menin Gate.[45]

Captain William Bunning, 22nd Battalion, AIF

In all, the British took some 5,000 prisoners. The Battle of Broodseinde had proved another great success, although again, British and Australian casualties were still painfully high at a total of around 20,600. Nevertheless, the Germans had by no means given up, and their artillery was still lethal.

One of the beauties of oral history is having the chance to hear the authentic voice of a man better known as a writer. Charles Carrington was the author of two of the finest books on the Great War: *A Subaltern's War*[46] and *Soldier from the Wars Returning*, and he was also interviewed for the BBC Great War series. As one might expect from someone who became a distinguished academic, he had a thoughtful perspective as the shells crashed down all around.

We settled down on our objective in a group of shell holes and there we sat for three days. On the second day it began to rain and rained continuously, so that the bog of Passchendaele spread out into a lake. All day long one had nothing to do but sit in the mud, shivering, wet and cold, with no hot food, very short of sleep and having been rather mentally shattered by the fighting of the previous day. The Germans did not in fact counter-attack us; however, they shelled us very scientifically, mostly from their 150mm guns which we called 5.9s. You could hear these shells coming – they took five or six seconds perhaps to come – and in five or six seconds you can pass through quite a number of psychological changes. Your mind can get through various phases. You'd hear in the distance quite a mild 'pop' as the gun is fired 5 miles away. Then a 'humming' sound as it approached you through the air, with a noise rather like an aeroplane, growing louder and louder. As it grew nearer you begin to calculate with yourself whether this one has got your name on it or not. The noise would grow into a great crescendo and at a certain point your nerve would break – in this flash of time, in a fifth of a second – you'd decide that this was the one, throw yourself down into the mud and cringe in the bottom of the shell hole. All the other people around would do the same. Well, you may save your life by doing that. Sometimes you miscalculate and this is a shell which isn't for you at all but it goes sailing busily on and plunks down on somebody else, 300–400 yards away. When a shell arrived it would plump into the mud and burst with a shattering shock. The splinters of the shell flew off, killing splinters, which might fly 50 yards away from the point of impact. You might find a fragment of jagged iron, nearly red hot and weighing half a pound, arriving in your shell hole. They would take another second or two before they would all settle down in the mud. Then you get up and roar with laughter and the others laugh at you for having been the first one to throw yourself down. This of course is hysterics! It becomes a kind of game in which you cling on and try not to let the tension break. The first person in a group who shows a sign of fear by giving way and taking cover – he's lost a point and it counts against him. The one who holds out longest has gained a point – but in what game? What is this for? After eighteen months in France I was still trying to pretend to be brave and not succeeding very well and so were we all. All the time one was saying to oneself, 'If they can take it – I can take it!' The awful thing being that this is not an isolated experience but it goes on continuously, minute after minute and even hour after hour.[47]

Lieutenant Charles Carrington, 1/5th Royal Warwickshire Regiment

Almost unnoticeable in Carrington's statement is a reference to rain. During the fighting on 4 October it had indeed begun to rain again, and once more the battlefield descended into a morass of mud and stagnant water. Rain in October was perhaps not surprising, but it did reveal one of the weaknesses of 'bite and hold' and why it was not a war-winning tactical solution. Advances of just 1,000 to 1,500 yards meant that they were getting nowhere fast. Put simply: it was a long way to Berlin at

1,000 yards a week. Now the cold and rain of late autumn weather was upon them, slowing progress still further, and time was fast running out. There was no longer any chance of reaching Roulers or clearing the Belgian ports. All that was left was the determination to keep on hammering away to secure the Passchendaele Ridge as a springboard to possible future offensive operations in 1918. But the rain threatened even that achievement.

Miles of glutinous mud impeded the gunners as they struggled to bring up the millions of shells needed to press home the assault. The guns themselves were trapped in place, often wearing out with little chance of any major repairs. The photographic and artillery observation aircraft of the Royal Flying Corps were also grounded by the bad weather. The Germans were up on drier land, where the drainage was still intact, and slowly they began to gain parity in the grim artillery duel.

The last six weeks of the fighting in the Salient were as close to hell as most people could ever imagine. For Bombardier John Palmer, an artillery signaller who had fought at the Battle of Mons, been awarded the Distinguished Conduct Medal and served through the Somme, it was the end of the line. This recording I have played many times at talks up and down the country. The tone of his voice and his phrasing may elude us on the printed page, but even so this is a revealing glimpse into the horrors of Passchendaele.

It was mud, mud, everywhere: mud in the trenches, mud in front of the trenches, mud behind the trenches. Every shell hole was a sea of filthy oozing mud. I suppose there is a limit to everything, but the mud of Passchendaele – to see men keep on sinking into the slime, dying in the slime – I think it absolutely finished me off. I 'knew' for three months before I was wounded that I was going to get – I knew jolly well, the only thing was I thought I was going to get killed. Every time I went out to mend the wire I think I was the biggest coward on God's earth. Nobody knew when a wire would go but we knew that it had to be mended, the infantrymen's lives depended on these wires working. It didn't matter whether we'd had sleep, we just had to keep those wires through. There were many days when I don't remember what happened because I was so damned tired. The fatigue in that mud was something terrible. You reached a point where there was no beyond, you just could not go any further. This night I reached my lowest ebb. I'd been out on the wires all day, all night, I hadn't had any sleep it seemed for weeks and no rest. It was very, very difficult to mend a telephone wire in this mud. You'd find one end and then you'd try and trudge through the mud to find the other end. As you got one foot out the other one would go down. It was somewhere near midnight. The Germans were sending over quite a barrage and I crouched down in one of these dirty shell holes. I began to think of those poor devils who had been punished for self-inflicted wounds, some had even been shot. I began to wonder how I could get out of it. I sat there and kept thinking. It's very lonely when you're on your own. Then in the distance I heard the rattle of harness, I didn't hear much of the wheels but I knew there were ammunition wagons coming up. I thought, 'Well, here's a way out – when they get level with me I'll ease out and put my leg under the wheel and I can plead it was an accident.' I waited and the sound of the harness got nearer and nearer. Eventually I saw the leading horses' heads in front of me and I thought, 'This is it!' I began to ease my way out and the first wagon reached me. You know, I never even had the guts to do that, I just couldn't do it. I think I was broken in spirit and mind.[48]

Bombardier John Palmer, 118th Battery, 26th Brigade, RFA

He would not have long to wait for relief of a kind from the intolerable fatigue and stress.

The next night my pal came out with me. We heard one of their big ones coming over. Normally, within reason, you could tell if one was going to land anywhere near or not. If it was, the normal procedure was to throw yourself down and avoid the shell fragments. This one we knew was going to drop near. My pal shouted and threw himself down. I was too damned tired even to fall down. I stood there. Next I had a terrific pain in the back and the chest and I found myself face down in the mud. My pal came to me; he tried to lift me up. I said to him, 'Don't touch me – leave me! I've had enough, just leave me!' The next thing I found myself sinking down in the mud and I didn't worry about the mud. I didn't hate it any more – it seemed like a protective blanket covering me. I thought, 'Well, if this is death, it's not so bad!' Then I found myself being bumped about and I realised I was on a stretcher. I thought, 'Poor devils these stretcher bearers

– I wouldn't be a stretcher bearer for anything.' I suddenly realised I wasn't dead, I realised I was alive. I realised that if these wounds didn't prove fatal that I should get back to my parents, to my sister, to the girl that I was going to marry. The girl that had sent me a letter every day from the beginning of the war. I thought, 'Thank God for that!' Then the dressing station, morphia and the sleep that I so badly needed. I didn't recollect any more till I found myself in a bed with white sheets and I heard the lovely wonderful voices of our nurses: English, Scots and Irish. Then I completely broke down.[49]

Bombardier John Palmer, 118th Battery, 26th Brigade, RFA

This is truly the authentic voice of the British soldier in 1917.

THE END GAME AT YPRES was not just a tragedy for individuals. It was a collective horror for the British Army. Pressed for time by the approach of the midwinter, the British were tempted to cut corners, which was inopportune, coinciding as it did with a reduction in the effectiveness of the guns on which everything depended.

The next 'step' was the Battle of Poelcappelle, launched on 9 October. This involved the Fifth Army assaulting the German lines between Houthulst Forest and Poelcappelle, while the Second Army pushed further along the Passchendaele Ridge. It was a disaster, as they failed to breach any of the major defensive works that remained in the dark fastness of Houthulst Forest. Conditions were such that no one knew what was happening and yet another assault was ordered.

The First Battle of Passchendaele, which followed on 12 October, marked a final abrogation of all the tenets of 'bite and hold'. The artillery preparations were totally inadequate and the poor battered divisions were expected to advance up to 1,000 yards further than they had achieved at the Battle of Menin Road three weeks earlier. The result was more disaster: too much ventured; nothing gained. Further attacks were postponed until the weather improved sufficiently to allow proper preparations to be made.

The next attempt would be the Second Battle of Passchendaele, launched at 05.40 on 26 October. The horizons at Ypres had closed in to such an extent that the intention was solely to capture the remnants of Passchendaele village up on the ridge. The Canadian Corps would lead the charge, with the planning devolved to its commander, Lieutenant General Sir Arthur Currie. There was an element of returning to the basic principles of 'bite and hold', as Currie was given plenty of time to prepare and split the offensive into two stages. However, the underlying problems of the dreadful state of the ground and prevailing bad weather remained. After hard fighting, the 3rd and 4th Canadian Divisions managed to push forward another vital 500 yards towards Passchendaele. Almost there.

To their left, the Fifth Army was required to make yet another attack on Houthulst Forest. It was a forlorn hope. Private Joe Pickard found himself up to his neck in trouble.

> The so-called front line was a series of shell holes with maybe one or two men in each shell hole. They were not linked – all separate. Our barrage opened early morning and within a couple of minutes at the outside, the German barrage opened. You were just sitting on the edge of this shell hole with your feet in the water. When the whistle went and you went forward it was a toss-up whether your legs would come or not! The ground was yellowy green soft quicksand. I got one leg in there and two fellows got hold of my rifle and pulled me out. You were plunging forward – you couldn't walk – there was nothing to be seen, your mind and thoughts were on the ground you were struggling across, wanting to avoid quicksands. There wasn't any cover. The shell holes were full of water, I wasn't going to bury myself. It was raining all the time; if you sat on the edge of a shell hole, if you didn't slide down the water came up to meet you. I don't suppose you had more than about 12 inches of soil going about the top. We couldn't walk across the water. You were staggering on; staggering on – all you did was to go forward. There was a whole roof of shells and God knows what going on top of you. Machine guns whistling past your ear, whizz bangs, God there was everything! You could see them dropping. If a chap got badly wounded and got in one of these shell holes he was finished. There was hardly anybody left when we got to the wire. You were no further forward – it was worse than a stone wall. There was no hopes of getting through. We just thought, 'God, we've got here. How are we going to get back?'[50]

Private Joe Pickard, 1/5th Northumberland Fusiliers

These attacks failed, along with simultaneous Second Army assaults pushing out from the Gheluvelt Plateau. Overall, the casualties were appalling: the Canadians lost approximately 3,400 men while the Second Army lost over 8,500. The next assault came at 05.50 on 30 October. In savage fighting the Canadians took the crest of the hill while the Fifth Army flailed away in the swamps to no effect. Individual trenches and pillboxes now defined progress as the fighting spluttered on. Finally, on 6 November, the Canadians managed to capture the mud and bloodstained rubble of Passchendaele itself. On 10 November they pushed forward another 500 yards before it was finally accepted that the long agony was over.

WAS IT WORTH IT? A difficult and emotive question. In a sense this is not a question that should be asked of Haig, Plumer or Gough. They were soldiers carrying out their duty as best they could. Once continental armies are set against each other the results are going to be unquestionably bloody. Haig had good strategic grounds for fighting the Third Battle of Ypres: the question that still resounds is whether the campaign should have ended in early October, when everything started to go wrong for a second time. The problem here was that the British positions, stuck halfway up the Passchendaele Ridge, were not really tenable: they either had to take the ridge or retire to the line of the Pilckem Ridge. This last may have been a feasible military solution, but it was almost impossible to envisage after all the painful losses already suffered.

Once Haig had embarked upon the campaign it all became part of the great 'wearing down battle' that sought to drain all strength from the monolithic might of the German Army. This was part of the classical Staff College analysis of any battle: the opening engagements, the battle of attrition till the enemy falters, and then the decisive blow to shatter the remnants and secure victory. The Somme and Verdun, coupled with the entry into the war of the United States, meant that the Germans were going to lose the war; the question was whether this could be finalised in 1917. The Germans feared that the British offensives would continue; indeed they expected they would, and they, too, were suffering agonies in Flanders. Haig feared that if the offensive was not pursued, despite the undoubted pain of Passchendaele, then the Germans would simply bounce back and he wanted to finish the job as soon as possible. He pressed on in the hope and partial expectation that the Germans were close to the brink, but as it turned out he was wrong; desperation did not dissipate the German fighting skills, nor was the German Army yet worn out. Haig has been greatly criticised for that conviction in 1917; but it was the same conviction from the same man that would drive the British-led offensives to ultimate victory in 1918.

Tanks for Cambrai

There was one last battle for the BEF in 1917. The genesis for this lay in a proposal by a brilliant British artillery specialist, Brigadier General Hugh Tudor, who came up with a plan for a surprise attack in the Cambrai area to exploit the recent developments in artillery techniques. Despite all the myths, it was the Royal Artillery that took the greatest step forward at the Battle of Cambrai.[51] Advances in direct fire had been driven forward, step by destructive step, by experts like Tudor, and the mathematics and paraphernalia of gunnery had together achieved a considerable degree of accuracy in both theory and practice. But the experts were on the verge of taking the next great step forward. Up until now, guns had needed to register by firing test shells and using the bracketing system to adjust range and direction in order to ensure that when they opened fire 'for real' at Zero Hour they would hit their target. But when hundreds of extra guns registered it rather gave the game away that an attack was imminent. What was needed was some way of opening fire and hitting the target area 'first time' without the need for preliminary registering. Before that could happen there were two fundamental prerequisites, and by November 1917 both had been achieved. First, the BEF needed accurate maps. The existing French maps were simply not up to standard and it took a good deal of time before the survey companies of the Royal Engineers could complete their work and produce the necessary accuracy. This meant that when a gun position had been surveyed and the location of target identified, by using an artillery board they could work out the firing orders required to bring the shells crashing down around the target. However, this would only work if the guns fired accurately, or with a known deviation. This second necessity was achieved by the laborious process of calibrating every artillery piece so that, when calculating the angle and elevation of fire to hit the target, allowance could be made for each gun's individual performance. This was then combined with various technological advances that allowed the effect of meteorological conditions to be measured and the exact position of German gun batteries to be located, using a mixture of aerial observation, sound ranging and flash spotting. The end result was that the guns could be moved up in secrecy, carefully surveyed 'on the map' and then hidden until the moment came to fire a 'predicted' hurricane bombardment onto the German batteries and other identified targets. With this artillery advance came the potential, lost since trench warfare began, for real tactical surprise. There was one big problem remaining: what to do about the barbed wire which would normally have been cleared by a long preliminary bombardment. Here Tudor found his answer: he had grasped the implication of tank-crew battle action reports which stated that tanks could crush massed barbed wire under their tracks and thereby clear a way for the infantry. In view of this, it was fortuitous that Lieutenant Colonel John Fuller and Brigadier General Hugh Ellis at the Tank Corps headquarters were simultaneously feeling their way towards the idea of making a giant forty-eight-hour 'tank raid' on the German lines in the Cambrai area. These two half-formed plans were both under consideration at General Sir Julian Byng's Third Army headquarters, and by September had been hammered into a coherent plan for what would become the Battle of Cambrai. This was duly approved by Haig in early October.

In all, 1,003 guns would fire in support of an assaulting force of six infantry divisions and nine tank battalions (476 tanks) which were covertly amassed in the Cambrai sector – with no less than five cavalry divisions standing by to exploit any breakthrough. Byng's plan was, in the end, fairly simple. The assaulting divisions would break through both the Hindenburg Line and the German second line, enabling the cavalry to advance into the gap and push across the St Quentin Canal. It was intended that the offensive would end after forty-eight hours, thus giving insufficient time for German reserves to arrive. Secrecy was all important if the Third Army was to have any chance of success.

Right from the start there had been problems in the deployment of tanks. At the Battle of Flers-Courcelette back in 15 September 1916 Haig had been expecting to deploy some hundreds of the first Mark I tanks, but eventually had to settle for just fifty. Their performance had been very mixed, but Haig saw their hidden potential and had ordered a thousand – in the circumstances a massive gesture of faith. However, although proving of value in some isolated incidents, they were generally unreliable and the tactics of employing them had not been worked out, so that they had little real impact.

Once the ground work was complete, however, tanks would be a vital component in securing surprise at Cambrai. The bombardment would only crash out at the moment the infantry went over the top, the tanks then being required to burst through and flatten the masses of barbed wire in front of the German trenches. But they had a huge problem to overcome. The Hindenburg Line had been built with tanks in mind and the trenches were both very wide and very deep. The answer lay in another throwback to ancient warfare – fascines. To maximise the use of each of these and to enable each tank commander to know exactly what he was meant to be doing, the Tank Corps headquarters came up with a simple tactical format.

> Fascines were enormous bundles of brushwood about 5 feet in diameter, like an enormous toilet roll carried on the nose of the tank. As the tank came to the trench this bundle was released – it fell into the bottom of the trench and enabled the tank to nose down, rest on it and crawl up over the other side. In this way the uncrossable Hindenburg Line was crossed! For the first time we had some form of tactical manoeuvre. At Point 'X' the leading tank would cross and move on towards the next trench. The next two tanks would cross over the same fascine, thus economising in fascines, and would turn right and left and clear the trenches on each side. The infantry would then come up and take it over. The last tank would follow along, overtake the first one so that the process could be repeated at the next line of trenches.[52]
>
> Captain Norman Dillon, B Battalion, Tank Corps

Everything was ready for the moment. The only question was: had the Germans discerned what was going on?

The predicted barrage crashed out at 06.20 on 20 November and at first everything went like clockwork. The shells slathered across their targets, the tanks rumbled forward and the infantry followed them through the wire and smashed through the German lines.

> The guns opened up on the German trenches and lay down a terrific barrage. We went forward as fast as we could – which wasn't very fast. We were under fire, but not so much, because they were taken so much by surprise and a lot of the Germans got down into the dugouts. We sort of picked them off as we went along. The tanks were shooting along the German trenches, then the infantry were coming on behind so the infantry mopped them up. We went straight over. You felt you were alright in a tank. I suppose there must've been a certain amount of excitement naturally: excitement and noise! Barbed wire flying past you and that sort of thing. We got slightly ditched in one of these small communication trenches. They just give way. They were partly underground, these communication trenches and the tank coming down on them, they gave way slightly. After a bit we managed to get out.[53]
>
> Private Eric Potten, F Battalion, Tank Corps

Everything seemed to be working perfectly. Behind them special tanks crushed the barbed wire, clearing the way for the infantry and cavalry.

> I had never seen such a depth of barbed wire. I suppose it was 10 yards deep and about 4 feet high. So dense that you could hardly poke a broom handle through it. It was quite impassable to any man or beast and could never be destroyed by artillery fire in a month of Sundays. The tanks went through it and I personally followed their tracks and walked straight through without any trouble at all – as though it had been a carpet! There were tanks with anchors on the end of steel ropes. These cleared the wire for the crossing of cavalry by driving into the wire two abreast, dropping their anchors, turning away from each other and going down the length of the wire dragging the anchor after them. The result was to drag those enormous barbed wire fences into balls of wire about 20 feet big. It cleared the ground as clear as a whistle![54]
>
> Captain Norman Dillon, B Battalion, Tank Corps

In front, the tanks pushed on until they reached the St Quentin Canal, but there their attempts to cross were thwarted.

> We got up to the objective – that was the bridge at Masnières. When we got there, we were about the third or fourth tank there and one of the tanks had tried to go over the bridge over the canal to get to the other side where the Germans were ensconced and the bridge had been partially blown and with the weight of the tank, it fell in. They managed to scramble out. We then patrolled up and down for an hour or two because the Germans were in houses on the other side of the canal and they were firing and we were trying to keep them down.[55]
>
> Private Eric Potten, F Battalion, Tank Corps

The canal proved a serious obstacle, as indeed had been expected. While they waited for the infantry to arrive, Potten's tank crew took the opportunity to take a breather.

> It was very hot, very stuffy, of course. The smell of oil and the machine guns. Soon after we got there, we got a chance to get out on one side. We were firing across the canal, so if you got out the other side of the tank, you were shielded. They'd only got machine guns there at that time so we were pretty safe there, you could get out for a breather and then get back in again. We were very glad to get out and get a breath of fresh air. Then the infantry came up. They managed to get across a wooden bridge that had been left and got into the houses. We knew it had been a success because we'd got our objective and that was a good 5 miles in and that was further than they'd ever done in the whole war at that time.[56]
>
> Private Eric Potten, F Battalion, Tank Corps

All over the battlefield the tank crews were congratulating themselves on what had been achieved. It truly seemed like a miracle.

> I found the tank crews all sitting down having mugs of tea! People were walking all about the open countryside. The infantry were just sculling about wondering at having got through so easily. The crews were saying, 'It was a piece of cake!' and 'Where are the cavalry?' That was the main theme: where are the cavalry that were supposed

to burst through? We were expecting to see them coming through in hordes![57]

Captain Norman Dillon, B Battalion, Tank Corps

Overall the tanks and infantry managed to crash through the Hindenburg Line and make advances that stretched up to 5 miles, although, with problems encountered at Flesquières, progress was not uniform. They also failed to capture the tactically significant Bourlon Wood Ridge, while the cavalry achieved little or nothing. The fighting continued, and as the German reserves moved up, the advance stalled completely and a prolonged and vicious battle began for Bourlon Wood.

By the time the British offensive was suspended on 28 November, the new British line was left forming an ugly salient. The Germans soon recognised that this would offer the perfect opportunity to try out their stormtrooper tactics for the first time on the Western Front, and they launched a full-scale counter-attack at 07.00 on 30 November. The new tactics relied on a sudden devastating barrage, followed up by squads of specially trained troops who would use infiltration methods to avoid centres of resistance, which, left isolated, could be 'mopped up' by later waves. The British were caught unprepared, and as they tumbled back there was panicky desperation. The Germans were attempting to cut off the head of the salient by attacking the 'neck' from either side. The fighting was chaotic in the extreme with heavy casualties approaching 45,000 suffered by both sides. Eventually, on 5 December, Haig was forced to order a withdrawal and the vast majority of the gains of 20 November had to be surrendered.

IN THE END the Battle of Cambrai achieved very little. For all the much vaunted ringing of church bells back in England, for all the propaganda of unstoppable tanks and stormtroopers, the situation had not really changed. The British and Germans had premiered their new attacking techniques; but at the same time neither had yet attained the elusive solution to a sustainable and decisive breakthrough. The Western Front was still unbroken. Yet the ground was shifting beneath their feet. Both sides had almost mastered the grammar and syntax of trench warfare;

both were ready for the next great leap forward. But did they still have strength left, after more than three years of war?

10

UP IN THE AIR, 1914–18

WAR IN THE AIR was a new phenomenon. Although the main combatant countries had all monitored developments in aviation and established their own air forces, they had not yet really got off the ground in anything but a literal sense. They had aircraft, they had balloons, they even had airships, they might have some inkling of the potential, but no one really knew how to use aerial resources effectively in war. All that lay in the future.

For Britain, that future began with the formation of the Royal Flying Corps (RFC) in April 1912. This was originally intended to serve both the army and navy, but the senior service chose to retain control over its own aviation and created the Royal Naval Air Service (RNAS) in July 1914. The pre-war years were marked by much experimentation as they sought to identify the best and most reliable types of flying machine, while simultaneously struggling to understand the science of controlling aircraft in flight.

When the RFC deployed with the BEF in August 1914 it sent just four squadrons totalling sixty-three aircraft to France. At first they were employed on reconnaissance missions to locate the position of the

German columns, rather in the fashion of aerial cavalry. Once located, they would scribble down the details and drop a message bag as close as possible to the nearest headquarters. But war was an extraordinary catalyst for rapid technical development, and within a couple of months the RFC had developed the capability of taking photos that recorded the layout and position of German trenches. Despite early efforts being blurred, they carried on, experimenting to determine the best methodology. Progress was rapid.

> The pilot had to look after the camera because at least from his seat you could look straight down. Good square mahogany box with a leather concertina pullout with a good big lens and a little handle that you pushed and pulled to change the plates. Real good old glass plates. In addition to that a bit of wire or string with a ring on it – which was skittering around in the wind – to pull every time you wanted to take a picture. The whole thing was strapped on the outside of the aeroplane and you had a sort of ball and ring sight at the back. To take the photo you had to lean over the side of the cockpit and look down through this ball sight, fly the aeroplane with the left hand, move the camera handle changing the plates with the right. Every time you change the plate you pull the string, wait until you'd flown along a bit more, judge the overlap and do it again.[1]
>
> Second Lieutenant Cecil Lewis, 9 Squadron, RFC

When they got the glass plates back to their airfield, the images could be blown up to make visible the intricate details of the German lines. By trial and error a whole new skill of photographic interpretation was created to decipher the tell-tale clues and accurately determine the locations of artillery batteries, machine-gun posts, trench mortars, dugouts, mineshafts and the signs of a communications centre that revealed headquarters. Once identified, they could be destroyed by the British artillery. The guns were greatly assisted by aerial artillery observation. Here again there was much rapid experimentation to establish the best means of communicating corrections from observers in the sky to Royal Artillery guns on the ground. Once a wireless had been successfully taken aloft then the 'clock code' was devised – a simple method of guiding the shells right onto their targets. Captain Archibald James explains.

You then, from a height of probably about 5,000 feet, proceeded to give the signal to fire, which was the letter 'G'. Having given the signal 'G' you watched the battery and you saw the flash of the guns. You then knew pretty well exactly how many seconds it would take for those shells to arrive at the target. You then shifted the wing of your aeroplane to have an unrestricted view of the target and you saw the fall of the shell or shells. The system of correcting faults was this. You had imaginary circles drawn round the target, 25 yards, 50 yards, 150, 200, 250, 300, 350, 400 – and you had a simple letter and figure code to indicate two things: the clock-face point at which the shells were falling, in other words whether they were falling at 1 o'clock or 3 o'clock from the target; and the distance as expressed in the imaginary circles which you visualised without much difficulty. With a good battery – batteries varied enormously – you should get them right on target at about the third salvo. They then fired as many shells as they had been instructed by the artillery authorities to fire.[2]

Captain Archibald James, 2 Squadron, RFC

Aircraft began to be defined by their purpose, with the development of 'corps' aircraft specifically devoted to the functions of reconnaissance and artillery observation. For this role the British mass-produced a two-seater aircraft prosaically known as the BE2c.

Neither side could allow free rein to their opponents' aviators, and it was inevitable that aircraft would be armed to do battle with each other; at first with just revolvers or rifles, but soon machine guns were in common use. One incident typical of these early days left James spluttering with frustration at the 'one that got away'.

One day I was ranging a battery and I was on our side of the lines over our battery, the visibility being very good. I looked over the side before sending a signal to our battery to fire and to my surprise saw a German two-seater almost directly below me, well on our side of the lines and about 1,000 feet below me. I had in the front seat of the BE2c as my observer and air gunner a corporal in my squadron who hadn't much experience in the air. So I throttled back, shouted to him what was happening, showed him the aeroplane and said, 'Get your Lewis gun!' I omitted to say, 'Don't start shooting till I tell you to!' With that I proceeded to go down, circling on top of the all-unsuspecting German. Unfortunately, my corporal got excited and when we were at least 150 yards away he opened fire and discharged the whole drum of his Lewis gun without any effect at all. Indeed the range was excessive. I then flattened out, very, very, close echeloned above the German. And I shall never forget the look of horrified surprise on the Germans' faces when they looked up, alerted by the rattle of my machine gun, and looked at me in sort of open-mouthed astonishment. The German observer recovered his composure in probably two or three seconds and swung round the rotating mounting round his cockpit and pointed the gun at me and opened fire. Meanwhile my idiot corporal was fumbling to try and get another drum on. We were so close that I actually saw the oil burning off the recoiling portions of the German machine gun. Well naturally, after two or three shots had been fired I banked steeply away at the same moment the German banked in the same direction. And we almighty nearly collided. That was the end of a thoroughly unsatisfactory episode.[3]

Captain Archibald James, 2 Squadron, RFC

The BE2c gave sterling service and by means of its wireless and camera brought untold havoc, death and general mayhem to the Germans – but it was designed as a stable observation platform rather than as a 'fighting aircraft'.

The BE2c had the observer in front and the pilot behind, whereas, with any sense it should have been the pilot in front and the observer behind, but it wasn't! So the observer sat in a cockpit, with four struts very close each side of him, wires to brace him well in and in front, none behind. And a little seat he could just get in to. And really he could do nothing at all except keep a look out. When it got at all hot and you were liable to be attacked from the tail as much as from anywhere else, he simply had to get up on his seat, kneel on his seat, which was a jolly cold, draughty business at 8,000 feet, even in the summer.[4]

Lieutenant Cecil Lewis, 9 Squadron, RFC

The inflexibility of the nascent British aircraft manufacturing industry meant that the RFC had little alternative other than to carry on using the BE2c right into 1917, by which time it was entirely obsolescent. The long-delayed replacement corps aircraft was the RE8, a much-criticised machine, which nevertheless performed valuable work as the eyes of the Royal Artillery, right until the end of the war.

The aircraft designed to prey on the reconnaissance aircraft were known as 'scouts'. In the summer of 1915 the first generic British scout squadron reached the Western Front equipped with the two-seater Vickers Fighter. This was a 'pusher' aircraft with its engine behind the nacelle, which had the advantage of a clear field of fire directly ahead with no whirling propeller to get in the way. The Germans countered with the Fokker Eindecker (E1), a single-seater monoplane that had the inestimable virtue of an interrupter gear, which allowed the machine gun to fire through the propeller. This meant that to aim the machine gun accurately you just flew directly at your target.

Two young German pilots, Leutnants Max Immelmann and Oswald Boelcke, took advantage of this and, diving down behind their prospective victims, created the 'Fokker scourge'. While not involving great numbers of casualties, this did hamper the operations of British corps aircraft. Brigadier General Hugh Trenchard (commander of the RFC on the Western Front) ordered his men to press on regardless, and by 1916 he had developed a coherent aerial philosophy based on a willingness to accept casualties in order to achieve the desired levels of reconnaissance and artillery observation. Trenchard believed that air losses numbered in dozens could not compare to the tens of thousands of lives that would be placed at risk if the artillery were not able to identify and destroy artillery and machine-gun targets before the infantry went over the top. He always required his aircraft to push out well over the German lines to achieve domination of the skies over the disputed battlefield.

It was fortunate for the RFC that the next generation of British aircraft arrived just in time for the preparations for the Battle of the Somme in the summer of 1916. Of these, the two-seater FE2b was a far more powerful version of the concept behind the Vickers Fighter. The FE2b would prove a fantastic workhorse: first as a scout, then as a general all-purpose aircraft and finally, when obsolescent, as a night-bomber.

The pilot was behind the observer in front of the engine and the observer was in the front nacelle or cockpit. In that cockpit I had three clips for the gun mounting to be assembled in. One for nose firing down, one firing to the right and one firing to the left. If you wanted to use the left gun, the mounting used to be pulled out of its clip and it was swivelled round onto the left-hand clip. When you fired you had to put your knee against the mounting, otherwise it would blow out with the explosion. In the rear you had one gun firing over the top plane on a moveable mounting, and a plunger arrangement where you just pressed the plunger underneath and the gun would go as high as possible to fire over the back plane. In the cockpit you had spare drums and it was one of your duties to make certain that, when you were firing the Lewis gun, to see that you carry out all the necessary things for safe flying. For instance, if you changed a drum you had to get hold of the drum on the gun, hold it very tightly, take it off the gun, bend down and lay it very carefully in its compartment as an empty drum. We also had on the Lewis gun an ejector bag where the empty cartridge cases fell into. On one occasion my clip on my cartridge case gave way, and all the rounds were whisked through the propeller in the wind stream. The observer's job was to in the main keep his eye on enemy aircraft and if necessary to ask the pilot to move the plane into position if they spotted an enemy plane, to make sure that he could get into a position to fire at it.[5]

Sergeant Harold Taylor, 25 Squadron, RFC

Another pusher aircraft arriving on the scene was the single-seater DH2, a small, relatively fast and manoeuvrable machine that would prove superior to the Fokker E1. In the early summer of 1916 the DH2 and FE2b squadrons were able to sweep the Germans from the sky, thereby allowing the BE2c corps aircraft to carry out their missions in relative peace.

On 1 July, when the infantry went over the top at 07.30, Lieutenant Cecil Lewis was up aloft in a Morane Parasol, carrying out another of the ever-increasing roles assigned to the RFC: that of contact patrols, charting the advances made and reporting progress to headquarters. Here he had a unique perspective as the huge mines detonated.

I was on the first patrol on the northern part of the salient from Pozières down to Fricourt. They'd put down two enormous mines right on the front line, hoping to clear the whole of the front line with this enormous burst. This was what we were looking for. We had our watches synchronised. We were up at about 8,000 feet and really it was a fantastic sight because when the hurricane bombardment started, every gun we had, and there were thousands of them, had all been let loose at once. It was wild. You could hear the roar of the guns above the noise of the aircraft like rain on a pane. Extraordinary, this roll of thousands of guns at the same time. Then came the blast when we were looking at the La Boisselle Salient – suddenly the whole earth heaved and up from the ground came great cone-shaped lifts of earth up to 3, 4, 5,000 feet. A moment later we struck the repercussion wave of the blast which flung us over right away backwards, over on one side away from the blast.[6]

Second Lieutenant Cecil Lewis, 3 Squadron, RFC

As the infantry charged, Lewis came right down to 3,000 feet so that he could see what was happening.

We had a klaxon horn on the undercarriage of the Morane – a great big 12 volt klaxon and I had a button with which I used to press out a letter to tell the infantry that we wanted to know where they were. When they heard us hawking at them from above, they had little red Bengal flares – they carried them in their pockets – they would put a match to their flares. All along the line wherever there was a chap there would be a flare and we would note these flares down on the map and Bob's your uncle! It was one thing to practise this but quite another thing for them to really do it when they were under fire and particularly when things began to go a bit badly. Then they jolly well wouldn't light anything and small blame to them, because it drew the fire of the enemy on to them at once. So we went down looking for flares and we only got about two flares on the whole front. We were bitterly disappointed because this we hoped was our part to help the infantry and we weren't able to do it.[7]

Second Lieutenant Cecil Lewis, 3 Squadron, RFC

Lewis may have been thwarted, but the RFC had done a brilliant job in their photographic and artillery observation duties that would continue throughout the long battle. The Germans fumed impotently, but there was little they could do to stop the British from peering deep behind their lines and dropping shells at will onto identified targets. The Somme fighting was devastating for the British infantry, but it very probably would have been worse still, but for the efforts of the RFC pilots.

In late September 1916 the German aviators were revitalised by the arrival of a potent new scout: the Albatros DI. This marked the beginning of a new generation of aircraft with its powerful engine, a sleek stream-lined design and armament of twin-synchronised machine guns firing through the propeller. The DI and its successor the DII were faster, could fly higher, were more manoeuvrable and much better armed than any British scout. RFC casualties began to mount from the autumn of 1916, but, as during the 'Fokker scourge', the British just gritted their teeth and continued to carry out their core functions regardless of casualties.

The worst period for the RFC occurred during the Battle of Arras in April 1917, when they were caught flying outmoded aircraft against the far superior German scouts, brilliantly led by the fearsome German 'ace' popularly known as the 'Red Baron': Oberleutnant Manfred von Rich-thofen.[8] Casualties rocketed, but the RFC was proud of the fact that it still managed to carry out the vast majority of missions required by the army below. When at last the next generation of British fighters typi-fied by the SE5a, the Sopwith Camel and the two-seater Bristol Fighter arrived on the Western Front, the two sides reached a rough equilibrium in aircraft quality – a situation that would endure until the end of the war.

By late 1917, many more young pilots had begun to master the techniques and tactics of aerial warfare. One such was Captain Gwilym Lewis of 40 Squadron. Although an ace, Lewis took most pleasure from his success in avoiding casualties among his flight.

> I was very keen on an efficient flight. That was my job. We became especially good with our formation flying. Perhaps we weren't a star turn, but I liked everyone to have got a Hun. It wasn't so easy getting Huns as all that. Fellows would fight quite hard and still not make the final hit. It was an extraordinary thing that a new fellow coming out here couldn't see half the things that were going on. Their eyes didn't register into the far distance. We had to see things – just a twinkle

of the sun on a bit of metal – that's all we would need to make us conscious that there was something in the sky way in the distance. From that we might manoeuvre our position. But we would get into dogfights and [new pilots] hardly knew what was going on. They were shot down pretty freely. I didn't like this, so any fellow coming out new to my flight, as soon as he was ready to go over the lines, flew next to me and outside him was an experienced man. So I never lost one of these boys who was new to the game. I kept my own eye on them and other people did too. As soon as they became better acquainted to what was going on, then they were on their own.[9]

Captain Gwilym Lewis, 40 Squadron

Lewis learnt a great deal from the example of the pilot sometimes described as the 'British Richthofen', Captain Edward Mannock, more often known as 'Mick' or 'Paddy' due to his Irish origins.

Mannock was the hero of the squadron at that time. He left the squadron with twenty-one victories and his victories were good. He came on to form having been older than most of us and a more mature man. He had given great, deep thought to the fighting and had re-orientated his mental attitudes, which was necessary for a top fighter pilot. He had got his confidence and he had thought out the way he was going to tackle things. He became a very good friend of mine and I owed a lot to him that he was so friendly. I was unnecessarily reserved and he liked to give people nicknames – he called me 'Noisy'! He was a lot of fun.[10]

Captain Gwilym Lewis, 40 Squadron

Although the corps pilots were the men carrying out the missions that seriously harmed the German Army, they had come to depend, at least in part, on the RFC scouts to preserve their existence in the dangerous skies. The most clichéd defining symbol of the scout's life was the 'dawn patrol'. By the summer of 1917, Lieutenant Cecil Lewis was flying an SE5a with 56 Squadron and on many such missions.

We were about 20 miles behind the lines, so we had time to climb up on our way over to get height this side of the lines. We usually got up to 15 or 16,000 feet before we actually crossed the lines into enemy territory looking for trouble. Our eyes were continually focusing;

looking, craning our heads round, moving all the time looking for those black specks which would mean enemy aircraft at a great distance. Between clouds we would be able to see the ground or only parts of it which would sort of slide into view like a magic lantern screen far, far beneath. Clinging close together about 20 or 30 yards between each machine, swaying, looking at our neighbours; setting ourselves just right so that we were all in position.[11]

Lieutenant Cecil Lewis, 56 Squadron, RFC

Scouts like Lewis would actively seek out German aircraft, looking to shoot down any reconnaissance aircraft and, of course, attacking their opposite numbers. The Imperial German Air Force was severely outnumbered on the Western Front by 1917, so it chose to concentrate what resources it had in larger formations than the British usually adopted. This meant that the Germans could cover far less air space, but if they were encountered it could be a dangerous business.

Sooner or later we would spot the enemy. If we were lucky it would be below us, but we were [usually] under the enemy. Our machines, good as they were, were still not up to the Huns who usually had a 1,000 to 2,000 feet ceiling clear above us. Even at 16,000 feet we were liable to be jumped from on top. That didn't have to worry us. We were usually out-numbered two or three to one. We used to engage irrespective if there was anybody above or not – just chance it. Usually the top flight of enemy aircraft who were above us would come down and jump us as we went down.[12]

Lieutenant Cecil Lewis, 56 Squadron, RFC

The most efficient kind of aerial combat had more in common with an execution than a fair fight. The whole object was to approach unseen, from clouds, out of the sun, or from an unexpected position. The predator would move in to close range, and then announce his presence with a stream of machine-gun bullets aimed at his hapless victim. This was how the great aces scored many of their 'kills'. But of course sometimes their approach was detected – experienced pilots were constantly scanning the sky looking for enemies. At this point a chaotic mêlée would ensue, popularly known as a 'dogfight', a term which neatly summed up the snarling action.

It's not really possible to describe the action of a fight like that.
Having no communication with each other we simply had to go in
and take our man and chance our arm – keep our eyes in the backs
of our heads to see if anybody was trying to get us as we went down.
But there was always the point where you had to go down anyway
whether there was anybody on your tail or not. The fight would begin
– engage and disengage with burst of thirty or forty rounds, three in
one tracer, so there was always some idea of where you were firing
because your sights were really no good in these dogfights – there
wasn't time to focus – it was just snap shooting. The whole squadron
would enter the fight in good formation but within half a minute the
whole formation had gone to hell. Just chaps wheeling and zooming
and diving. On each other's tails – perhaps four in a row even – a
German going down, one of our chaps on his tail, another German
on his tail, another Hun behind that – extraordinary glimpses. People
approaching head on, firing at each other as they came, and then just
at the last moment turning and slipping away.[13]

Lieutenant Cecil Lewis, 56 Squadron, RFC

Parachutes were not issued to the British pilots, so there was little
chance of escape from a plummeting burning aircraft if they were hit.
The unremitting tension of patrols coupled with the occasional frenetic
excitement of a dogfight was a rich mixture, and these young pilots were
under great stress.

You did have this strain that could occur if you never could get out
of gunfire and the possibility of being hit even when you were asleep.
So we lived always in the stretch or sag of nerves. We were either in
deadly danger or no danger at all. This conflict between something
like being at home, and being in really a quite tight position, had a
great effect on us all and produced a certain strain, probably because
of the change.[14]

Lieutenant Cecil Lewis, 56 Squadron, RFC

This level of pressure caused many pilots and observers to break down,
and they would then be sent home to recover.

THERE IS NO DOUBT that the RFC personnel lived in relative luxury compared to the average infantry subalterns stuck in muddy dugouts. They usually lived in huts or tents and their squadron mess would be in a farmhouse close to the airfield.

> Old simple, whitewashed rooms with terrible old furniture and the food good, but rough. Lamps hanging on strings from the ceiling, thick with dead flies and a general rudimentary primitive sort of life. Sometimes an old upright piano in the mess with keys so yellow they looked as if the keyboard had been smoking for about fifty years! And we had one chap who played the piano and he'd sit down in the evenings and there were two or three notes missing, it was out of tune and it was a terrible piano – but it didn't matter. He'd play the tunes of the time, the revues of the time, the things we knew by heart, we used to sing in chorus. Occasionally a bit of Chopin or something like that on the nights when we felt that that sort of thing was appropriate. All very easy and go as you please. Usually after that, turning in fairly early and going to bed, because one might be up on the dawn patrol the day after, perhaps up at 4 o'clock or more in the morning and wanting to get some sleep in. It was a quiet life really on the airfields themselves.[15]
>
> Lieutenant Cecil Lewis, 56 Squadron, RFC

The different squadrons in the RFC had a variety of approaches to the drinking of alcohol. Most pilots had the sense to generally restrict themselves to 'social drinking' in the mess bar, but some young officers definitely used alcohol as a 'crutch' to help them through the bad times.

> The centre of the squadron seemed to be in the bar. When you think of the tensions they lived through day to day – they would come in in the evening and ask about their best friend, 'Where's old George?' 'Oh, he bought it this afternoon!' 'Oh heavens!' The gloom would come, the morale would die and the reaction was immediate, 'Well, come on, chaps, what are you going to have?' That was the sort of spirit that kept you going and although people are against alcohol I think that it played a magnificent part in keeping up morale.[16]
>
> Lieutenant Frederick Powell, 40 Squadron, RFC

Every so often they would indulge in a jaunt into the nearest town for a chance to let their hair down – in no uncertain fashion.

> When the squadron had perhaps a particularly bad time, or a particularly good time, either was an excuse to go in and whoop it up a bit. We used to take a tender and go off to the nearest town. There we'd find some sort of an estaminet or restaurant, probably a girl or two around the place. We'd begin to have a drink or two and start singing songs and enjoying ourselves. Whooping it up to say midnight, and then get into the tender and come back to the airfield again. One mustn't think of it entirely as being 'lived up' because people were being killed every day. My best friend was there one evening, and he wasn't there next day at lunch and this was going on all the time.[17]
>
> Lieutenant Cecil Lewis, 56 Squadron, RFC

MEANWHILE, BACK HOME there was a desperate rush to produce the thousands of pilots that were needed for the RFC. Acceptance of casualties was all well and good in theory, but they still had to be replaced. At first flying training was rudimentary, as the instructors barely understood the mechanics of staying aloft themselves. But by 1917 the process was well understood. After being wounded at Gallipoli, Ernest Haire had been commissioned and served with the 12th Lancashire Fusiliers in Salonika. Invalided home again, he then began to train as a pilot.

> I had straight flying and turns. Feet at the rudder bar and keep the nose of the machine on the horizon; if you do that you're flying level. If you put the joystick forward the nose goes down; back the nose goes up. Right you banked to the right; left you banked to the left. It was sort of ball and socketed. You turned using both the rudder and the stick; in other words you turn and bank. I could always turn better to the left than I could to the right![18]
>
> Lieutenant Ernest Haire

I was also lucky enough to interview Laurie Field who, after service with the infantry on the Western Front, had been commissioned and transferred into the RFC where he learnt to fly on a Maurice Farnham

Shorthorn. Field certainly put his finger on one of the true essentials of flying.

> Landing is the most difficult thing of any, because it's the one thing that matters! If you make a mistake in the air it doesn't matter – if you make a mistake in landing, you're in trouble! Anybody can fly, but the whole art is to learn to land, isn't it – to get down on Mother Earth again. The knack of the landing is that when you come down you've got your gliding height, your engine is off. An ideal landing is that you gradually pull your nose up as you lose flying speed, it really stalls your aeroplane and the perfect landing is to have the wheels and the tail skid hit the ground together. That is the perfect landing, which happens once in twenty times. A bad landing is when you pull up your nose too early and you're perhaps not near enough the ground and your plane then drops. If it drops sufficiently badly your undercarriage is gone.[19]
>
> Second Lieutenant Laurie Field

Field later went on to fly on the Avro 504 at London Colney. The Avro was a superb aircraft but, even better, they received lectures from Captain Edward Mannock.

> We used to worship him, we thought he was the 'King of Air Pilots', absolutely the ideal man for air scrapping. He was the life and soul of the mess. I well remember him one day, the pilots had one ante-room and the instructors had another one which used to open onto our room. One day he burst through and said, 'All tickets please!' as though he was on a bus. He never approved of it; he thought that the pilots and those learning to be pilots should be altogether.[20]
>
> Second Lieutenant Laurie Field

Unfortunately, Mannock was desperate to return to the front, where he would be killed in action on 26 July 1918.[21]

THE WAR IN THE AIR ON THE WESTERN FRONT boiled up to a climax in 1918. Although a lot of new pilots were being funnelled through the system, experience was the most valuable of all assets. The training may have been excellent, the lectures and advice entirely appropriate, but nothing could match time in the air in a combat situation. Major Frederick Powell had almost too much experience. He had flown in the Vickers Fighter and single-seater pusher scouts back in 1915 and 1916 before taking his turn as an instructor. Now he was back on the Western Front in command of 41 Squadron, RFC, and flying an SE5a. Here, he too found that his new pilots lacked the crucial ability to spot their enemies in the open skies. Time and again the youngsters' patrols came back reporting that they had made no enemy contacts. Chafing at the bit, on 2 February 1918, Powell decided to lead a patrol himself to ensure contact with the German scouts, and if all else failed, he resolved to make a low-level raid on a German airfield. He was determined to 'blood' his men in combat.

> I would lead the patrol at 14,000 feet when I would cross the lines. The other flight of four machines, led by the flight commander, would fly at 17,000 feet, 3,000 feet above me, the object being that when I was attacked by Albatros then the top flight would dive down on the Germans. In effect I was the bait.[22]
>
> Major Frederick Powell, 41 Squadron, RFC

Powell led his ingénues in a patrol towards Douai and at first his frustration increased as, even to his experienced eyes, the skies seemed empty of German aircraft.

> To my horror we had not been attacked and I thought, 'Oh damn! I'll have to lose height and carry out this hazardous trip to shoot the people in the aerodromes!' But I had only just turned about – and then the sky seemed filled with black crosses – there were Germans everywhere! My flight commander fired a red light which was the signal for hostile aircraft – well I'd seen them! I got down on the tail of a German and I got him in my Aldis telescopic sight but I thought, 'No, I'm not going to pull the trigger and blast off a load of ammunition; I'll get this fellow so easily in the back of the head with the first three rounds.' But first I had to get him right in the centre of the Aldis sight. This fellow, he just slipped out of the sight to one side; I counter-ruddered and brought him back – I was just about to fire when another German who was on my tail fired and he hit my

instrument board, hit me through the leg and hit me through the arm – at the time I didn't notice this – except I just felt a bang. That was my first experience of getting a bullet through me. I had often visualised what the heck it was going to feel like, but of course one doesn't feel it – it is just a blow. He was using armour-piercing bullets of which one went through the 'V' of the engine and cut out one entire block of cylinders. There was a cloud of steam and water that went up as it had gone through the radiator and my first reaction was, 'My God, fire!' I knew I was at 14,000 feet and I had to get down to the ground before the thing disintegrated entirely in flames – remember we had no parachutes. I dived down as hard as I could go and looked back and saw that I had three German Albatros on my tail. Well they were heavy machines not so manoeuvrable as the SE5 and I was able to turn quickly in an Immelmann turn, quickly, and go underneath them on my way down with no engine. They took a long time to get round before their guns came on to me, then I whipped round quickly the other way and went down. After I seemed to have been going down for about four weeks I had to drag my eyes from these Boche and look where I was. I was only about 400 feet up in the air and passing over a marvellous field which turned out to be a German aerodrome – where I landed. The German who shot me down came and landed on the aerodrome as well, while the other two went round and round in circles, leaving a gun on my machine all the time. It was rather well done. I got out of the machine, went to the little locker in the back, pulled off my flying helmet and put my cap on. Then I walked across to the German who was sitting there in his machine with the engine ticking over. I had forgotten I had been hit. I went up to him and I put my hand out, because there was that sort of friendship, and he leant out to shake my hand. As he did so he suddenly said, '*Verwundert?*' That sounded like wounded and I looked down and saw blood running out of my sleeve – then of course I felt it.[23]

Major Frederick Powell, 41 Squadron, RFC

Powell had been shot down by Leutnant Max Kühn of Jasta 10. This regrettable affair demonstrated that while experience was of great value, it also could date very quickly in the hurly-burly of the air war. Tactics that might have been appropriate in 1916 were outmoded, and Powell's over-confidence in his own abilities had led him to make a series of errors from which he was fortunate to emerge with his life.

The RFC and RNAS had been amalgamated to form the Royal Air Force (RAF) on 1 April 1918. During the German spring offensives, the war in the air matched the frenzy of the war on the ground, and on 21 April 1918 Manfred von Richthofen was shot down in circumstances that remain controversial.[24] Richthofen's death was emblematic of the demise in 1918 of many of the great aces of both sides, including Major Edward Mannock, Major James McCudden and many others. Battle-fatigued, chancing their arm once too often, they ignored their own rules and thus crashed from the skies. Their deaths reflected a change in the status of military aviation, which had moved by 1918 onto another stage of development. The work of the great aces was done. Individual enterprise and well-honed skills became secondary in an aerial war increasingly dominated by sheer numbers of pilots and machines.

Aviation was no longer an added extra, but a fully integrated part of the 'All Arms Battle' that the British would finally unleash on a tottering German Army in August 1918. Aircraft seemed to be everywhere, probing deep behind the lines and hitting the Germans just where it really hurt.

> If you could shoot up transport and block the road, that was a fine thing – you stopped the whole lot. I used to try and attack them from the front; that is to say from the direction to which they were proceeding. If you could manage to shoot up a couple of transport wagons, the whole road was blocked for some time – then they were just cold meat – you just went along with the 20-pound Cooper bombs.[25]
>
> Lieutenant James Gascoyne, 92 Squadron, RAF

Gascoyne had a well-developed sense of humour and even in these circumstances he did not miss the chance for a laugh.

> I discovered a line of infantry behind a hedge. Riding towards them was a big fat German on a horse going across a ploughed field; there was plenty of mud and dirt about. It suddenly appealed to me to see what I could do about it. I didn't want to hurt the horse so I dived down. He saw me coming and jumped off the horse holding the

reins. Well I frightened this poor horse so much that it started to gallop across the field – the fat German hung on to the reins for 10 or 15 yards – dragged through all the mud and mire. He looked a proper sight![26]

Lieutenant James Gascoyne, 92 Squadron, RAF

But this kind of low-level ground-strafing was a dangerous business. Anyone with a rifle or machine gun could take a shot at you, and even an infantryman ignorant of the principles of deflection shooting could sometimes hit your aircraft if you carelessly gave them a clear shot.

I came across a village where the German troops were retreating. A whole line of transport in a very straight street and at the bottom of the street a church tower. I was so intent in having a go at this transport I was not flying at more than about 200 feet and I foolishly went absolutely straight down this village street. Suddenly there was a burst of machine-gun fire right into my machine. One bullet came through the windscreen, hit my helmet, made a little hole, a mark on my head – it felt just like being hit with a brick. I put my hand up and found there was blood. I stuck my head over the side and I regained consciousness very quickly. I discovered where the firing was coming from – the church tower at around the height I was flying, straight into him.[27]

Lieutenant James Gascoyne, 92 Squadron, RAF

Of course even during the new 'All Arms Battle' the RAF were required to carry out all its usual tasks. The artillery observation role was as important as ever in a war increasingly dominated by the guns of the Royal Artillery, while the photographic reconnaissance aircraft worked overtime recording the manifold changes in the German line, identifying new defended positions. And still the scouts had to fly their dawn patrols, grinding down and suppressing the German Imperial Air Force at every opportunity. Young Second Lieutenant Laurie Field finally got out to join 40 Squadron in the high summer of 1918, and he was to retain a vivid impression of what it was like to be up in the skies with the early birds.

It always depended really on the weather, but particularly in the summer we would get up very early because there were always patrols first thing, mostly round about dawn. The sun rose in the east and it was in your eyes. We wore a Sidcot suit and a pair of flying gloves which had a piece you could put over your fingers. Cold was always the greatest enemy for us because we had open cockpits. On the hottest summer's day, as soon as you got up to about 2,000, you'd feel it, you were shivering to death. I did have a little thing that some girl I knew in England made me – it was a little sort of rabbit made of wool and I always took it up, but I don't think I was ever very superstitious. I flew an SE5a, which was a scout, and we didn't have any job at all to do except look for trouble. We always flew in a 'V' shape: that would be the Flight Commander Chidlaw Roberts, then one on his left and one on his right. I was always on the left, Smith was the right wingman – he came from Nottingham. We would first of all make height, by circling the aerodrome, which took a little time. We mostly did our patrols at 15,000, anything between 15,000 and 20,000. As soon as you got to your height, then we knew which part of the line we had to patrol over the German lines. Of course, unless you're very careful you can't tell from the air which is German and which is your territory, you've got to go by the map. You were looking for trouble. Our tanks held two hours' petrol, so that was the limit, but the centre-plane gravity tank held an extra quarter of an hour. The whole time you were on patrol you're on the lookout, you have no minute off at all or otherwise you're likely to get attacked. I am afraid I was never very good at seeing things and Chidlaw Roberts would waggle his wings and point down. I would look over the side and right down there you would see the enemy aircraft, it looked as if they were crawling on the ground. Then it would depend what he decided – you really felt you were protecting him. So he would attack and you stayed with him. You could come out of the sun; the thing to do was to keep your shadow on the aeroplane and then you come out of the sun then. We could dive at a tremendous speed. It was always said of the SE5a that it always remained intact; some machines would come to pieces in the air when you took evasive action.[28]

Second Lieutenant Laurie Field, 40 Squadron, RAF

But it was better by far to attack aircraft on the ground where they were helpless. Soon squadrons were combining together to launch coordinated raids on German airfields. This was a glimpse of the future.

THERE WAS ANOTHER DIMENSION TO AIR WARFARE. In the early years of the war the Germans had introduced long-range bombing of British towns and cities using first their Zeppelins and then the Gotha or Giant heavy bombers. The damage and casualties seemed terrible at the time, but some of the greatest harm was done by the air-raid warnings which closed factories and caused whole regions of the country to lose industrial productivity. But the British had developed effective countermeasures: first the German bombers were restricted by the increasing presence of British scouts to night raids, and then the British developed the skills to allow a force of night scouts to defend the homeland. When the Germans switched their focus to send instead their heavy bombers to seek out targets behind the Western Front, they would find the specialist night-fighting pilots of 151 Squadron waiting for them. Among the most successful of these intrepid pilots was Lieutenant Archibald Yuille, who neatly described what it was like to fly the dangerously unstable Sopwith Camel in the dark.

> We had the enamel basic instruments: a compass, clock, air speed tube and altimeter, but there wasn't much else. These weren't electrically lit but had luminous paint on the dials. You could just decipher them when you had to. We had to fly the aeroplane by feel and instinct. It's very funny night flying. You get a very good horizon to fly against and you can see water very clearly underneath you, but of course you can't pick out roads or railways or anything like that. The main thing is to keep your eye on the horizon and not find yourself getting into a dive when you don't mean to. You had to have cat's eyes – you had no aids. You were just there up by yourself, in the dark for two hours on a patrol. One of the things one did was sing, quite unconsciously and you'd come down absolutely hoarse! Well it's lonely, two hours up there seeing absolutely nothing. The bomber pilot had a crew, but you were by yourself.[29]
>
> Lieutenant Archibald Yuille, 151 Squadron, RAF

The Camel pilots bobbing about in the night skies had no wireless to 'guide' them onto any intruder. As they gained in experience, they took an increasing toll on the German bombers. Archibald Yuille had already shot a Gotha down over Étaples when on 10 August 1918 he scored a truly memorable success above Amiens.

> We knew that they would be flying at 8,000 feet so we always flew at about 7,500 so that we could see him against the sky which was always light, whereas you could never see him beneath you against the ground which was always dark. We could only tell that there were raiders there by what I call the 'mess' – the searchlights and the flak. So we used to fly into that area and switch on our light underneath the aircraft that was to stop the Archie shooting whilst the searchlights went on hunting for the Hun. If we were lucky – and that wasn't very often – we would see the Hun up above us. A black streak going in front of you and you went to try and get behind him. It wasn't very easy, but we were faster than he was, which let us catch up. This was the whole art of night flying. The aeroplane throws out a slip-stream from the propellers and we used to come up behind feeling the slip-stream on our top wing which just shook the Camel a little bit. Then you knew you were just underneath the slip-stream coming up straight behind him and he couldn't shoot you because he had no gun actually in his tail. That gave you a narrow angle which got narrower as you got in where you were immune from being hit. If you could control yourself enough to get up little bit by little bit by little bit he couldn't hit you, and probably didn't know you were there, because he couldn't see you either. Then you opened fire from about 25 yards range if you had the nerve to get in as near as that. If you shot from further away you would probably miss. We had tracer bullets, armour piercing bullets with two machine guns firing through the propeller at 600 rounds a minute each. A pretty good volume of fire, which would go on about two minutes. If you shot straight you only needed one or two short bursts. You could see where the bullets were going because the tracers would tell you. If you were too much to the right or left you adjusted the aeroplane so that you were on target. That really was the whole secret of the thing – to have the patience to get in close after you had been lucky enough to find your Hun – but that was easier said than done. North of Amiens I found

a Hun and I got in behind him, went very close, opened fire and he just went up in flames. I identified myself by shooting a Very pistol out of my Camel then I went down to watch him crash and it turned out afterwards that this Hun was a very special one – one of the Giant aeroplanes that they were using – with five engines and eight men in it. It had been making an unusual noise so that the whole of France was watching, including the King who was visiting.[30]

Lieutenant Archibald Yuille, 151 Squadron, RAF

His victim was the first Giant aircraft to be shot down behind British lines.

In war, any offensive action usually brings a reaction and the bombing of London triggered a retaliatory campaign by the British. The Independent Air Force (IAF) was formed especially for the strategic bombing campaign against the German heartland. At first it used a combination of the daytime and night raids. Among the night-bombers was Second Lieutenant Roy Shillinglaw, who in 1918 was still flying in one of the trusty old two-seater FE2bs.

I don't think anybody deliberately bombed civilian houses or people. So far as my colleagues and myself were concerned we were very, very keen to be on our target. There is no doubt that our raids on German towns – railway stations and factories in those towns – must have been demoralising to some of the civilian inhabitants. In our night-bombing it was difficult to see our results – we would see a fire burning or the explosion in a works. But next day the day-bombers would be over at dawn and as they passed over our targets they photographed them and within twenty-four hours we would see pictures of our targets and where perhaps we'd hit, or whether we'd just missed and so forth. So that we were very keen to be on target because our errors were shown up on those photographs – there was no kidding the authorities. I think we were pretty accurate on the whole.[31]

Second Lieutenant Roy Shillinglaw, 100 Squadron, IAF

The IAF was also moving forward into the modern age with the Handley Page bombers.

One felt absolutely confident that the Germans could never bring it down. The pilot and the observer sat side by side in the front with the gunlayer at the rear. He had two platforms: one higher, one lower, with three Lewis guns, one at the bottom for firing back underneath the tail and two at the top. The observer had two Lewis guns in the front cockpit and was also responsible for the bomb-dropping equipment. He lay almost prone and had five pushes, like bell pushes, with five lights – two red, two green and one white. The white being the centre, the two green meant veer to the right and so on. By this method the pilot was able to see exactly what the observer wanted and try and get lined up on the target.[32]

Gunlayer William Wardrop, 207 Squadron, IAF

The actual physical damage caused by the bombs probably did not justify the occasional heavy losses suffered by the bombers and their diversion from tactically significant targets on the Western Front. Yet the knock-on effects of the air-raid alarms on German industry and the impact on civilian morale were considered to make the raids well worth-while. The future of twentieth-century warfare was taking shape.

WHEREVER THEY WENT THE GERMANS were harassed from the air. Their front-line trenches and artillery batteries were mercilessly targeted by the combination of the corps aircraft and the Royal Artillery, their rear positions were remorselessly probed, their supply chain and rein-forcements bombed, their communications infrastructure threatened and even the factories and inhabitants of the German homelands were brought face-to-face with the all-encompassing nature of modern war. The RAF numbered nearly 300,000 officers and men by November 1918, a sharp contrast to the strength of just over 2,000 for the entire RFC and RNAS back in August 1914.

11

1918: GERMAN SPRING OFFENSIVES

THE GREAT WAR would be decided by the fighting on the Western Front in 1918. That is not ignore the significant part played by the Russian Army in draining strength from the mighty German Army – the heart and soul of the Central Powers. For three years the Russians had hammered away on the Eastern Front, before the Bolshevik revolution in November 1917 had finally brought the country to its knees. The titanic battles fought almost alone by the French Army on the Western Front from 1914 to mid 1916 had also clawed away at the Germans, but the French had faltered after the ordeal of Verdun and the failure of the Nivelle Offensive in April 1917. The resulting mutinies had left them in a badly weakened state.

The British, too, had been drained by their ordeals on the Somme and at Ypres in 1916–17. But if the three great Allied Empires had almost fought themselves to a standstill by the end of 1917, the results of their collective attritional efforts were still evident: Germany was doomed. Her manpower reserves were fast eroding, her economy was staggering, raw materials of all sorts were scarce and her population was overwhelmed by war weariness. When the United States joined the war on the side of the

Allies in April 1917, things could only get worse for Germany. As with the British Empire, it would take over a year to convert military potential into actual soldiers on the ground, but by the summer of 1918, millions of Americans would be recruited, equipped, trained and finally delivered to the Western Front. It was evident to Hindenburg and Ludendorff that Germany would be defeated unless she could end the war before the Americans arrived in strength. The Germans could either give up, or try to knock Britain or France out of the war by utilising the manpower freed up by the Russian surrender to launch a decisive spring offensive. So the Germans geared up for a huge onslaught between the Somme and Arras, designed to knock Britain out of the war once and for all.

Unfortunately, the British Prime Minister, David Lloyd George, was unable to grasp the firmness of purpose required to concentrate resources for the decisive battle looming on the Western Front. Although responsible for great things in his management of the civilian war effort, Lloyd George recoiled from the excruciating casualties inevitable in facing the German Army head-on, and by 1918 he had lost all faith in Haig as commander of the BEF. Regrettably, as an Easterner, not only did Lloyd George support the frittering away of vital resources on campaigns that were peripheral to the result of the war, but he also tried to starve the Western Front of the reinforcements that were needed to maintain the strength of the BEF in the face of its mounting losses. He was later to portray this as saving manpower from any future Haig offensives which he had considered murderous and futile exercises. What he actually achieved was to weaken the BEF just as it faced its greatest test.

DRAFTS OF NEWCOMERS still daily arrived on the Western Front to fill the gaps torn in the ranks by the battles raging at Passchendaele and Cambrai. By this stage of the war, most of them were conscripts. The men who had been out at the front for years could not help but look at the excitable new arrivals with a jaundiced eye. The veterans did not find war exciting; they found it bloody terrifying. Some found that their courage had been eroded by the horrors they had already experienced and had begun to rely on artificial stimulants to keep them going. The picture of young officers drowning their fears in alcohol, as portrayed by war veteran R. C. Sherriff in his popular post-war play *Journey's End*, had a basis in reality.

> I knew one or two cases, sadly enough very young chaps – 22, 23 – who depended on alcohol. The odd thing was it didn't make them drunk and staggering about or anything like that. It simply cured the nerves that caused fear. Every man has got a certain quantity of courage. It varies tremendously. When you've used that up, you've got to replace it with something else. Army discipline and training lends you the ability to carry on to some extent and drink does the rest. My morale was good enough to keep me going: I didn't like it very much towards the end of the war, I was getting worn down, I'd twice been wounded and I was beginning to run out of my supplies of courage, but I managed to get through to the end. I always carried some whisky about in my water flask, but more as a reviver than anything! I didn't resort to heavy drinking.[1]
>
> Captain Norman Dillon, B Battalion, Tank Corps

Morale in the BEF was not high, in the sense that grumbling was widespread and despair was beginning to creep in. Yet overall there was still confidence that eventually they would prevail, although many had lost faith in believing that they themselves would be there to see it. Somehow most of them kept on going.

To make matters worse, everything around them seemed to be changing. Thanks to Lloyd George's insistence on retaining vitally needed reinforcements in Britain, the manpower of the BEF fell to such an extent that its existing organisational structure was undermined and it seemed likely that whole divisions might have to be broken up and the men redistributed. Instead, it was decided to reorganise the brigades, reducing from four battalions to three and using the redundant battalion to replenish the ranks. In itself this was perhaps not such a bad thing; the three-battalion brigade was the standard unit in many armies. The problem was the timing. Long-established working patterns and relationships between units were pulled asunder and would take time to rebuild – time which the Germans would not give them. At the same time, the BEF was required to assimilate the new defensive tactics necessary to have any real chance of withholding an imminent German offensive. Simple lines of trenches were now outmoded, rendered vulnerable by the huge power of the massed guns. To be effective there had to be a system of defence in depth to keep the guns at a distance. The front line would be made up of a series of strongly fortified redoubts, with barbed wire, machine guns and artillery covering the gaps. Two or three miles behind would be the main defence lines of the Battle Zone, and further back still the Rear Zone. The only problem was the same manpower shortages which dogged the army at large meant that labour was at a premium, and much had yet to be done by the time the Germans attacked.

As the two sides prepared, ordinary soldiers continued in the deadly routines of trench warfare. The fighting never stopped and a moment's bad luck could still kill, cripple or wound soldiers. Recently promoted Lance Corporal Ivor Watkins had a terrifying experience of mustard gas in a relatively quiet sector near Houplines on 16 March 1918. He was sheltering asleep in some cellar dugouts when the damage was done.

> There was an 18-pounder battery behind us, further back. The Germans were seeking them out and he started shelling with mustard gas. Our gas guard must have got killed, the shells dropped and the gas – heavier than air – must have got down into the cellars. When we woke up in the morning we felt our eyes burning terribly. We thought it was the smoke from the brazier. Naturally we started rubbing our eyes – what we were doing was rubbing the mustard gas into our eyes. With the smell – which is very akin to horseradish – we realised what we had done. Our eyes were running profusely, burning like hell they were, nothing but water running from our eyes. I could just see a mist in front of me. We came up and somebody from another section got hold of us and we were rushed down to the casualty clearing station and from there to the 2nd Canadian Hospital near Étaples. They washed my eyes, bandaged my eyes up – on my ticket that was attached to me, 'Gas shell, very severe!'[2]
>
> Lance Corporal Ivor Watkins, 15th Welsh Regiment

I can never see the wonderful picture 'Gassed' by John Singer Sargent at the IWM without remembering Watkins telling the story of how he and his friends felt their way back to safety. Within four days he was back in St Luke's Hospital in Bradford.

I couldn't see when I got to the hospital. That was the most terrifying experience I have ever had. I was 19 – what was I going to do – my trade, my employment gone. My whole life was in ruins. It hit me pretty hard, very, very hard. I cannot say what they did: there was a certain amount of bathing, there was a certain amount of ointment put in the eyes. I had a Scottish army sister and I always remember her intoning, 'Taffy, I'll get your sight back, don't worry!' My eyelids weren't shut but I couldn't recognise anything for the first month or so. Then there was a gradual haze. I was given goggles with a metal fine mesh grille to keep the glare out. A gradual process – I recovered my sight. The most horrible thing I have experienced and yet it's still used as a means of war. They're still manufacturing mustard gas today and selling it at a profit to countries. Horrible! Horrible! Saddam used it on the Kurds: burnt, blinded, the most horrible thing I can think of mustard gas. Banned! I'd murder the people that manufactured it![3]

Lance Corporal Ivor Watkins, St Luke's Hospital, Bradford

THE GERMAN OFFENSIVE, OPERATION MICHAEL, began at 04.40 on 21 March 1918. The bombardment, fired by 6,608 guns and a further 3,534 heavy trench mortars, opened up on the section of the front line held by the troops of General Sir Hubert Gough's Fifth Army and the neighbouring Third Army commanded by General Sir Julian Byng. Waves of shells smothered the British positions, a symphony of destruction, passing in phases over front-line redoubts, machine-gun posts and artillery batteries, while at the same time deluging the communications and command centres to prevent any coordinated response. The barrage was ferocious and, to make matters worse for the British defenders, dawn that morning brought a thick fog that completely obscured their view as the Germans emerged into No Man's Land at 09.40. The Germans pushed forward, using their elite stormtroopers to infiltrate the British lines, passing between centres of resistance and looking to hit the headquarters and overrun gun batteries before the British knew what was happening. In these circumstances it is not surprising that many positions in the front-line zone were cut off and overwhelmed with little effective resistance. Sergeant Joe Fitzpatrick was with his Lewis gun team in a support line.

I said, 'Come on, get ready!' Two officers came along, I think they were as drunk as lords because they were waving their revolvers and singing, 'Here's the Boche, here's the Boche, the Boche is here!' I thought, 'You silly buggers!' They went up the front. I was waiting and waiting. Jerry must have come past the front line and I looked right and left and I saw them swooping down the valley. The lieutenant sent an order, 'Tell Sergeant Fitz to bring twenty men up.' I got about a dozen and says, 'Come on with me.' I'm walking up this communication trench and my brains working all the time, I said to myself, 'You're a silly bugger – you're leading the way!' So I said to the runner, 'Run on and tell him we're coming.' He hadn't gone half a minute before he came running back: no tin hat, no rifle, 'They're here, Sergeant, they're here!' I looked and I saw this head so I let go with my rifle, 'BANG'. I looked round and they'd scarpered. I don't blame them really. I ran back and I got behind my Lewis gun team and I'm saying, 'Keep the bastards there – keep on that opening!' I've got my rifle and bayonet in my left hand and 'BANG' I thought I'd lost all my fingers on my left hand. My nose hit the floor, I rolled into the trench, got my phial of iodine, broke it, smeared it over and put a bandage on it. I turned round, I picked a rifle up and I got firing away to my left. No need to take aim. You only had to fire straight at them. I must have done about hundred rounds; changed the rifle when it was white hot. Picking the other one up, I looked behind me and he's coming back up the valley, I thought, 'Well, we're buggered here, we've had it!' I turned to the left and I saw a Jerry officer, 30 yards away on the other side of the wire. I always carried my cap up my shirt so I threw my helmet away, put me cap on, discarded my equipment and I walked through the wire to him. We stood face to face and we stared at each other. He stuck his revolver in my stomach, fully a minute. I thought, 'I've had my chips here!' He looked and said, 'Go!' That's the way that I got copped.[4]

Sergeant Joe Fitzpatrick, 2/6th Manchester Regiment

The British plan involved counter-attacks by reserve units after the Battle Zone had been made secure. This collapsed as the Germans pushed rapidly through the lines and the small number of divisions designated for the counter-attack role found themselves caught up in the main defensive battle. All along the line the Royal Artillery did their best to help, but for the most part their observation officers were blinded by the fog, or their guns were overrun before they could open fire. The experiences of Lieutenant Ernest Millard in the Epéhy sector were typical.

> I was in bed in the dugout. Of course they'd got our battery position and they shelled us. There were shells all round us. There was a heavy mist that morning and a concentration of gas. Visibility was very short indeed; in fact I lost my way from the dugout to the guns! I found myself in front of the guns – it didn't matter because they were 4.5-inch howitzers! But I had to walk back to get to the gunpits. We were on SOS lines, as soon as they opened fire we had our line of fire on No Man's Land. There was no communication from the observation post because there was no observation; the subaltern just got hold of a rifle and acted as an infantryman. There was no question of doing any counter-battery or observation work.[5]
>
> Second Lieutenant Ernest Millard, D Battery, 95th Brigade, RFA

Second Lieutenant Cyril Dennys had moved up under heavy shell fire to his forward observation post facing St Quentin. Here he found that, despite the bombardment, he still had an uncut telephone line through to his mighty 8-inch guns. Through a gap in the fading mists he was able to see the Germans massing – and then it was time for vengeance.

> I saw grey figures, obviously German, going to and fro from Dum and Dee Copses. This struck me as a target worth having and I phoned through to brigade and said that I could see German infantry massing in these copses. I think they were preparing to make an attack on one of the surviving redoubts. The brigade turned all the surviving guns that we had onto the two copses. There was a most gratifying sight from my point of view – flashes then large bursts of smoke and debris. When the smoke cleared away I could see no more German infantry at all; I hoped that I had got them, I was really feeling rather vindictive. I'd been frightened in the morning and it was time I frightened somebody else![6]
>
> Second Lieutenant Cyril Dennys, 212 Siege Battery, RGA

The next few days were a desperate affair as the Germans pressed home their advantage and the British fell back in considerable disarray, but just about holding the line together. Dennys found that his triumph was short lived, for on 22 March it was clear that the Germans had not only broken through the Battle Zone but were fast approaching his gun positions.

> I suggested to the captain in charge of my section that I might go out in front and see what I could see – how long we'd got! I went out in front and I saw at some considerable distance small parties of our troops slowly retiring one after another from one position to another followed by larger groups of Germans. A lot of machine-gun fire. I realised that our time was going to be very short. So I came back and said, 'Look, I think we'd better have these guns out of action seeing as we can't take them away! At any rate prevent them from being used?' The captain said, 'Yes, we will, we'll let all the pressure out of the gun cylinders then fire them with a full charge, so that they'll break the cylinder! If we attack the screw part of the breach with a cold chisel that will make it impossible to shut the breech!'[7]

> Second Lieutenant Cyril Dennys, 212 Siege Battery, RGA

With their guns destroyed they joined in the general retreat. One of the reserve divisions moving forward to try to stem the tide was the 50th Division. With them was Private Joe Pickard of the 1/5th Northumberland Fusiliers.

> It was a nerve-racking thing when they were attacking you. They used come like a house, like bonded together. Our idea of attacking was extended order – a good bit between each man – so that if a shell burst it only maybe took one man, it might take two. The Jerries came across like the side of a house, heavy and they used to fire off the hip, the leading man. I suppose trying to put the wind up you. But that didn't take much effect; I mean the thicker they were together the more the bullet was taking – the bullet would take two men instead of one.[8]

> Private Joe Pickard, 1/5th Northumberland Fusiliers

Somewhere nearby was Private George Thompson of the 1/5th Durham Light Infantry. They were caught in positions with a poor field of fire and the Germans were on them in a flash.

The Germans appeared suddenly from dead ground in front of us: it was a badly positioned trench as a matter of fact. They drove straight at us with their bayonets fixed and their rifles going. We fell back – there so many of them – into a ditch about 50 yards further back. From the ditch we held them. We just blazed at them and they stopped. Before daylight we retreated to another trench further back. Then just about dawn we retreated again and this time for most of the day, right across the River Somme. It was carried out as a retreat should be carried out. You laid down on the ground and when the enemy appeared in sight, you opened fire on them. That drove them down and then you got up and retreated. Then you stopped and held them a bit, then retreated – it went on all day.[9]

Private George Thompson, 1/5th Durham Light Infantry

Although most units kept some appearance of order, there were inevitably stragglers, while the walking wounded were left to make their way back as best as they could. As the Fifth Army fell back, small parties of men were ordered to fight to the end to cover the retreat. Private Walter Hare of the 15th West Yorkshire Regiment found himself engaged in one such desperate holding action. He was lucky to survive.

The Germans were advancing wave after wave after wave. What few machine guns we had we were using and we fired at them with our rifles. We were short of firepower but we did the best we could. We knew we'd done them a lot of damage. They couldn't get any more ammunition or food up to us, so we went two days with no food. The Germans got a lot of machine guns up; there was tremendous fire. We kept getting up and having a shot at them, then bobbing down again quick. The chap next to me got up and fell back, he'd got a bullet through his head and he was dead. I thought, 'No. I'd better not fire!' Our biggest problem was they got round our flanks. There was a farm on the left-hand flank and they got machine guns in there. We couldn't understand how they managed to do that, because we thought there was a Guards Battalion on our left and we knew Guards weren't famous for retiring. They were firing into our backs down this road. No cover at all except for what we'd dug into the embankment. Sergeant Major George Cussins said to me, 'We can't stay here! We'll have to retire, have to get back! After the next burst of machine gun

329

fire, we'll dash for it!' There was a burst of fire and the sergeant major ran. I maybe wasn't quick enough off the mark, but he ran, I didn't – I stayed where I was and I thought I'd make the next rush. I saw him fall down in the field behind us. I thought I'd better wait until it was a bit darker, then I'd try to get away. But I was too late, by that time they were around us, surrounded us. A German was coming for me with his bayonet. I put my hands up and dropped my gun, that's all you can do in a case like that. I was surprised to see my brother. Two days ago I'd been told he'd been killed as we retired. There was about thirty of our chaps go forward with their hands in the air, but more surprising, my brother was amongst them – I couldn't believe it![10]

Private Walter Hare, 15th West Yorkshire Regiment

A couple of days later Sergeant William Collins was caught up in a defensive action at Le Hamel.

I was bandaging the wounded on the top of the hill at Le Hamel. Casualties were streaming onto my post. Captain Swan, the medical officer, was as busy as he could be dressing casualties. We were right in the front line; down below was a trench full of 300 fellows from the 16th Irish Division firing their Lewis guns. While having a breather, I went to a bank next to this Lewis gunner; he was firing and I was sat with my back to the bank and my head back. I'd got my tin hat on – having a rest you see. A shell came and I was blown unconscious. How long I was unconscious I don't know – it must have been two or three hours. When I came to, I got up and I looked at the other end of the bank and there was infantry dug in slit trenches. They'd dug themselves in while I was unconscious. I stood there looking at them. An officer looked up at me and said, 'What the hell do you think you're doing? Get away, farther up there!' I was half woozy – off my head. My tin hat had been forced down on my head, I was badly concussed and I was wounded round the back of the neck and over the shoulder. My coat was all torn ragged by the bits of shell. All of a sudden a stream of machine-gun bullets came by. I've never heard a more horrifying sound in my life. It was like a thousand gas taps turned on, 'PSSSST! HSSST! HSSST! HSST! PSSSST! HSSST! HSSST! HSST!' Magnified a hundred times going hissing past! I had sufficient consciousness to go down – I was flat on my face – instinct. I got up, walked around and eventually I found myself back with the field ambulance. I was very shocked – there's no doubt about that. Heavy in the head and not thinking clearly. I still couldn't tell you exactly what I did to this day. But I couldn't bear to hear a sound. Couldn't bear to hear a pin drop. Every explosion, my heart jumped out of my skin. In three weeks I lost nearly all my hair. I used to have to take a firm grip of myself and just stand it. Gradually it diminished.[11]

Sergeant William Collins, No. 1 Cavalry Field Ambulance

Private Joe Pickard faced a terrifying predicament on 31 March 1918, when he was caught near Moreuil in a concentrated box barrage of German shells.

He boxed us and they started to 'harrow' the box – like harrowing a field – searching the box with shells. The first lot was alright and it was coming through the second time when I got hit. I remember seeing this big black cloud go up the side of the ditch. When I came to myself I was lying back up the road amongst a lot of dead Frenchmen. There was a Frenchman, he was just like a pepper pot hit about the head. I jumped straight up – I went straight down again and I thought, 'Well, the leg's away!' I found out where I was hit, tore the trousers down. I thought, 'Well, if I stop here it's either a bullet or a bayonet!' They wouldn't pick you up you know, couldn't afford it, they were trying to travel fast. I got me first aid packet out and all there was in there was a lot of gauze, a little tube of stuff and a big safety pin – that was your first aid. I tore the trousers down; I was hit underneath the joint of the leg and I tied it on there. The piece of shrapnel had cut the sciatic nerve, chipped both hip joints, smashed the left side of the pelvis, three holes in the bladder and I lost my nose – a right bloody mess. I crawled down the road on my hands and knees. I saw a fellow I knew on one of these ridges and I gave him a shout – fellow called Craig came from Darlington. He got two little fellows, two little Durhams, to come out. I was about head and shoulders above them. Somehow or other they got a stretcher and there was a Red Cross van pulled up somewhere near the bottom of the road. They carried us through the barrage a third time and I got into the wagon and the fellow said, 'You'll be alright now, chum!' The ambulance took me to an old farmhouse, the roof was blown off – and everything else. I wanted a drink. Well they wouldn't give us any water – abdominal wounds you see. You never get water. They

331

must have bandaged us there. When I came round it was dark and I was lying on a stretcher. I didn't know what was the matter with us – it turned out there was a blanket over the top of us. I was left for dead. The old lady got the number of my grave and the King and Queen's sympathy.[12]

Private Joe Pickard, 1/5th Northumberland Fusiliers

Alive he may have been, but what was left of Pickard's poor mangled body was in a dreadful state. Yet the terrible disfigurement caused by the loss of his nose was the very least of his concerns.

I knew there was something the matter with my face – I was bound to – I knew the blood was running. I never bothered about it. Well I mean in a case like that you think whether you want to live – and to hell with what you look like.[13]

Private Joe Pickard, 1/5th Northumberland Fusiliers

A series of operations removed the shrapnel from Pickard's abdominal wounds and legs, and after being kept in Rouen Hospital for six weeks, he was eventually evacuated to the 3rd Western General Hospital in Neath where he would remain until January 1919. As his body slowly healed he began to take more of an interest in what was left of his nose.

With the blinking bandages you could nearly always tell what meal I'd had – it always showed on there. I used to get shaved across there. I got fed up with this so one day as the sister was standing at the table and we were just chatting away I said, 'Have you got a mirror, Sister?' She said, 'Yes,' I said, 'Do you mind if have a loan of it?' I said, 'Give us a loan of your scissors.' I cut all the blinking bandages off to have a look at it. The nose was off to about halfway up the bridge. She was a bit dubious about it and she said, 'What do you think about it?' 'Well,' I said, 'What can I do – it's off, it's gone – you don't think I'm going to travel up the line to look for it!' She said, 'You'll get better!'[14]

Private Joe Pickard, 3rd Western General Hospital, Neath

MEANWHILE, ON THE SOMME BATTLEFRONT the roads leading back to Amiens were chaotic, but one sign of hope was the sight of the French troops arriving to help the British stem the German advance. From 26 March, the British and French divisions had been placed under a more centralised direction after the appointment – by mutual agreement, not a Lloyd George inspired coup – of a Supreme Commander in the august form of Marshal Ferdinand Foch. Although Haig and Pétain would still retain considerable autonomy, Foch would hold the ring and set the overall direction to ensure that the French, British and, ultimately, the American armies, all acted as one.

One of the British units moved up to plug the gaps opened up by the German advance was the 9th Royal Fusiliers. Among them was Lieutenant Jim Davies, who had been transferred when his own 8th Royal Fusiliers had been broken up during the brigade reorganisation earlier in 1918. He claimed to have been present when the famous 'Leaning Virgin' at Albert was finally brought down to earth.

> I was enfiladed – a chap was hit on my left, the bullet must have passed me to get him in the face. I was enfiladed from the tower of the 'Leaning Virgin' at Albert. I said, 'Anybody here who can run fast?' A boy said 'I can!' He was about 18 years old – his name was Hayes. He ran and I saw him go down, I think it was fright more than anything; he wasn't shot in the legs, he was shot in the arm. He got up and came in and he said, 'I've eaten the message!' I said, 'You've been reading the *Boy's Own Paper*!' The second runner I sent back down the communication trench to battalion headquarters, who got onto the artillery through brigade. After a time they started to shell the tower and down came the Virgin![15]
>
> Lieutenant Jim Davies, 9th Royal Fusiliers

The British line was further stiffened by the arrival of the Australian Corps, who had developed from the brave but inexperienced troops thrust into action at Gallipoli into war-hardened, tactically brilliant soldiers ready to stand centre stage. Their relationship with the British Army was always a source of amusement.

> I called out, 'Halt, who are you?' He said, 'Fucking Australian! Who the fucking hell are you?' So I realised he was drunk and I said, 'You realise you're talking to an officer?' and he told me to go and fuck myself! My troops were watching this and I wondered how to handle

it. You can't say, 'Fall in two men, take his name and number!' So I hit him! I knocked him down. I can see him now sitting with his knees up and his head at the back. I never saw him again; I didn't want to. He probably had a vague idea he'd been hit, that somebody had knocked him into the mud. It was the only thing to do.[16]

Lieutenant Jim Davies, 9th Royal Fusiliers

But the Australians could fight sure enough and they successfully stabilised the line in the vital Villers-Bretonneux sector in front of Amiens.

The German spring offensive on the Somme had failed. It had not knocked the British out of the war, it had not broken through and rolled up the line to the north of Arras, it had failed to drive a wedge between the British and French Armies and, with the failure to reach the Amiens rail junctions, it had not taken any strategically significant objective. All the German Army had done was carve out a huge bulbous 40-mile deep salient totalling some 1,200 square miles, much of it devastated by war. These meaningless gains would be a hostage to fortune in their vulnerability to future Allied counter-attacks. And the clock was still ticking inexorably towards the advent of the American hordes in the summer. Spring would not last forever.

THE GERMAN HIGH COMMAND HAD LITTLE CHOICE but to try again. This time, Ludendorff resolved to strike in Flanders, seeking to knock the British out of the war with Operation Georgette. Here there was a real strategic focus, in that the vital Hazebrouck rail junction was just 20 miles from the front lines, while a little further back were the essential Channel ports. The German divisions would assault between Armentières and the La Bassée Canal on 9 April 1918, then attack next day all along the Messines Ridge with the aim of punching through the lines and encircling the whole Ypres Salient. Haig was well aware of the threat of any German advance in Flanders, but his forces had already been stretched to their limits. The German barrage began at 04.15 with their infantry attacking at 08.45, again blessed by thick fog. The Portuguese troops (the Portuguese had joined the war in March 1916 and sent two weak divisions to serve on the Western Front) in the front line had little stomach for a murderous fight with which they could not readily identify, and they gave way with little effective resistance, although it should be noted that some of the British divisions already mauled during Operation Michael did little better. The German attacks followed, thick and fast. Sergeant Henry Mabbott was wounded defending the La Bassée Canal on 18 April.

> We got as far back as the La Bassée Canal and we had six machine guns on the German side of the canal and everybody was evacuated onto the other side. That six was reduced to four, reduced to two and then to one. I had the one Lewis gun with one man. He fed the gun for me while I used it. By this time the other five guns were able to open up, giving me a chance to get over the bridge. When the signal had been given, everything opened up and I ran across the bridge. But just before I got to the other side, there was a blinding white light and a second afterwards I was swallowing water. I struck out for the side, was pulled out and got up to run – something happened to my right leg – I went down. I got up again to run and once again I went down crash, I felt for my leg from somewhere round about halfway up the calf – there was nothing – it wasn't there. Of course it was bleeding very badly and I cut the string of my gas mask and put it round my thigh, tied it as tight as I could. Put the dirk back into the sheath, put the sheath in and turned it until such time as the blood had stopped flowing and I hung on to it. Somebody found me and carried me a distance until they could get me onto a stretcher. There was an awful amount of shelling going on at the time and it took an awful long time to get me down to a dressing station. The doctor put a needle into my wrist and I knew no more.[17]

> Sergeant Henry Mabbott, 1st Cameron Highlanders

The imperturbable Haig issued his 'Backs to the Wall' order to try to stiffen the general resolve. In the end the line held and the Germans were held back from Hazebrouck. It had been a close-run thing, but the Germans again failed to achieve any really significant objectives, despite their consuming desperation to end the war. And time kept marching on.

THE WESTERN FRONT could no longer be seen as a futile struggle. Everyone could grasp the fundamental importance of the deadly battles being waged across France and Belgium. Yet as the reserves were mobilised for drafts to the front, in keeping with human nature not everyone wanted to go. Strangely absent from contemporary accounts are the stories of men who did not relish the thought of imminent action, but oral history highlights many different reactions to the clarion battle-cry. Some had been wounded in earlier battles and baulked at the thought of a return to the Western Front to face the same dangers. One such was Sapper George Clayton who was at the Royal Engineers Command Depot in the Thetford area.

> You had to pass your digging test. They used to record the time that it took you to dig a hole and fill it up again. When you completed that job in a certain length of time you were eligible to go back to France again. There was a lot of lead-slinging, a lot didn't want to go back – I was one! I knew that if I filled that up in a certain length of time I'd be going back to France. I never raced to dig a hole. I'd been out there about two and a half years and I'd done my share of front-line work. We had to go to a medical board. They had the records of how far I'd progressed with this digging and I hadn't very good marks. I thought I'd be sent back, because I felt fit and looked well, but I was discharged. So they marked us for a discharge – valvular disease heart – that's what I was given a discharge with. I was given a pension of 40 per cent. I think my heart's better now than it was then![18]
>
> Sapper George Clayton, Royal Engineers Depot, Thetford

Others, such as the splendidly irascible Jack Hepplestone, would only go back to the front in their own time. After service on the Western Front he had volunteered for the Tank Corps and was at Wareham Camp, being trained as a driver. When his leave was cancelled Hepplestone simply went absent without leave.

> They said that we could have a seven-day leave but the Germans made an advance and we were ordered back sharp. I thought to myself, 'Well, I'm going to have mine!' I went down to the station and got on the train to London and Sheffield, that's how I came to be absent without leave. They locked me up and the Military Police

came and escorted me back to Wareham. They fetched me out of the compound and paraded me in front of the orderly officer as to the reason why you been absent. This sergeant major, he'd been out of the Guards, he came very close to me and said, 'You're the man that's been absent? You've caused us a lot of trouble, you. Do you know what I'd like to do with you if I had my way?' I said, 'I don't know! If I knew I'd write home and tell me mother!' I think that upset him. He says, 'I'd put you on the parapet and let the Germans use you for a target!' I said, 'They've been trying that for nearly three years and missed me every time – but I'll not miss thee!' Smack! And I gave him one! These two Red Caps never tried to stop me – they wanted me to give him some more actually – they didn't say so but that was their attitude. He looked like getting up so I jumped on him, gave him a bit of knee business and I bit his ear-hole. I was remanded for a court martial.[19]

Private Jack Hepplestone, Tank Corps, Wareham Camp

Punishment was inevitable and Hepplestone was sentenced to six months in Maybrick Military Prison in April 1918. Here the warders were more than willing to accommodate his predilection for violence.

First day it was really funny. 'Get undressed, everything off, you've got to get bathed.' All right, I get everything off and it was cold water, so I splashed some about, wet my hair – knocked at the door and said, 'I've had my bath!' This Sergeant Billy Williams came in, a bit of a Cockney fellow he was, he said, 'Have you been in your bath?' So I says, 'Yes!' 'You bloody liar!' Smack! He hit me and knocked me in it, 'Ahhhhrr!' It took me breath. Then they took me round to the cell I was going in. You had to put your kit on a shelf, folded up in regimental style. I folded it up as I thought was perfect – which it was. This Sergeant Williams walked in, hands behind him, looked round. He said, 'Is that your way of putting your kit up?' He pulled it down all on the floor and said, 'Put it up again!' I said, 'Well, tha's knocked it down; now thee pick it up!' He went out and came back in with three more; shut the door and gave me the biggest hammering I'd ever had in my life. He said, 'I shall always remember you!' Another sergeant, he knew all about this and he said, 'I'll show you something!' He took me down on the ground floor and there were two cells knocked in one. There were straitjackets, handcuffs, a

337

cat-o'-nine tails. He said, 'We can tame lions here. We'll not stand for 'owt like that here – be a good lad and you'll be all right!'[20]

Private Jack Hepplestone, Maybrick Prison

Hepplestone wisely swallowed his pride and for the rest of his sentence became a model prisoner.

The response to the emergency demand for replenishments at the front was complicated by the impact of the influenza virus that swept across the world in the summer of 1918. The mortality rate was dreadful and Nurse Bird found the constant funerals deeply depressing.

> We had the Spanish Flu epidemic. Every morning before we went on duty we had to go through the fumigation department and also before we left at night. The mortuaries were so full we had the patients lying one on top of the other. The funerals were going all day long; the boys were dying off like flies. Walking from the hospital we had to stand and we bowed heads while the funerals were passing by. Sometimes it took so long to get there I had to give up going. It was so terrible; funerals were going on all the time.[21]

Nurse Bird, Colchester Hospital

The flu pandemic lasted from early in 1918 until well into 1920. The disease seemed to trigger an over-reaction of the body's immune system, which meant that perversely it preyed on the young and strong as well as the very young, the old and those weakened by the ravages of war. It was a global phenomenon, far greater than the Great War, and before it was finished it is estimated that it killed over 50 million worldwide. It was fatal for some 10 per cent of all those it infected. In India alone some 17 million died. It was cruel that so many who had survived all the terrible horrors of war were brought down and destroyed by a microscopic virus.

MANY OF THE MEN SENT OUT in emergency drafts in the spring and early summer of 1918 had been unwilling conscripts, never keen to join the army in the first place. Private Jim Fox certainly did not consider himself a soldier, but while on embarkation leave back home in Durham during the spring of 1918, he managed to convince himself that no harm would come to him.

> I had to go to the south side of Durham station to entrain for Stockton. It was a brilliant morning, the sun was shining. Just before I entered the station I turned round and from that area you got a very good view of Durham castle and cathedral. The sun was shining lovely on those two wonderful buildings and I said to myself and loudly too, 'I'm sure to come back and see this view that I'm looking at now!' And do you know I never forgot it. Many, many times I was in danger of being shot, maybe blown to smithereens, but that thought always came to happen to my mind, 'That'll never happen to me because I'm sure to get back to see the cathedral and castle!' That thought always kept me going.[22]
>
> Private Jim Fox, 51st (Young Soldiers) Battalion, Durham Light Infantry

When he got out to the front he was posted to the 11th Durham Light Infantry who were in the then relatively 'quiet' sector of Arras. Here he was caught up in the outcry over the question of 18-year-olds being allowed to fight at the front. Fox and another young soldier saw their chance.

> My friend Charlie Ford was the man that led me astray. In June, one morning we were called on parade. The purpose was, 'Anyone not yet 19 years of age, step two paces forward!' So Charlie Ford instantly thought, 'Well, it's one way of getting out of this mess – I'll step two paces forward!' He pulled me forward with him. But the difficulty was he was 19 in April and this was in June – and I was 19 on 4th May. This being in June, both of us were 19 years of age – we weren't 18. The corporal came round and asked various particulars, 'Name and date of your birthday?' I told him mine was 4th July and Charlie said 16th July. We were both telling an untruth – I was worried to death. When we got back to billets and I said, 'Look here, Charlie, by stepping those two paces forward you've landed us both into a hell of a mess. The authorities have only got to look up the records and they'll soon see we're both 19. One of these days in the very near future someone will collar us both by the scruff of the neck and take us to the guardroom to be punished!' The days went over, nothing happened and in about ten days we were called on parade again.

The officer then said, 'These names I now read out, step two paces forward!' Charles Ford and my names were included – there was about forty all together.[23]

Private Jim Fox, 11th Durham Light Infantry

These forty young soldiers were sent back to the Infantry Base Depot at Étaples. Here they came into contact with a measles victim in their tent and as a result Fox and Ford were sent on to an isolation camp. When they finally got back to Étaples, the two incorrigible malingerers tried it on again.

We were wondering what to do and I said, to Charles, 'We might get two or three days here if we report sick!' The next morning the usual request came, 'Anyone sick two paces forward!' We stepped two paces forward, Charlie and I. There was about forty or fifty of us, all different regiments all congregated together. The sergeant in charge marched us to the medical hut at Étaples. He asked everyone of us to strip and we came out into the big hall of the hut. We waited about five minutes for the medical officer who was an old colonel, very gruff old fellow. He just came down the line and he didn't stop very long at any one person. He looked at the corporal with him and said, 'Fox, what's the matter with you?' 'Well, Sir, I've had trouble with recurring pains in the back!' He said, 'Whereabouts?' I put my hand behind my back, 'About here, Colonel!' He says, 'You say they recur quite frequently?' 'Yes!' 'When are these pains the worst, morning, afternoon or during the night?' 'Well, not all the time but the greater part of the time, morning, afternoon and night.' He paused for about five seconds that seemed like five minutes and then he said, 'Look, there's only one thing the matter with you, Fox!' 'What's that, Colonel?' 'You want your bloody hair cut!' That was the medical examination. We got no sympathy at all – that was a waste of time.[24]

Private Jim Fox, Base Depot, Étaples

When they were finally sent back to the 11th Durham Light Infantry they discovered the unit had suffered severe casualties in their absence.

Others were not so lucky in their encounters with army discipline. Private Jack Earl of the 1/7th Lancashire Fusiliers was one of those executed for desertion in 1918.

We only had one lad that deserted. He did it twice and he got
sentenced to death. They stripped him of his medal – he had a medal
– and he was sentenced to be shot. We all had to go and see it, every
one of us. That was as good as to say, 'Now you know!' That's about
what it was. The whole battalion was on parade, whether you shut
your eyes was up to you, but we were all there. We were all up the
hill, down below they'd got like a little stage. I just watched it. It
only took a minute or two. There was a chair in the middle of the
stage and he was brought out, sat on the chair. He was in just a shirt
and his trousers. His identification was there dangling on his chest.
He must have asked about being blindfolded, and they did blindfold
him. They had to take the firing squad out of his own platoon. They
took eight of them. One of them was his mate and he refused to
take part in it. He was told that if he didn't he'd be court-martialled
and get a really bad sentence. They told him, 'There's nothing to
worry about because you won't shoot him!' The thing was there were
eight rifles and one had a dummy bullet, but none of the eight men
knew which of them had got the dummy bullet. So as the officer
said, 'Each one of you have got it there that you didn't shoot him!'
As a matter of fact some of them must have missed deliberately,
but that was unfortunate because he just slumped forward, but he
wasn't dead. That's when the Provost Marshal had his revolver and
he shot him. He was a lad that lived not far from here – Jack Earl.[25]
I felt very miserable because he was a friend of mine. He was a very
good lad. The trouble with him was he deserted the once – that was
when we were going back – and then later on he pushed off again. Of
course you can't do that twice, not during the war. When it comes to
desertion there was only one sentence: he was lucky to have got away
with it the first time. But when it comes to the second – well they
had to. He asked for it more or less! We didn't have any crying parties
on his behalf or anything like that. I was relieving as company clerk
and I had to send a telegram home to his people. The procedure was
that if anybody was killed I used to send this telegram, 'We regret to
inform you that your son killed in action.' With him I had to send a
telegram just 'Killed'. The words in action were not in the telegram.
Unfortunately, this lad lived in the same street as him, and when he
got home on leave he told young Earl's parents that he'd deserted and
been shot. That was the most horrible thing to do. It got round to us

and one or two of the lads gave this bloke a right piling up, battered
the bloody daylights out of him.[26]

Private John Grainger, 1/7th Lancashire Fusiliers

The twin emotions of sympathy for poor young Earl and acceptance of
the sentence are evident.

As the drafts of new soldiers reached the front they found themselves joining units that had been put through the mill just too often.
Private Bill Gillman joined the 2/2nd London Regiment in the Somme
area. What he found was fairly typical.

It was a mixed bag. There were so many casualties and replacements
that there was only very few of the old sweats left. Most of those
were NCOs, for which we were glad. I had one special pal, from
Bermondsey, he'd been wounded and he got a big dent in his head.
He'd been home to England and been sent out again. Now he was an
old sweat. I used to look up to those men. Because they knew their
onions, all the snags, what to look for – or look out for! I used to be
careful to listen to them. You soon found out that you didn't know
it all – there was quite a lot you didn't know. If you started slinging
your weight about you were reminded that you'd only just come up.[27]

Private Bill Gillman, 2/2nd London Regiment

The quality of the British soldier may have been declining as enthusiasm
for the war waned, but there was also clear evidence that the German
Army was a diminishing force.

One thing I noticed was that the Boche had had it just as much as
we had: the German troops I saw were not the same blokes that we
had fought at Loos. They were not the same type, not organised like
the Boche usually was. There didn't seem to be the strong discipline
that there'd been at the Battle of Loos. Their equipment too was very
backward. They were getting towards the end.[28]

Lieutenant Jim Davies, 9th Royal Fusiliers

Both sides were suffering.

IN MAY 1918 THERE WAS A LULL on the Western Front while the Germans pondered their diminishing options. Taking due advantage, the British juggled their divisions around as Foch attempted to create a strategic reserve of British and French divisions able to respond to a German attack. As part of this process, some of the most exhausted British divisions were sent to recuperate as part of the XI Corps under the command of the French Sixth Army, in the then relatively quiet Chemin des Dames sector in front of the River Aisne. It was thus unfortunate that this was the very place chosen by the Germans to launch a third great offensive on 27 May 1918: Operation Blücher. The bombardment opened at 01.00.

> As we entered the woods of the Chemin des Dames the bombardment started. We went into dugouts at first. It was a terrific bombardment, a thundering noise going on all the time. If they're bombarding you they can't attack, or they'd be bombarding themselves, so you wait until the bombardment subsided and then you come out. We were standing in the trench waiting for the attack to come and we got heavy rifle fire from the left, not in front. I got a bullet through my shoulder and another one in beside my spine and out at the side – that knocked me down in the trench. Next thing I knew, I was being rolled over by two German Red Cross soldiers, young lads about my age I should think. They were quite pleasant: they stole all my cigarettes, like, but they dressed my wounds. My legs I couldn't use at all at first, because the spine had been touched by the bullet. Gradually the feeling came back again and I was able to walk – with difficulty. These two pointed which way to go. I walked back and it wasn't long before I found a big group of our prisoners. All ranks: officers, sergeant majors, privates – all together – prisoners![29]
>
> Private George Thompson, 1/5th Durham Light Infantry

Among the captured was Signaller George Cole, who was set to work as an impromptu stretcher bearer carrying back the German wounded. As such, they were forbidden to take their own British wounded and this caused an untoward reaction.

> Mark Carr and me were carrying a big German – oh, he was a big feller. And there was no stretchers; we were just carrying him in

blankets. Big heavy feller. We kept looking at one another and putting him down to rest. All he could say was, 'Wasser! Wasser! Wasser!' He was wanting a drink. As it got so far back there was one of our lads, one of the 6th Durhams, lying wounded next to a bloody big shell hole. Without any thought, I said, 'Marky, put him down!' And I motioned to him. We just tipped this German in the hole, 'Get in there!' He rolled in the hole, you'd think it had been rehearsed. We picked this lad up, the 6th Durham and ran off like hell. Even now I never have any regrets at what I did. It was only common sense, you look after your own first.[30]

Signaller George Cole, A Battery, 250 Brigade, RFA

Cole and Carr could have been shot for their ruthless action. But they got away with it.

The British and the French Sixth Army fell back, surrendering the Chemin des Dames and withdrawing across the River Aisne before retreating in confusion across successive valleys and ridges. The German advance was finally held on the River Marne by a combination of newly arrived French divisions and, most significantly of all, by two new American divisions. The frantic Germans would attack once more on 9 June with Operation Gneisenau, which was directed against the French and sought to expand the salient bequeathed by Operation Blücher. The French at first pulled back, but on 11 June they viciously counter-attacked the exposed German western flank and suddenly the long agony of the German 1918 offensives was over. The Germans had expended their reserves of manpower and could attack no more. The American Army began to feed more and more divisions into the line, taking over the quieter sectors and learning the grim trade of trench warfare. They had a lot to learn in a short time, but there were an awful lot of them and the trickle of fresh divisions became a flood in the early summer of 1918. The Germans had finally reached the end of their rope.

12

1918: ADVANCE TO VICTORY

THE BRITISH FOURTH ARMY in the Somme area had become aware that the German troops in front of them were not behaving in accordance with their normal high standard of military efficiency. In order to test the situation, General Sir Henry Rawlinson ordered a local attack by the Australian Corps under Lieutenant General Sir John Monash. This assault, in July 1918, would also trial the new tactics of the 'All Arms Battle' that had been under development by the British Army for more than a year. This was a collective new vision of twentieth-century warfare: the replacement where possible of vulnerable and increasingly scarce human bodies with massed firepower and mechanised weapons. An excruciating number of casualties had been suffered in 1918, and with a shrinking British Army, manpower had to be conserved.

However, although there were fewer infantrymen available, the ones they had were far better armed than their predecessors. They had plenty of Lewis light machine guns, a copious number of hand grenades and their own 'artillery' in the form of rifle grenades or mortars. Not too far behind them, they could call on the support of heavy mortars and Vickers machine guns. They no longer advanced in lines, but in short strings of men with a screening of skirmishers ahead. By August 1918, the Royal Artillery had no shortage of guns of all calibres and all the ammunition they required. British gunners could now dominate the battlefield and had a complete grasp of their deadly trade. Rather than aiming to destroy, they sought to suppress the ability of the German Army to mount any effective resistance. The German gunners and formation headquarters were sprayed liberally with gas shells, strongpoints identified by aerial reconnaissance were pounded relentlessly, and when the British infantry emerged into No Man's Land they were preceded by complex creeping barrages that lashed down curtains of shrapnel and high explosive shells. The infantry would be accompanied by tanks, still unreliable, but now given a realistic auxiliary role in the attack, crunching flat any remaining barbed wire and dealing with any surviving machine-gun posts and pillboxes. The Whippet light tanks would forage ahead seeking gaps in the German defences, while supply tanks, in an equally important role, could ferry copious quantities of ammunition across No Man's Land in relative safety. Above them were the RAF, not only photographing, directing the artillery and carrying out contact patrols, but now directly intervening by ground strafing, and attempting to cut vital German communications and transport links through bombing missions.

In the event, as a practical experiment, the Battle of Hamel on 4 July 1918 was a huge success. Objectives were quickly seized as the Germans seemed to fall apart in front of the attack and suffered nearly 2,500 casualties, many of whom were taken prisoner, while the Allies lost only around 1,000 men. This stunning triumph cleared the way for a much larger attack using the same principles – what would become the Battle of Amiens, launched on 8 August 1918. Rawlinson's plans would eventually involve the entire Tank Corps of some 324 heavy tanks and 96 of the lighter Whippets – indeed this would be the greatest tank battle of the war. Yet although the tanks were an important element of the plans, there should be no confusion as to where the key to success lay: it was the performance of the gunners that would be crucial, as it was essential that the German artillery be silenced.

The British had developed a reliable system of identifying German batteries, no matter how hard the Germans tried to conceal their presence. The aerial photographic interpretation experts had improved their skills year on year, and the slightest sign visible from the air would be swiftly spotted. Then there were specialist units who used science to thwart any camouflage attempts. One example was the flash spotters. This sounds simple – and indeed the concept is – but a variety of refinements had made it a lethal science for the German gunners, who would find themselves suddenly deluged with shells as their 'cover' was blown. Private Victor Polhill was one of this new breed of scientific warriors who had volunteered to join the Observation Group of the Royal Engineers after being slightly gassed. He was posted to Chateau des Trois Tours at Brielen in the northern Ypres sector where they manned an intimidatingly tall observation tower.

> It was about 112 foot, a triangular shape and held up by big steel cables to hold it in position. We formed ourselves into batches of three. You would get onto the little seat at the bottom of this tower and the other two would wind you right up to a little platform near the top. As I was going up I did think, 'Suppose the rope or the seat breaks – it would be a nasty death down there!' You could see a little triangle of grass and this winding gear. As it went up I used to grab the sides, so that if anything happened I could grab the struts at the side. You get out onto this platform and there was a rope ladder which led up to the top storey where the theodolite was and the bench. That was above the tops of the trees and the whole of the outside was camouflaged by bits of branches. You could look out over Ypres right across to these ridges behind where the enemy guns were. The theodolite was miles better than binoculars. We registered them on churches behind the German lines – fixing a point and making sure that the four instruments were all in line and accurate. So we all knew exactly where everything was. As soon as you saw a gun fire, you switched the theodolite round on to it, said, 'German gun firing at a so and so' – so that the other three posts and headquarters who were all listening knew there was a gun firing. Then you give a rough idea of where it might be – not only a bearing – but you might say it looked like it's on the ridge, even the type of gun, a 5.9-inch, or a bigger type of gun. You could tell by the appearance of the flash some idea of distance. You pressed a buzzer when it went off so if there were several other guns they'd

know which one I was looking at. So they all switched round and gave a bearing and I gave my bearing. The headquarters had a board with threads coming through – each post had a thread and a pin. They pulled that thread out and stuck it there on a bearing, this one on the bearing, that one at a bearing and if they were lucky they all crossed at a certain point. It was all done within a few seconds. We reckoned we could check a German gun to within 5 yards of its position, especially if more than two were on it.[1]

Private Victor Polhill, No. 1 Observation Group, Field Survey Company, Royal Engineers

This kind of sophisticated operation was carried out all along the line. It was backed up by the Sound Rangers who employed a similar system using microphones to accurately determine a gun's location. By these means the British had identified 504 of the 530 German guns facing the Fourth Army before the infantry finally went over the top.

The attack was launched south of the River Somme at 04.20 on 8 August by the Australian Corps, the Canadian Corps and the British III Corps. The Australians and Canadians were unstoppable that day, and surged forward some 8 miles south of the dividing line of the River Somme. The Germans suffered some 27,700 casualties of which 15,000 were prisoners of war. They also lost well over 400 guns and a considerable number of mortars and machine guns. Ludendorff summed it up thus: 'August 8 was the black day of the German Army in the history of this war.'[2]

The tanks were going forward and taking position after position, the infantry following up behind and, even though the Germans brought their artillery up out of their pits, it was to no avail as the Australians got all round them. The German prisoners were coming up and I saw one Australian private actually prodding the rear of a German brigadier – much to the amusement of everybody at the time. But it was a morning of victory. You felt the hair prickling up your spine with excitement because we knew that this was going to be the end of the war.[3]

Captain Stanley Evers, 30th Battalion, AIF

The new Whippet tanks played a significant role, but Private Eric Potten, who came from my home town of Chesterfield, was lucky that he missed the battle, having been injured in a prior accident. Shortly afterwards he heard his usual Whippet had been hit by a shell during the fighting. The consequences were stomach turning.

> I had to go up and see what we could manage to save from the tank. We had to get the instruments out, the guns, had to salvage anything we could. The tank was completely smashed up; it had had a direct hit right at the front. I never ate any bully beef after that for years. They were splashed all over the inside of the tank. Blast and fire. Terrible. Awful.[4]
>
> Private Eric Potten, 6th Battalion, Tank Corps

To the north of the Somme, the III Corps encountered more problems, as they had not only been allotted far less tanks, but also faced a series of ridges running down to the River Somme. The ebullient Lieutenant Jim Davies found everything wreathed in confusion.

> We arrived there at night, short of officers again. We got into position and I didn't know quite what was going to happen, what my objective was now. There was quite a barrage going on from us and one tank came out and went on. An SOS went up from the Boche I presumed so I made up my mind. I went forward and I suppose I'd been going forward for about ten minutes. It was dark and I'd never seen that part of the line before. The Boche had got light machine guns out in the front and one of those got me. It got me through both legs, I went down and the bloke next to me was killed, he was lying about 4 feet away from me. I took my scarf off, put a tourniquet on my left leg with my pistol through and tightened up. I was lying there, day broke, then I saw about thirty or forty men coming back. I couldn't see anybody in command of them and I called out, 'Who are you?' They were West Kents. 'What are you coming back for?' They said, 'He's too strong for us!' I said, 'He's not too strong, my troops are forward, go forward!' They didn't take any notice of me; I couldn't do anything! A sergeant and about four fusiliers appeared, not my company, but I had a shrewd guess that they were 'shell hole droppers'. They go over in the attack, but they've got no loyalties and they would drop down into a shell hole. I had been wounded again, a piece of shrapnel through the knee, and I told them to move me

to a shell hole. They tried to move me, but by then it was painful, I couldn't move. One of the boys came back with four prisoners including two German stretcher bearers. They started to look at my legs, there were little bits of bone all sticking out. The knee was completely shattered. I didn't try to move it; it was bloody painful! I said, 'It's hopeless, leave it alone!' All they'd got was paper bandages. They lifted me up on their shoulders and took me down. They started to run when there was shelling and I shouted out to a corporal to stop these Boches from running. My stretcher was saturated with blood.[5]

Lieutenant Jim Davies, 9th Royal Fusiliers

When at last he reached the casualty clearing station it was evident that at least one of his legs was beyond hope, now attached to his body only by a meagre scrap of skin and sinew. Amputation was inevitable.

I don't remember being undressed, I don't remember going into the operating theatre. But I do remember coming to and seeing a table with a chap with his side all open. There was a sister giving anaesthetics and she said, 'Somebody come and help me hold this officer down!' And that was it. I didn't know any more till about 9 o'clock the next morning. I was all bandaged up and the first thing I did was reach down and I felt a stump. The sister said, 'Anything you want?' I said, 'Yes, I want to be sick!' She brought a kidney bowl and there was lot of brown stuff I brought up. She said, 'Anything else you want?' 'Yes, can I have a drink of whisky!' She brought me a large whisky. It had been a guillotine amputation, straight through, plug the bone marrow and bind it all up.[6]

Lieutenant Jim Davies, 9th Royal Fusiliers

Although his war was done for now, Davies would enlist and serve his country again during the Second World War.

On the second day of the offensive, Private Bill Gillman went into action with the 2/2nd Londons against Chipilly Ridge. It proved a daunting prospect.

We had to attack the ridge. It was a fairly long ridge. Unknown to us there was from ten to twenty heavy German machine guns in emplacements. My God, he really opened up! He let us have it. He just swept us. I looked round as I was advancing and you could see the numbers of our people melting away, just dropping all around you. Those that fell were still shot over again. There were no orders – nothing. There was nothing you could do. It was getting so bad, as I took my steps I thought, 'The next one will be it!' But of course you didn't know what being hit was. I jumped for this big shell hole. Fortunately it was empty, no water in it. I wouldn't have minded if it had, I'd have gone in. I knew there was no hope of getting any orders because there was nobody to give any. The bullets were hitting the back of the shell hole; it was raining bullets. I don't know how I got missed.[7]

Private Bill Gillman, 2/2nd London Regiment

It was indeed hard going for the III Corps as they slogged across the ridges. But even south of the river the Australians and Canadians began to run out of steam as the Germans fell back onto lines occupied earlier in the war and brought up their reserves. It was at this point that the last great step was taken in developing the 'All Arms Battle' into the ultimate war-winning system. When the German opposition began to stiffen, Haig's corps commanders persuaded him to shift the focus of the attacks to the neighbouring Third Army, just to the north in front of Albert. This would allow the Fourth Army to reorganise, move forward its guns and thoroughly reconnoitre the opposing German defences. Foch objected at first, but Haig insisted. The attack would continue – but further north.

The tactical conundrum of the Great War had finally been solved. In 1918 there were enough guns to allow huge barrages at any point in the front, barrages that would have been unthinkable in 1916. Each of the five British armies had sufficient artillery resources to launch a devastating attack. From this point on, the pace of the war was unrelenting. Orchestrated by Foch and Haig, the focus of attacks switched constantly; the Germans found they could never relax for a moment. This was real manoeuvrist warfare. Striking here, there and everywhere, up and down the Western Front, the British, French and American Armies succeeded in getting inside the 'command loop' of the German High Command to such an extent that Ludendorff himself suffered a nervous breakdown. The Germans simply did not have sufficient time to plan their response to the latest attack. By the time they had worked out what was happening and what to do, the focus of the attack had moved and they were once again clutching at straws.

The British guns were truly *ubique*, a thunderous backdrop to every British advance. But the infantry still found it hard going at times. The German Army was a determined foe and though its ultimate defeat was no longer in doubt, many fought on to deadly effect. British casualty rates soared as relentless attacks took them out of their trenches and into open warfare conditions. In September 1918, Private Bill Gillman had a close escape during street fighting in misty conditions at Epéhy in the approach to the Hindenburg Line.

> You couldn't see what you were doing. Your mind was on like a razor edge, every move, even the swirling mist used to seem like something human. You could see about 3 or 4 yards clear as a bell – and then it would come swirling round again. You were trigger-happy then. That saved me; this fog opened and there was couple or three Jerries with a machine gun in a front garden and the bloody gun was pointing at me. I opened up fire first; it was split second stuff, swung the Lewis gun round automatically and that was it – I'd saved my life. If they'd opened up just a fraction before, me and my tea would have gone – I wouldn't have known anything about it. I took a quick glance and they were finished.[8]
>
> Private Bill Gillman, 2/2nd London Regiment

Private Horace Calvert had been in the army since 1914, but had been so under-age that he was still only 18 when he was finally drafted back to the front with the 2nd Grenadier Guards in 1918. In September, he was delighted as he saw the scale of the artillery preparations for their imminent attack on the fearsome German Hindenburg Line defences in the Cambrai area.

> We marched towards the jumping off place for attacking the Canal du Nord, which was a dry canal, and the Hindenburg Line. On the way up the 18-pounders were wheel to wheel – I've never seen as many guns on a front. The ammunition was stacked up. The gunners who were busy getting ready told us that they were going to put a shell on every 3 yards of trench. They said, 'You won't have any difficulty if we can keep that up!'[9]
>
> Private Horace Calvert, 2nd Grenadier Guards

In the end, when they attacked they found the gunners were right: the German opposition could not be sustained long against such a bombardment and by the time Calvert reached the canal the fighting was over.

> At five past four in the morning, there was one gun fired, no blowing whistles, that was the signal for the attack and off we went. The barrage opened – it was deafening. The Coldstream Guards were leading – we were the battalion behind them. There was this big concrete-lined empty canal, about 20 feet deep. There were scaling ladders, we had to go down and then climb up the other side with full equipment. The Coldstreams had done a good job because there was no opposition to us. We got into the Hindenburg Trench, the Coldstreams were going ahead and we had to turn to the flank to face any attack from the left. We looked towards Bourlon Wood. In the distance we could see the German artillery being pulled out of the outskirts of the wood. They were galloping on the road with their guns, but we couldn't do anything; it was too far off for effective rifle fire, so they got away. I went across an open field – there were no hedges it was just open. Right in the centre was a big sunken emplacement for a howitzer, probably a 5.9-inch, you couldn't see it till you got on top of it nearly. It had never been fired. It was one of the defences of the Hindenburg Line, only to be used in case of an attack, but it failed. We were too quick.[10]

Private Horace Calvert, 2nd Grenadier Guards

Even when there was significant resistance the British were still able to keep moving remorselessly forward. Captain F. W. S. Jourdain had the responsibility of ordering a divisional advance in his then capacity as a junior staff officer with the headquarters of 16th Division in 1918.

> The division had been advancing 10 to 15 miles every other day with very little opposition. Everybody was out one day: the GSO2 and GSO1 were going round the line or somewhere. For some reason it became imperative to tell the division to move 10 to 15 miles forward tomorrow. As likely as not the divisional clerks told me. 'You'd better get something out!' So I issued the order, but forgot to make arrangements for the rations. Of course they got their rations, but from the formal point of view the arrangements had not been made

to deliver their rations 15 miles further on. Which was pointed out to me when various people came back – and no doubt would have been pointed out to me in no uncertain way if I'd gone any way near the line.[11]

Captain F. W. S. Jourdain, Headquarters, 16th Division

Sometimes the advance may have seemed easy; but it was all a matter of the localised tactical situation at the time they attacked – and it could be bad. When troops were out in the open they were incredibly vulnerable if anything went wrong even for a moment. A burst of machine-gun fire, a single well-placed shell could spell disaster for an individual. Corporal Donald Price was wounded leading his section into the attack at Caudry on 8 October 1918.

We got to a place called Caudry. We were in a sunken road. I'd got a section about eight men! We were going over and I said, 'Now you fellows look: you're going to be spread out in this field, when you see this khaki handkerchief on top of my bayonet that's me!' So over we go. It wasn't bad. Somebody said, 'That farm has got to be taken!' A tank came along, and 'Chick' Edgar and I, we went behind this tank. It was easy, walking along, hardly anything happening. On the other side of the valley we could see three Germans and they'd just come out of a trench. Old 'Chick' Edgar he puts his rifle up and he has a go. One of these fellows dropped. Just before we got to the top, I got one. A bloody bullet got me in the leg: it went straight through my leg and blew a great big hole in the back – it didn't hurt. I was really thankful that I'd got hit. I said to 'Chick', 'I've got one!' He'd gone white, he wasn't looking very well; he knew he'd killed or hit somebody. Off I went. I sat down for a bit and six Germans helped me down – and I robbed them. I got another six watches from these fellows who helped me down! I put them in a sandbag. I'd got all these watches. When we got to this first aid post, the officer said, 'What have you got in there?' I said, 'Oh, I've got a few watches!' He said, 'Well, give me one!'[12]

Corporal Donald Price, 13th Royal Fusiliers

Price was taken back to hospital at Boulogne. Here he found that the wound, although impressive looking, was not actually that serious. But having done his duty and served on the Western Front for three long years, Price was now determined to postpone his return to active service for as long as possible.

> There was only a little bullet wound at the front, it was the back that was the trouble; there was a great hole. It had gone right smack in the middle of the leg and the bullet had gone right round the bone and blew a hole right out of the back, it didn't even crack the bone. I was a very, very healthy lad and my wounds were healing too quickly. So I decided to keep the wound open. I tried to keep the back open, knocked the scab off one or twice and used my toothbrush to rub the scab off. But I healed very quickly; the whole thing was healed. I was limping a bit about the 10th November and that was about all.[13]
>
> Corporal Donald Price, 13th Royal Fusiliers

Private Jim Fox, never an enthusiastic soldier to say the least, had by this time been involved in a fair amount of fighting. In one close-fought affair he found himself isolated with a small party of men as an attack broke down under heavy fire. Here, although he tried his best, he fell foul of an unsympathetic officer.

> We got to about 80 yards from this village and three German machine guns fired. We lost quite a lot of men on the first burst and the rest dashed for cover in shell holes. There's no great joy in being in a large shell hole about 10 feet deep with 2 foot of water at the bottom of it. We had messages sent to us by paper and a bit of stone, throwing it you see. It said, 'Lieutenant Black: Blow whistle 11 o'clock, rush for trench about 60 yards behind us!' We waited for this whistle at 11 o'clock. It was very slippy and I was struggling to get out of this shell hole and in the effort my rifle slipped from my shoulder into the bottom of the shell hole – so I left it there and rushed back without it. When I got to the trench, Lieutenant Dunn said to me, 'Where's your rifle?' 'I'm sorry on the dash it fell off my shoulder into the bottom of the shell hole!' He said, 'Well, what are you going to do now without a rifle?' 'Well, there's plenty of spare rifles, we've had a few lads killed. I'll use one of them!' 'Oh no you won't! It's an order! You'll have to go back for it!' I crept on my belly the 60 yards, getting round different shell holes, now and again they would see us and the bullets were whizzing over my head. I had to do the same the 60 yards back! It

took me over three-quarters of an hour to do it. But I got back at the finish and I'd got my rifle.[14]

Private Jim Fox, 11th Durham Light Infantry

The German artillery, though, had a long reach, and the casualties were not just in the front line. The incident that most affected Private Bill Gillman occurred when they were marching out of the line to what he thought was safety.

We came out on rest for a couple of weeks. We were marching down the road and old Jerry was poking some long-range stuff over – he dropped a bloody shell right in the middle of our No. 3 Company! It was a big one. It was hell! There was eighteen to twenty casualties. We halted and took cover straight away in case any more are following at the same range. You did that automatically, you don't wait for orders when a bloody shell comes over like that and gets in amongst you. Down we went on our faces by the side of the road. I sat by the side of the road and I sobbed my heart out. Having been in these scraps, days of fighting, constantly tensed up, we were war weary with the constant action. What hit me was that having got away, marching back, no more casualties, really free of it: in fact we were singing, going along the road when this bloody thing came over, carefree away from the front, fighting and scrapping with your finger on the trigger. Then from all that bloody distance they lob a shell onto us. One shell, there was no more, it was the only one. That solitary bloody shell! From miles away and it knocks out our mates. Having got so far: I thought I couldn't cry – I didn't feel like crying till then.[15]

Private Bill Gillman, 2/2nd London Regiment

Gillman was a thoughtful man and pondered a good deal on the response to the trials and tribulations of active service.

Generally there was no despondency, this is what amazed me about it all. We took it in our stride as a sort of accepted fact and I think we were all instilled with the idea that this was war and we'd got to kill the Germans. The kind of usual brainwashing that you get in war. They said it of the old British 'Tommy' – and it's true – he's unconquerable. It's not understandable, because it doesn't seem natural for people under those conditions to accept things like they did. Of course it was the same in the German Army – I think they accepted the position in the same way. I don't think it was just because we were British. But we always have had a knack for standing up best when we've got our back to the wall.[16]

Private Bill Gillman, 2/2nd London Regiment

But it wasn't the British with their backs to the wall in November 1918. Germany was utterly done: her army was on its last legs, her navy was mutinous, the air force ground down by sheer numbers, her economy in ruins and the German people turning to revolution. It had been a war fought on many fronts, in many ways – it was, after all, the first total war. In the end, Germany lost on every level.

THE END OF THE WAR was negotiated using President Woodrow Wilson's Fourteen Points as an initial point of reference. After a great deal of ardent posturing, the Allied leaders hammered out their conditions for an Armistice. These were stringent, demanding the surrender of all the German conquests in Russia and Rumania, the immediate evacuation of French and Belgian territory, the surrender of Alsace-Lorraine and huge financial reparations. In addition, German military forces would be stripped to the bare bones to prevent any possibility of military action in the foreseeable future. An Allied military force would occupy the west bank of the Rhine, with bridgeheads and a neutral zone on the eastern bank of the Rhine. The German government fell as Kaiser Wilhelm abdicated on 9 November and a socialist leader, Friedrich Ebert, took over as Chancellor. Ludendorff, too, had been replaced: the architects of defeat had been swept away. The final signing of the Armistice took place in a railway carriage in the Forest of Compiègne at 05.15 on the morning of 11 November. The war would end at the eleventh hour of the eleventh day of the eleventh month.

Fighting continued up until the very end of the war and many men could not help but feel an enhanced fear at the idea of being killed or maimed just as the long agony was nearly over.

You don't know the feeling you have. Everybody had the wind up. Really afraid, really windy. When ten to eleven came I was really windy. He started shelling, one or two long range stuff, expending his shells instead of carrying it back, getting rid of it. I just threw myself under an embankment; all of a sudden I felt a crack on my steel helmet – shrapnel. It jerked my head a bit, gave me a bit of a headache, but it didn't penetrate the helmet itself. I looked up and there was a girl at the side of me. I thought, 'My God, I've gone mad now! A damned girl beside me in the midst of a war!' Anyhow it seems this girl was in a local farmhouse, heard the shelling, saw me dart under this embankment and she'd come out and done likewise. The shelling finished right on the dot at 11 o'clock. Not another thing.[17]

Private Bill Smedley, 14th Worcestershire Regiment

And some men were not so lucky. A few would have to make the last, the greatest sacrifice, even when it was all but over.

From about 6 o'clock that morning there was only the occasional shell that was sent either by us or the Germans – maybe one an hour. At about 10 o'clock a shell came down and killed a sergeant of ours that had been out since 1915. Killed by the shrapnel. We thought that was very unlucky – to think he'd served nearly four years and then to be killed within an hour of the armistice.[18]

Private Jim Fox, 11th Durham Light Infantry

For me, one of the strangest stories of Armistice Day originated from the straitlaced figure of Air Mechanic Ernest Hancock, who had been serving in Italy but who on that fateful day was back home on leave and paying a visit to his old factory in Luton.

On the 11th November I had been invited by the directors of Vauxhall Motors to have a farewell lunch with them at the works. In the morning I was walking towards the works down Kempton Road where the factory was. Nobody about. I was kitted up in my best uniform to present myself to the board. Near the works the sirens were sounding all over Luton and Vauxhall Motors. I thought it was rather early for lunch because it was about 11 o'clock. But I carried on. Then to my horror a sea of females: young, middle-aged and old, girls and women, came out of the factory and descended upon me like a hive of bees. Being in full naval uniform they used me as a target to express their joy: they kissed me, tried to pull my buttons off, they nearly had my trousers off! I fought like a maniac because I didn't know what this was about! When they told me armistice had been declared I kissed the lot of them! When it was all over I staggered down to the works.[19]

Air Mechanic Ernest Hancock

The Great War was over. For those who survived there would always be the question: what was it all for?

13

AFTERMATH OF WAR

AS THE GUNS FELL SILENT on 11 November 1918 there were a number
of different reactions. Where men had the opportunity, wild drunken
celebrations featured prominently, but this was by no means a universal response to the Armistice. Many were underwhelmed by the occasion and could not help but contemplate their family, pre-war friends
and wartime comrades who had not survived to share the victory. Vast
empires had fallen and millions of men had died; millions more were
crippled or maimed. Most men seem to have found it nigh on impossible to articulate the tangle of emotions that ran through their heads.
No more mud and blood; no more desperate attacks amid the bullets
and shells; no more sudden death. And no more eking out their lives in
holes in the ground. Yet hard upon those feelings of freedom came the
question: what were they going to do now? Men had simply presumed
that they would not live to see the end of the war, and the idea that they
had nothing to look forward to was part of their mental defences – as
dead men walking they did not have much to lose if they were killed. In
a flash their mental landscape had changed; they had a future. But what
kind of a future would it be?

One wonderful anecdote illuminated the final reels of my interview with Raynor Taylor, as it provided me with a strangely emotive link with someone often considered one of the true greats of English literature. It also brought home the anguish of loss that overwhelmed so many people in the aftermath of war. Taylor had been medically downgraded and sent to act as a guard at various prisoner of war camps in late 1918 while awaiting demobilisation. Here he had a strange encounter while strolling off-duty near Burwash in East Sussex.

> There were four of us and we were walking down a country road when we were accosted by an elderly gentleman. In my mind's eye I can see him now. He had on a Norfolk suit. He bid us the time of the day, asked us how we were going on, what we were doing, where did we come from? Suddenly he said, 'I wonder if you boys would like to have tea with me?' Just imagine somebody offering you a civilised tea instead of going back to jam and cheese! 'Oooh yes!' He walked back, we went with him and we turned in at a big house. He said, 'We've four boys for tea!' He took us into a big room, with a long table and we sat talking. I noticed round this room was a lot of pictures. Ever such a lot. We talked about what we did, where we'd been and where we came from. Eventually this lady set the tea things and we had our tea, bread and butter thinly cut, jam and cakes. No limit to what you could eat. Afterwards we sat chatting. I was able to get up and have a look at these pictures. In the main they were historical – battle scenes and things like that. Very interesting. One in particular, I'd seen in an art gallery. It was a picture of a man on a white horse; he looked all in and it was a picture of Doctor Brydon, the sole survivor coming from the Khyber Pass. I went round and came to the fireplace. There was a framed print. It was a poem. I stood there, looked at it and I knew the poem. Without a noise I was mouthing it. Suddenly a voice alongside me said, 'Do you like that?' 'Yes, I do!' 'Do you know it?' 'Yes, I do!' He said, 'Could you recite it?' And I did. The poem was called 'If'. Just the tail end:

If you can take up all your winnings
And risk them on one turn of pitch and toss
And lose and start again at the beginning
And never say a word about your loss
If you can fill the unforgiving minute

With sixty seconds full of distance run
Then yours is the Earth and everything that's in it
And – what is more – you will be a man, my son!

I got to the end and he said, 'Very good, you like that?' I said, 'Yes!'
He said, 'So do I! In fact I like it better now than the day I wrote it!'
Kipling! If I live to be a thousand I'll never forget that. That part of
the poem that says, 'And never say a word about your loss'. Do you
know he never said he lost his only son – he never mentioned it
while we were there. But he had.[1]

Private Raynor Taylor

Lieutenant John Kipling had been killed at the Battle of Loos back in
1915 and had no known grave. Great Imperial poet or not, Kipling
seems to have felt a considerable degree of guilt over the death of his
son – for whom he had pulled strings to secure a commission in the
Irish Guards after the 18-year-old had initially been rejected. One can
perhaps guess what was in Kipling's mind as he penned the memorable
lines in his *Epitaphs of War*: 'If any question why we died, Tell them,
because our fathers lied.'[2] During the Great War the British Empire lost
a total of 956,703 killed in action: every one a son, a father, a loved one.

For those that survived, the war had been a searing experience
that overwhelmed their former selves. Everything had changed: callow
schoolboys were now hardened soldiers; timid clerks had become
experienced NCOs or officers; brave men had been shell-shocked into
twitching invalids; strong labourers, proud of their physique, had been
disabled for life. Would they even want to return to a civilian existence
that had once seemed a remote idyllic dream but in practice often
proved a dreary humdrum existence after all the frenetic excitements
they had endured? The end of the war was the culmination of all their
hopes, but it was also a tremendous anticlimax.

For a while, at least, most soldiers were protected from adjusting to
the reality of post-war life by the requirements of their continued service
in the armed forces. The Germans had been given just fourteen days to
evacuate French and Belgian territory and they seem to have retreated
in good order, although at least one of them was endowed with a sense
of humour.

We met a little bit of psychological warfare, because two or three of us went into a estaminet to get a cup of coffee while we were waiting and there was quite a good looking girl there. *'Bonjour mamselle!'* 'You can kiss my bottom, Sir!' The Germans had taught them to say this as a suitable greeting.[3]

Lance Corporal Harry Hopthrow, Signal Service, Headquarters, 30th Division

Many of the British force would be based in the Cologne bridgehead area of the Rhineland. After the formal ending of the war at the Treaty of Versailles in 1919, the occupation continued under the auspices of the Inter-Allied Rhineland High Commission. A staged withdrawal, conditional on 'good behaviour', only ended with the final evacuation of Allied forces from the Rhineland in 1930.

DEMOBILISATION WAS GOING TO BE A LENGTHY PROCESS. Almost all of the men serving in the British Army just wanted to get out of khaki and safely back into their civilian lives as soon as possible. This, though, would prove to be a staggering administrative task. Millions of men would have to be returned to their former employments, and if this was not handled carefully then economic chaos and mass unemployment loomed large. Any demobilisation system had to be both transparently fair and carried out as soon as possible. Thus it was decided that men who were needed urgently to help restock the workforce of key industries at home would be returned first, after which release groups would be organised according to category and length of service, with priority for those who had volunteered early in the war. Regular soldiers were required to serve out their time, while Territorial and conscripted men simply had to wait their turn. Among the thousands of bored men, chafing under a discipline that now seemed redundant, there were many disturbances which could have been easily characterised as mutiny if the bulk of officers, NCOs and men had not kept their heads. Private Horace Calvert witnessed a typical 'spot of bother' at the Harfleur Base Camp in December.

I heard this shouting. Lower down the road there was this huge gathering of soldiers. I saw staff officers surrounded by a lot of troops

– all sorts of regiments – and they were telling them they wanted money being paid every week – they hadn't been paid for weeks, they wanted the right to go into Le Havre and they wanted the Military Police easing up a bit on them. The rumour was around that the last to be called up would be the first to be demobilised because they were the key men to get industry going. Some of the chaps in this disturbance said they hadn't been home for four years. They said it was time they were allowed to go home. That caused a lot of ill feeling. They shouted at these officers. I was on the outskirts, I didn't join in. I listened. I thought, 'I'm not getting mixed up in that lot!' I knew that these men were trying to give their demands in an improper way. There were two or three ringleaders. They were doing all the talking and waving everyone around to come and join them – there was two or three hundred there. I wouldn't call it a mutiny or anything like that – I would call it a disturbance. They managed to disperse them eventually, they told them they couldn't do anything, they'd have to take up this matter with the senior officers above them. What happened was they got everybody out of that camp – in twenty-four hours they were all lining up, getting into trains and off – they cleared the lot out.[4]

Private Horace Calvert, 2nd Grenadier Guards

It was not unnatural that men resented their continued service, especially as the army soon returned to its default state: a peacetime regime where 'spit and polish' ruled. But these men were not 'natural' soldiers. Many had joined for the duration of the war and for no longer; others had joined under duress through conscription. The system may have been fair enough in principle, but it was inevitable that thousands of individual cases fell through the net. Everyone seemed to be dissatisfied with a demobilisation process that seemed to last forever.

When a man was finally due for demobilisation he was medically examined and given documentary evidence of his service. He would then be sent to an Infantry Base Depot prior to sailing back to Britain. On arrival he would attend a demobilisation centre where he got more documentation, a war gratuity based on rank and length of service, a railway warrant to his local station and a 'demob' suit (or the equivalent monetary value of 52 shillings and sixpence). He would then go on his final leave still in uniform and although technically still a soldier for a further month, he was effectively free to begin his new life as a civilian. A serious national emergency could still trigger a recall to the colours, as everyone was still considered to be in the Class 'Z' Army Reserve, though in practice this would prove irrelevant.

EVENTUALLY THE SURVIVORS WOULD ALL RETURN HOME, free at long last to try and pick up the elusive traces of their civilian lives. Too much had changed: the world had changed; *they* had changed. As a result many of the men had great difficulty in settling back down into civilian life. The army training programme they had all undergone as recruits was designed to break them down as individuals and rebuild them as soldiers: disciplined, obeying orders instinctively without question and able to cope with the violent physical and mental pressures of war. There was no such de-programming on their demobilisation. Life had not stopped in the absence and not all families had survived psychologically, or physically, intact. When Joseph Napier got home he received a somewhat muted reception. His father had been killed at Gallipoli and there is no doubt that his mother was still emotionally traumatised.

> The only reception I got from my mother when I got home was almost one of anger. Saying, 'Well, what are you going to do now? There you were in the army clothed and fed and paid! And here you are with nothing to do!'[5]
>
> Joseph Napier

Many also became deeply aware of the suffering undergone by the families left behind while they were away. One Oldham mother had certainly been reduced to a shadow of her former self by the stress of war. She had three sons in the services: Albert Taylor, who had joined the 7th East Lancashire Regiment, Jack Taylor serving with the RND at Gallipoli and Raynor Taylor, who fought on the Western Front with the 24th Welsh Regiment. For four long years this poor woman suffered torments every time there was a knock on the door.

365

Pretty shattering, you know. During the war, casualties were always notified by telegram. As the war went on, the sight of a telegram boy on the road – it frightened everybody to death. He used to come on a bike! They used to stop and look which street he was going up. Where was he going, because you knew something had happened. Do you know how many times he came to our house? Ten times! Now just try and think about that. Ten times! Our Albert got wounded four times, our Jack got wounded three times, I was wounded twice. Ten times a knock on the door … it was during the day and my dad would be at work and invariably it was my mother that answered it. She'd go to the door – telegram boy and she knows that something's happened. Words can't describe what she must have felt, to open the telegram and find out that they were only wounded. Until the last one she got was our Albert was missing, believed to be killed, in 1918. We all gave him up as dead; his platoon officer said he 'Couldn't hold out much hope for him being alive!' We thought, 'No chance!' But my mother wouldn't give way. No she wouldn't give way at all, 'He's not dead!' And funnily enough she was bolstered by Spiritualism. She'd go to these meetings and she came back one time and even said they'd told her that he was a prisoner somewhere. The war finished and one Saturday, I was in hospital, our Jack wasn't home, mother went to the door and there was our Albert at the door! She lived long enough to see us home and that was it – she became very frail and she died of cancer. It took her three months to die in awful agony.[6]

Raynor Taylor

One more victim of the war.

Many soldiers returned to the realities of fatherhood with children they had conceived on leave, or who were babies at the time of their enlistment and who barely knew their fathers. Norman Kirby had never met his father and remembered the shock of fear that ran through him when he first saw his father home on leave when he was about 4 years old.

My father was away at the front in the Royal West Kents and Middlesex. He got some of the words of the mud and the noise – the nerve-wracking experiences. I didn't know about him when I was very little. I would be one when he joined up and there wasn't much leave. This man, ever so dirty, covered in mud, came into our dining room. I ran and hid behind the curtains at the French windows. I can only have been a toddler. I was absolutely scared to death because I'd never seen a man like this, all covered in mud. He kissed my mother! I came out from behind the curtain, 'How dare you kiss my mummy!' The idea of him touching her was awful. Years later I thought what a terrible thing for this man – he'd gone through all the hell of Passchendaele – to be rejected.[7]

Norman Kirby

And, of course, human nature being what it is, some soldiers returned to find children that could not possibly be their own progeny.

In the aftermath of war the returning soldier was forced to earn a living in the real world: a world filled with jobs that seemed meaningless and the dark spectre of mass unemployment; a world that seemed venal and corrupt; a world full of women who required far more from a relationship than their army mates did; a world that seemed ungrateful for all their sacrifices. Underlying everything was a deep feeling of disappointment that life was not 'better' for them as veterans. Men had not really joined up for 'King and Country' or to fight the 'War to end War'. Their real motivations had usually been far more complex, mixing noble sentiments with more basic desires for excitement and an all-too human vulnerability to peer-group pressure. But now the war was over there were just too many of them to be all hailed as heroes, and thus the demobilised ex-soldier found he was nothing special in society at large on his return. Often the veterans found that life had moved on in their absence. They had missed any opportunity of a better education; lost their best chances of significant promotion at work and their fond pre-war ambitions were often cruelly dashed. Before the war James Snailham had dreamed of a career in professional football.

The war made me bitter, because I'd been denied of the thing I'd lived for: football. I got playing with teams, but they weren't where I wanted to be. I'd had a trial with Preston, but I couldn't stick it – the malaria and dysentery had taken the guts out of me. I could play, but I wasn't strong enough.[8]

James Snailham

Football had been the very cornerstone of Snailham's life and he struggled to fill the void it left.

Few, if any, allowances were made for the returning veterans as they struggled to readjust to the constraints and petty humiliations of civilian life.

> I applied for a job at Whitehall, at the Ministry of Labour as a temporary clerk. I went before a man, he was chairman and a lot of bearded old men round a board. The old men were in the saddle again and you just didn't stand a chance. He said, 'I'm sorry, Mr Dixon, but you've had no experience!' Why didn't I see red. I got up on my hind legs and said, 'Pardon me, Sir, but I've had more experience than anybody in this room, but the thing is it's been the wrong sort! When I joined the army in 1914, I told the recruiting sergeant I couldn't ride a horse and he said, "We'll bloody soon teach you!" They did and they spared no pains over it. Apparently I could be fitted for war, but I can't be fitted for peace. I shall know what to do another time, gentlemen!'[9]
>
> Fred Dixon

Though sorely tried, Dixon at least had kept control; other men found that they had developed a hair-trigger that could make them explode into violence when placed under stress.

> I think it sent me crackers a bit. One day the gaffer came, he said something to me and it just got right on top of me. I grabbed hold of him by the blinking lapel of his coat and I said, 'I'll split you top to bottom!' Stupid of me. I think he thought, 'Here's a crackpot come out from the war!' I calmed down after a while.[10]
>
> Albert Birtwhistle

The apparent tranquillity of civilian life concealed its own pressures where the instinctive violent response of a soldier is almost never appropriate. Terms like 'post-traumatic stress disorder' were unknown, but the bottled-up fears and emotions, suppressed during the long years of war or concealed beneath a blanket of unthinking male comradeship, began to show after demobilisation. Norman Kirby remembered how his father struggled.

His nerves were very bad. I don't want to say anything negative about my father because he was such a lovely person, but he used to get very irritable at times. I used to say to my mother, 'Mummy, why do we have to be so quiet?' She used to put her fingers to her lips, 'Well dear, it's because of Daddy's nerves!' At school, boys would say, 'What's the matter with your Dad?' He was never violent, he was a gentle man, but he used to get very on edge. It was called neurasthenia in those days. He had a kind of worry complex; he was always worried and anxious. He got better – I think it was the warmth of family life helped.[11]

Norman Kirby

Despite it all, most ex-soldiers coped, but a proportion did not and there were horrendous bouts of domestic violence. For obvious reasons this is little mentioned in oral interviews, but there were thousands of battered wives and slapped down children, all victims of frustrations and traumas that originated in the war.

The response of individual servicemen took many forms. Some just suffered a general feeling of dislocation which gradually dissipated with no real ill effects. Perhaps they drank a bit more for a while, left their former job, or just took a while to settle down. Some suffered minor mental problems, such as this case of mild claustrophobia experienced by former aviator Laurie Field.

What I used to notice more than anything was after living for most of the war in the open, I couldn't bear to be in bed and at home. When I went to live with my parents we had a 50- or 60-yard garden and at the bottom there was a stable which had no doors and I had my bunk under there. I couldn't bear to be under a roof. It lasted two or three months; I suppose I got fed up of it in the end.[12]

Laurie Field

War-related nightmares were certainly a common phenomenon, capable of disturbing men's sleep decades later. Indeed many veterans found our interviews triggered new bouts of disturbing dreams as an echo of long-buried traumas. Men also ceased to believe in the very tenets of their previous existence. A few lost their patriotism and turned against the concepts of duty to 'crown and country' that they felt had led them to so much suffering. It was also very difficult for men to reconcile religious faith and the concept of a benevolent deity with the excruciating horrors they had experienced.

> The war made a great deal of difference in my thinking. I went through the prayer book with a comb and found half the things I didn't like. Phrases like, 'Give peace in our time, Oh Lord, because there is none other that fighteth for us'. I mean there's just no sense in it. I went through lots of things – resurrection of the body: well I don't believe it – I'd seen so many bodies.[13]
>
> Eric Wolton

Others went the other way and sought a mental safe harbour in religion, taking succour in the belief that there must be some sort of underlying divine purpose even to the mayhem of war. Some turned in desperation to spiritualist charlatans who appeared to offer the chance to contact those who had died.

Some found the scars of war ran far deeper. There had been 2,272,998 wounded casualties (if a man was wounded twice he was double-counted in the statistics). Approximately 182,000 had been discharged from the services as invalids. Indeed many men were still fighting for their very lives as a result of their mangled bodies. One such was Private George Dray, who had been badly wounded while serving with the 6th Northamptonshires in Trônes Wood in 1916. His injuries had not properly healed and his son, John Dray (whom I interviewed in connection with his service in the Italian Campaign during the Second World War), recounted how his father lost his final battle.

> He was the deputy pier master on the Woolwich ferry. I was born in 1926 and in December 1928, 2 years old I was, he came home from work, just before Christmas and he said, 'I've got a headache. I think I'm going to bed!' It was December 23rd. My sister went up with a cup of tea for him and she came running down, 'There's something funny with daddy's eye!' The eye was bulging on one side. They ran him into hospital and this blood clot was pushing the eye from behind. They took the eye away and they thought that was the end – that he'd be 'One-Eyed George' for the rest of his life. But the blood clot had turned and was going back. The next day 24th December, was my

mother's birthday. About eight at night she went up to the hospital. He was dozy, half unconscious. All of a sudden he became very clear and he said, 'Elsie, have you hung the children's stockings up?' She said, 'Not yet!' He said, 'I would go home if I was you and do the stockings – I'll see you tomorrow!' Well she did and before she got home he was dead – this blood clot had touched his brain and killed him. Christmas Eve, my mother's birthday and she was six months pregnant with my last sister.[14]

John Dray

A tragic tale, but by no means unusual in the two decades after the war, as bodies collapsed in a delayed reaction to damage suffered during the conflict. Hospital wards up and down the country were full of men who were gasping their last breaths as the after-effects of gas poisoning were exacerbated to a fatal degree by the pernicious impact of diseases like bronchitis or pneumonia. Crippled men were everywhere in the 1920s: armless, legless, terrible gashes ripped into their bodies that would never heal. Joe Pickard had at least partially recovered from his leg and pelvic wounds, but he remained terribly facially disfigured after the loss of most of his nose. At first, he hid from the stares of the curious and mocking that surrounded him as he convalesced in Neath.

It was the first time I was out of the hospital. I wanted to go down and have a look at the place. All the houses are built on the hillside in rows. I was going along the bottom and there were some kids playing about. As I went past, a short time after they got up and galloped past me. I passed about two or three streets and when I got there all the kids in the blinking neighbourhood had gathered. Talking, looking, gawping at you. I still had this little bit of white plastic stuff. I could have taken the crutch and hit the whole blinking lot of them! I knew what they were looking at. So I turned round and went back to the hospital. Talk about confidence. I was sitting one day and I thought, 'Well, it's no good, I can stop like this for the rest of my life – I've got to face it sometime!' So I went out again – people staring – I used to turn round and look at them. I find if you're not a one that talks about what's the matter with you, nobody will be bothered about it.[15]

Private Joe Pickard, 3rd Western General Hospital, Neath

In the end Pickard was to be one of the lucky ones, for he was the beneficiary of an early form of plastic surgery at the Queen Mary's Hospital in Sidcup.

> They cut down the right ribs and took a lot of cartilage out, then they buried it in my stomach to keep it alive. Then when they wanted it they took it out, cut a piece off and put it in the bridge of my nose to build it up. The first lot went wrong – it curved – it mustn't have been properly cured. Dr Kilner said, 'What have you been doing? It shouldn't go like that!' 'Well,' I said, 'You put it in!' He said, 'What do you want? A Wellington nose or a Roman nose?' I said, 'I don't care what it is as long as I get one!' I went in at 9 o'clock the next morning and the next thing I remembered it was in the middle of the next night. All of the night staff used to come down and have a rub at the nose – that was to keep the circulation. They used to say they would have a rub at the 'lucky' nose. This pal of mine came up and said, 'By God, what a lovely little nose you've got!' I couldn't raise my head off the pillow – I had two black eyes, a square chin. He went away and got a mirror. He showed me the magnifying side – the blinking nose seemed to fill the mirror. I didn't care as long as I've got one. Can you ever imagine being without one?[16]
>
> Private Joe Pickard

He was eventually discharged from the army in January 1921. His leg and pelvic injuries were such that he could never run, so sport or any kind of athletic pursuit was an impossibility. But Pickard was the kind of man to always make the best of his lot and he lived a long and fulfilling life. Even when I interviewed him in 1986 he still had the piece of spare cartilage in his stomach which he let (or rather made!) me feel – a strange little gristly lump and a physical echo of his past. But by then his nose looked little stranger than the majority of gnarled noses besported by 90-year-old men.

The men who had lost their legs often faced a long wait before they could get themselves fitted with an artificial limb. Then it could be a tortuous business learning to walk again. Some men had almost no assistance and had to learn from scratch themselves.

They measure you from this hip to the floor and from the knee,
round the stumps and all like that. We were just sat there in this
grubby old ward. One day a railwayman came in and said, 'Mr
Towers?' I said, 'Yes, me!' 'Oh right, there that's yours!' That was
the leg! 'These are yours and these are yours!' Straps and socks!
'Sign here!' I signed. I looked – what the devil do I do with this. No
instructions. I'm trying it on, trying to fit it on – these straps I didn't
know what the devil they did. In the afternoon the doctor came,
'Now then you've got your leg, haven't you? You can go home this
afternoon!' Nobody to tell me how. No! You have to find out! I put
this leg on, I didn't tighten it up long enough and it was trailing; I
was on crutches and I had a kitbag. It was quarter of a mile to go to
a tram and nobody helped me. Who could we complain to, nobody
wanted to know. But I'd got the leg – and I was determined – I wanted
to walk.[17]

Driver William Towers

It was a painful process, but he stuck to it and was soon able to walk
miles with just the aid of his stick. When he was discharged in 1919 he
generally found that most people back in his home town were sympathetic to his plight. But one thoroughly unpleasant individual provoked
him so much that in defiance he resolved to rise above his physical
problems.

He eyed me up and down, he said, 'I suppose you'll have to be living
on other people's generosity for the rest of your life?' I said, 'Well,
it won't be your bloody generosity I want. Goodbye!' And I walked
away. I thought, 'Well, I'll show that fellow if nobody else – I don't
want their generosity!' And do you know it spurred me on, that did.[18]

William Towers

Men like Towers were not prepared to be passive victims and sought to
improve their condition by joining together to publicise their plight.
Not everything went smoothly, as he discovered when he attended the
inaugural meeting of the Limbless Ex-Servicemen's Association at Leeds
Town Hall in the 1920s.

'Oooh Bill, there's going to be a meeting at the Town Hall, we're
going to form a union!' 'Right, I'll be there!' We went and there was

a chap there signing you in as a member of LESMA, the Limbless
Ex-Servicemen's Association. You paid your shilling entrance fee and
they gave you a little white button with LS on it in red. We had this
meeting and there were several ex-officers all sat there: accountants,
solicitors and barrister – all big people. And we were down here
– the common troops. We all had a leg, an arm or an eye out. Mr
Cyril Stevens, who was an accountant, he said, 'Someone nominate
somebody for chairman!' It must have been cut and dried because
some bright spark said, 'I propose Mr Holden!' A fellow said, 'Well,
I second that!' Mr Holden was the manufacturer of cheap legs and
we were having a lot of trouble with limb fitting. That was like a big
factory forming a union and putting the manager in as chairman of
the union. They had me beat.[19]

William Towers

But Towers persevered and for the rest of his life he would remain committed to the fight to secure better conditions for limbless ex-servicemen.

The seriously wounded faced an extremely uncertain future in a
world where there was little or no concept of a welfare state. In the post-
war years, men simply had to earn a living, or be consigned to a pov-
erty-stricken existence eked out by a minimal pension. They were also
subject to constant re-examinations, after which their pension could be
cut back or abolished entirely if it was considered they had 'improved'.
George Peake had suffered a bad leg wound and was initially awarded a
30 per cent disability pension. He went back to work at the iron foundry,
but was soon recalled to appear in front of a medical board.

I was trying to walk without a stick and I managed it. Later on I had
to go on what they called the House of Lords Board. I was supposed to
be represented by a solicitor to further my case. A solicitor pal of mine
didn't turn up. They asked me who I was voting for, I said, 'That's
my business!' A bit cheeky you know. They said, 'Right!' So they cut
my pension off – I'd been drawing it for four years – they cut it off
and gave me a lump sum of £12. I was only getting 12 shillings and
sixpence a week but 12 shillings and sixpence in those days was quite
an amount. I missed my pension.[20]

George Peake

Many men were 'offered' and accepted a lump-sum payment, after which their pension would cease. Stephen Moyle had his pension removed by a medical board in 1920. It was sixty years before further medical examinations finally proved he still had significant bone and tissue loss from his leg.

> I got notice for a Medical Board in Princess Road, Liverpool. I stripped off and there were three doctors there. I was marching up and down the room, I didn't put on a limp or anything like that. They muttered amongst themselves and I got dressed and came home. I don't think they put a finger on my wound in the leg. After that I got a notice which meant that I got nothing. Well, being a young fellow and being active again, able to do things, 'Oh to hell with it!' I said. I never appealed again until 1980. I had three admissions and three denials. After admitting that there had been damage to the veins they eventually gave me a grant of £1,600 – lovely! I had it in my bank book. Then another examination, another board, another doctor and they decided I would have a 30 per cent pension. But they informed me, 'You can't have both!' So until the grant was 'absorbed' they'd stop my pension from 1980–81. I'd left it so long I can't blame them altogether; it's my fault for not claiming earlier. I do feel a bit rattled when you come to reckon the number of men like me who never groused in their lives.[21]
>
> Stephen Moyle

Moyle was right: a large number of ex-servicemen were proud men, determined to stand on their own feet as best they could. As a result many left it too late to seek help as they found old age exacerbating the health problems caused by their wounds; indeed many died without receiving the disability pensions that they should have received. We often criticise the cruelty and lack of caring displayed by society in the 1920s, but society in the 1980s proved no more sympathetic to the plight of old soldiers.

THE VETERANS NEVER FORGOT the Great War, but joined regimental associations to preserve the memory of their service, their old comrades and most of all the achievements of their units. It used to be considered a truism that veterans never talked about the war: the reality was that more often their family and younger post-war acquaintances had swiftly tired of hearing their stories. Generally the veterans didn't talk about 'it' because nobody wanted to know – at least not until it was too late.[22] But at their regimental reunions they talked of little else other than the war: revelling in all the old stories and mourning the friends they lost along the way. Many of these associations commissioned a permanent record of their deeds. Eric Wolton became determined to write a history of his battalion.

> I came to write it for one main reason and that is I was determined that the deeds of the 1/5th Suffolks should not be forgotten. That it should be on record. They were a wonderful battalion. I was determined that there will always be a book with their names and a record of what they had done. I went to Worley Barracks and copied out the battalion war diary, which took me a week, so I could get all my facts. Got them roughly into order and then what I remembered of myself and other people also helped in writing it. Fairs lived in New Zealand so I used to write a rough draft to send out to him and he would put in any comments he had and rewrite it – then it would come back to me. It was quite a job. I was determined that the 5th Suffolks would forever be known if people were interested.[23]
>
> Eric Wolton

His book was the first regimental history I ever bought, inspired to the purchase after conducting a five-hour interview with Wolton himself back in 1986. It was a slippery slope to a library that over the years has cost me tens of thousands of pounds, but I have never regretted that first step. Above all, it is still a wonderfully evocative book and is indeed a worthy tribute to the men of the 5th Suffolks.

Some veterans turned away from war, looking towards pacifism as an answer to the horrors they had witnessed. Victor Polhill was one such, but although his views were undoubtedly sincerely held, his interview exposed that he was not a pacifist in any accepted sense of the word.

I felt anti-war. I'd lost all my friends, the ones I'd been to school with, they'd all been killed. People with wonderful brains, wonderful mothers and fathers – I thought, 'Well, what a complete waste!' So I used to go and hear Donald Soper and I joined the Peace Pledge Union. I used to think that if the League of Nations was going to do any good they've got to nip in when anything happens. I remember when Japan went into Manchuria and I thought, 'What are we going to do about it? Aren't we going to do anything?' Then Italy went into Abyssinia and nobody did anything; everybody was frightened to do anything. I thought, 'That's not much good – that's just nothing!' When Hitler came on the job I thought something ought to be done about that. I thought that instead of having George Lansbury saying, 'Disarm!' and Soper saying, 'Disarm!' If only we'd built up a jolly good Army and Navy then Hitler could have been stopped long before he was – but of course he had a free run. I think you've got to watch what's happening in other countries.[24]

Victor Polhill

What Polhill seems to be advocating is akin to an early intervention policy to defuse a threatening international situation.

In the 1920s there was a surge in battlefield tourism, but most men were far too poor to afford such a trip. Many never got out to see the dreadful battlefields of their youth; others only got to see them again when they were very old men. Malcolm Hancock was around 86 years old when he finally managed to get out to Suvla Bay at Gallipoli in 1983. Having reached his old stamping grounds around Hill 60, Hancock began searching for traces of their front line.

I was able to identify the very place where the mine was exploded under the Turkish lines. Having found that crater I was able to retrace twenty-five to thirty paces and found just the faint indentations of our front line and our machine-gun post – there it jolly was! After all those years it was rather a relief to actually see it again; almost like laying a ghost.[25]

Malcolm Hancock

He left a rough diagram of his position and, as a result, nearly twenty years later, in 2000 Nigel Steel and I were able to retrace his steps during

377

our own visit to Hill 60. We could only imagine what it must have been like for Malcolm Hancock to be there once again. The war was so long ago, but its traces had by no means vanished into the haze: bullets could still be found in the ploughed fields. We even found a skeletal leg buried alongside the track running past the north side of the cemetery. Perhaps Hancock had known – or killed – or buried – its owner eighty-five years before?

Most of the men I interviewed were in their late eighties and early nineties and were looking back across almost their whole life span. By this time, one way or another, most of them had come to terms with their war service. Jim Fox, for instance, knew he had been a pretty ordinary soldier, but having been called up he had tried as best he could to make the grade.

> Army life is like any other sphere of activity: some people are made to be soldiers, some people aren't. There are professional soldiers who seem to be born to be a soldier. I was never born to be a soldier. Men of that calibre could stand war, the traumatic conditions, mud, slush and blood. But I wasn't of that frame of mind. A few months of that and nine out of ten men would lose their sense of balance. Now I was never cut out to be a fighting man. While I did give of my best, I'm quite sure that there were far better soldiers in the army than I ever was.[26]
>
> Jim Fox

As they looked back, some veterans came to see the war as a gigantic blunder perpetrated on the whole of mankind. In this they were certainly influenced by the changes that occurred in the popular attitude to the war. When Haig died in 1928 his funeral procession was attended by dense crowds, most of them veterans more than eager to pay their respects. Once Haig was dead his reputation was attacked by politicians such as Lloyd George and Churchill, who began to retell the story of the war through the prism of their eloquent, but deeply suspect, personal memoirs. They sought to pour scorn on Haig, putting forward an illusion of the lost possibility of a near pain-free war victory, if only anyone had listened to their brilliant schemes to shift the war away from the Western Front. At the same time, the underlying deep-seated pain rooted in the dreadful casualties began to curdle, stirred up by the much anthologised war poets and a series of anguished memoirs. The darkening mood was seized upon by journalistic commentators led by Basil Liddell Hart. As the years passed, popular opinion began to perceive the war as utterly futile and this culminated in the idea of 'lions led by donkeys'. After all, the tragedy of the Second World War certainly did seem to call into question whether anything worthwhile had been achieved. Veterans like George Ashurst came to doubt the justification of all the hell their generation had suffered.

> I think it was a daft excursion. It was absolutely silly, that war. It was absolutely ridiculous. I never knew what I was fighting for. I didn't even know about that prince or something that got assassinated. When I think about the Battle of the Somme I think it's a huge joke – apart from the sadness of it.[27]
>
> George Ashurst

But there was still an older, prouder tradition that I find more authentic to the underlying spirit of most of the veterans that I interviewed. They may have been bowed by age, cast down perhaps by the trials and tribulations they had undergone during the rest of the twentieth century, but they were still proud of what they and their comrades had achieved in the Great War. These men did not see themselves as helpless victims, mere mannequins to be slaughtered in some pointless game – they were soldiers fighting as best they could in defence of their country against a formidable enemy. To one such old soldier should go the very last words:

> It made a man of me! I've no regrets at all. I'm proud to be able to say that I fought at Loos, I fought on the Somme, I fought at Passchendaele and I fought when the Germans broke through in 1918. To me that's an honour.[28]
>
> Richard Trafford

ACKNOWLEDGEMENTS

Firstly I must express my gratitude to the long-standing Keeper of the IWM Sound Archive, Margaret Brooks, her predecessor David Lance and the current Section Head, Tony Richards. Together they have been responsible for the creation of a wonderful archive that will continue to bear rich fruits for any historian willing to make an effort. I would also like to thank Richard Hughes, Richard McDonough, Laura Kamel, Rosemary Tudge and James Atkinson, my colleagues at the Documents and Sound Archive of the Imperial War Museum. I am a huge admirer of the sheer professionalism and skills of the other oral history interviewers quoted here, including the aforementioned Margaret Brooks and David Lance, but also Lyn Smith, Martin Brice, Conrad Wood, Peter Simkins, Chris Thistlethwaite, Bill Brooke and the usually unsung anonymous interviewers and technicians who recorded the BBC Great War Series. I would also pay tribute to the sagacity of my old chums John Paylor and George Webster who have been kind enough to cast an eye over the text to ensure that I have not strayed from the path of righteousness! The Profile team, including my editor Cecily Gayford and my copy editor Penny Gardiner, have been brilliant and a pleasure to work with! Thanks also to my lovely family: Polly, Lily and Ruby. They are – as they frequently tell me – very patient with my many failings and inform me that I am very lucky to have them. But most of all I acknowledge the wonderful men who are the real authors of this book: the veterans themselves.

All interviews were carried out by the author unless otherwise noted.

NOTES

Preface

1. I have, however, included some excerpts from interviews as a rightful tribute to the wonderful work carried out by my colleagues, or where necessary to reflect crucial incidents not covered in my own interviews. This is clearly indicated in the endnotes.

1. All over by Christmas!

1. William Holbrook AC 9339 Reel 1.
2. William Collins AC 9434 Reel 2.
3. Cyril Dennys AC 9876 Reel 2.
4. Keir Hardie was the first Independent Labour Party MP and a prominent founder of the Labour Party. As a socialist pacifist he campaigned against the Great War.
5. Harold Bing AC 00358 Reel 1. Interview recorded by Margaret Brooks.
6. Jim Davies AC 9750 Reel 2.
7. Jim Davies AC 9750 Reel 2.
8. Horace Calvert AC 9955 Reel 1.
9. Eric Wolton AC 9090 Reel 1.

2. 1914: The Death of an Army

1. Thomas Painting AC 212 Reel 3. Interview recorded by Martin Brice.

2. Basil Farrer AC 9552 Reel 4.
3. Basil Farrer AC 9552 Reel 5.
4. Euan Rabagliati, SR 4208 Reel 1. Interview recorded for the BBC Great War Series broadcast in 1964. This ground-breaking twenty-six-episode documentary series was a joint production by the BBC, ABC, CBC and the IWM. The series is widely acclaimed as one of the finest documentaries ever made. A team of excellent historians led by John Terraine and Corelli Barnet (including Peter Simkins, later Senior Historian at the IWM) provided a clear narrative, while the interviews carried out were with veterans who were still relatively young. The IWM Sound Archive programme would not start until the early 1970s and I did most of my interviews in the 1980s.
5. Lieutenant Maurice Dease, 4th Royal Fusiliers, who was awarded the first VC of the Great War for his heroic defence of Nimy Bridge where he was killed on 23 August 1914. Buried in St Symphorien Military Cemetery.
6. Private Sidney Godley, 4th Royal Fusiliers. He was awarded the VC for his courage at Nimy Bridge where he was captured by the Germans on 23 August 1914. Survived the war.
7. William Holbrook AC 9339 Reel 7.
8. Henry Dally AC 4070 Reel 1. Interview recorded for the BBC Great War Series broadcast in 1964.
9. Lance Sergeant John Fair, 2nd Argyll and Sutherland Highlanders, killed on 26 August 1914. He is listed on the La Ferté-sous-Jouarre Memorial. This rectangular block of stone, 62 x 30 x 24 feet high, commemorates nearly 4,000 officers and men of the BEF who died in August, September and the early part of October 1914 and who have no known grave.
10. Charles Ditcham AC 374 Reel 6. Interview recorded for the IWM by David Lance.
11. Thomas Painting AC 212 Reel 4. Interview recorded for the IWM by Martin Brice.
12. Captain Thomas Bridges of the 4th Dragoon Guards performed great feats in motivating the masses of dispirited troops milling around in St Quentin.
13. William Holbrook AC 9339 Reel 7.
14. Thomas Painting AC 212 Reel 4. Interview recorded for the IWM by Martin Brice.
15. William Holbrook AC 9339 Reel 8.
16. Thomas Painting AC 212 Reel 5. Interview recorded for the IWM by Martin Brice.
17. Joe Armstrong AC 10920 Reel 2.
18. Joe Armstrong AC 10920 Reel 3.
19. Joe Armstrong AC 10920 Reel 3.

20. Thomas Painting AC 212 Reel 6. Interview recorded for the IWM by Martin Brice.
21. Joe Armstrong AC 10920 Reel 3.
22. William Finch AC 8280: edited from Reel 2–3.
23. William Finch AC 8280: edited from Reel 2–3.
24. William Finch AC 8280: edited from Reel 2–3.
25. William Finch AC 8280: edited from Reel 2–3.
26. Thomas Painting AC 212 Reel 6. Interview recorded for the IWM by Martin Brice.
27. Thomas Painting AC 212 Reel 6. Interview recorded for the IWM by Martin Brice.
28. Thomas Painting AC 212 Reel 7. Interview recorded for the IWM by Martin Brice.
29. Colonel Norman McMahon, killed 11 November 1914. He has no known grave and is commemorated on Panel 1 of the Ploegsteert Memorial.
30. William Holbrook AC 9339 Reel 8.
31. Philip Neame AC 48 Reel 8. Interview recorded by David Lance.
32. George Ashurst AC 9875 Reel 6.
33. Henry Williamson AC 4297 Reel 1. Interview recorded for the BBC Great War Series broadcast in 1964.
34. George Ashurst AC 9875 Reel 6.

3. Ready for War?

1. Horace Calvert AC 9955 Reel 1.
2. Harold Hayward AC 9422 Reel 1.
3. It is indeed. A photo and listing of the memorial at the New Seaham Recreation Grounds can be seen on this excellent website commemorating the War Memorials of the North East. http://www.newmp.org.uk/memorial_image.php?contentId=8564
4. George Cole AC 9535 Reel 1.
5. James Snailham AC 9954 Reel 1.
6. Ernie Rhodes AC 10914 Reel 1.
7. Raynor Taylor AC 11113 Reel 3.
8. Raynor Taylor AC 11113 Reel 3.
9. Sapper Harry Rhodes, 17th Field Company, Royal Engineers, who died aged 23 on 19 April 1915. The son of John and Mary Ann Rhodes, of 19 Fox Street, Eccles, Manchester. He has no known grave and is commemorated on the Ypres Menin Gate Memorial.
10. Ernie Rhodes AC 10914 Reel 1 and 4.

11. Rifleman Albert Cawthorne, 8th London Regiment (Post Office Rifles), who died aged 22 on 17 May 1915. Albert Cawthorne is buried in the Post Office Rifles Cemetery at Festubert.
12. Alan Short AC 15353 Reel 1.
13. Victor Polhill AC 9254 Reel 1.
14. Sibbald Stewart AC 10169 Reel 1.
15. I thoroughly recommend Lyn Smith's wonderful book, *Voices Against War: A Century of Protest* (Edinburgh: Mainstream Publishing, 2009).
16. Howard Marten AC 00383 Reel 2. Interview recorded by Margaret Brooks.
17. Howard Marten AC 00383 Reel 2. Interview recorded by Margaret Brooks.
18. Francis Meynell AC 00383 Reel 4. Interview recorded by Margaret Brooks.
19. Howard Marten AC 00383 Reel 2. Interview recorded by Margaret Brooks.
20. Thomas Baker AC 8721 Reel 2.
21. Malcolm Hancock AC 7396 Reel 2.
22. Joe Murray AC 8201 Reel 2.
23. Henry Williamson AC 4297 Reel 1. Interview recorded for the BBC Great War Series broadcast in 1964.
24. Arthur Watts AC 8278 Reel 1.
25. Eric Wolton AC 9090 Reel 1–2 and 11.
26. Joe Pickard AC 8946 Reel 2.
27. Basil Farrer AC 9552 Reel 13.
28. Raynor Taylor AC 11113 Reel 6.
29. Malcolm Hancock AC 7396 Reel 1.
30. George Thompson AC 9549 Reel 1.
31. Norman Edwards AC 14932 Reel 2.
32. John Grainger AC 10768 Reel 7.
33. Norman Dillon AC 9752 Reel 2.
34. Eric Wolton AC 9090 Reel 2.
35. Reginald Johnson AC 9172 Reel 1.
36. Ivor Watkins AC 12232 Reel 3.
37. Thomas Baker AC 8721 Reel 1.
38. William Davies AC 8320 Reel 2.
39. Ernie Rhodes AC 10914 Reel 6.
40. Tom Williamson AC 9317 Reel 2.
41. Malcolm Hancock AC 7396 Reel 2.
42. Company Sergeant Major George Harp.
43. William Davies AC 8320 Reel 2.
44. Jim Crow AC 9118 Reel 2.

4. 1915: Western Front

1. John Wedderburn-Maxwell AC 9146 Reel 4. Interview recorded by Lyn Smith for the IWM.
2. William Underwood, AC 4247 Reel 1. Interview recorded for the BBC Great War Series broadcast in 1964.
3. Jack Dorgan AC 9253 Reel 9.
4. George Harbottle AC 9474 Reel 3.
5. Lieutenant A. R. Garton. Killed 26 April 1915. He has no known grave and is commemorated on the Menin Gate Memorial at Ypres.
6. George Harbottle AC 9474 Reel 3.
7. John Oliver died 26 April 1915. He has no known grave and is commemorated on the Menin Gate Memorial at Ypres.
8. Robert Young died 26 April 1915. He has no known grave and is commemorated on the Menin Gate Memorial at Ypres.
9. Jack Dorgan AC 9253 Reel 10.
10. George Harbottle AC 9474 Reel 3.
11. William Watson Armstrong actually wrote the following: 'Bob Young, as he was carried away, minus his legs, called upon an officer, who was almost overcome by the sight, to "be a man"; and I was further told that he died kissing his wife's photograph, with the word "Tipperary" on his lips. Such were the men the Germans failed to break – men with an unconquerable spirit which no human horror could overcome.' *My First Week in Flanders* (London: Smith, Elder & Co., 1916), p. 20
12. Jack Dorgan AC 9253 Reel 22.
13. George Ashurst AC 9875 Reel 9.
14. Victor Hawkins AC 4130 Reel 1. Interview recorded for the BBC Great War Series broadcast in 1964.
15. Alfred Bromfield AC 4038 Reel 1. Interview recorded for the BBC Great War Series broadcast in 1964.
16. William Tyrrell was an interesting character. Born on 20 November 1885, before the war he had played as an international for Ireland and as a British Lion on a tour of South Africa in 1910. A reservist, he served as a medical officer but then progressed to command the RAMC School of Instructors. After the war ended he transferred to the RAF and rose to the dizzy heights of air vice marshal and honorary surgeon to King George VI. He died in 1968.
17. Victor Hawkins AC 4130 Reel 1. Interview recorded for the BBC Great War Series broadcast in 1964.
18. W. Tyrrell quoted in *Report of the War Office Committee of Enquiry into 'Shell Shock'*, (London, IWM, 2004), p. 8.
19. George Ashurst AC 9875 Reel 9.

20. Private John Lynn was aged 27 when he was killed on 2 May 1915. He was buried in the Grootebeek British Cemetery.
21. Victor Hawkins AC 4130 Reel 1. Interview recorded for the BBC Great War Series broadcast in 1964.
22. Alex Thompson AC 11460 Reel 4.
23. Martin Greener AC 8945 Reel 2.
24. George Clayton AC 10012: edited from Reel 5–6, 7 and 10.
25. Martin Greener AC 8945 Reel 5–6.
26. Gordon Carey AC 4050 Reel 1. Interview recorded for the BBC Great War Series broadcast in 1964.
27. Patrick Horrigan AC 860 Reel 2. Interview recorded by M. E. Anfilogoff in 1976.
28. William Edington AC 4093 Reel 1. Interview recorded for the BBC Great War Series broadcast in 1964.
29. John Palmer AC 4198 Reel 1: edited from two versions on tape. Interview recorded for the BBC Great War Series broadcast in 1964.
30. Walter Cook AC 9352 Reel 2. Interview recorded by Lyn Smith.
31. Jim Davies AC 9750 Reel 4.
32. William Hildred AC 9199 Reel 1. Interview recorded by Lyn Smith.
33. Walter Spencer AC 10170 Reel 2–3.
34. Walter Spencer AC 10170 Reel 2–3.
35. Walter Spencer AC 10170 Reel 2–3.
36. George Craik AC 4116 Reel 1. Interview recorded for the BBC Great War Series broadcast in 1964.

5. Way out East, 1914–18

1. William Jones AC 4141 Reel 1. Interview recorded for the BBC Great War Series broadcast in 1964.
2. Thomas Baker AC 8721 Reel 3.
3. Frank Brent AC 4037 Reel 1. Interview recorded for the BBC Great War Series broadcast in 1964.
4. Listed as Sergeant Robert Robinson of 6th Battalion, AIF, killed on 25 April 1915. He has no known grave and is commemorated on the Lone Pine Memorial at Anzac.
5. Frank Brent AC 4037 Reel 1. Interview recorded for the BBC Great War Series broadcast in 1964.
6. Thomas Baker AC 8721 Reel 3–4.
7. Joseph Clements AC 11268 Reel 3.
8. Thomas Baker AC 8721 Reel 3–4.
9. Thomas Baker AC 8721 Reel 4.
10. Thomas Baker AC 8721 Reel 4.

11. Sidney Hall AC 10412 Reel 1.
12. Stephen Moyle AC 8227 Reel 2.
13. Reginald Gillett AC 7377 Reel 1. Interview recorded for the BBC Great War Series broadcast in 1964.
14. Joe Murray AC 8201 Reel 7.
15. Joe Murray AC 8201 Reel 7. Although referring to real people and actual events, when he wrote his book *Gallipoli – As I Saw It* (London: William Kimber, 1965), Joe Murray changed the names of his friends so as not to distress the families with details of their deaths. From then on, he used the altered names whenever describing these events and he never told me what the real names were.
16. Frank Brent AC 4037. Interview recorded for the BBC Great War Series broadcast in 1964.
17. Harold Pilling AC 7496 Reel 2.
18. Joe Murray AC 8201 Reel 11.
19. Joe Murray AC 8201 Reel 12.
20. Stephen Moyle AC 8227 Reel 4.
21. This could be Private John Mitchell, killed on 5 June 1915, whose date of birth is unclear. It could also be Private Walter Mitchell, aged 24, killed on 7 August 1915. Both have no known grave and are commemorated on the Helles Memorial. Another possibility is Private Malcolm Mitchell of the 1/8th Lancashire Fusiliers, killed on 7 August 1915. He is buried in the Skew Bridge Cemetery; but as he was only 19 it seems unlikely that he had two children.
22. George Peake AC 10648 Reel 4.
23. Joe Murray AC 8201 Reel 9.
24. Lieutenant Commander Raymond Parsons, killed on 4 June 1915. He has no known grave and is commemorated on the Helles Memorial.
25. Joe Murray AC 8201 Reel 9.
26. Joe Murray AC 8201 Reel 10.
27. Thomas Baker AC 8721 Reel 5.
28. Company Sergeant Major George Harp, aged 33, killed on 7 August 1915. He is buried at Ari Burnu Cemetery, Anzac Cove.
29. William Davies AC 8320 Reel 4.
30. Joseph Napier AC 7499 Reel 4.
31. Lieutenant Tudor Jenkins.
32. Joseph Napier AC 7499 Reel 4.
33. Lieutenant Colonel Sir William Lennox Napier, aged 47, killed on 13 August 1915. He is buried in the 7th Field Ambulance Cemetery.
34. Joseph Napier AC 7499 Reel 4.
35. Ernest Haire AC 10401 Reel 7.
36. Ernest Haire AC 10401 Reel 8.
37. Ernest Haire AC 10401 Reel 8.

38. Tom Williamson AC 9317 Reel 2.
39. Arthur Bull AC 10410 Reel 2.
40. Malcolm Hancock AC 7396 Reel 4–8.
41. Eric Wolton AC 9090 Reel 4.
42. Malcolm Hancock AC 7396 Reel 6.
43. Malcolm Hancock AC 7396 Reel 8.
44. Eric Wolton AC 9090 Reel 5.
45. Joe Murray AC 8201 Reel 27.
46. Joe Murray AC 8201 Reel 28.
47. Jack Callaway AC 3277 Reel 1.
48. William Finch AC 4100. Interview recorded for the BBC Great War Series broadcast in 1964.
49. Jack Callaway AC 3277: edited from Reel 4–4.
50. William Finch AC 4100. Interview recorded for the BBC Great War Series broadcast in 1964.
51. Joseph Napier AC 7499 Reel 4.
52. James Snailham AC 9954 Reel 5–6.
53. Ian Macdonald AC 9149 Reel 3.
54. Joseph Napier AC 7499 Reel 6.
55. Joseph Napier AC 7499 Reel 6.
56. Ian Macdonald AC 9149: edited from Reel 3.
57. Henry Rich AC 766 Reel 1. This is by an anonymous interviewer.
58. Jack Callaway AC 3277, Reel 4.
59. Charles Barber AC 4005 Reel 1. Interview recorded for the BBC Great War Series broadcast in 1964.
60. Humphrey De Verd Leigh AC 0037 Reel 3. Interview recorded by ??? for IWM.
61. Ralph Hockaday AC 4123. Interview recorded for the BBC Great War Series broadcast in 1964.
62. F. G. Ponting AC 4203. Interview recorded for the BBC Great War Series broadcast in 1964.
63. Captain Edward Staples.
64. Captain Tudor Jenkins – the same officer who had nearly bayoneted Napier at Gallipoli.
65. Joseph Napier AC 7499 Reel 9.
66. C. T. Atkinson, *The History of the South Wales Borderers* (London: The Medici Society Ltd, 1931), p. 326.
67. Ernest Jones AC 12678 Reel 8.
68. Ernest Jones AC 12678 Reel 8.
69. Ernest Haire AC 10401 Reel 12–13.
70. Terence Verschoyle AC 8185 Reel 3.
71. Walter Ostler AC 39 Reel 5. Interview recorded by David Lance.
72. Walter Ostler AC 39 Reel 6–7. Interview recorded by David Lance.

73. Captain Charles Gimingham, who died aged 26 on 9 November 1917. He is buried in the Struma Military Cemetery.
74. Walter Ostler AC 39 Reel 6–7. Interview recorded by David Lance.
75. Walter Ostler AC 39 Reel 6–7. Interview recorded by David Lance.
76. Leutnant Rudolf von Eschwege, who died aged 22 on 21 November 1917. Originally buried in Struma Military Cemetery, his body was moved in 1922.
77. Walter Ostler AC 39 Reel 6–7. Interview recorded by David Lance.
78. If you want to read more on Salonika, then I thoroughly recommend *Under the Devil's Eye: The British Military Experience in Macedonia 1915–1918* by Alan Wakefield and Simon Moody and recently republished by Pen & Sword, Barnsley, 2011.
79. Lawrence Pollock AC 4200 Reel 1. Interview recorded for the BBC Great War Series broadcast in 1964.
80. Eric Wolton AC 9090 Reel 9.
81. Eric Wolton AC 9090 Reel 10.
82. Lawrence Pollock AC 4200 Reel 1. Interview recorded for the BBC Great War Series broadcast in 1964.

6. 1916: Western Front

1. Norman Edwards AC 14932 Reel 7.
2. Montague Cleeve AC 7310 Reel 3. Interview recorded by Lyn Smith.
3. George Ashurst AC 9875 Reel 15.
4. Murray Rymer Jones AC 10699 Reel 2
5. Ralph Miller AC 11961 Reel 4.
6. Frederick Glanville AC 14720 Reel 1–2.
7. James Snailham AC 9954 Reel 4.
8. George Ashurst AC 9875 Reel 15.
9. Alfred Irwin AC 211 Reel 1. Interview recorded by Martin Brice.
10. Captain Wilfred Nevill died at the age of 21 on 1 July 1916. He is buried in Carnoy Military Cemetery.
11. Albert Hurst AC 11582 Reel 7.
12. Stewart Jordan AC 10391 Reel 4.
13. Norman Edwards AC 14932 Reel 7.
14. Ms Llewellyn AC 4163 Reel 1. Interview recorded for the BBC Great War Series broadcast in 1964.
15. Leonard Ounsworth AC 332 Reel 6. Interview recorded by David Lance.
16. Norman Edwards AC 14932 Reel 8.
17. Arthur Roughton Smith died of wounds at the age of 23 on 22 July 1916. He is buried in the Warloy-Baillon Communal Cemetery Extension.
18. Richard Trafford AC 11218 Reel 7.

19. Harold Hayward AC 9422 Reel 11.
20. Harold Hayward AC 9422 Reel 12.
21. Cyril Jourdain AC 11214 Reel 3.
22. R. Feilding, *War Letters to a Wife* (London: The Medici Society, 1929).
23. Cyril Jourdain AC 11214 Reel 3–4.
24. R. Feilding, *War Letters to a Wife*, p. 114.
25. R. Feilding, *War Letters to a Wife*, p. 119.
26. George Cole AC 9535 Reel 4.
27. George Cole AC 9535 Reel 4.
28. Stuart Hastie AC 4126 Reel 1. Interview recorded for the BBC Great War Series broadcast in 1964.
29. Joe Murray AC 8201 Reel 35.
30. Joe Murray AC 8201 Reel 36.
31. Frederick Kelly was a well-known musician and well-known rower who had won a gold medal at the 1908 Olympics. He was a prominent member of that talented group of officers who had gathered around Rupert Brooke in the Hood Battalion during the lead-up to the Gallipoli campaign. Kelly was killed at the age of 36 in the attack on Beaucourt on 13 November 1916. He is buried in the Martinsart Military Cemetery.
32. Joe Murray AC 8201 Reel 37.
33. Joe Murray AC 8201 Reel 37.
34. Joe Murray AC 8201 Reel 37.
35. Joe Murray AC 8201 Reel 37.
36. Martin Greener AC 8945 Reel 8.

7. All at Sea, 1914–18

1. George Wainford AC 9953 Reel 4 and 6.
2. Ernest Amis AC 4003 Reel 1. Interview recorded for the BBC Great War Series broadcast in 1964.
3. Sylvester Pawley AC 4189: edited from Reel 1. Interview recorded for the BBC Great War Series broadcast in 1964.
4. John Ouvry AC 9260 Reel 1. Interview recorded by Conrad Wood.
5. John Ouvry AC 9260 Reel 1. Interview recorded by Conrad Wood.
6. Lieutenant Gordon Steele was later awarded the VC for his actions taking command of Coastal Motor Boat 88 and torpedoing and damaging the Russian pre-dreadnought *Andrei Pervozvanny* during a night attack on Kronstadt harbour during the North Russian intervention in 1919.
7. George Hempenstall AC 9534 Reel 3.
8. George Hempenstall AC 9534 Reel 3.
9. George Hempenstall AC 9534 Reel 4.
10. George Hempenstall AC 9534 Reel 5.

11. Charles Falmer AC 4096 Reel 1. Interview recorded for the BBC Great War Series broadcast in 1964.
12. Charles Falmer AC 4096: edited from Reel 1. Interview recorded for the BBC Great War Series broadcast in 1964.
13. Alfred Blackmore AC 4025 Reel 1. Interview recorded for the BBC Great War Series broadcast in 1964.
14. George Betsworth AC 9004 Reels 1–2. Interview recorded by Henry Baynham in 1973.
15. John Ouvry AC 9260 Reel 2. Interview recorded by Conrad Wood.
16. Brian de Courcy Ireland AC 12243 Reel 6.
17. William Fell AC 30917 Reel 1. Interview recorded by Roger Hill in 1978.
18. John Ouvry AC 9260 Reel 2. Interview recorded by Conrad Wood.
19. George Wainford AC 9953 Reel 7.
20. George Wainford AC 9953 Reel 7–8.
21. George Wainford AC 9953 Reel 7–8.
22. Lieutenant Commander Arthur Onslow of HMS *Onslaught* died on 1 June 1916. Commemorated at the Queensferry Cemetery, West Lothian.
23. George Wainford AC 9953 Reel 7.
24. Sid Bell AC 10915 Reel 7–8.
25. William Piggott AC 12235 Reel 7.
26. H. Clegg AC 4062: edited from Reel 1. Interview recorded for the BBC Great War Series broadcast in 1964.
27. H. Clegg AC 4062: edited from Reel 1. Interview recorded for the BBC Great War Series broadcast in 1964.
28. Brian de Courcy Ireland AC 12243 Reel 8.
29. Brian de Courcy Ireland AC 12243 Reel 8.
30. George Wainford AC 9953 Reel 7.

8. Life in the Trenches

1. Alfred West AC 12236 Reel 4.
2. Donald Price AC 10168 Reel 5.
3. George Harbottle AC 9474 Reel 5.
4. Ivor Watkins AC 12232 Reel 5
5. Jack Dorgan AC 9253 Reel 14.
6. Donald Price AC 10168 Reel 4.
7. Horace Calvert AC 9955 Reel 7.
8. George Ashurst AC 9875 Reel 4.
9. Harold Hayward AC 9422 Reel 5.
10. Horace Calvert AC 9955 Reel 7–8.
11. Horace Calvert AC 9955 Reel 8.
12. Jack Dorgan AC 9253 Reel 15.

13. Horace Calvert AC 9955 Reel 8.
14. Horace Calvert AC 9955 Reel 10.
15. George Ashurst AC 9875 Reel 19.
16. Edward Race AC 13081 Reel 3.
17. Charles Austin AC 11116 Reel 9.
18. Jim Davies AC 9750 Reel 8.
19. Charles Gee AC 13717 Reel 2–3 and 5.
20. Brigadier General Roland Bradford was born on 23 February 1892 in Witton Park, Bishop Auckland. When the war began he was just a second lieutenant with the 2nd Durham Light Infantry. He was the youngest of four brothers of whom only one survived the war. His elder brother George won a posthumous VC for his actions at Zeebrugge on 23 April 1918 making them the only brothers to win the VC in the Great War. Roland Bradford is buried in the Hermies Military Cemetery.
21. Jack Dorgan AC 9253 Reel 19.
22. George Ashurst AC 9875 Reel 3–4.
23. George Ashurst AC 9875 Reel 4.
24. Alfred West AC 12236 Reel 4.
25. William Collins AC 9434 Reel 10.
26. Donald Price AC 10168 Reel 6.
27. George Ashurst AC 9875 Reel 7.
28. George Ashurst AC 9875 Reel 7.
29. Alfred West AC 12236 Reel 5.
30. Ivor Watkins AC 12232 Reel 5.
31. Private Charlie Reid of 238 Machine Gun Company was killed on 25 September 1917. He is buried in the Larch Wood (Railway Cutting) Cemetery.
32. Sibbald Stewart AC 10169 Reel 6.
33. Alfred West AC 12236 Reel 5.
34. Ralph Miller AC 11961 Reel 4.
35. Norman Edwards AC 14932 Reel 3.
36. Albert Hurst AC 11582 Reel 6.
37. Ivor Watkins AC 12232 Reel 6.
38. Joe Fitzpatrick AC 10767 Reel 10.
39. John Mallalieu AC 9417 Reel 2.
40. William Holbrook AC 9339 Reel 13.
41. Leonard Ounsworth AC 332 Reel 10. Interview recorded by David Lance.
42. Joe Pickard AC 8946 Reel 7.
43. Philip Neame AC 48 Reel 2.
44. Basil Farrer AC 9552 Reel 8.
45. Joe Yarwood AC 12231 Reel 5.
46. Private Robert Dunsire VC was serving with the 13th Royal Scots when he was killed in action on 30 January 1916 at the age of 24. He had earlier

been awarded the VC for his courage on Hill 70 during the Battle of Loos on 26 September 1915, when he went out and rescued two wounded men from No Man's Land despite being under very heavy fire. He is buried in the Mazingarbe Communal Cemetery.

47. William Collins AC 9434 Reel 10.
48. William Collins AC 9434 Reel 10–11.
49. William Collins AC 9434 Reel 9.
50. Basil Farrer AC 9552 Reel 16.
51. Joe Yarwood AC 12231 Reel 4.
52. Nurse Bird AC 7376 Reel 1–2.
53. Jack Dorgan AC 9253 Reel 14.
54. Private Richard Westmacott of the 20th Royal Fusiliers. Considering the nature of this quote it is interesting to note that he was commissioned into the RAMC in 1917!
55. Donald Price AC 10168 Reel 5.
56. Sidney Taylor AC 10615 Reel 3.
57. This story is perhaps worth noticing as an example particularly common in oral history, of private soldiers being given direct orders by senior officers in a manner which rarely happens in real life. But then again, Private James Snailham was the runner for Lieutenant Colonel Arthur Rickman.
58. James Snailham AC 9954 Reel 2–3.
59. Jack Dorgan AC 9253 Reel 19.
60. Harold Hayward AC 9422 Reel 6.
61. Jack Dorgan AC 9253 Reel 19.
62. Ivor Watkins AC 12232 Reel 6.
63. William Holbrook AC 9339 Reel 12.
64. Jack Dorgan AC 9253 Reel 18.
65. Jack Dorgan AC 9253 Reel 18.
66. Jack Hepplestone AC 9575 Reel 5.
67. Frank Raine AC 9751 Reel 7.
68. Lieutenant Colonel Ralph Husey had a great reputation as a fire-eater! Commanded the 1/5th London Regiment and subsequently promoted to command the 25th Brigade which was part of the 8th Division. Husey was badly wounded and captured during the German offensive on the Aisne on 27 May 1918 and died in captivity three days later. He was 36 years old.
69. Victor Polhill AC 9254 Reel 4.
70. Tom Bracey AC 9419 Reel 5.
71. Donald Price AC 10168 Reel 7.
72. William Holbrook AC 9339 Reel 14.
73. This incident recorded by Holbrook probably occurred in 1917.
74. George Harbottle AC 9474 Reel 5.

75. Norman Dillon AC 9752 Reel 10.
76. Edmund Williams AC 10604 Reel 19. Interview recorded by Chris Thistlethwaite.
77. Basil Farrer AC 9552 Reel 14.
78. Joe Pickard AC 8946 Reel 14.
79. Ernie Rhodes AC 10914 Reel 5.
80. Frank Raine AC 9751 Reel 5.
81. Ernest Millard AC 14985 Reel 4.
82. Joe Yarwood AC 12231 Reel 8.
83. Nurse Bird, AC 7376 Reel 2.
84. William Holbrook AC 9339 Reel 13.
85. James Watson AC 11040 Reel 3.
86. Charles Gee AC 13717 Reel 7.
87. Private William Roberts of the 4th Royal Fusiliers was executed for desertion on 29 May 1916 and is buried in the Renninghelst Cemetery.
88. William Holbrook AC 9339 Reel 14.
89. Jim Davies AC 9750: edited from Reel 8–9.
90. Ivor Watkins AC 12232 Reel 5.
91. George Ashurst AC 9875 Reel 8–9.
92. Tom Bracey AC 9419 Reel 6.
93. Jim Davies AC 9750 Reel 7.
94. Basil Farrer AC 9552 Reel 8.
95. Joe Pickard AC 8946 Reel 2.
96. Jack Dorgan AC 9253 Reel 16.
97. Victor Polhill AC 9254 Reel 3.
98. Jack Dorgan AC 9253: edited from Reel 16 and 23.
99. Jack Dorgan AC 9253 Reel 16.
100. Raynor Taylor AC 11113 Reel 14.
101. Anonymous interview due to the subject matter quoted.
102. George Ashurst AC 9875 Reel 6.
103. Donald Price AC 10168 Reel 4.
104. Alfred West AC 12236 Reel 6.
105. George Ashurst AC 9875 Reel 8.
106. Jack Dorgan AC 9253 Reel 15.
107. George Cole AC 9535 Reel 17.
108. Joe Fitzpatrick AC 10767 Reel 10.

9. 1917: Western Front

1. John Fell AC 9151 Reel 3–4.
2. John Fell AC 9151 Reel 4.
3. John Fell AC 9151 Reel 4.

4. Robert Cook AC 7397 Reel 3.
5. Martin Greener AC 8945 Reel 8.
6. Kenneth Page AC 717 Reel 2–3. Interview recorded by Peter Simkins.
7. George Hancox AC 4129 Reel 1. Interview recorded for the BBC Great War Series broadcast in 1964.
8. Victor Polhill AC 9254 Reel 6.
9. Major Arthur Asquith was the son of Prime Minister Herbert Asquith and served with the Hood Battalion at Gallipoli where he had been wounded. He would attain the rank of brigadier commanding the 189th Brigade in December 1916 but was severely wounded and had his leg amputated in December 1917.
10. Joe Murray AC 8201 Reel 42.
11. Joe Murray AC 8201 Reel 42.
12. Joe Murray AC 8201 Reel 42.
13. Bryan Frayling AC 4105 Reel 1. Interview recorded for the BBC Great War Series broadcast in 1964.
14. John Royle AC 4215 Reel 1. Interview recorded for the BBC Great War Series broadcast in 1964.
15. John Royle AC 4215 Reel 1. Interview recorded for the BBC Great War Series broadcast in 1964.
16. John Royle AC 4215 Reel 1. Interview recorded for the BBC Great War Series broadcast in 1964.
17. Bryan Frayling AC 4105 Reel 1. Interview recorded for the BBC Great War Series broadcast in 1964.
18. George Thompson AC 9549 Reel 4.
19. Frederick Collins AC 8229 Reel 4. Recorded by Lyn Smith.
20. Ivor Watkins AC 12232 Reel 5.
21. Horace Birks AC 4024 Reel 1. Interview recorded for the BBC Great War Series broadcast in 1964.
22. Horace Birks AC 4024 Reel 1. Interview recorded for the BBC Great War Series broadcast in 1964.
23. Ulrich Burke AC 569 Reel 14–15. Interview recorded by David Lance.
24. Ulrich Burke AC 569 Reel 14–15. Interview recorded by David Lance.
25. Ulrich Burke AC 569 Reel 14–15. Interview recorded by David Lance.
26. George Thompson AC 9549 Reel 4.
27. Alan Hanbury-Sparrow AC 4131 Reel 1. Interview recorded for the BBC Great War Series broadcast in 1964.
28. Alan Hanbury-Sparrow AC 4131 Reel 1. Interview recorded for the BBC Great War Series broadcast in 1964.
29. Alfred Griffin AC 9101 Reel 3.
30. Lieutenant Thomas Mashiter attached to 1/5th Lancashire Fusiliers. Died aged 26 on 31 August 1917. No known grave. He is commemorated on the Tyne Cot Memorial.

31. Captain Austin Hudson was killed on 31 August 1917 at the age of 24. No known grave. He is commemorated on the Tyne Cot Memorial.

32. Although Thomas Mashiter and Austin Hudson are reported as having been killed on 31 August 1918, there are no other reported casualties that day. There are only five other rank fatalities for the period 30 August 1917 to 2 September 1917, all of whom were killed on 1 September, which is also the date that Hudson is recorded as having been killed in 'Soldiers Died'. These are Private Richard Smethurst, Private Sydney Lowe, Private John Maughan, Private William Livesey and Lance Corporal William Taylor. I presume the incident occurred on the night of 31 August/1 September 1917. Thanks to Steve Chambers who helped work out these details.

33. George Horridge AC 7498 Reel 7.

34. Sibbald Stewart AC 10169 Reel 5.

35. William Collins AC 9434 Reel 12.

36. Douglas Wimberley AC 4266 Reel 1. Interview recorded for the BBC Great War Series broadcast in 1964.

37. Alfred Griffin AC 9101 Reel 4.

38. Cyril Dennys AC 9876 Reel 6–7.

39. Sibbald Stewart AC 10169 Reel 7.

40. Charles Austin AC 11116 Reel 8.

41. Donald Price AC 10168 Reel 11.

42. William Towers AC 11038 Reel 7–8.

43. William Towers AC 11038 Reel 8.

44. William Towers AC 11038 Reel 8.

45. William Bunning AC 4046 Reel 1. Interview recorded for the BBC Great War Series broadcast in 1964.

46. Written under the pseudonym Charles Edmonds.

47. Charles Carrington AC 4057. Interview recorded for the BBC Great War Series broadcast in 1964.

48. John Palmer AC 4198 Reel 1. Interview recorded for the BBC Great War Series broadcast in 1964.

49. John Palmer AC 4198 Reel 1. Interview recorded for the BBC Great War Series broadcast in 1964.

50. Joe Pickard AC 8946 Reel 14.

51. I am of course indebted to Bryn Hammond who has explored this battle in fascinating detail in his *Cambrai 1917: The Myth of the Great Tank Battle*, published by Weidenfeld & Nicolson, London, in 2008.

52. Norman Dillon AC 9752 Reel 11.

53. Eric Potten AC 11042: edited from Reel 2.

54. Norman Dillon AC 9752 Reel 11.

55. Eric Potten AC 11042: edited from Reel 2.

56. Eric Potten AC 11042: edited from Reel 2.

57. Norman Dillon AC 9752 Reel 11.

10. Up in the Air, 1914–18

1. Cecil Lewis AC 4162 Reel 2. Interview recorded for the BBC Great War Series broadcast in 1964.
2. Archibald James AC 24 Reel 13. Interview recorded by David Lance. Strangely, although the war in the air has always been one of my defining historical passions, I only ever recorded a few Great War aviators. Part of the reason was the excellence of the very first IWM oral history project on the Royal Flying Corps (RFC) and the Royal Naval Air Service (RNAS) carried out by David Lance as the first Keeper of the IWM Sound Archive.
3. Archibald James AC 24 Reel 9. Interview recorded by David Lance.
4. Cecil Lewis AC 4162 Reel 2. Interview recorded for the BBC Great War Series broadcast in 1964.
5. Harold Taylor AC 307 Reel 1. Interview recorded by David Lance.
6. Cecil Lewis AC 4162 Reel 2. Interview recorded for the BBC Great War Series broadcast in 1964.
7. Cecil Lewis AC 4162 Reel 2. Interview recorded for the BBC Great War Series broadcast in 1964.
8. An ace had been given credit for shooting down five victims. Manfred von Richthofen would eventually claim eighty victims.
9. Gwilym Lewis AC 11308 Reel 4. Interview recorded by Brad King. Brad was a truly inspirational expert on Great War aviation; my 'mentor' in that subject!
10. Gwilym Lewis AC 11308 Reel 3. Interview recorded by Brad King.
11. Cecil Lewis AC 4162 Reel 1. Interview recorded for the BBC Great War Series broadcast in 1964.
12. Cecil Lewis AC 4162 Reel 1. Interview recorded for the BBC Great War Series broadcast in 1964.
13. Cecil Lewis AC 4162 Reel 1. Interview recorded for the BBC Great War Series broadcast in 1964.
14. Cecil Lewis AC 4162 Reel 1. Interview recorded for the BBC Great War Series broadcast in 1964.
15. Cecil Lewis, AC 4162, Reel 1. Interview recorded for the BBC Great War Series broadcast in 1964.
16. Frederick Powell SR 87 Reel 6. Interview recorded by David Lance.
17. Cecil Lewis SR 4162 Reel 1. Interview recorded for the BBC Great War Series broadcast in 1964.
18. Ernest Haire AC 10401 Reel 15.
19. Laurie Field AC 11376 Reel 7–8.
20. Laurie Field AC 11376 Reel 8.

21. Major Edward Mannock died at the age of 31 on 26 July 1918. He was awarded a posthumous VC in 1919. He was acclaimed as the highest scoring British Empire pilot with some seventy-three claimed victories. He has no known grave and is commemorated on the Flying Service Memorial to the Missing at the Faubourg d'Amiens Cemetery at Arras.
22. Frederick Powell AC 87 Reel 8. Interview recorded by David Lance.
23. Frederick Powell AC 87 Reel 8. Interview recorded by David Lance.
24. Sadly, I never interviewed anyone who claimed to have fired that 'magic' bullet.
25. James Gascoyne AC 16 Reel 3. Interview recorded by David Lance.
26. James Gascoyne AC 16 Reel 3. Interview recorded by David Lance.
27. James Gascoyne AC 16 Reel 4. Interview recorded by David Lance.
28. Laurie Field AC 11376 Reel 9–10
29. Archibald Yuille AC 320 Reel 2 and 4. Interview recorded by David Lance.
30. Archibald Yuille AC 320 Reel 3. Interview recorded by David Lance.
31. Roy Shillinglaw AC 4224 Reel 1. Interview recorded for the BBC Great War Series broadcast in 1964.
32. William Wardrop AC 29 Reel 3–5. Interview recorded by Martin Brice.

11. 1918: German Spring Offensives

1. Norman Dillon AC 9752 Reel 12.
2. Ivor Watkins AC 12232 Reel 8.
3. Ivor Watkins AC 12232 Reel 8.
4. Joe Fitzpatrick AC 10767 Reel 13.
5. Ernest Millard AC 14985 Reel 6.
6. Cyril Dennys AC 9876 Reel 10–11.
7. Cyril Dennys AC 9876 Reel 10–11.
8. Joe Pickard AC 8946 Reel 11.
9. George Thompson AC 9549 Reel 5.
10. Walter Hare AC 11440 Reel 8–9.
11. William Collins AC 9434 Reel 14–15.
12. Joe Pickard AC 8946 Reel 16–17.
13. Joe Pickard AC 8946 Reel 17.
14. Joe Pickard AC 8946 Reel 17.
15. Jim Davies AC 9750 Reel 13.
16. Jim Davies AC 9750 Reel 13.
17. Henry Mabbott AC 860 Reel 1. Interview recorded by M. E. Anfilogoff in 1976.
18. George Clayton AC 10012 Reel 12.
19. Jack Hepplestone AC 9575 Reel 7.
20. Jack Hepplestone AC 9575 Reel 7.

21. Nurse Bird AC 7376 Reel 2.
22. Jim Fox AC 9546 Reel 4–5.
23. Jim Fox AC 9546 Reel 5.
24. Jim Fox AC 9546 Reel 5.
25. Private W. J. Earl served with the 1/7th Lancashire Fusiliers. He was executed by firing squad on 27 May 1918 and he is buried in the Warlincourt Cemetery.
26. John Grainger AC 10768 Reel 8.
27. Bill Gillman AC 9420 Reel 4–7.
28. Jim Davies AC 9750 Reel 13.
29. George Thompson AC 9549 Reel 5.
30. George Cole AC 9535 Reel 13.

12. 1918: Advance to Victory

1. Victor Polhill AC 9254 Reel 11.
2. E. Ludendorff, *Ludendorff's Own Story: August 1914–November 1918* (New York & London: Harper & Bros, 1919), p. 326.
3. Stanley Evers AC 4099 Reel 1. Interview recorded for the BBC Great War Series broadcast in 1964.
4. Eric Potten AC 8946 Reel 17.
5. Jim Davies AC 9750 Reel 13.
6. Jim Davies AC 9750 Reel 13.
7. Bill Gillman AC 9420 Reel 12.
8. Bill Gillman AC 9420: edited from Reel 11–12.
9. Horace Calvert AC 9955 Reel 16.
10. Horace Calvert AC 9955 Reel 16.
11. Cyril Jourdain AC 11214 Reel 6.
12. Donald Price AC 10168 Reel 14.
13. Donald Price AC 10168 Reel 14.
14. Jim Fox AC 9546 Reel 5.
15. Bill Gillman AC 9420 Reel 12.
16. Bill Gillman AC 9420 Reel 4 and 6.
17. Bill Smedley AC 10917 Reel 9.
18. Jim Fox AC 9546 Reel 6.
19. Ernest Hancock AC 8950 Reel 5.

13. Aftermath of War

1. Raynor Taylor AC 11113 Reel 17–18.
2. R. Kipling, *The Years Between* (London: Methuen & Co., 1919), p. 137.
3. Harry Hopthrow AC 11581 Reel 14.

4. Horace Calvert AC 9955: edited from material in Reel 17 and 18–19.
5. Joseph Napier AC 7499 Reel 15.
6. Raynor Taylor AC 11113 Reel 3 and 19.
7. Norman Kirby AC 16084 Reel 1.
8. James Snailham AC 9954 Reel 5–6.
9. Fred Dixon AC 737 Reel 15. Interview recorded by B. P. Wilkins.
10. Albert Birtwhistle AC 11970 Reel 10.
11. Norman Kirby AC 16084 Reel 1.
12. Laurie Field AC 11376 Reel 11.
13. Eric Wolton AC 9090 Reel 11.
14. John Dray AC 9090 Reel 11.
15. Joe Pickard AC 8946 Reel 18.
16. Joe Pickard AC 8946 Reel 18.
17. William Towers AC 11038 Reel 9.
18. William Towers AC 11038 Reel 9.
19. William Towers AC 11038 Reel 10.
20. George Peake AC 10648 Reel 9.
21. Stephen Moyle AC 8227 Reel 6.
22. The veterans were certainly keen to record their memories for posterity when interviewed by the IWM. Recording in two-hour sessions is hard work for men in their late eighties and nineties and they had to show a considerable amount of commitment to get the job done properly.
23. Eric Wolton AC 9090 Reel 11.
24. Victor Polhill AC 9254 Reel 13.
25. Malcolm Hancock AC 7396 Reel 14.
26. Jim Fox AC 9546: edited from Reel 1 and 5.
27. George Ashurst AC 9875 Reel 22.
28. Richard Trafford AC 11218 Reel 8.

INDEX